FREEDOM

Also Available from Bloomsbury

The Challenge of Bergsonism, Leonard Lawlor
Bergson: Thinking Beyond the Human Condition, Keith Ansell-Pearson
Henri Bergson: Key Writings, eds. Keith Ansell-Pearson, John Ó Maoilearca

FREEDOM

LECTURES AT THE COLLÈGE DE FRANCE, 1904–1905

Henri Bergson

Edited, with an Introduction, by Nils F. Schott and Alexandre Lefebvre, based on the French edition by Arnaud François

Translated by Leonard Lawlor

BLOOMSBURY ACADEMIC
LONDON • NEW YORK • OXFORD • NEW DELHI • SYDNEY

BLOOMSBURY ACADEMIC
Bloomsbury Publishing Plc
50 Bedford Square, London, WC1B 3DP, UK
1385 Broadway, New York, NY 10018, USA
29 Earlsfort Terrace, Dublin 2, Ireland

BLOOMSBURY, BLOOMSBURY ACADEMIC and the Diana logo are trademarks of Bloomsbury Publishing Plc

First published in Great Britain 2024

Series design: Ben Anslow
Cover image: ETIENNE MAREY (1830-1904). / Etienne-Jules Marey. French physiologist. Bird in flight photographed with 'Marey's rifle,' a portable motion picture camera in the shape of a rifle he invented in 1882.
(Contributor: GRANGER- Historical Picture Archive / Alamy Stock Photo)

A catalogue record for this book is available from the British Library.

A catalog record for this book is available from the Library of Congress.

ISBN: HB: 978-1-3500-2916-3
PB: 978-1-3500-2917-0
ePDF: 978-1-3500-2915-6
eBook: 978-1-3500-2918-7

Typeset by Deanta Global Publishing Services, Chennai, India
Printed and bound in Great Britain

To find out more about our authors and books visit www.bloomsbury.com and sign up for our newsletters.

CONTENTS

SERIES PREFACE

HENRI BERGSON AT THE COLLÈGE DE FRANCE

Alexandre Lefebvre and Nils F. Schott

Henri Bergson (1859–1941) was the most important philosopher of the early twentieth century in France and for fifteen years taught at its most prestigious academic institution, the Collège de France. From 1900 to 1904 he held the Chair of Greek and Latin Philosophy and then, until his effective retirement in 1914, the Chair of Modern Philosophy. Twice a week during the teaching semester, he would deliver one course on a philosophical problem (on Fridays) and then another on a great philosophical text (on Saturdays). While there is no complete list of the texts he taught on Saturdays, the topics of his Friday courses are known:

- *The Idea of Causality* (1900–1)
- *The Idea of Time* (1901–2)
- *The History of the Idea of Time* (1902–3)
- *The History of Theories of Memory* (1903–4)
- *The Evolution of the Problem of Freedom* (1904–5)
- *Theories of the Will* (1906–7)
- *General Ideas* (1907–8)
- *On the Nature of Spirit and the Relation of Thought and the Brain* (1908–9)
- *Personality* (1910–11)
- *The Idea of Evolution* (1911–12)
- *On Philosophical Method, Concept and Intuition* (1913–14)[1]

Founded in 1530, the Collège is a very old institution. It is also unique in that it has always been open to the public and confers no degrees. Then as now, courses can be enjoyed by specialists and enthusiasts alike without having to pay or register. Today, lectures can be attended in person or online. And the Collège keeps excellent records of past courses, many of which are faithfully preserved in audio or video format. The same cannot be said for those courses delivered before the recording era, as the majority are lost to history. Indeed, the fact that we have perfect transcriptions of a handful of Bergson's courses is something of a miracle. For, you see, he lectured without notes and well before recording devices had made their way into classrooms.[2]

A scheduling conflict is to thank. One of Bergson's most devoted students was the writer Charles Péguy. He attended almost all the courses in person. Yet there were four years when he couldn't make the Friday sessions. And so he did what any sensible student would have done in his position—he hired legal stenographers, the brothers Raoul and Fernand Corcos, to capture the lectures verbatim. These notes were stored and forgotten in three red cardboard boxes until 1997, when they were donated by Péguy's estate to the Jacques Doucet Library and eventually published by the Presses universitaires de France.[3] Those four courses are *The Idea of Time* (1901–2, published in 2019),[4] *The History of the Idea of Time* (1902–3, published in 2016), *The History of Theories of Memory* (1903–4, published in 2018), and *The Evolution of the Problem of Freedom* (1904–5, published in 2017). They are the only complete records we have of Bergson's teaching at the Collège. Yet courtesy of Péguy and the Corcos brothers, they are a perfect record, unblemished by the usual worries of a pre-recording era. We don't need to wonder if Bergson actually said this or whether a student made a mistake, or took an interpretive liberty, in noting it down. Nor do we miss any of the important asides or spontaneous observations of a spoken lecture, which so often convey its essence. It is all there, preserved as it was spoken more than a century ago.

Bergson's lectures at the Collège will interest several audiences. For philosophers, they give a fuller picture of his thought. So often, Bergson uses the lectures to recapitulate ideas from his previously published books, as well as to prepare the ground for those ahead. His lectures also contain deep reflections on many core topics in contemporary philosophy such as the nature of time, the difference between brain and mind, the relation of memory to perception, and the vindication of freedom over determinism. Last but not least, Bergson's lectures are part of an exceedingly rare genre of modern philosophy: spoken and not written philosophy, expressed as thinking in the making that is nevertheless remarkably structured and analytically lucid.

For intellectual historians, the lectures are a feast: they are a slice of the living thought of a great thinker and a rich commentary on the history of ancient and modern philosophy. This last point is worth emphasizing. All of Bergson's published books are based on a close engagement with a cutting-edge natural or social science of his day: psychophysics and neuroscience in *Time and Free Will* (1889) and *Matter and Memory* (1896), evolutionary biology in *Creative Evolution* (1907), relativity theory in *Duration and Simultaneity* (1922), and sociology and anthropology in *The Two Sources of Morality and Religion* (1932). Yet in those books, Bergson is virtually silent about his philosophical antecedents—which can give the impression, as commentators have often remarked, that he springs from the ground as if without any predecessors at all.[5] The lectures offer an indispensable corrective as they provide Bergson's engagement with philosophy and philosophers and his accounts of how, for example, Plato, Aristotle, the Stoics, Plotinus, Descartes, Berkeley, Spinoza, Leibniz, and Kant wrestled with similar metaphysical, psychological, biological, and social and political issues. In this sense, we recommend reading Bergson's lectures alongside his published books as a two-pronged approach, with the books engaging the leading sciences, and the lectures the history of philosophy, to tackle wickedly difficult interdisciplinary problems.

Finally, for cultural historians, the lectures are a marvelous artifact of Belle Époque France. From about 1905 and building from there, Bergson had become a celebrity, and his lectures were the cultural capital of the day. Thanks in part to the quality and accessibility of those lectures, the fashionable and wealthy flocked to hear him speak, including—a new phenomenon for the time—women too.[6] The truly rich sent valets hours in advance to secure seats, and the minutes before Bergson's Friday lecture course could be riotous, with seven hundred or so people jostling to secure one of 350 seats. For a decade, Paris was well and truly gripped by Bergsonmania.[7]

Those were the later courses. But the ones that Péguy was unable to attend, and for which we have transcripts, were given early in Bergson's tenure. The atmosphere back then was, shall we say, much more low-key. In 1900 he was not yet a star and, as the historian François Azouvi puts it, his early listeners had the feeling of being the chosen few of a new church. Here is how the poet Tancrède de Visan describes the 1900–1 course on causality:

> We were a half-dozen faithful who met together in this small poorly-lit room, almost a sanctuary. Bergson entered quickly—in a hurry, one might say—like a lion tamer, and a very plain one at that. He was short but, behind that meagre pulpit of grimy wood, he seemed very tall, with his outstretched neck and bird-like head thrown in front, as if attracted by the pull of our friendly attention. Sitting on uncomfortable benches, benches for choir boys, and using our knees as desks, we listened with reverence to that small pinched voice that reached down to the bottom of our restless hearts. Ah, with what thirst we gulped it down, that voice flowing with poetry! For while most philosophers write well, many speak poorly; and we who navigated through doctrines only to reach the harbor of lofty and serious literature—the literature of ideas, loaded with the heavy baggage of methods—we could not remain indifferent to the expression of a thought that wished to be poetic in order to be even truer.
>
> His eyes focused on his own inner vision, Bergson spoke without notes, without any paper at all, now worrying a tiny handkerchief, now joining his hands in front of him, with the look of a diver who wished to plunge further into the mind. His words escaped, admirably linked, and, on their elegant and subtle metaphors, lifted whirlwinds of evocative thoughts and whiffs of suggestions.[8]

Fame can change a thinker. An adoring crowd, a magazine profile, or an online following can easily turn a bookish academic into a different sort of public intellectual. We think it safe to assume, however, that this wasn't the case with Bergson. He always shunned the limelight, and while notoriety never bothered him, popularity did. "Odious" was the word he used, and he meant it.[9] The later lectures that made Paris swoon were likely of a similar kind as those spoken to a faithful few, even if the friendly attention Visan speaks of was no longer quite as intimate.

The standard view in philosophy is that the popularity of a doctrine is secondary—a distant second—to the merit of its content. Ideas are one thing, uptake another. Yet Azouvi is quite correct to claim that the popularity of a doctrine is proof of the author's capacity to read and interpret his or her own milieu. "Bergson's philosophy," he observes, "more than any other, struck contemporaries as capable of providing a means to understand the world appearing before their eyes in 1900, this world that we today also call *modern*, and whose richness and muchness still strikes us today, a century on. Were they wrong to believe it?"[10] In this respect, Bergson's lectures provide a picture of his own world and, so long as we continue to be its heirs, of ours as well.

* * *

Our concern in editing Bergson's lectures for publication in English was to make them not just readable but audible. This meant transposing them from the format of an oral presentation in French—which, however improvised, is still quite polished—into a form that an English-speaking audience will recognize as something spoken, something meant to be listened to rather than read. Hence, for example, sentences that begin with an adverb or a conjunction, or the use of contractions.

It also required special attention to the flow of Bergson's periods and to their construction on the spot. The elaboration and logical connection of ideas and concepts with one another and with their antecedents in the history of philosophy is buttressed by a wealth of recurring images, expressions, and turns of phrase that will be familiar to his readers. But these ideas are also, and importantly, linked by a host of adverbial phrases (such as *en somme*), conjunctions (such as *donc*), and the like, that serve a connecting function and characterize the spoken word. These have, therefore, been retained even where, in the comparable enterprise of turning a talk into a book chapter or article, they would have been cut.

A central feature of these lectures—inextricably tied in with Bergson's philosophy as an effort to describe reality "in the making"[11]—is that, speaking without notes, Bergson articulates the points he is making as he is talking. He often does not leave it at the initial expression, however, and rearticulates a thought by starting anew or by inserting explanations of one of the terms he began with. Sometimes this leads to a sentence being left unfinished or to its changing subjects as it is spoken.

It thus bears emphasizing once more that these courses were not intended to take the written form in which they survive, nor were these transcripts meant to be published.

The typescripts, for instance, are not always consistent in their punctuation, nor generally in the way the sentences are structured on the page. Basing ourselves on the conventions of English usage, we have sought to remedy such inconsistencies and strike a balance between the oral and the written word. For instance, we intentionally refrained from introducing additional ellipses to mark the development of a thought. All ellipses thus either mark suspension points from the French transcript or are used to adapt existing translations to Bergson's use of a given passage. None of them are used to indicate cuts to the French text.

Punctuation, however, is just one set of problems that arises only on the page, as it were. Spellings and capitalizations are another. Here we followed the conventions of philosophical writing.

A third, important set is homophones. One prominent example is the fact that in spoken French, the future tense and the conditional in the first-person singular (*–ai* and *-ais*, respectively) are indistinguishable. Here, too, we chose the solution most likely adapted had these lectures been given in English. Where ambiguities exist, these are pointed out in the notes.

All notes are editors' or translator's notes, and most are based on the tremendous scholarly work of the French editors.

Occasionally, we simply shifted something Bergson said into the notes for ease of reading. When he cites a passage using the page number in a particular French edition, for example, we moved such specifics and provided references to an English version instead.

The majority of notes contain references to Bergson's books and lectures. Bergson does refer to earlier work of his, but only ever in passing. References to such work, both earlier and, in the case of *Creative Evolution*, contemporaneous, thus do not mark self-quotations (except, of course, where Bergson explicitly cites himself) but indicate parallel passages that draw from the same source.

There are several additions beyond the notes. For easy comparison, the page numbers of the French editions are given in the margins. And for ease of orientation, we added descriptive tables of contents and detailed indexes.

Where the usefulness of an interpolated term (the original French, the referent of a pronoun, and the like) is such that it justifies the disruption caused, it is inserted in square brackets.

Some minor mistakes were silently corrected.

Another silent change is the choice of generic and thus gender-neutral terms for generic uses, "human being" rather than "man," for example, and the use of plurals rather than gendered singulars and their respective pronouns. Where that was not possible, we retained Bergson's gendered—and that, overwhelmingly, means masculine—nouns and pronouns.

In presenting English editions of Bergson's lectures at the Collège de France, we acknowledge a great debt of gratitude to their French editors—to Arnaud François for *Freedom* and *Memory*, to Camille Riquier for *Time*, and to Frédéric Worms for overseeing the entire project.[12]

Notes

1. Bergson was on leave several times, hence the lacunae. See also below, 21–22n1–2.
2. For more on the institutional context of Bergson's lectures on the Collège de France, see Céline Surprenant, "Bergson at the Collège de France," in *The Bergsonian Mind*, ed. Mark Sinclair and Yaron Wolf, 28–41 (London: Routledge, 2021).
3. Camille Riquier, "Présentation," in *Histoire de l'idée de temps: Cours au Collège de France 1902-1903*, by Henri Bergson, 7–16 (Paris: Press universitaires de France, 2016), 13–16.
4. Of this course, only the last few sessions were recorded stenographically, though some students' notes survive that have allowed for a reconstruction.
5. See Mark Sinclair, *Bergson* (London: Routledge, 2019), 4, as well as several essays in Sinclair and Wolf, eds., *The Bergsonian Mind*, and in Lefebvre and Schott, eds., *Interpreting Bergson: Critical Essays* (Cambridge: Cambridge University Press, 2020).

6. Emily Herring, “Henri Bergson, Celebrity,” *Aeon*, May 6, 2019, https://aeon.co/essays/henri-bergson-the-philosopher-damned-for-his-female-fans
7. See Philippe Soulez and Frédéric Worms, *Bergson* (Paris: Presses universitaires de France, 2002), 95–101.
8. François Azouvi, *La Gloire de Bergson: Essai sur le magistère philosophique* (Paris: Gallimard, 2007), 99–100.
9. M, 1555.
10. Azouvi, *Gloire de Bergson*, 15–16.
11. See below, 15–16 and 49–50, and CE, 210/238.
12. There are at present no plans to prepare an English edition of the remaining lecture course, *The Idea of Time* (1901–2), reconstructed and edited by Gabriel Meyer-Bisch.

ACKNOWLEDGMENTS

The translator would like to thank colleagues at Penn State University for helping locate certain of Bergson's quotations from the history of philosophy: Uygar Abaci, Brady Bowman, and Mark Sentesy.

The editors would like to thank the team at Bloomsbury Academic. Donald Landes and Tony Bruce at Routledge were very kind to share the new translation of *Creative Evolution* before it went into print. Thanks also to Henning Schmidgen for his insights on Bergson and experimental psychology. Special thanks are due to Melanie White. The editors and translator are deeply grateful to Arnaud François, whose clarifications were invaluable.

INTRODUCTION

HENRI BERGSON, FREEDOMIST

Alexandre Lefebvre and Nils F. Schott

Henri Bergson produced two major works on freedom and gave both rather technical titles. The first was his first book, *Essay on the Immediate Givens of Consciousness* (1889), and the second is the present volume of his 1904–5 lectures at the Collège de France, *The Evolution of the Problem of Freedom*. In both cases, the English publisher opted for punchier titles—*Time and Free Will* and *Freedom*, respectively—which have their merits. Still, there is something to be said for the precision of the original versions.

Take the title of the *Essay*. With the term "immediate givens" Bergson states his thesis: direct contact, without distance or mediation, is possible with reality. Today, this might seem plausible (or at least arguable), but Bergson knew that it would ruffle the philosophical orthodoxy of his day. For he asserted precisely what the reigning Kantianism denied, which is that we can access a level of experience unmediated by language or conceptual frameworks—something really real, as it were. Hence the reason why an *essai* was needed, the word in French meaning an attempt as well as a literary form. Linguistic animals that we humans are, and living as we moderns do in a world that privileges science, measurement, and quantity, an effort is needed to roll back the symbols and categories we impose on ourselves and the world. It takes an essay (*un essai*) to regain the immediate givens (*les données immédiates*) we deny ourselves.[1]

That's quite a title. So too is *The Evolution of the Problem of Freedom*. Simple enough on the surface, each term marks a concept that receives philosophical treatment in Bergson's oeuvre: evolution, problem, freedom. Our introduction will address all three and explain their interconnection, starting with *problem*.

The Evolution of the Problem *of Freedom*

Midway through his lecture course (on February 10, 1905, to be precise), Bergson pauses to reflect on what reasoning actually consists of. It starts and finishes, he says, with one person's intention to communicate a unified and integral thought to someone else. Unfortunately (or perhaps fortunately) the person with the idea cannot simply beam it into the minds of other people. He or she must break it up into propositions that build on one another, and which, if successful, the listener pieces back together into an approximation of the original idea.

> They want to prove something, they have an intention. This intention subdivides in the person's mind into a series of propositions, which, understood by us and

> admitted into our mind, are going to reconstitute and reproduce the idea, the original intention of the person who spoke. We thus have an intention in the one who reasons, an intention, that is, something simple, indivisible, undivided, concentrated, something that is then scattered into a series of propositions, which represent the same thing in a diffuse state and that, when they are heard and understood by the person who is looking to be convinced, merge, concentrate themselves again, and reproduce the original unity of the intention from which they emerged. (99)

These remarks are made in the context of Bergson's examination of the different meanings of that trickiest of Greek words, *logos*. At the same time, they can stand for the purpose of the lecture course more generally. Not so much because Bergson has an idea to get across (that would be true of any of his utterances) but, more specifically, because his first lecture on freedom begins with the claim that all his auditors—and really, all of us who continue to inhabit roughly the same modern dispensation of culture and society as him—share an intuitive understanding of what freedom means. Bergson's opening gambit is that his simple idea matches our own.

"No matter what opinion people hold in this regard and no matter what theory they advance on the subject of freedom," Bergson announces in the opening minutes of his course, "there's one point on which everyone agrees: freedom is a certain characteristic that is inherent or that seems to be inherent to our action such as it immediately appears to us, such as it's given to our immediate consciousness" (12).

What exactly this certain something called freedom is will have to be defined. For now, the claim is that we all intuitively know what it is: a quality, one that is lived and felt, internal to our action. And yet—here comes *the problem of* freedom—Bergson is not blind to the fact, nor does he think we are blind to it either, that in modern times the very notion of freedom seems dubious. Doesn't scientific necessity explain everything? Don't astonishing advances in the human, medical, and biological sciences (including psychology, physiology, and neurology) herald a future where all thoughts and actions, human or otherwise, can be accounted for by determinate causes?[2]

The problem of freedom, in other words, is that we live in a time of tremendous scientific understanding of the natural world; what's more, we widely accept that this understanding can (or with further progress, will eventually) bear on human beings and provide accurate causal explanations of all our forms of life; and nevertheless, Bergson insists, our belief in freedom not only endures, it intensifies. The problem of freedom is the problem that our action, which we believe is free, poses to our speculation, which we believe denies the possibility of freedom.

How did we get here? Why do we oscillate between two contradictory ideas that are nevertheless simple, intuitive, and compelling? We know and feel that freedom is real; we think and reason that freedom is an illusion (16–17). This is what the lecture course seeks to explain. And to do that, Bergson will need to produce an elaborate series of propositions—a chain of reasoning that spans twenty two-hour sessions—to explain how the problem of freedom has evolved over the long course of Western philosophy, religion, society, and science, from antiquity to the present.

The Evolution *of the Problem of Freedom*

"Are we really free?" seems to be one of those timeless questions of philosophy and religion, on par with "how do I know if what I believe is true?", "what's the right thing to do?", and "what happens when we die?" But Bergson is crystal clear that this question, along with any other that commands enduring attention, had to be asked in the first place. It doesn't spring ready-made from the essence of the human mind. It takes a creative act from someone working within a specific intellectual tradition and social context.

This insight is based on thoughts Bergson would later elaborate on in his final published book. There he observes that philosophical breakthroughs occur not when some age-old problem is finally solved but when a new problem comes along to displace it. This takes effort and ingenuity; it is also when the real fireworks of thinking happen. "Stating the problem," he writes, "is not simply uncovering, it is inventing. . . . In mathematics and still more in [philosophy], the effort of invention consists most often in raising the problem, in creating the terms in which it will be stated."[3]

Bergson's course on freedom implicitly begins from this insight about the creation of philosophical problems. In his opening lectures he insists that ancient philosophers did not, one fine day, simply start talking about the nature of freedom as if that were an established and set topic. Something was required for freedom to become a live concept and concern. What was it? Well, Bergson explains, it took the advent of cogent theories of determinism. The proverbial chicken of freedom needed to hatch from the egg of determinism. Consider his summary reflections on Socrates, which set up his upcoming treatment of Stoicism, the first consistently determinist doctrine:

> Socrates didn't speak of freedom, he didn't pronounce the word, he didn't discuss the thing. We can only discuss freedom—I've said this many times already in relation to other questions—when we're face to face with determinist doctrines. Freedom only becomes aware of itself, only seeks to articulate itself when it faces doctrines that aim to deny it. Now, the question was not yet posed in Socrates's time; it's thus natural that we find in Socrates neither a discussion nor a formal exposition of freedom. (52)

The problem of freedom that Bergson announces in his title turns out to be, in fact, two twinned problems: the problem of determinism and, in its wake, the problem of freedom. While it is clear that the former came before the latter, it is equally apparent that egg and chicken will continually interact and reshape one another through the history of philosophy. This ongoing dynamic, and its many twists and turns, constitute what Bergson will call the *evolution* of the problem of freedom (and, had he wished to say so, the *evolution* of the problem of determinism).

Bergson's lectures on freedom were contemporaneous with the writing of the book that would make him an intellectual and cultural superstar, *Creative Evolution* (1907). Innumerable points of reference, allusion, and anticipation can be found between the two—and the reader will discover many in the editorial notes to this volume.[4] Stepping back from the details, we believe that Bergson's lectures are indebted in two main ways to his theory of biological evolution.

The first pertains to our topic from a moment ago: problems and the evolution of problems. That the history of philosophy proceeds by a process of problematization is not so astonishing. One thinker's solution swiftly becomes another's problem, which then launches a tradition in a new direction.[5] It is, on the other hand, surprising to hear biological evolution described in the same manner. Yet this is exactly what Bergson proposes in chapter 2 of *Creative Evolution*—each and every organism, right down to its individual qualities and capabilities, represents a solution to a problem posed by evolution. Why, for example, do insects have such marvelously well-adapted instincts? The answer is clear: to solve a particular problem posed by its environment over the course of an unfathomably long history. And why, he continues, do human beings have such developed intellectual powers? Well, perhaps to solve the same vital problem that confronts insects, albeit in a completely different manner. The instinct of insects and the intellect of human beings, he goes so far as to say, "represent two equally elegant but diverging solutions to one and the same problem."[6] Yet the broader point is that all these solutions will, over the expanse of evolutionary time, cumulatively and continually modify the problems that confront future species. Life never stops moving, with microbes, plants, animals, and all organisms great and small trying to scratch out ways to survive and reproduce that will alter the problems faced by their successors, who will then have to evolve their own vital solutions, and so on forever and always.

The evolution of the problem of freedom is of a kind, albeit less dizzying in size and scope. Determinists will generate a theory of cosmic and human necessity, to which defenders of freedom—*libertistes*, "freedomists," Bergson calls them and counts himself among (18)—rally with renewed theories of their own and set the terms for subsequent doctrines of necessity. It is an endless process, and Bergson has no illusions that his own contributions will bring it to a halt.

That said, there is a key difference between how evolution in life and evolution in philosophy proceed. In *Creative Evolution*, Bergson criticizes a biological theory that had powerful adherents in his day: *saltation*, a conception of evolution where new species appear by sudden breakthroughs rather than the continuous accumulation of minor variations—*saltare* in Latin meaning to dance or leap.[7] But when it comes to his discussion of the problem of freedom, Bergson does not hesitate to employ such a notion. Determinist doctrines, he observes, make slow and steady progress, only to be interrupted by eruptions of new theories and reclamations of freedom. The progress of the idea of freedom "didn't take place in a continuous manner, as it did for the idea of necessity," he says. "It took place in a discontinuous manner, in fits and starts, I'd almost say in explosions, in two or three great explosions, no more than that" (19). And slightly later, "So there we have what will be striking in this history, the progressive and continuous character of the evolution of the idea of necessity and the rather explosive character of the idea or, rather, the intuition of freedom" (20).

The tortoise and Achilles, the plodder and the dancer—these are the crisscrossing rhythms that make up the evolution of the problem of freedom. But before we discuss the explosions of freedom identified by Bergson, there is a second respect in which his conception of freedom is indebted to his contemporary work on evolution. And it marks a departure from (or more precisely, an addition to) his early conception of freedom in *Essay on the Immediate Givens of Consciousness.*

In that book, the enemy of freedom is not so much determinism or necessity as inauthenticity. Being free for the young Bergson means to act from our deepest self, the self that carries forward the whole of its unique past in every thought, feeling, and action. The trouble, however, is that most of us most of the time do not own and live up to our singularity, opting instead for the ease of ready-made opinions, convenient clichés and symbolizations, and plans of life stamped with the imprimatur of social convention. The situation seems so dire to Bergson that he concludes, "many live this kind of life, and die without having known true freedom."[8] And so, when he urges on his reader to reclaim their freedom, he doesn't exactly mean for people to behave more spontaneously. He instead calls for us to be authors of ourselves. To be free in this special sense is not to be un-determined (whatever that would mean). It is to be determined by a very special cause: myself, me who overflows with a past that is uniquely mine and prepares for a future life and self with no other model.[9]

Bergson never abandoned this subjectivist conception of freedom. But as he worked on biological evolution, he layered it with another: freedom understood as creativity, novelty, and unforeseeability. And this kind of freedom—unlike his earlier notion of self-determination, which requires a subject able to retain in memory and consciously claim the whole of their past—is something found in much more than human beings. Bergson even came to believe that this aspect of freedom is present in all biological life and serves to distinguish it from inorganic matter:

> [I]f by "freedom" we mean the creation of certain absolutely unforeseeable actions, of actions that add something to the conditions in which they are given, then this indetermination is found everywhere where there is consciousness, and de jure, at least de jure, everywhere where there is organic life [*organisation*]. For the conclusion I'm going to propose is this: organic life, life, in short, is consciousness; organic life appears in the world at the same time as consciousness; and the raison d'être of organic life, like the raison d'être of consciousness, is choice, that is, the creation of something. If there's choice, there's creation, since with the elements of reflection we cannot say a priori what will happen. What will happen adds something to the elements; consequently, there is genuine creation. (78)

Here we have, two years prior to its publication, the great thesis of *Creative Evolution*: life is consciousness and consciousness is life, because both are free in the sense of creative unpredictable abundance. Duration, which Bergson had previously located only in human consciousness, is now co-extensive with life itself; and the lecture course on freedom is the site where Bergson begins to work out these implications. It is a rare glimpse of a philosophy in the making, where a topic that Bergson may have seemed to be done with (freedom) is reinvigorated by a theory (of biology and life) he is busy building.

A charming aside in the lectures makes the point. Near the end of the course, in a session on Leibniz, Bergson imagines a mathematician who is given a choice. He (and Bergson is of his era in speaking of men only) can either choose to discover a one-sheet version of a beautiful new theorem, or else he can be given the "thousand little slips of paper" on which it had been developed (188). It's a no-brainer for the mathematician: he'll take the sheet. Historians of philosophy (and historically minded philosophers), however, are built differently. Gluttons for punishment, the thousand pages of working-out seem preferable.

Luckily, readers of Bergson today are not confronted by this dilemma. His books are elegant theorems—not single-page versions, of course, but polished and complete. The lectures, by contrast, are akin to slips of paper, a veritable "laboratory" as Arnaud François aptly puts it, where Bergson cooks up new ideas and also puts parts of his oeuvre into dialogue that are either absent from, or only receive a highly compressed treatment, in his published work.[10] In this case, Bergson will connect the problem of freedom and indetermination to great theories of necessity and determinism from the history of philosophy (with Stoicism leading the ancient and Spinoza and Leibniz the modern charge). How freedom is vindicated in the face of such formidable challengers is the final topic of our introduction.

The Evolution of the Problem of Freedom

"Two or three great explosions, no more than that," says Bergson about the history of freedom. But what does he mean? What are these great moments when freedom breaks through the barricades of determinism?

The lecture course is not always consistent on this point (or at any rate, it does not fully follow through on its original suggestion). When Bergson initially makes the comment about explosions of freedom, he has specific events and delimited historical periods in mind (19–20). They are: Golden Age Athens, from Pericles to Aristotle; a Judeo-Christian moment, which seems to refer to early Christianity; and the 1789 French Revolution. Bang, bang, bang—these, Bergson declares in his opening lecture, are the explosions of freedom from millennia of Western history.

Perhaps this declaration served as a placeholder for Bergson to pick up thirty years down the road. In *The Two Sources of Morality and Religion* (1932), he argues that a very special emotion—love, which shares many qualities with freedom—bursts through at punctual moments in history to generate enduring religious and political doctrines and institutions.[11] Yet the fact is that his 1904–5 course on freedom does not proceed in this manner. First of all, beyond the first lecture, Bergson focuses almost exclusively on intellectual history. Social, political, and religious contexts and events hardly factor. Second, more importantly, while Bergson does indeed divide his lectures into three historical periods, they are long expanses of time, not explosions in any recognizable sense. The majority are dedicated to ancient thinkers (lectures 1–12, as expected given that Bergson held the Chair of Greek and Latin Philosophy until just a few weeks before the beginning of the course); next is a short yet crucial section on Descartes, which serves to transition from ancient to modern philosophy (lectures 13–14); and finally come the modern thinkers who bring us to Bergson's historical present (lectures 15–20). Three periods, yes. But explosions? Not exactly.

How then should we interpret Bergson's remark? We believe it is useful to separate the words "two or three" from "explosions." On the one hand, Bergson distinguishes between two vast historical periods—ancient and modern—which pose qualitatively different problems of freedom and determinism. And it is within these two periods, on the other hand, that he presents the many explosions of freedom that challenge the deterministic doctrines of their day.

Bergson naturally begins with the ancients and devotes much time to showing how they locate freedom in a different place than us moderns. Moderns tend to think of freedom in terms of action and will: it is a quality and feeling that accompanies what we say and do. That notion would have been foreign to ancient thinkers. Freedom, for them, is a question of knowledge and consists in the choice either to remain ignorant (which would determine one's life in an ignoble and unhappy direction) or to seek wisdom (which would determine one's life in a worthy and happy direction). Human life is determined one way or the other. Where we have a say in the matter is how we direct our attention and learning.

The story thus begins with the famous trio of Socrates, Plato, and Aristotle, all of whom believed (albeit in often incompatible ways) that remaining ignorant or becoming wise was a human choice—perhaps the only meaningful and fateful choice we ever make. But the problem of freedom, as we suggested earlier, only truly takes flight with the advent of determinism. Bergson will thus devote the crucial seventh, eighth, and ninth lectures to Stoicism and the theory of universal necessity. In many ways a modern doctrine, Stoicism sets the stage for later thinkers who would either deny that nature was a closed and predictable causal system (such as Epicurus) or who would concede the point yet retain a place for freedom in a life devoted to contemplation (such as Plotinus). Moves and countermoves, the evolution of the problems of freedom and determinism in antiquity proceeds apace.

But then, late in the final session on Plotinus, Bergson introduces the great plot twist of the lectures: a paradigm shift brought on by Christianity and developed by medieval and early modern theologians and philosophers (143–6). "This idea," he explains, is that "action prevails over speculation, that the will is superior to the intellect in the sense that the intellect can be considered a creation of the will" (143). Metaphysically, action is superior to speculation: the divine will and creation are prior to everything. Ethically speaking, the charitable, not the contemplative, life is godly. Thus a new evolution is set into motion. Descartes is the great mover here; a figure at once old and new, he returns to the voluntarist roots of Christianity while also planting the seeds of modern psychology. And from there Bergson will set out the modern problem of freedom and determinism as it is waged on the ground of will and action rather than intellect and contemplation.

Spinoza and Leibniz are the great determinists, with Rousseau and Kant asserting that human freedom is the one reality we can really know and experience.

With his lectures on Kant, we reach the last of the "thousand slips of paper" on which Bergson had developed the philosophical antecedents for his views on freedom. But if the reader likes, he or she can then turn to the "one-sheet" theorems that precede and succeed these lectures: *Essay on the Givens of Consciousness* and *Creative Evolution*, both of which begin from a critique of the Kantian orthodoxy of his time on issues of freedom and knowledge. It is a large program of reading, granted. But we recommend it on two counts.

First, taken together, this volume of lectures and those two books capture the complete view of Bergson's conception of freedom. Second, the lectures and the books present two different modes of doing philosophy that have a direct bearing on the topic of freedom. Bergson's books, like all great works of philosophy, are products of painstaking craft. A first draft is written, then another, and another—and through this process pieces are assembled, screws tightened, and coats of polish applied until, finally, a book is ready to be sent into the world. The lectures, by contrast, have a different rhythm, even a different timing and temporality. They were delivered and recorded on the spot, with all the open-endedness and unpredictability that Bergson taught us to regard as defining qualities of the present moment. Seen from this perspective, the lectures are not simply more of Bergson's thoughts on freedom. These thousand slips of paper are a philosophy in the making as well as, perhaps, a philosopher in the making, one who in telling the grand history of the problem of freedom and determinism in Western philosophy is well on his way to becoming a freedomist.

Notes

1. On the title of *Essai sur les données immédiates de la conscience*, see Frédéric Worms, "Présentation," in *Essai sur les données immédiates de la conscience*, by Henri Bergson (Paris: Presses universitaires de France, 2007), 7–13 and Suzanne Guerlac, *Thinking in Time: An Introduction to Henri Berson* (Ithaca, NY: Cornell University Press, 2006), 42–4.
2. On the scientific milieu of Bergson's time, against which he and others sought to vindicate freedom, see Larry S. McGrath, *Making Spirit Matter: Neurology, Psychology, and Selfhood in Modern France* (Chicago, IL: Chicago University Press, 2020). McGrath is especially adept at showing the neurophysiological form that determinism took (both then and now) in the challenge to human freedom and that Bergson discusses at length in *Time and Free Will*, *Matter and Memory*, and elsewhere.
3. CM, 59/52.
4. The editor of the French edition of these lectures, Arnaud François, was also responsible for the magisterial critical edition of *L'évolution créatrice* (Paris: Presses universitaires de France, 2007).
5. For a Bergsonian treatment of the history of philosophy as the history of its problematizations, see Gilles Deleuze and Félix Guattari, *What Is Philosophy?* trans. Hugh Tomlinson and Graham Burchell (New York: Columbia University Press, 1994).

6. CE, 131/144.
7. CE, 63–4/63–4. In this regard Bergson, who has the theories of Hugo de Vries and William Bateson in mind, agrees with Leibniz's dictum, *natura non facit saltus* ("nature does not jump"); compare his remark on the *saltus* below, 164.
8. TFW, 166/125.
9. Vladimir Jankélévitch provides an excellent commentary on this aspect of Bergson's theory of freedom. See his *Henri Bergson*, ed. Alexandre Lefebvre and Nils F. Schott, trans. Nils F. Schott (Durham, NC: Duke University Press, 2015), 49–65 and 221–2.
10. See his Introduction, "Vie et liberté" to the French edition of *L'évolution du problème de la liberté: Cours au Collège de France*, by Henri Bergson, 7–14 (Paris: Presses universitaires de France, 2017), 10.
11. TS, ch. 3, 209–65/221–82; Alexandre Lefebvre, *Human Rights as a Way of Life: On Bergson's Political Philosophy* (Stanford, CA: Stanford University Press, 2013), 83–109; and Alexandre Lefebvre and Nils F. Schott, "Closed and Open Societies," in *The Bergsonian Mind*, ed. Sinclair and Wolf, 251–63.

LECTURE 1
DECEMBER 6, 1904

Gentlemen, I ought to begin by devoting the first lecture of this course to the work of the [15] philosopher who held, unfortunately for far too few years, the chair to which I've been transferred: Gabriel Tarde, whose memory we preserve with great reverence.[1]

As I was re-reading his work, I realized that it is difficult, not to say impossible, to summarize in a single lecture, and that this oeuvre, which is dominated by ideas and views of the utmost importance, is perhaps still more important, thanks to the detailed views and the suggestions of all kinds with which it is filled. For Tarde was above all a great evocator of ideas. It seemed to me that it would be better to devote not just one lecture this year to the study of this oeuvre but one of the courses next year or one of the later years to it; probably next year, the Saturday course, the one I'm devoting this year to commenting on one of Herbert Spencer's works. I'll do for *The Laws of Imitation*, Tarde's most important work, what I'm going to do this year for Spencer's *First Principles*, a critical commentary.[2]

It's not without reason that I bring these two names, Tarde and Spencer, together. One name calls forth the other; one oeuvre completes the other. The conclusions of these two philosophers are as opposed to one another as conclusions can be. One could oppose Tarde to Spencer on nearly every point, just as the intellectual temperament, if we can say this, the intellectual temperament of these two philosophers differs profoundly. [16] Spencer, as we'll see, is a deducer [*un déductif*], a great deducer and above all a deducer, despite the huge mass of facts his work is full of. But a closer look at this work indeed shows, as does the study of his biography, that he was above all a great constructor of systems. He started as a mechanical engineer and he remained a constructor all his life, with a mechanical *je ne sais quoi* at work in the way he proceeded. Tarde on the contrary was an intuitor [*un intuitif*], a great intuitor, unlike Spencer who, as we'll see, formulated a program in 1860 that already noted, chapter by chapter, all the books that he was to write, and who fulfilled his program, who put forty years into implementing the program he conceived, always moving straight ahead. Tarde on the contrary went here and there, strolling across ideas, strolling for his own pleasure, it seems, for his own pleasure and for the pleasure of others. He started in poetry, he started by composing verse, and one can say that he remained a poet all his life.

In terms of intellectual temperament and from the viewpoint of the conclusions they reach, Tarde and Spencer are very far apart. Yet there is a kinship between them, and this kinship is due to two causes. The objective of the two philosophies is the same. Like Spencer, Tarde started from considering societies; he observed certain fundamental conditions of the existence of societies, and he extended what he had observed about societies by generalizing it, step by step, thereby constructing a system of the world whose starting point is sociological. This is what Tarde did and this is what Spencer did, and this enterprise, it seems to me, is without precedent in the history of philosophy. That's the first point.

Then there's another resemblance, very profound as well, the resemblance in their methods, despite the diversity of the conclusions, a resemblance all the more striking to the extent that the enterprises are hardly different from one another, and that to reach their results, they resorted, above all, to analogical reasoning. Tarde and Spencer are the two philosophers who have made the greatest, I can say the most wonderful, use of reasoning by analogy. So they resemble one another both in terms of objective and in
[17] terms of method. This is why I said that one name calls forth the other; this is why I'm adding that studying one of them calls for studying the other, and undoubtedly, too, later historians of philosophy will associate them very closely.

Gentlemen, as I announced last year, we're going to be concerned this year with the classic problem of freedom.

Immediately, starting with this first lecture, which is necessarily devoted to generalities that are themselves a bit vague, a question arises: What is the problem of freedom? It's hard to define *freedom* if we want to avoid favoring a particular theory and prejudging the solution. It might be easier to define the *problem* of freedom.[3] No matter what opinion people hold in this regard and no matter what theory they advance on the subject of freedom, there's one point on which everyone agrees: freedom is a certain characteristic that is inherent or that seems to be inherent to our action such as it immediately appears to us, such as it's given to our immediate consciousness.

We will[4] to do something, and within this will, immanent to this will, so to speak, there is a certain feeling that we call the feeling of freedom. So freedom is a certain feeling, real or apparent, given forth by immediate consciousness when the will acts. Yet if there is a problem of freedom—and there is a problem of freedom—it's obviously because reflection intervenes: it's a problem only for reflection, for reflective thought. So the problem of freedom is obviously a problem that comes about, that springs from the encounter of immediate consciousness and reflective thought. This is how I'll define it: it is the problem that our action poses for our speculation.

But why does action pose this problem for speculation? Probably because they don't agree. If they agreed, the one would not be a problem for the other. It's probably because the two faculties or the two functions are not absolutely aligned with one another. In fact,
[18] without prejudging the solution to the problem of freedom in any way, it's easy to see that "immediate consciousness" and "reflective consciousness," "action," and "speculation" are not and cannot be aligned with one another.

I'm looking at action, and I'm taking as simple an example as possible, a voluntary act, the act of standing up: I want to stand up; I stand up. Here we have a voluntary act that appears to immediate consciousness as free. The most obvious characteristic of this act is that it's something simple and self-sufficient. We'll say, employing a philosophical term, that this act is an absolute, [that] it can be an absolute.[5] In fact, the voluntary act seems to be self-sufficient; it's something closed, it's a closed system. I'm not saying that the act is undivided. You'll be able to distinguish very clearly the intention of standing up, followed by the act itself of standing up, by the execution—we'd be able to distinguish still other moments, but these are successive, different viewpoints on one and the same simple act, and we can say that the willful act is something simple.[6]

We could take examples that are a lot more complicated. We could take acts that extend over a long time: for example, the act of talking about freedom for an hour. Here we have an act that splinters, that subdivides into as many parts as you like. Yet for all that, it's a simple act in the sense that it's one self-same intention, a single intention, we could almost say an undivided intention that refracts into as many moments as there are words, a bit like a fertilized germ cell subdivides indefinitely and produces living beings. Yet for all that, it's always the same movement, the same thrust.

This is true of [any] voluntary act: however complicated it may be, it is simple, and in any case it appears as something closed, self-sufficient. This is what I'll formulate by saying that the will always appears in units; the will is always dealing with units.[7] The reflective intellect, for its part, always needs two things, it must have two. The reflective intellect, intellect in general, for that matter, could be defined, in opposition to the will, by the prominent characteristic that it needs two terms, that it doesn't bear on unities but [19] on pairs. It must have a pair. We can see this in the entire field of intellectual operations, but if we want to spare ourselves the task of listing all the different intellectual functions, we need only look at the common expression of all intellectual acts, their common measure: every intellectual act can be formulated in a proposition, and a proposition contains two terms, a subject and an attribute, and it's no use saying that a term is something intellectual. No, a term is only half of what the intellect considers. It always needs to complete this term with another term. It must have a pair.

I reach for the lamp. You'll say to me: "Well, what? What's with the lamp?" If I've lit . . . You'll say to me: "What has been lit, what?" It takes two terms for the intellect to be satisfied: "The lamp is lit." Ah, now we have a proposition where the mind comes to rest, it's face to face with a pair, with two terms that complete one another.

So there's a radical, fundamental, clear, external difference—it goes without saying that I am limiting myself to external differences so as not to enter into the core of the question—there's a very clear external difference between the will and the intellect, and what I'd call a difference in equilibrium conditions.[8] The equilibrium conditions are not the same. The will keeps its balance on a single point, like a person who is standing upright: it occupies one single place, the place where the person's feet touch the floor. I'd compare the equilibrium of the intellect with the equilibrium of a tightrope walker with his balance pole. This equilibrium consists in an oscillation between two possible falls, to the right or to the left, between two possible movements, and it's this duality of possible positions, as it were, that his equilibrium consists in. In a word, the intellect always needs two terms; the will only needs one.

The intellect needs two terms, I must add something: the intellect needs to unite the two terms, precisely to find its equilibrium. I was speaking of the tightrope walker's balance pole. This balance pole, in short, is a link[9] between the two possible falls I was speaking of. Likewise, the intellect always needs a link, it needs to establish a link [20] between the two terms it's dealing with.

This amounts to saying that every intellectual act is a synthesis, quite simply the synthesis of two terms. In a proposition like the one I stated earlier, there's the subject, "the lamp," and there's the attribute, "lit," and then there's a relation established by the mind between the two terms. So every intellectual act is the synthesis of two terms that thereby form a whole.

This is precisely the point that interests us when it comes to events, to facts that succeed one another in time. The mind always considers pairs that present a particular characteristic, which we'll have to try and define, namely that one is called *cause*, the other *effect*.

So to think facts, to think events, is to establish a causal relation between two terms and, ultimately, between an infinity of terms, since each term in turn becomes a cause or an effect depending on our point of view.

Let's return to the example I used earlier. I said: I want to stand up; I stand up. From the viewpoint of immediate consciousness, there's something simple here, an intention realized, something self-sufficient. That's what immediate consciousness says. But reflective thought says something else, it must have a pair. Thought is going to connect this action with a prior situation. I stand up because . . . because I'm hot . . . because I don't like the heat. I stand up for a whole series of reasons that, taken together, constitute a certain situation, and this situation forms a pair with the action on which intelligence comes to rest. So, while for immediate intelligence, the action is self-sufficient, the action is an absolute, for reflective thought, on the contrary, the action, like everything that's the object of reflective thought, is part of a pair such that by taking one of the two terms, we determine the other.

This amounts to saying, in a form that is more precise but not absolutely different, it amounts to saying that our intellect is made above all in order to think what we call a nature, that is, a tangle of causes and effects, a fabric of causes and effects, where cause
[21] and effect always form a pair whose two terms cling together. Our intellect is thus made for thinking a nature whose elements, whose events, if you like, determine one another, while our immediate consciousness, on the contrary—insofar as it bears on our actions—is made for linking up with terms that are self-sufficient, each of which appears to immediate consciousness as a kind of absolute.

The problem of freedom arises from the encounter of these two functions of the intellect, of immediate consciousness and reflective thought, immediate consciousness bearing on self-sufficient terms, on unities, and reflective thought bearing on dualities, on pairs that, connected to one another, constitute a nature in which everything clings together and everything is determined.

I said that these two functions immediately appear as having different characteristics, which even, in certain aspects, exclude one another. We could, gentlemen, take a closer look at the gap I just pointed out between the two functions: rather than narrow, this gap would become wider and wider the more we tried to measure it.

I'll present right away one of the conclusions we'll reach—a conclusion, incidentally, we already reached in an earlier course[10]—I'll present right away what appears to be the most precise formulation of this gap between the will and the understanding, between the will, or the immediate consciousness that we have of the will, and the understanding that works on the products of this will, which products, like all the rest, come to be part of nature.

The difference is this: action takes place in time, that's self-evident; to act is to do something that takes time, that endures and occupies a certain place in the whole of time. Action thus happens in time. Reflection, the intellect, for its part, does not and cannot have time as its object: time is a thing that absolutely escapes the grip of reflective thought.

I've already devoted a whole year, gentlemen, two years, even, to establishing and developing the consequences of this point. Despite appearances, the intellect cannot grasp time. When we want to picture time, we see a line in space, that is, in short, [22]
something that doesn't endure, something already made [*tout fait*]. Of course, we immediately correct ourselves, we say to ourselves: we have to introduce movement into this, and we then see something like a point moving in space. That will then be time. Yes, but when our thought wants to grasp this movement, grasp what there is in time, what happens? It only ever grasps a position, the position of a point, then another position, and then another position, and so on, always positions, never the movement. However, if the moving thing has changed positions, there must indeed have been some movement, at least from one position to the next. Yes, but if we want to grasp this movement, this transition from one position to the next, what are we going to do? We're going to introduce ever more positions into the interval we're considering, an indefinitely increasing number of positions, indefinitely approximating, it seems, the image or the counterfeit of movement, for the movement itself escapes us. We narrow the interval, or we believe we grasp it, just as a child grasps at smoke to catch it, but the smoke escapes and so does the movement between the two positions where we'd like to catch it.

So we cannot grasp time itself by thought, and the symbols by which we express it necessarily are inadequate symbols. If I take inner life, this life that flows in time, but perhaps there is no real duration . . .[11] This is a point to which I should have perhaps returned to earlier. I've shown that the time at issue in the positive sciences is not something that endures. The time in question in the positive sciences is simply a length measured on a certain straight line or on a certain curve starting from a point of origin, and what science considers is always simultaneities, correspondences between points of this line and points of all the other lines, yet nothing but correspondences, nothing but simultaneities.[12]

This is exactly the same for metaphysics when it presupposes that within time properly speaking, there is no time, that there is only space, only lines and curves. External time [23]
is first of all a thing that escapes from the grips of science and the intellect. I said that the inner life is a life that flows in time, that *is* the very flowing of duration. Action takes place in this duration, but the intellect, when it is fixated on action, immobilizes the action, fixates it as well.

To speak more clearly: the intellect cannot grasp the inner life, that which is in the making; it grasps only what is already made. The intellect is made for thinking what is already made, it is not made for thinking what is in the making.[13]

Our action, I said, is in time, I could say that our action is time itself, it's our present.[14] Action is the present, and the present is already the future. What we call the present is a perpetual encroachment on the future, the present leans toward the future, it's an inclination toward the future.[15] That's the very definition of the present, and the intellect, if it were in time, would be in the past and not in the future because it needs something already made.[16] But in reality, it's no more in the past than it's in the present: it takes place outside of time. As I said earlier, it needs pairs, pairs between which the relation, at the moment we consider it, is timeless or supposedly timeless.

With this, gentlemen, I am only repeating, in a somewhat different way, what all philosophers have said since Aristotle, namely, that the intellect thinks in the universal, in the general. The intellect is made for thinking generalities—it is no more in a given time than it is in a determinate place—while consciousness is made for something else. Immediate consciousness, for its part, grasps the singular: it is concerned with time, with what constitutes the development of time itself.

This is why, as I was telling you earlier, there's a gap, and a considerable one that widens the closer we get to it, the closer we think we are getting to it, a gap between intuition such as it is given to immediate consciousness and reflective thought as it usually works.

[24] The history I'm going to sketch in broad strokes in the first part of this course, the history of the problem of freedom, is none other than the history of the mind's oscillations between the testimony of immediate consciousness, which we'll call intuition, if you like, between intuition and the demands of reflective thought insofar as it engages with these givens of intuition.

I'm going to limit myself to sketching this history in very broad strokes because I want to save some time for a theoretical study of the problem. I'm saying it right away, we're making our way toward this theoretical study, and I want to reach the theoretical conclusion toward which we'll be moving without distorting, it goes without saying, the givens of the history of philosophy.

In this history of the human mind's oscillation—between the givens of intuition, which, in short, is freedom, and the conclusions of reflective consciousness, which are always facts that have happened necessarily—in this history, as you'd expect given all I just said, the necessitarian doctrines will always have the lead role. I'll state right away—and I don't need to say this—that my conclusion will not fall on the side of necessity. My conclusion will be entirely different: it will be oriented in the direction of freedom.

At this point, I cannot summarize—moreover, it wouldn't be helpful—the reasons that I'll bring forward, that I'll provide, that I'll allege in support of my conclusions, but I'd like to point right away to one common sense reason in favor of freedom, a reason that is obvious as soon as the problem has been posed in the form we see it posed, a simple good sense reason in favor of freedom. And, I'm saying this right away, this is the reason that will guide us as we make our way to our conclusion. Here's the reason: a priori and considering only the exterior of a problem such as I just posed it, all the chances, all the probabilities are on the side of freedom and not of necessity, and if we wanted to make a bet, we'd have to bet on freedom. And here's why: if reflective thought is right, and if everything is necessity, then I don't understand why I think I'm free, why

I feel free. If reflective thought is right, I don't understand why I have this testimony of [25] immediate and spontaneous consciousness, I don't understand the illusion of freedom. They'll explain it to me, they've provided analyses, they've provided reasons . . . Yes, they'll explain the origin of this illusion to me, but what they won't make me understand is why this illusion persists and endures, why it endures across history. I'll show, in fact, that in this history of theories, to the extent that the human mind has made progress in science, the idea of necessity, of natural laws, has become more and more precise, strengthened, and intensified. We believe a lot more, a lot better in the necessity of nature than Thales of Miletus did, for example. How is it, if the doctrine of necessity has become clearer and clearer, if it imposed itself more and more on the intellect, how is it that the illusion of freedom, that is, in short, a breach of universal necessity, has endured? More than that, how is it that it became stronger? For that, too, will be one of the results of this historical study, as we go across the ages: we'll see that this illusion, this feeling, too, intensifies. However, while it's true that life, as the theory of evolution says, is a perpetual and ever more perfect renewal of internal correspondences and external correspondences, we ought to align ourselves ever more with the objective truth, which is necessity. It's necessity we ought to believe in inwardly. Well, we don't: we continue to believe in our freedom, we believe in it more and more.

So if everything is necessity, I don't understand why we have the illusion of free will, but in contrast, if I really am free, I understand very well why everything appears to me and must appear to me to be necessary.

Do note, gentlemen, that we still consider the intellect to be a kind of *deus ex machina*,[17] something we are given so that we can do philosophy, do science. But philosophy and science are fairly recent products of the intellect. We can maintain that the intellect, at least at its origin, is not made for that. The intellect is made for guiding the will, for the benefit of action. The will, whose role is to act and even to act freely, needs, [26] absolutely needs to have a certain support added to it, whose role will be to enlighten it [*l'éclairer*]. How? What does that mean, to enlighten? To show the will in each case the possible consequences of what it is going to do, that is, it needs certain faculties that work on pairs, that tell it: *In this situation, that is going to follow; if you do this, here's what it's going to result in*, that show it the consequences that necessarily follow, as it were, from the premises.[18] The will must thus enlist a certain faculty, in other words a faculty whose role is to extract repetitions from the surrounding world, to extract cycles that are analogous to what happened in the past, [and] to warn the will about the consequences of its current action.

But note, gentlemen, that the human intellect is not a kingdom within a kingdom[19] and that animals already have a certain kind of intellect, but what constitutes the intellect in animals is the faculty of associating ideas. But what is association?[20] Association, the psychologists say, occurs through resemblance and through contiguity. That is to say, in a given case the animal is able to associate by resemblance, that is, to remember situations analogous to the current situation. And then the animal also associates them by contiguity, that is, it recalls what preceded and especially what followed. So association by resemblance and association by contiguity are what guides action in animals.

In humans, these two associations cling together but without losing their original character, which is above all to serve as a guide for practice and especially for action.

Let's suppose a will like the human will acting in a nature that is chaotic. If this will wants to act, and by definition it does, it needs solid supports. It cannot act if it doesn't form next to itself, around itself, as it were, something like an atmosphere of pairs, of paired elements, such that one [element] being given, the other follows necessarily. We can conceive of this will as creating or constructing centers for itself, such that everything that isn't repetition or similarity is either eliminated or it's as if, for the will, it didn't exist.
[27] What's left then is a little world of causes and effects that follow each other quite regularly and that will be the base, the sustentation, as it were, for its actions, but I don't want to go that far. There's no need for this kind of hypothesis. I'm only saying that if the will is free, it can exercise its freedom, it can will, only on the condition that it enlists an intellect that inevitably bears necessity in itself, that always sees similarities, that establishes necessary relations of cause and effect between all the given terms, such that the very actions of this will, which are effects, appear necessary. Thus, as some people say, everything here below is necessity. If necessity is everywhere, I don't understand how the feeling of freedom takes shape and especially why it persists. But if there is freedom, I understand very well why everything appears to the intellect in the form of necessity.

This is why I said that, a priori, and consulting simple good sense alone, all the chances, all the probabilities, or at least the highest number of probabilities are on the side of free will and that if we must make a bet, we must bet on freedom. But that, gentlemen, is a simple good sense argument, and all in all, good sense is action much more than speculation, and the theories of philosophers are forms of speculation.[21] We mustn't be surprised, then, that in the very brief, very truncated history of the problem I am going to present, the theories of necessity dominate, that they have, as I was saying earlier, the lead role.

This is basically what still happens in all of the debates.[22] You can listen to a debate between a partisan of freedom, that is, a "freedomist," if this word existed,[23] and a partisan of necessity, a determinist. In a debate between a freedomist and a determinist, the determinist always seems to be right. And it's easy to understand why: the determinist always has the frameworks, the habits of thought, of thought in the proper sense, on his side; thought is what intervenes in the debate; he has the frameworks, the habits of thought, language on his side. The freedomist has none of all that. He is forced to appeal to an inner feeling, and this inner feeling, as soon as it wants to express itself, is forced
[28] to borrow terms from reflective thought, terms that are its enemies, as it were. The freedomist is always on the defensive, he cannot go on the offensive; it's the determinist who is on the offensive. The argumentation of the freedomist is necessarily negative, it can only ever consist in denying what the determinist claims. The thesis of freedom doesn't lend itself to a positive formula. It can be expressed, as I'll show, only in terms of the negation of determinism. This is why the freedomist is always on the defensive and is always caught up in negations, while the determinist can be on the offensive and he affirms. At the end of a debate between these two adversaries, the determinist always seems to have the edge.

It's nearly the same thing in the history of philosophy: the leading role is always found on the side of the theories of necessity. It is they that have presented the most complete evolution. I'd even say that in reality the theories of necessity are the only ones to have evolved, they're the only ones to have really evolved in the history of philosophy.

We'll see that from the first Greek thinkers up to our times the idea of necessity progressed by ever making itself more precise, by ever perfecting itself. For the first philosophers of the Ionian school, necessity was only the idea of a vague regularity of nature, like a rhythmic movement of things, a *circulus*, a circle that periodically brings back the same objects and the same event.[24] Then, as we go forward, we see the clear idea of a causal chain emerge, and this idea acquires a certain precision already with the Stoics who formulated, with the greatest clarity, the idea of a universal interdependence of all things and of all phenomena, everything being a function of everything, as it were.

This idea becomes still more precise in antiquity in a philosopher like Plotinus, who, however, is an enemy of the thesis of necessity and who fought the Stoics. We'll see, however, in Plotinus formulations of determinism, of necessity, that are more precise than the ones Stoicism left us.

Then, across the Middle Ages and the Renaissance going up to modernity, this idea becomes ever more precise and transforms. Among the ancients, necessity is simply that of a qualitative determination, as we would say: under certain given conditions a [29] phenomenon produces a given effect in regard to the quality, an effect of a certain kind. But we'll see that in modernity the idea of a quantitative determination is added to the causal relation. We'll see how following the great discoveries of the Renaissance and especially following the discoveries of Galileo and Kepler, the causal relation becomes a relation between magnitudes, a relation of such a nature that if a quantity of certain prior phenomena is given, we can deduce the quantity of the resulting phenomena.

To be sure, in this form the idea is not very clear, nor is it of any philosophical use. But we'll see how philosophers used it and how they led it to its greatest clarity, how it was formulated first by Descartes, how, in theories like those of Spinoza and Leibniz, the idea of necessity takes on its greatest clarity and its greatest strength.

So the idea of necessity evolved in a regular manner across the history of philosophy. It's entirely different for freedom. History will show you—unfortunately I won't be able to show this in great detail—that undoubtedly, the idea of freedom became more perfect and progressed, but in a way entirely different from the idea of necessity.

First of all, the ways in which this idea made progress never came from speculation, never from science. Such progress always came from the outside, by an intrusion of certain foreign elements into philosophy, certain social, sociopolitical elements, which, to be sure, conceal other much more profound elements, elements of intuition.

That's a first point. The second point is this: the progress didn't take place in a continuous manner, as it did for the idea of necessity, it didn't take place in a continuous manner. It took place in a discontinuous manner, in fits and starts, I'd almost say in explosions, in two or three great explosions, no more than that. I'll count three explosions in the history of philosophy.

The first dates from the Socratic period, from the century of Pericles.[25] The great
[30] movement of social ideas in this period, the attention drawn to social problems suggested to Socrates not a theory of freedom—he's generally, albeit mistakenly, considered a determinist;[26] the truth is that he didn't address the problem—but suggested to Socrates a certain philosophy from which emerged a certain conception of freedom contained in it. In fact, this latent intuition of freedom, this intuition developed by Plato, would find its precise form in Aristotle, a form that would no longer change, that, at the very most, put up with, or rather, put itself in a position to defend itself against the Stoics' determinism.

This was the first eruption of the idea of freedom in the history of philosophy. I'll link the second up with the movement of ideas that followed Christianity or Judaism—by Christianity I mean Judaism as well, the two doctrines coinciding at the origin.[27] There's no need to investigate the origins of this movement and of its propagation across the world of rejuvenated Jewish ideas, but these origins, as everyone acknowledges, are not scientific or speculative. No, it's totally different, and it links up with certain social relations, with certain well-defined social circumstances.

This conception of freedom persisted through the Middle Ages. We'll see how Descartes, as a philosopher of the will, adopted it, modifying it, to be sure, and it then stays more or less in that form across modernity.

Finally, there is a third explosion—grant me this word since this is about an instantaneous process like an explosion. This one is connected to the movement of ideas and feelings from which the 1789 Revolution was to erupt. In Rousseau—who is, as all agree, one of those who prepared this revolution in feelings and in ideas[28]—we'll see an already quite clear formulation for this conception of freedom. To be sure, it finds its fully philosophical formulation only in Kant, but Kant, as I'll show, was directly influenced by Rousseau on this point.[29]

So there we have the third intuition of freedom, I don't see any others. I said these
[31] intuitions are making progress from one to the next—that's not entirely accurate, for if progress here is to be progress in the formulas, in the theories, then no, there is no perceptible progress. The formulas are more or less the same, even in Kant. And yet there's already a notable difference; you won't find in Rousseau formulas like [Kant's]—they're nearly the same formulas but there's something else, it's—how do I put this—it's like the feeling of freedom taking on greater and greater importance, as if the impression was still going in the same direction but already deeper, and as if each time, the philosopher had excavated a deeper layer of personality and brought it out into the open.

So there we have what will be striking in this history, the progressive and continuous character of the evolution of the idea of necessity and the rather explosive character of the idea or, rather, the intuition of freedom.

I'll add that the study of the doctrines of necessity face to face with those of freedom is very intriguing. Earlier I was speaking of a debate between a freedomist and a determinist. In the history of philosophy, things don't take the form of a debate at all. No, we're always witnessing the following operation: the theories of necessity, instead of being simply opposed to the theories of freedom, these theories always try to absorb the theories of

freedom into themselves to come to a formula of freedom, a definition of freedom that could contain freedom but that, in reality, is able to coincide with necessity. I compared the appearance of each new conception or each new intuition of freedom to a kind of explosion, to a kind of eruption, as the geologists say. The theories of necessity can be compared to the forces the geologists talk about, forces of water streams, forces of the seas that work on volcanic rocks, that perform a labor of erosion, of disintegration such that sedimentary layers are constituted. The theories of necessity have always acted on these intuitions of freedom by disintegrating them and by assimilating them, such that each new intuition of freedom appears to have provided the earlier theories of necessity
with new material to work on. All we have to do is take up this comparison between [32]
explosive forces and forces of sedimentation. The causes of sedimentation are those we generally talk about when we talk about the evolution of ideas. They are causes that work slowly, in a continuous, imperceptible manner, and many historians of philosophy recognize or accept only those sorts of forces. There are others, there are forces we could call eruptive, there are causes of eruption, and, in the domain of thought, as in geology, these eruptions provide the forces of disintegration with the material they work on.

There we have some of the conclusions this history will provide us with. In the next lecture, gentlemen, we'll take on the idea of freedom in Greek philosophy, and, in the second part of the lecture at least, we'll leave the relatively vague generalities, where this first lecture has remained, behind.

Notes

1. Gabriel Tarde (1843–1904), sociologist and philosopher, author of, in particular, *Les Lois de l'imitation* (1890, *The Laws of Imitation*, trans. Elsie Clews Parsons [New York: Holt, 1903]); *Monadologie et sociologie* (1893), and *L'Opposition universelle: Essai d'une théorie des contraires* (1897). From 1900 until his death four years later, Tarde held the Chair in Modern Philosophy at the Collège de France. Bergson had sought to occupy this position himself at the same time as Tarde, and he had even been nominated for it by Charles Lévêque, the Chair in Greek and Latin Philosophy, for whom he had been substituting as early as 1897 (lecturing on "Plotinus's Psychology" on Tuesdays and on the Fourth Ennead on Saturdays). Lévêque died three days after he wrote the letter recommending Bergson—who then succeeded him permanently. Following Tarde's death in 1904, Bergson requested, and was granted, the (unusual) transfer to the Chair of Modern Philosophy in November 1904, just weeks before the beginning of this course (see Christophe Labaune, "Bergson au Collège de France (exposition virtuelle)," *Colligere*, March 12, 2020, https://archibibscdf.hypotheses.org/?p=8177, and M, 413).

   Bergson sees in Tarde, whom he talks about several times ("Discours sur Gabriel Tarde," September 12, 1909, in EP, 375–7; "Préface aux Pages Choisies de Gabriel Tarde," 1909, EP, 377–9; "La Philosophie française," May 15, 1915, rewritten in 1933, EP, 452–79, here 466), a sociologist who spoke from the heart, quite different from an intellectualist sociologist like Durkheim. Bergson is struck by the diversity of disciplines Tarde studied (psychology, law, and economics, in particular), which translated into the creative unforeseeability of the path he took (contrasting with Spencer, as Bergson will explain in a moment). Mindful also of the poetical dimension of Tarde's work, Bergson willingly grants him the title of "philosopher," and even of "metaphysician." Particularly attentive to Tarde's division and correlation, within individual existence, between "imitation" and "invention," he is grateful to him for having rendered sociology relatively autonomous from the model of the physical and chemical sciences and of immutable laws, a philosophical gesture that, in Bergson's eyes, was also likely to stimulate our actions in the world.

2. Each year, Bergson would devote one of his two courses, on Fridays, to the history of a philosophical problem, and the other, on Saturdays, to the study of a work. The Saturday course the following year, 1905–6, continued the reading of Spencer's *First Principles*, those of subsequent years discussed several works by Berkeley, and it seems that Bergson never gave the course on Tarde announced here.

3. In *Time and Free Will*, Bergson does venture a definition of freedom, if only to then immediately assert that it must elude definition: "Freedom is the relation of the concrete self to the act which it performs. This relation is indefinable, just because we are free. . . . Thus any positive definition of freedom will ensure the victory of determinism" (TFW, 219–20/165).

4. The French verb *vouloir*, used here, means either "to want" or "to will"; the French word for the will is *volonté*, which is etymologically related to *vouloir*.

5. CM, 188/178.

6. CM, 190/180.

7. The term *unité* can also mean "unity" or "whole."

8. A notion borrowed from classical mechanics.

9. The expression Bergson uses here, *un trait d'union*, also means "hyphen," that which unites two terms.

10. Bergson is referring to the 1902–3 course "History of the Idea of Time" (forthcoming in this series), which in turn was an extension of the 1901–2 course on "The Idea of Time."

11. Here Bergson interrupts the argument for a few moments to explain its stages to his audience. His sentence would have ended with something like "but perhaps there is no real duration outside our consciousness."

12. TFW, 115–17/86–7.

13. CE, 210/238: "For our consciousness to coincide with something of its principle, it would have to detach itself from what is *ready-made* and attach itself to what is *being made*" (Bergson's emphases).

14. MM, 176–7/152–3.

15. ME, 5/8.

16. CE, 49/47.

17. Literally, "God out of a machine," *deus ex machina* designates theatrical devices—technical, narrative, or both—that unexpectedly and as if out of nowhere bring a figure (e.g., a god, a messenger) onto the stage to resolve a plot.

18. CE, 135–6/150–1.

19. *Imperium in imperio* is an expression from the preface to the third part of Spinoza's *Ethics* (in CWS, vol. 1, 401–617; Curley [491] translates "dominion within a dominion"), often used, and by Bergson himself, to criticize rigid dualisms or undue privileges.

20. For more on the association of ideas, see MM, 212–20/181–8.

21. MM, 198/170, and "Good Sense and Classical Studies" (1895), in KW, 245–53/EP, 152–64.

22. Bergson means "all the debates around freedom and necessity."
23. Bergson coins the term *libertiste*, which we are rendering as "freedomist." He makes the same point with the same example in CM, 41/37.
24. As we shall see later (in the lecture of February 10, 1905), Bergson is thinking in particular of Heraclitus. But we might add Thales, Anaximander, and Anaximenes, among others.
25. The fifth century BCE, usually considered the apex of Greek civilization.
26. In the following lecture, we learn that Bergson is especially thinking of Alfred Fouillée.
27. Bergson will refine his conception of the relations between Judaism and Christianity in *The Two Sources* (TS, 240/254–5).
28. *Cette révolution dans les sentiments et dans les idées* is an allusion (made explicitly in the next sentence) to Kant and his formula of a "revolution in the way of thinking."
29. This is very close to what Bergson says in *The Two Sources* (TS, 282/300).

LECTURE 2
DECEMBER 16, 1904

Gentlemen, as I said in the last lecture, we're going to enter into the history of the problem of freedom. I also announced that this history, if we consider the origins of the problem, is the history of the idea of necessity much more than of the idea of freedom. Before we consider—and we can do this only very briefly—before we consider the idea of necessity among the philosophers properly speaking, it's perhaps worthwhile to study the more popular idea of necessity among the ancients. [33]

The belief in fate was a very widespread belief, generally widespread, throughout all of antiquity. It's still a belief in necessity, but it's not entirely the belief I'll analyze in the next lecture. The belief that has its roots in the intellect, that comes from our reflective thought, the belief in that kind of necessity looks for laws that unfold in time: that, gentlemen, is necessity as the philosophers conceive it. But there's a belief in necessity whose origins aren't intellectual, aren't rational, but affective and, I might say, emotional. This belief seems to be the ancient, popular belief in destiny, in fate.

I don't know whether anyone has ever undertaken a deep scientific study of the origins of this idea nor even of its evolution across classical antiquity. This would be a study of great interest, though, since few ideas played as considerable a role in antiquity as this one did.

The ideas of the ancients on this subject, it must be said, are quite vague, as happens
with ideas that have a rather emotional origin. The belief in fate, moreover, must really be [34]
older than classical antiquity. However, in classical antiquity the idea is still very vague.

Defined in a general way, this belief is a belief in a blind force, rather more evil than good, that governs human affairs, that determines events in general and even our decisions insofar as they are made within the web of events. In the ancient poets, this force appears to be omnipotent, even more powerful than the gods. The gods are subject to fate. We could cite several ancient texts. Here is a dialogue between the chorus and Prometheus in Aeschylus's *Prometheus*:

> Chorus: Well, who is the steersman of Necessity?

—that is, the force that directs necessity—

> Prometheus: The triple Fates and the unforgetting Furies.
> Chorus: You mean Zeus is less strong than these.
> Prometheus: Certainly he cannot escape destiny.[1]

We find nearly the exact same words in Herodotus, *The Persian Wars*: "None may escape his destined lot, not even a god."[2] On this last point, the question of knowing whether it's necessary that the gods themselves be subject to fate, the view of the ancients isn't settled. In the poets and in particular in Homer, we discover passages both for and against this view. There are quite a few passages in favor of the gods being subject to fate, but there are some against, which are fairly typical. I'll just quote the passage from book 16 of the *Iliad*, in which Jupiter, or rather Zeus, states that fate wants that Sarpedon be killed by Patroclus. Will he let this happen? He hesitates. Juno, or rather Hera, intervenes and asks him to let it happen. Nevertheless, she recognizes that Zeus has the power, if he wants, to send Sarpedon back to Lykia unscathed, delivered or rather dispensed from death, from "ill-sounding death."[3]

There are even one or two passages in Homer where the poet goes further. In certain
[35] cases, it seems, he attributes to humans themselves the power to evade what fate has decreed. Thus, still in book 16, we see Patroclus chasing after the Trojans and the Lykians, and then we have these two lines: "Besotted: had he only kept the command of Peleiades / he might have got clear away from the evil spirit of black death."[4]

Thus, gentlemen, popular thought, like the poets, the popular thought the poets express is rather uncertain on this point, as is, for that matter, the genealogy of this divinity superior to all others. Certain authors make the goddess of fate, destiny, the daughter of Zeus himself; others make her the daughter of Chronos; still others the daughter of the Ocean. There's one point, however, on which all of them agree: they all make destiny the daughter of the night. There is a passage in Plato's *Republic* where he says something analogous.[5] For Plato, fate is the daughter of *anankē*, of necessity, and in Plato's system, necessity is the principle opposed to the Good, which is, as you know, the light, the sun. For this reason, too, fate is the daughter of the night, the principle of obscurity.

The thought of the ancients in itself is thus very imprecise. What are its origins? It's very hard to say. If what we're trying to determine is the accidental, historical origins, we don't currently have the documents. As you know, right now some people are engaged in a scholarly investigation into the historical, or rather the prehistorical, origins of certain very profound beliefs, like the belief in fate. They put forward a thesis, which, incidentally, we'll have to criticize, the thesis that a lot of these beliefs can be explained by causes that are entirely accidental, by parallels [*rapprochements*], by associations of ideas that point to a very inferior mentality, a mentality like the one we find today in certain primitive tribes [*sauvages*], which are in a state . . . how do I put this . . . of stupefaction in the face of the things around them.[6] We mustn't disdain an explanation of this kind, but when the issue is a belief as profound and as widespread as fate, we can imagine that the origins are profound as well, psychological origins. In fact, when we turn to psychological analysis, we come upon a certain number of
[36] elements. There's not just one cause, not just one reason for this belief in fate, there are a lot of them. First in line, we'd have to put what I would call the ineluctability of death.[7] The idea of death must have played the major role here or, rather, humanity's feeling in relation to death.

In fact, we should note that the characteristics that classical antiquity attributes to fate are the very characteristics of death. Death is inevitable. Among all human events, it is the only one whose ineluctability is beyond doubt. It is, therefore, absolutely inevitable. It is unforeseeable.[8] While we know that we must die, we generally never know when, we don't know when or how, so death is a simultaneously unforeseeable and inevitable event. And then it's an event that seems to take no kind of human scheming into account, an event that takes place independently of every kind of human event, in the sense that death might strike at any time. It might strike when a great enterprise that could be useful to humanity is about to be completed, or it might happen before, as in Balzac's novel, *The Search for the Absolute*, when the main character dies at the very moment that he is going to disclose the secret of nature, the secret of the philosopher's stone.[9] So there is an event that takes place as if it had been marked out independently of anything we might think of as human considerations. It's a thread that is cut at a given moment because it was necessary that it be cut at that exact moment.[10]

The three essential characteristics of death are precisely the three characteristics of fate in general such as the ancients pictured it: it is implacable, destiny is inevitable; we cannot know it, it's unforeseeable; finally, it takes nothing into account, fate is blind.

On top of that, we should note—and this is a telltale sign—we should note that the Greek words to designate the goddesses of death—the Parcae, the Moirai, the Kēres—are the very words that, in the singular, designate fate and, in the plural, death. Indeed, destiny is called *moira, kēr*. So it's the same words, and it's likely that, basically, it's the [37]
same thing. Death, then, is what first inspired this feeling or, rather, this emotional idea. It then is probable that this idea of the fatality of death, so to speak, radiated, opened up onto all the rest of existence. It reascended the entire slope of life and the characteristics of the outcome reflected little by little onto the entire drama or comedy. This is how, after having been perhaps only an idea limited to the final event, the idea of fate was extended to life as a whole.

So there's that origin, but undoubtedly, as I was telling you, there are many others. Right here, while explicating Alexander of Aphrodisias's *On Fate*, I happened to discuss his opinion (which isn't lacking in subtlety) that in general, we attribute our successes to ourselves, but the lack of success, the failures, we like better to attribute to a foreign force.[11] We believe in forces antagonistic to ours. What are these forces? First of all, there are wills, undoubtedly, human wills that are opposed to our will, but there are also forces of nature that are opposed to our force, but there is, moreover, something like the encounter or the combination of all of these elements together. This combination occurs in a given place, at a given moment, and it's this combination that is truly efficacious, because if these elements hadn't met where they met and hadn't met when they met, what happened probably wouldn't have happened. Well, this coincidence, this encounter is something unforeseeable in general and something that constitutes what we've always called chance, the ancients' *tukhē*. Luck is something unforeseeable, irrational, unreasonable.

Let me note in passing that we've always sought to conjure chance by means of irrational, nonreasonable practices. The magic we find in all ancient religions is nothing other than this set of irrational practices intended to conjure the irrational force that is chance.

The idea of chance forms rather naturally from all this, and then especially from the
[38] conviction that humanity is not entirely the cause of its failures and lacks of success. And then logic is brought to bear on this, originally rather emotional, idea. The demarcation line between success and lack of success is very difficult to draw, that is, the limit between what is beneficial and what is not beneficial, and thus the idea of fate, which at first was limited to characterizing the collection of obstacles placed in the way of human activity, could be extended, and it ended up engulfing not only what goes against our activity but even what in turn benefits this activity. At that point, our actions themselves, all of our ways of getting things done became effects of fate, movements intended to lead to and facilitate the event marked out by destiny. In short, it's what I was saying earlier: an unfavorable event or a series of unforeseeable unfavorable events suggests the idea, and the idea radiates, opens up, and little by little reaches a very large number of events to which it did not at first apply.

Gentlemen, it's likely that this idea wouldn't have had so much credence in antiquity, that the conviction, the belief in fate wouldn't have been so widespread if it hadn't had even deeper emotional roots. All in all, a belief in general and its tenacity can be explained only if it is compatible with humanity. If the belief in fate didn't contain something compatible with us, we likely wouldn't accept it so easily. It's clear that the belief in destiny is a belief that has something consoling in it. From the moment that humanity is endowed with memory, from the moment that it is endowed with foresight (two attributes that distinguish it from animals), humanity's joys and pains are infinitely multiplied. That's often been said: joy is multiplied by expectation and also by memory. It is multiplied by expectation because hope always presents to us the future in a beneficial light. Even if hope doesn't make things more beautiful, it multiplies: we imagine many possible futures all of which might be happy when only one among them will be realized. In regard to the recollection of the past, people have often spoken of the poetry in memory: memory makes things more beautiful.

[39] We might even wonder—this is another question—whether the idea of happiness does not come, to a large extent, from the faculty of foresight and from the faculty of remembering, whether the complete idea of happiness is only ever realized in the future or in the past.

Even when sorrow and sadness are at issue, foresight and regret, or rather memory, are still forces of multiplication, multiplying forces. Everyone says—this is a banal truth—that a misfortune happening is still better than a misfortune feared. When the misfortune is upon us and we feel its blow, we feel less anxiety than when we don't know where the blow is going to land and where to ward it off. When what's at issue is past, there's no pain more harrowing than the regret, in many cases, of realizing that simply doing something different from what we did would have sufficed for something different to happen from what did happen.

The belief in fate is a consoling belief because of the very simple reason that we no longer have to be concerned about the future. It's marked out in advance, so there's no uncertainty. And there's no reason to regret the past because, no matter what we did, what did happen would have happened. That's a very consoling belief, this. Moreover, we see in antiquity that it forms the leitmotiv, so to speak, of all the consolations, for the consolation was a literary genre in antiquity.[12] Consolations were treatises or letters a philosopher sent to someone who had suffered a severe misfortune. We know that this genre flourished especially during the Stoic period, that is, among people who were convinced of universal determinism. Their argument par excellence was the argument from fate.

The belief in fate is a belief that must arise naturally and as if spontaneously in beings like humans, who are emotional, who have foresight of the future and at the same time memory of the past. Today we would say that it's an antidote, an antitoxin.[13] Today we are told that bacteria are generated in the organism, that they produce poisons or toxins. Then, by means of its natural force of defense, the organism produces antitoxins, that [40]
is, it secretes substances intended to neutralize the damage that those other substances have produced.

Let's take an animal soul, and let's make it human by introducing into it memory [and] the foresight that we find in humans: we'll produce suffering and mental illness [*maladies de l'âme*], or, as the ancient moralists said, anxiety and regret.[14] Then, by itself, the moral organism is going to react and secrete some sort of antitoxin, and its ultimate reaction against suffering will be the belief in fate.

This reason explains the belief in fate quite naturally. We'd find many others—if we had the time to develop this analysis further—we'd find other emotional causes.

We could—this would perhaps be more subtle—we could discover still more reasons coming from self-love [*amour-propre*], since one must always look for it as a reason not only for human actions but also for human beliefs. It's the great motivation [*mobile*] and one of the great sources of beliefs, a lot more than interest, regardless of what philosophers have said about this.[15] When they present humanity—perhaps we'll be able to return to this later in relation to the different kinds of determinism—when they present humanity to us as determined by its interests, and this is the case with utilitarian ethics, they exaggerate the value of this motivation.[16] Very often, this is the motive [*motif*] we put at the top of the list. We prefer confessing to a motive like this one, even though at bottom self-interest is less admissible morally, we prefer confessing to this motive to confessing to pride, but pride, or self-love, is the main motive.

At first sight, though, this belief certainly seems to testify to a certain feeling of humility. It's indeed a force that goes beyond the human; it would thus be an expression of its modesty. But looking at it more closely, we see that in this belief in fate there's something that raises us up, that encourages our pride because we feel that we are in league with this superhuman force that governs everything: while we suffer its effects, we also participate in it.[17] Our actions, our entire life thus lose their contingency, their accidental character. It pains us to admit that a small change in circumstances would [41]
have been enough for us not to have been born, for our existence not to have come about, that the slightest thing would have been enough for such and such an act, which may have decided our existence, not to have come about. The belief in fate [*à la fatalité*,

au destin] immediately gives our actions and our situations an importance they perhaps wouldn't have had without it, as if they were so many cosmic events, human actions and situations take on the same importance as a cosmic event.

There is thus, at the bottom of this belief, a point of pride that we end up untangling all the same. In all of this, there's a lot of other things yet; I'm not insisting on all the elements, emotional as well, that we'd find in this idea. I've insisted on this as much as I have because the idea of fate is even more alive than we think. When we speak of fate, we like to say that it's an ancient idea, that it's part of paganism. Paganism is gone, but this idea remains, a lot less visible, no doubt, a lot less explicit, latent deep in souls and in a state of torpor. But it surfaces at certain times, especially in circumstances that are serious; and then, among the very people who reject it where the events of individual lives are concerned, we find this idea to be as alive, as intense as ever, when it comes to no longer individual events but collective events and actions. We no longer believe in fate concerning the individual, but we believe in fate as soon as what's at issue are peoples. The story of sociology is that of the old fatalism in general—there are exceptions but at its core it's fatalism. What reasons are given for this determinism in the history of peoples? We're going to have to concern ourselves with this question over the course of this study,[18] but I'll say right away that historical determinism, historical fatalism generally reasons as if it were up to those who believe in the contingency of historical events, in the contingency of human events, to prove or demonstrate freedom, the freedom of the
[42] people in what we could call the creation of its history. The burden of proof here, the *onus probandi*, would thus be incumbent on the freedomists.

Yet the appearances speak in favor of an efficacy of human action and of individual action. History shows us that we would be mistaken if we trusted the appearances. It shows us that it was possible to push back or deflect the currents that seemed the hardest to resist every time there was a certain number—there doesn't have to be a lot of them—a certain number of energetic wills convinced of their rights. That's what history demonstrates.[19]

As soon as the appearance is there, it falls to those who deny the reality of the appearance to provide a counterproof. Now, they try to give us these proofs. In the Saturday course, we'll be able to discuss these proofs in relation to Herbert Spencer. They generally are a lot more metaphysical than they seem. At the bottom of these apparently scientific arguments, there's a metaphysics, and a very old metaphysics at that, a latent metaphysics.[20]

How are we to explain the fact, though, that we are so ready to accept theories like this? It's because science demands a certain kind of determinism, and if there isn't some kind of determinism in the course of history, then history isn't a science. Obviously, we have to accept determinism to some extent, but, in the end, we wouldn't accept it so easily if our souls had no incentive to welcome this belief. And even the feelings that are at the origin of the ancient belief in individual destiny, the same feelings come together here, namely, first of all, a certain indolence: we much prefer believing that things will happen by fate, like they must happen. Then, there's also pride because it pains us to admit that a people of which we are a part, that a people is something accidental, or at

least that the course of the evolution of this people is something absolutely accidental and contingent. We prefer to see in it something whose place is absolutely marked out in nature, something that's as ineluctable as the orbit a planet traces in space. In our own eyes, that raises us up, that puts us at a higher level. That's because it pains us to admit the contingency of the collective actions of humanity, for this contingency appears to us [43]
to introduce something accidental into them that diminishes and demeans them. That's why we welcome historical fatalism so easily.

So the belief in fate belongs to all epochs, it belongs to ours as much as to the epoch of the ancients. It's been worthwhile to look for its intellectual and emotional origins. Now, gentlemen, we turn to the idea of necessity such as we find it in the first phases of Greek thought and such as we find it, no longer in popular thought, but in the philosophers. As I was saying the other day, among the ancients, this idea is far from taking the precise and rigorous form it has among the moderns. When we speak of necessity, we immediately think of a natural law, and a natural law, a physical law, is something we define very easily and very precisely: it is a constant relation between variable magnitudes. Such a conception of physical laws was possible only after the discoveries made in modernity. It presupposed the idea of varying, simultaneously, physical phenomena from the viewpoint of magnitude.[21] This is not to say that the ancients didn't come into contact with this kind of experiments, as far back as the most remote periods of classical antiquity. The Pythagoreans discovered the law that links the pitch of the sound to the length of the vibrating string. This law was indeed analogous to physical laws such as we understand them today.[22] However, pitch for them was not a quantity, not a magnitude. They didn't manage to define pitch by the frequency of the vibrations; they didn't manage to generalize this idea; they didn't reach the idea of laws in general such as we understand them because, quite simply, their mathematics were not advanced enough. This isn't due at all, as some people say, to the ancients being incapable of observation and experimentation. It's simply because they didn't experiment with the aim of measuring and because they didn't have the mathematical tools for measurement that we have at our disposal, and, finally, because they hadn't managed to unearth what [44]
we call the idea of function, for that's what laws are.[23]

This idea could thus not have existed in antiquity, and the very idea of necessity in the sense of reciprocal dependence in general—the reciprocal dependence of the parts of the universe in relation to one another—this idea, as I said, is hardly encountered except in the Stoics. We don't find the idea of universal reciprocal dependence of all phenomena, of all things of nature in relation to one another, until Chrysippus.[24] However, in these first attempts by Greek philosophy, we find an idea of necessity. This idea appears to be above all the idea of a determinate place, marked out in advance, of all facts, of all cosmic events in time. This idea of the regularity of the course of nature is, in the ancients, strictly tied to the regularity of astronomical revolutions. The process is circular like the revolution of the heavens. At the end of a certain number of years, after thousands of years, things are back at exactly the same point in relation to one another, all the parts of matter, of the universe, are at the same point in relation to one another, and then everything starts over again in the same way. The same events are reproduced in the same order, which is always circular. This idea is completely opposed to our modern idea of evolution. In contrast to the ancient idea, our modern idea of evolution, of progress, is the idea of an indefinite movement in a straight line. Their idea of evolution—and this idea subsists across antiquity—is the idea of a circular process and consequently of a limited progress, of the return of all things to the same place at the end of a determinate amount of time, and of a universal starting over.

So we have what was, among the first philosophers—as much as we can surmise from the small number of texts related to this question that have been handed down to us—the idea of universal necessity. We have some passages that sufficiently show that the ancients resolved the problem of freedom such as we have posed it in the direction of necessity. For example, we have two passages—very distant from the source, unfortunately—on
[45] Heraclitus's philosophy, one from Plutarch and one from Joannes Stobaeus, which agree absolutely.[25] This is what Plutarch says: "Heraclitus says that all things are made by destiny."[26] Stobaeus tells us that "Heraclitus has shown that the essence of fate is reason circulating throughout time." I should note, parenthetically, that it's not certain that it's "reason" or *logos*; it's very possible that Stobaeus attributes a Stoic view to Heraclitus here: "The Logos is the ethereal cause"—the famous ether—"the many of universal becoming, the measure of fixed periods." *Periodos* is the cyclical course of things. He adds: "According to Heraclitus, everything comes about by destiny."[27]

As much as we can judge from these fragments, this shows that according to Heraclitus there is a universal regularity, a universal necessity. And in all likelihood humans are caught in the gears of all things. However, this is not said explicitly.

There's also one of Democritus's claims that has come down to us. However, Democritus represents a philosophical tendency quite different from that of Heraclitus: "All things happen by virtue of necessity. Necessity is the same thing as destiny."[28]

Thus, gentlemen, at the beginning, the idea of universal necessity dominates. It would be an exaggeration to say that we're dealing with fatalist or determinist theories here, since the fatalist solution is born only once we have posed the problem of freedom. When the problem is not even posed, we cannot find any solution for it. But what we must say is that there is, implicitly contained in this first philosophy, the belief in universal necessity, which, undoubtedly, it would have been quite difficult for these first thinkers to reconcile with the belief in freedom had they been led to pose the problem. But the problem isn't posed until the day when the idea comes to slice very small circles out of the immense networks of the events that compose reality, very small regions to which we then attach
[46] a privileged importance: I mean human actions. From the day the idea came to isolate human actions, the necessity arises as well to wonder whether or not human actions must be lumped in with the rest of the events, with the changes produced in nature. From that day, the problem was posed.

It is Socrates—what I'm saying here is a banal truth—it's Socrates who took up human events, who separated them out from all other events, and who said: we are going to concern ourselves with them, we are going to concern ourselves with human events, and those first of all and those alone. Nature, that's the gods' business; it's they who made nature and it's up to them to take care of it. The impossibility of physics itself has been demonstrated by the contradictions that the Stoic philosophers have presented to us and at which they have ended up. And even if physics were possible, it would be useless since what must concern humans are human things. Humans must be concerned with human things and consequently human things, human events, must be separated out from all the rest of reality and must be considered by themselves.

Socrates added that the inward gaze of consciousness must be turned toward human things. Certainly this formula doesn't mean that we must do psychology, that we must analyze ourselves. Socrates gives this formula a much more practical and down to earth sense. "Know thyself" means: look for what you can do; be aware of what you can do, of what you know. Don't think you have what you don't know; analyze yourself from the viewpoint of what you can do. Take stock of yourself, weigh up your value. This above all is what Socrates meant, judging by the dialogue we find reported by Xenophon.[29] However, it's possible that it was something more; it's hard not to see in Socrates something of what we call psychological analysis and, especially, not to consider that he attributed the highest importance to inner observation. It's very hard when we think of the importance he attributed to that daemon, or rather to demonic signs, to this inner law that we probably shouldn't compare to the law of the mystics, yet which, from a certain angle, is already a mystical phenomenon.[30] Certainly, this inner law does not [47]
teach him at all about the things beyond, about mystical things. It intervenes only in order to advise, and especially to warn against certain things. Nevertheless, it's true that the entire Platonic and Neoplatonic philosophy comes from this Socratic idea of the daemon. The concept of the daemon in general is thus indeed a concept with a mystical nature. And, without attributing to Socrates all that emerged from this idea, we can nonetheless say that what emerged from it at least indicates the direction in which the idea was leaning. In Socrates, in Socrates's philosophy, we find what I'd call the external symptoms of a doctrine of freedom since the theory of freedom, all in all, is always characterized, is always distinguished by means of these characteristics: it opposes human things to natural things in general or at least it separates out human things from natural things in general. Then, in varying degrees, the doctrine of freedom is always a call to inner observation. It's not rare that a mystical element joins it. Then, finally, it presents a characteristic that some people have exaggerated a lot in relation to the current doctrines of freedom but that we see even more in the ancient conception of freedom. It's been said that the belief in freedom is necessarily the sign of a reaction against positive science. That's not true. One can certainly say that this belief limits positive science to some extent, but in no way is it a reactionary belief against science. Nevertheless, there's a tendency in "freedomist" philosophers to diminish science in the strict sense, the natural sciences. Well, no one can go further down this path than Socrates, since he declares that knowledge of nature is first of all useless, then impossible, and even sacrilegious.[31]

We thus have the external symptoms of a belief in freedom, of a theory of freedom. You know that the historians of philosophy agree that there is in Socrates's philosophy, implicitly at least, a certain conception of human activity, a well-defined conception even. Fouillée goes very far in this direction. In his very remarkable book on Socrates, [48]
he allows us to see, in Socrates, the creator, the founder of determinism, at least of a

certain kind of determinism, psychological determinism.[32] The symptoms, the external appearances are contrary to the texts, and yet the passages I invoked are ones from which we might, at a pinch, draw this conclusion. Must we draw it? We don't have the time today to resolve this question. We'll attempt to respond to it at the beginning of the next lecture, only at the beginning, since we have to move on to Plato's opinion on this point.

Notes

1. This is Alan H. Sommerstein's English translation of verses 517–20 of *Prometheus Bound* (the full title of the play) in *Aeschylus, Persians, Seven against Thebes, Suppliants, Prometheus Bound* (Cambridge, MA: Harvard University Press, 2008), 499.
2. This A. D. Godley's translation (Herodotus, *Herodotus in Four Volumes I: Books I and II* [Cambridge, MA: Harvard University Press, 1926], I.91: 117).
3. The passage spans verses 433–43, the quotation comes from verse 442. See *The Iliad of Homer*, trans. Richmond Lattimore (Chicago: University of Chicago Press, 2011), 363.
4. *Iliad* 16.685–8: 369. Achilles is also called Peleiades, after his father Peleus.
5. Plato, *Republic* 10, 617b–c: 1220.
6. The parallel with *The Two Sources* (TS, 103–4/106–7 and 143–52/149–59) suggests that Bergson is referring to his schoolmate Lucien Lévy-Bruhl, the author, in 1903, of *La Morale et la science des mœurs* (*Ethics and Moral Science*, not translated into English), and in 1922, of *La Mentalité primitive* (*Primitive Mentality*). On the then-widespread analogy between the prehistoric and the "primitive" generally and on Lévy-Bruhl in particular, see Erich Hörl, *Sacred Channels: The Archaic Illusion of Communication*, with a preface by Jean-Luc Nancy, trans. Nils F. Schott (Amsterdam: Amsterdam University Press, 2018), esp. ch. 4.
7. Recall that, according to *The Two Sources*, conjuring the representation of the inevitability of death constitutes one of the three functions of religion insofar as it aims at the preservation of the individual and society, that is, one of the three functions of "static religion" (TS, 129–38/134–44).
8. In *The Two Sources*, the third function of "static religion" consists in attenuating the depressing effects of the unforeseeability of death (TS, 138–40/144–6).
9. In Balzac's 1834 novel, "the absolute" designates the object of the alchemists' quest, the element common to all the chemical elements of nature.
10. Here Bergson takes up the image of the "thread" of human life, spun, drawn out, and cut by the three Fates (the Moirai in Greek, the Parcae in Roman mythology).
11. In 1900–1901, in the Saturday morning course. In *The Two Sources*, Bergson will refer to these lectures (saying mistakenly that they were given in 1898) and to the elements that, in the present lecture, he extracts from them (TS, 148n8/154n1).
12. One might think of *The Consolation of Philosophy* by Boethius (470–524 CE), but the Stoic philosopher Seneca (4 BCE–65 CE), for example, also wrote *Consolations* (to Marcia, to Polybius, and to Helvia).
13. This is vocabulary drawn from immunology, a medical and biological discipline rapidly developing at the turn of the twentieth century.
14. First of all Plato in the *Timaeus*, 86c–d: 1285–6.

15. At this time, Bergson leaned toward making "vanity" one of the main drivers of human activity. See L, 171–5/131–4.
16. This is probably an allusion to John Stuart Mill, who will be discussed in the lecture of February 15, 1905, but also, more broadly, to thinkers like Bentham, Smith, or Spencer.
17. See TS, 144–5/151–2.
18. Bergson will not have the time to keep this promise. We can nevertheless guess that he is thinking of Auguste Comte and his law of three states, as well as of the positivist sociologies he inspired (those of Spencer, who is mentioned a few moments later, or of Durkheim), as opposed to Tarde's sociology.
19. TS, 293/312–13.
20. ME, 51/41.
21. CE, 284–90/328–35.
22. In *Creative Evolution* (CE, 288/333), Bergson cites the example of Archimedes's buoyant force.
23. CE, 287/332.
24. Chrysippus of Soli, a Greek philosopher of the third century BCE, succeeded Cleanthes as the head of the Stoic school in Athens.
25. Joannes Stobaeus (fifth century CE) was a compiler of Greek texts, whose works preserved fragments from ancient authors found nowhere else. Bergson is citing *The Anthology*, though it is unclear what his exact source was. The standard edition is by Kurt Wachsmuth and Otto Hense, *Ioannis Stobaei Anthologium*, 5 vols. (Berlin: Weidmann, 1884–1912).
26. This is Bergson's very loose translation; compare Plutarch, *On the Generation of the Soul in the Timaeus*, trans. Harold Cherniss, in *Moralia, Volume XIII: Part 1: Platonic Essays* (Cambridge, MA: Harvard University Press, 1976), 27, 1026b: 253.
27. This translates Bergson's rendering of Stobaeus's *Eclogues*, bk. 1, ch. 5, sect. 15, p. 178, in the traditional numbering, p. 78 in vol. 1 of the Wachsmuth/Hense edition. In his edition of Heraclitus, G. T. W. Patrick translates Stobaeus's comment in a note: "Heraclitus declares that destiny is the all-pervading law. And this is the etherial body, the seed of the origin of all things, and the measure of the appointed course. All things are by fate, and this is the same as necessity. Thus he writes, 'For it is wholly destined———'" (*The Fragments of the Work of Heraclitus of Ephesus on Nature* [Baltimore, MD: Murray, 1889], 100nLXIII).
28. This is reported by Diogenes Laertius in the chapter devoted to Democritus in *Lives of the Eminent Philosophers*, trans. R. D. Hicks (Cambridge, MA: Harvard University Press, 2005), 9.45: 455. Only the first sentence is strictly a quotation. The second sentence is Bergson's gloss on it.
29. Bergson is referring to the "know thyself" inscribed in the portico of the temple at Delphi. On the role of the oracle at Delphi in making Socrates discover his own vocation, see Plato's *Apology*, 20c–23c: 20–2; the Delphic formula is also found in Plato's *Alcibiades* 124a, *Protagoras* 343b, and in *Philebus* 48c (*Plato: Complete Works*, 580, 774, 438). The reference to Xenophon is specifically to the dialogue between Socrates and Euthydemos in book 4, chapter 2 of *Memorabilia*; see Xenophon, *Memorabilia, Oeconomicus, Symposium, Apology*, trans. E. C. Marchant and O. J. Todd, rev. Jeffrey Henderson (Cambridge, MA: Harvard University Press, 2013), IV.2: 281–311.
30. On Socrates "daimon," which manifests itself only by way of negative warnings, see Plato's *Apology*, 31c–d: 29. Also, see Bergson, "Philosophical Intuition," in CM, 129/120, and TS, 61–3/59–62.

31. In Plato's *Phaedo* (96a), Socrates describes his early interest in natural science and his eventual rejection of the sorts of causal explanations offered in this field. Also, in the opening of *Phaedrus* (229d), Socrates criticizes those (including natural philosophers) who would criticize myth as pursuing something that he, at any rate, does not think is a high priority. See also *Phaedo*, 97b–102a: 84–7, or Aristotle's *Metaphysics*, 987b1, 1.6: 1561. Bergson was also struck by Xenophon's Socrates; here, in fact, he is paraphrasing *Memorabilia* IV.7: 363–9.
32. Alfred Fouillée, *La philosophie de Socrate*, 2 vols. (Paris: Ladrange, 1874). Fouillée (1838–1912) was not only a historian of philosophy (with studies of, among others, Nietzsche, Kant, and Guyau, his stepson) but also an important philosopher in his own right, who theorized what he called *idées-forces*. He began his philosophical career with a dissertation entitled *La Liberté et le déterminisme* and wrote extensively on social and political philosophy as well.

LECTURE 3
DECEMBER 22, 1904[1]

Gentlemen, let me remind you that at the end of the last session I said that Socrates's [49] philosophy externally presents certain features that are precisely the external characteristics of the philosophies we usually call the philosophies of freedom. In fact, if, in these philosophies in general, we leave aside the intuition (in the strict sense) at their center, certain external characteristics remain, which are like the mark of the doctrine's intuitive character. I listed these features at the end of the last session: they are, first, a tendency to isolate human things from the rest of nature, the tendency to consider the human as a kingdom within a kingdom, I said; second—and this, for that matter, is the consequence of the first—a tendency, I wouldn't say to demean, but to limit the natural sciences, to limit the scope of the natural sciences, those sciences that today we call the positive sciences; third, a call to inner observation, the soul's attention being turned from the outside to the inside; and then finally, a last feature, which isn't essential, which isn't inseparable from a theory of freedom, but which usually accompanies theories of freedom, and which we can consider, I think, to have a certain kinship with the essential characteristics of a theory of freedom, is—how do I put this—the idea or the feeling the philosopher has of a union with something that surpasses him, in a word, a certain mysticism. This, I repeat, isn't essential, isn't inseparable from the theories of freedom, but it's their usual companion, so much so that we can conclude that between mysticism [50] and the inner feeling of freedom, there is, I wouldn't say a kinship but at least a kind of sympathy, something like a natural affinity.[2] These are the four features we find in the two or three great philosophies that are unanimously admitted to be philosophies of freedom.

Now, we encounter these features in Socrates's philosophy: separating out the human from nature, considering the human realm to be a realm apart is what Socrates does, for, as you'll recall, the very principle of his philosophy is this: to consider human things, the *anthrōpeia*, to be privileged things and even to be the only things that merit the philosopher's concern.

The tendency to diminish the positive sciences—that is to say, what in Socrates's time could only be a very general physics—this tendency is very clear in Socrates since he declares that the knowledge of nature is first of all something impossible, and if it is possible, it's useless. One can't go further down this path, and Socrates, moreover, was entitled to talk this way by the arbitrary and fanciful character of the science of his time.

To lead human attention back to the inside by making an appeal to inner observation: in Socrates, the formula "know thyself," *gnōthi seauton*, indeed testifies to this tendency, even if it must still be interpreted as more of a practical advice, a call to observe ourselves, to consider ourselves with an eye to what we do know and what we don't know, what we are capable of doing. That's what it is at first, but it's perhaps, it's certainly, even, something else.

And then, finally, I said that we find in Socrates's teaching that touch of mysticism we encounter rather frequently in the theories of freedom, for although Socrates's daemon is a voice that alerts him only to what he has to do practically or, rather, to what he should not do, Socrates nevertheless speaks of this voice as of a divine thing. It's something divine, it's a god who is personal to him, with whom he is united personally, intimately,
[51] and this belief in a god personal to the philosopher, who is his own, who is within him, this vision or rather this inner voice[3] is something so singular in antiquity, and we can say certainly unique in the history of paganism, that it's impossible not to establish a connection between this characteristic feature of Socrates's philosophy and the no less singular feature that is the invention of a philosophy that appeals to inner observation.[4]

Thus we already discover in Socrates all the features that we find in the two or three great doctrines known for being philosophies of freedom. That said, it's generally acknowledged, or at least the historians of philosophy generally agree, that while Socrates didn't pose and consequently didn't solve the problem of freedom, the tendency of his philosophy such as it appears to us, in Xenophon's books in particular, is nonetheless a determinist tendency.

Before considering the passages and expressions that this interpretation aims at and that can be controversial, it'll be worthwhile to bring forward the points on which everyone agrees, those which raise no controversy, the two or three fundamental principles of Socrates's ethics.

The first of these principles is the proposition that everyone seeks happiness, everyone aims at happiness, and that happiness is a positive state, something definable and defined. This proposition strikes us as a banal truth, but that might be because today we live to a large degree on Platonic and consequently on Socratic ideas—but this truth hasn't always been banal, and with this specificity and in this form, it wasn't banal in Socrates's time.

Saying that happiness is the purpose everyone tends toward, and a positive and defined purpose, implies that there is, for happiness, something like an Idea in the Platonic sense, an Idea in the sense that Plato intended, something that, being objective, can moreover be defined in itself. But nothing is less evident than such a proposition.

First of all, happiness can be something personal to each person, variable from
[52] person to person. It's the generic name we give to the set of states that bring us a certain contentment, to the set of states we find pleasant. But there is no possible definition of happiness in general, more than that, we could maintain that happiness is not something positive, that it's only a negation, that it's something negative and consequently something that can't be defined.

Let's take a philosophy like that of Schopenhauer. In Schopenhauer's theory we are wills or, rather, we are phenomena of the will in general. We will in order to will, and when we have obtained what we willed for, we necessarily will something else, because by definition we are beings who are always in movement, who consequently always will. Consequently, happiness is nothing other than the endpoint that, by definition, is always receding. It's that toward which we think we are moving, but fundamentally it's only a movement, it's the direction of the movement, it's the symbol, it's the arrow that indicates the movement.

Let's take an object always in motion, for example, the hand of a watch: it turns, it turns indefinitely because it must turn, there's a spring unwinding. Let's imagine a metallic arrow attached to the hand indicating the direction it's turning in, the tip of the arrow indicating the direction it turns in. Well, if this hand became conscious of itself, it would see in front of itself the pointed tip of the arrow. It would tell itself that that's where it's going and that it's moving to reach this tip. But the tip always moves with the arrow and changes location with it.[5] Consequently, if it reflects, if it's endowed simultaneously with reflection and with consciousness, it will end up telling itself that this tip toward which it believes it is moving as its endpoint is nothing other than its very movement symbolized, that it's like its movement hypostatized.

So here we have, gentlemen, another conception of happiness. Happiness then isn't something real, positive, it's not the endpoint toward which we're going. We keep going simply because we keep going, we move in order to move. To speak of happiness is simply to say that we're moving.

You'll tell me that this conception is a fiction, that it's the conception of the [53]
philosopher, of the dilettante. Nevertheless, a large part of humanity has a conception that's, if not identical, then at least analogous to this. I also think that there's something of this in Buddhist philosophy, of happiness being considered as something negative and not positive.[6]

It is thus in no way evident a priori that happiness is a defined and definable endpoint for our activity. Immediate experience shows us that as soon as we possess what we're looking for, as soon as we are where we think we'll find happiness, we look for something else. All in all, this immediate experience would rather be in favor of a negative conception of happiness. This is worth repeating: if this conception doesn't look to us as natural as another, there are undoubtedly numerous reasons, but in particular, there's this reason: still today, our minds are turned, poured into Platonic molds, that is, into Socratic molds.

That's the first point: in Socrates's philosophy, happiness is something positive and definite. Everyone believes in happiness. The second point is that happiness is identical with virtue.[7] Morality and happiness are the same thing. That's the second proposition. I'd say that, if the first proposition can be called banal, the second can be called paradoxical. The great Socratic paradox, it's been said, is that happiness and virtue are something identical.[8] That's possible, but what's certain is that if we accept the first proposition, namely, that we can define happiness, then we will necessarily end up at the second. It'll be very easy to show this if we follow the pointers of ancient philosophy itself. Let's assume that happiness is indeed something that can be defined, that can fit into a universal definition: then in what way can we characterize the state of happiness? Necessarily, we must exclude from it all the elements that are, by definition, by essence, variable from person to person. If we look at violent passions, for example—assuming that they can make certain people temporarily happy and satisfied—then the same passions, passions

[54] of the same kind as we're considering, which will make another person unhappy, all of these movements coming from the soul will neutralize one another in the definition. Where the satisfaction of sensibility is concerned, all that remains are entirely moderate satisfactions. Consequently, we'll be led to recommend moderation, temperance, as the ancients said.[9] This will be the very base of virtue, the starting point for virtue. Then this temperance, which implies a moderate use of pleasures, this temperance will call for what the ancients called self-control, *enkrateia*.[10] We can take any of the directions of sensibility, but we must be sure to know when to stop, we must have self-possession. Then, when we've thus managed to secure the perfect calm of the soul, we're going to see higher pleasures develop on this bed of flowers, as it were, that we can cultivate: the pleasures of the mind, the pleasures of the arts, the pleasures of conversation, which for the ancient Greeks is the art par excellence, the art, moreover, that is accessible to everyone. So we have the higher and more refined pleasures of the mind, and these pleasures consist in cultivating oneself, in perfecting oneself. The Greek word, incidentally, means moral perfection as well, it is "to complete oneself."[11]

So we have what I'll call individual virtue. Now there's something else alongside this. The main effect and main objective of the virtue we call "temperance," "self-mastery," or "wisdom," is to give us inner peace or calm. To be complete, to even be possible, this peace presupposes outer peace. One must be at peace with others at the same time as with oneself, and then justice comes in as the natural complement of wisdom. We must be aware that for the ancients, and for the Greeks in particular, justice is, all in all, an individual virtue. It's a duty in relation to oneself as much as and perhaps more than a duty toward others.

It's hard for us today to place ourselves in this point of view, to see things this way, but that's because justice as we conceive it is something much broader, much more extensive than Greek justice. We must remember, in fact, that Greek society is a polity composed
[55] of a very small number of free men, it's a society based on slavery. The duties of justice, in short, are the obligations of a small number of free men in relation to one another, men who by this fact are privileged. They are privileged, and then being just consists, at its core, in cultivating one's privilege as a free man. This is not at all the conception of justice we have today, and what we would call the moral attitude of an ancient, the attitude of the just man among the ancients is not for the ancients what this attitude of justice is for us.[12]

If we wanted to think about this attitude, this state of mind, it would be necessary to cut some small, limited societies out of the large societies in which we live and to consider what happens in these limited circles, to take professional duties, for example, to take—this might be an exaggeration—to take the obligations of one upper class man toward other upper class men, the duties of a judge toward the judiciary, or of an officer toward the army. We'd have to consider what we call professional duties, the duties a limited number of men feel toward each other, men who form a closed circle and have, in short, certain special assignments and thereby also have certain privileges.

In these limited circles, obligation has a particular characteristic: an obligation toward others here immediately and naturally assumes the form of an obligation toward oneself.

We are indeed duty-bound to one another, but at bottom that's because we are duty-bound to ourselves.

Earlier, I used an example that I said was not quite fit for giving us a complete idea of the matter, the example of an upper class obligation: a clubman, a gentleman who is a member of a social club will not, when he enters the club, take the chair in which another member usually sits. He doesn't do this for the other man, since that man might like nothing better than letting him have his chair; he does this for himself, for his independence, because acting otherwise would bother him. So, by the very force of things, the obligations toward others in a limited circle become obligations toward oneself. This is what we call honor: the obligation toward others that succeeds in taking [56]
the form of an obligation toward oneself.

It has often been noted, and rightly so, that honor is a feeling that develops in small societies, in societies in which all men are equal and generally equal in pleasure. But it is wrong to say that the feeling of honor didn't exist among the ancients. They had no name for it, that's true, but that might be because something, precisely, of what we ourselves call honor, the feeling of honor, plays into all their moral notions, into all their moral feelings. Hence it wasn't necessary for them, as it is for us, to have a special word with which to designate it.

The proof that this is really so is that when society grows, when it becomes less limited, Roman society for example, then we find a word with which to designate honor. The word *decus* thus designates, or very nearly designates what we ourselves call "honor." It's not absolutely the same thing. I'm not saying that the ancients had exactly our idea, our notion of honor. Honor such as we conceive it is something rigid, a bit curt, a bit prim, while what the Greeks called "goodness" is something more supple, something, I would say, easy-going.[13] Nevertheless, the essence of what we call honor is, of course, an obligation in relation to others but an obligation that takes the form of an obligation toward oneself.

I'll add that because for them, justice is above all that, it appears to the ancient Greeks, to the ancient Athenians, as something much simpler and much easier to practice than it does to us. In fact, in a society in which men were probably not absolutely equal among themselves, it was a lot easier to be just, for there were inequalities in wealth, but they were a lot less accentuated than ours are and, above all, they didn't entail inequalities of culture, of instruction, of education, which are profound and important inequalities. So, in a society like this, justice was something easier to practice and, I imagine, easier to [57]
know. When society grows, when the barriers fall or are going to fall between classes, then the duties of justice become difficult not only to practice but also to know.

For the ancients, this was something a lot simpler. In Socrates's time, justice had neither the complexity nor the difficulties that it can have for the moderns and that it has for us.

Now, it's obvious that Socrates didn't accept the moral ideas of his time as they were. The very truth is that his moral horizon was much vaster than that of the men of his time. On slavery in particular, on the dignity of work, he has views that are quite ahead of the views of his contemporaries. In a word, Socrates is the creator of a morality in the sense that he replaced a conventional morality founded on tradition with a scientific morality, a philosophical morality that goes back to principles, that is founded on inner observation. All of that is certain. Nevertheless, he did not, of course, completely remove himself from the moral conceptions of his time, and if, for a Greek of this epoch, virtue and even justice are above all what provides calm and peace, the peace with oneself and with others, if, moreover, for Socrates happiness thus is something positive and can be defined, is something that can be given a definition, a universal definition, then naturally, by the very force of things, we'll come to say that virtue thus understood is what is most capable of bringing happiness and that virtue and morality are the same thing.

So if we start from these premises—that there is a positive, definable, defined state of happiness—we'll come to a conception of happiness nearly identical to the one a Greek society had of morality, virtue, and justice. The first proposition quite naturally entails the second.

The third proposition—and here we're approaching our conclusion—the third is that the intellect is at work above all in the search for and the discovery of happiness, consequently in the practice of virtue. Socrates always believed that everything we do,
[58] and everything we are able to do, can be evaluated, as it were, in relation to this standard, which is, call it what you will, happiness or virtue. And depending on whether a thing is more or less capable of bringing us happiness or capable of realizing virtue, he'll say that it is more or less useful: that's *to ōphelimon*. Socrates also calls it *to sumpheron*, literally what contributes to happiness or to virtue.[14] So we can measure or evaluate every real or possible step we take by this standard, and consequently, we also can, we must imagine a knowledge [*science*] whose objective is to take such measurements.[15] This knowledge will be the knowledge of virtue. Virtue is a kind of knowledge.

The texts agree on this point. The formulas vary but it's always more or less the same thing.[16] In the *Nicomachean Ethics*, Aristotle tells us that according to Socrates, "all virtues are forms of practical wisdom [*phronesis*]." A little later he says: "virtue is the state that implies the presence of reason [*logoi*]."[17] In the *Eudemian Ethics*, the word "knowledge" appears, "all the virtues [are] kinds of knowledge."[18] In the *Memorabilia*, Xenophon tells us that "for Socrates, justice and all the virtues are *sophia*," which is to say wisdom, which is to say knowledge.[19]

So virtue is knowledge. Here we have the principle of Socrates's ethics, which I'll call the third principle. Here we have a point that, all in all, everyone agrees on. Here we have the premises of ethics on which everyone is in agreement. Here we have the formula from which we infer Socrates's determinism: if happiness and virtue are identical things, if we naturally and even necessarily tend toward happiness, then we necessarily also always choose what appears to us to contribute most and best to happiness. So we never will anything but the best, and if we do evil, it's because the intellect has made a mistake, it's ignorance. No one wills evil.

In the *Magna Moralia*, Aristotle (assuming it was written by Aristotle) tells us that "if . . . one were to ask any one whatever whether he would wish to be just or unjust, no one would choose injustice."[20] Consequently, if we opt for injustice, it's because we lack knowledge of justice. There's a formula Aristotle attributes to Socrates in the

Nicomachean Ethics, although Socrates isn't mentioned in this passage, but the allusion [59]
to Socrates is obvious: "no one is voluntarily wicked."[21] So we conclude that being good or evil does not depend on us.

The historians of philosophy agree in seeing in this a formula that tends toward determinism. The thesis of Socratic determinism has been expounded many times, in particular in a very brilliant way in Fouillée's works on Socrates's philosophy. I must say that this thesis had its defenders already in antiquity. Aristotle himself is the first historian of philosophy, since in the *Magna Moralia* he attributes to Socrates the following proposition: "to be good or bad does not rest with us to come about." Then the passage I quoted earlier appears: "if . . . one were to ask anyone whatever whether he would wish to be just or unjust, no one would choose injustice."[22] So this thesis already has Aristotle as its defender. But there's one thing we mustn't forget when we're dealing with his texts: we needn't go by them in any absolute way. And here's why: Aristotle's constant habit is to interpret the doctrines of his predecessor and to interpret them in terms of the problems he is posing—in the passage just quoted in particular, Aristotle poses the problem relative to what depends or doesn't depend on us, and then he attributes to Socrates his own concern. The sentence Socrates is to have said, "being good or bad does not rest with us to come about," just like the conclusion Aristotle draws from this sentence, that "if one were to ask anyone whatever, do you want to be just or unjust?" then this someone will never say that he wants injustice, these are Aristotle's interpretations, they aren't quotations. In short, Aristotle interprets the Socratic formula that "no one does evil voluntarily," that wickedness is ignorance, in his own way.[23]

But, gentlemen, is this a determinist formula? And can we conclude from this formula—we don't do evil from the moment we know the good, and we do evil only out of ignorance—can we conclude that we are not free to do evil or good? Yes, we could conclude this if we weren't free to know or to not know. Ah, yes, if it didn't depend on us
to know or to not know, then it would follow from this thesis that virtue is knowledge, [60]
it would follow that we aren't free to be good or evil. But then Socrates would have had to tell us that we aren't free to choose between knowledge and ignorance. The formula, "no one does evil voluntarily," is not enough for me to see a determinist in Socrates, or a philosopher tending toward determinism. What I'd need is for Socrates to have said: "no one is voluntarily ignorant." Yet we do not find this formula in any of the texts from the historians who spoke about Socrates's philosophy, neither in Xenophon, nor in Plato, nor in Aristotle. Everything we know about Socrates and his teachings protests against such an assertion.

What does Socrates point to, above all, as the fault par excellence? Ignorance. What is the fault against which Socratic irony is directed? Ignorance. Ignorance is thus the precise point where, according to Socrates, our responsibility lies.

Socrates never said nor thought we weren't responsible for our ignorance, entirely the opposite. Someone will say: but we aren't free to choose to be knowledgeable or ignorant the way we are free to choose between good or evil, since to be knowledgeable, to know, you need to have favorable circumstances, you need to have external help, while to will well, it's enough that you will. There's only one good thing, Kant says, and that's the good will.[24] Socrates would have absolutely repudiated this formula. He would have said: "No, there's only one good thing, and that is the intellect, the intellect that knows [*l'intelligence connaissante*]."

Knowledge [*science*] as Socrates understands it is a kind of knowledge that is within the reach of everyone. For we have to remember what I said at the very beginning of this lecture, that the knowledge at issue is not the knowledge of external things, of the things of nature. For Socrates, that knowledge is impossible and useless. The knowledge par excellence, and the only kind of knowledge, is the knowledge that takes inward things for its object, moral things. Now, to acquire this knowledge, no teacher is needed: we can acquire it on our own. Socrates is indeed devoted to helping others acquire this kind of
[61] knowledge, but he begins by declaring that all he knows is nothing at all.[25] Consequently, he cannot teach anything, he simply helps others draw forth all that is in them.

You recall that he compared the procedure of his method to giving birth, it's the art of "maieutics."[26] The knowledge in question is thus within everyone's reach. To reach this knowledge, in short, it's enough that we want to reach it. Others can help us and certainly Socrates advises dialogue, conversation, or what we could call dialectic. It's better to partner up to improve oneself, but the simple fact that there's nothing to take from what comes from others does show that there's a way of proceeding within everyone's reach. Consequently, for Socrates, knowing is something within the reach of everyone and the knowledge he speaks of is a knowledge we can give to ourselves. The formula, "know thyself," aptly demonstrates that the issue, at bottom, is to dispel ignorance, which, no doubt, is a state we find ourselves in naturally. It's a kind of veil nature and, especially, tradition place over something that appears quite naturally as soon as the veil is lifted.

In the Alexandrians, in Plotinus and especially Porphyry (who devoted a whole treatise to the "know thyself," the *gnōthi seauton*), there are some very interesting commentaries on this Socratic slogan.[27] This philosopher[28] tells us that knowing ourselves consists in reascending from the personality we believe we have to the true personality that remains above. We've fallen: there's one half of ourselves that has fallen into space and time, it's what we commonly call our person; then, there's another part that remains above, they say, and this is the truly intelligent and intelligible part. Knowing ourselves consists in turning our gaze away from this self, which in reality is external to us, and turning the gaze back toward the true self, the one that remains above. To place ourselves back in the true self, they say, it's enough to look. That's why to do good, it's enough to know the good.

I'm not saying that there's a theory of this kind in Socrates. The Alexandrians, I've said it many times, are philosophers who enormously magnify everything they touch.[29]
[62] The Alexandrians push ideas that are only in the state of a proposition in Socrates or Plato, or in Aristotle, they push these ideas as far in their development as it is possible to push them. But it's precisely for this reason, as I've also said many times, that they are magnifying glasses, as it were, that allow us to see many things in the philosophers of the Socratic and Platonic period we wouldn't have seen without them. Even if Socrates says nothing of this kind, judging by what Xenophon tells us, there nevertheless is in Socrates a very clear distinction between two humans in each of us: the human who is made from

tradition and also from prejudices, the human who receives from those around him a certain number of ready-made ideas; and the human who comes up with his own ideas about all moral questions, and in coming up with them, he is finding himself. A labor like this is within everyone's reach, within the reach of those who want it. The proof, moreover—I'll return to this—that there's something like this in Socrates is that we can find intermediaries between Socratic ethics and the Platonic myth of the fall of the soul. That's what I'll try to show in the next lecture. The myth about the fall of the soul is sometimes considered to be a kind of *deus ex machina*, an invention of Plato's. I'll show that this myth emerges very naturally from Socratic ethics, that if we consider the human to be a kind of duality, to be, on one side, external to himself, made of prejudices, and on the other, internal to himself, we can consider the external self, the external human to be a kind of degradation, a kind of fall of the soul, such that it's sufficient to externalize Socratic thought, translate it into images, and into superb images, as Plato did, to get, quite naturally, to the idea of the fall of the soul, the Platonic myth of the fall of souls.

So there's a relation between the two things. To sum up, Socrates seems to have had, implicitly rather than explicitly, the conception of freedom I would formulate in the following way: it's a choice, not, perhaps, between doing and not doing, but between looking and not looking. The good is a kind of light, as Plato will say:[30] we can focus on [63]
it and we can avert our gaze. Undoubtedly, the act of freedom doesn't consist in doing or not doing, since once we have seen, we aren't free not to do. Rather, true freedom consists in the choice between seeing and not seeing, between looking and not looking.

Someone will say: but then it's a singular act, a unique decision. We choose once and for all between knowledge and ignorance. Then freedom is found, so to speak, in a single step.[31] Even if freedom were defined this way, Socrates wouldn't be a determinist. In those theories, which everyone considers to be theories of freedom, where freedom consists in one and the same single act (this act can be a nontemporal act, as Kant said[32]) that is refracted into the past and into time—there's no need to believe that Socrates uttered a proposition like this:[33] it's enough that to his mind, we are free at every moment to choose between knowledge and ignorance. We can choose to be ignorant: for that, it's enough that we avert our attention from what we should be looking at.

Although we have unfortunately only very few texts from which we might be able to draw this kind of conclusion, there's one passage that is rather significant, it's in the fourth book of Xenophon's *Memorabilia*, there's a dialogue between Socrates and Euthydemus. Socrates asks Euthydemus: "Which one is better, the one who deceives others voluntarily or the one who deceives others involuntarily?"[34]

Let me say in passing that, if we can deceive others voluntarily, I wonder what happens to the formula Aristotle attributes to Socrates, "No one is wicked voluntarily."

So, I was saying that we find the following formula: "Which one of the two is better, the one who deceives voluntarily or the one who deceives involuntarily?" Socrates answers: "It's the one who deceives voluntarily."[35] In my view, this response is quite paradoxical. That's because, if someone deceives voluntarily, this proves that he knows what is just. The other who deceives involuntarily doesn't know what is just, is ignorant of justice. Consequently, out of these two, there is one, the one who deceives voluntarily, who in

general sees right [*juste*], who pays attention to justice, yet, at a given moment it pleases him to avert his gaze from justice: he is wicked accidentally. But the other one, who has
[64] not beheld justice, doesn't know it at all: this one is wicked essentially, he turns his head not accidentally but essentially.

So there we have what appears to be the Socratic conception of freedom: a choice between turning your head toward the good and turning it away from it. You recall Plato's allegory of the cave.[36] There are people who look at shadows in front of them, who never see anything but shadows. Then there are others—the chosen few—who turn their heads and who see the light. Like most Platonic myths, the allegory of the cave is only the development of certain Socratic moral conceptions in images, in superb images, as I said a minute ago. Of course, these developments aren't in Socrates. But his successors, Plato and Aristotle, have externalized in images things that in Socrates were internal, purely internal. In Socrates, these things are virtually in the state of an inner intuition, a moral intuition. That's why I said that indeed, the first philosopher to have the intuition of freedom is Socrates. To summarize, in Plato and in Aristotle, we find very fine developments; we find, explicitly, what was implicit in Socrates; we find efforts to dispel certain difficulties such a theory gives rise to—but nothing more, for some at least, nothing more than that. One would have to wait a long time, search much further, to have a new inner intuition of moral freedom. This is what I'll show in the next lecture, which won't take place until January 13.

Notes

1. There is no reason to doubt the dates the typescript gives for the first three lectures (December 6, 16, and 22, 1904), which thus did not strictly follow the weekly rhythm. This would no longer be the case starting in January 1905.
2. "Affinity" is a term borrowed from chemistry, with a long history of literary appropriation, as in Goethe's novel *Elective Affinities* of 1809.
3. The word Bergson uses here is *audition*, literally "hearing," but he constructs it in analogy with *vision* in the sense of "something seen"—hence "voice" for what Socrates heard.
4. For the word "singular" in the "this no less singular feature," the typescript contains a strange *compliqué*, "complicated."
5. Here, with a bit of humor, Bergson is paraphrasing Schopenhauer, who in this passage is paraphrasing Spinoza. See Arthur Schopenhauer, *The World as Will and Representation 1*, ed. and trans. Judith Norman, Alistair Welchman, and Christopher Janaway (Cambridge: Cambridge University Press, 2010), I.§24: 151, and Spinoza, letter 58 to Schuller, CWS 2, 428.
6. For Bergson's analysis of Buddhism, see TS, 224–7/237–40. A different version can be found in Schopenhauer, for whom "the essence of inner virtue" is "diametrically opposed to . . . happiness" and "every satisfaction is only the removal of pain"; see *The World as Will and Representation 1*, IV.§65: 388 and IV.§67: 402.
7. On this point, see, in particular, Plato's *Protagoras* 351b–358d: 781–7.
8. He is referring again to Fouillée, who makes the point explicitly in *La philosophie de Socrate*, 1.3.4: 255.

9. Here, Bergson is thinking of *sophrosynē*, one of the four cardinal virtues Plato lists in book 4 of the *Republic* (427e: 1059 and 435b: 1066). Bergson goes on to discuss two more of these cardinal virtues, wisdom and justice; he does not comment on courage.
10. See Plato's *Republic*, for example book 3, 390b: 1028, and book 4, 430e: 1062, and Aristotle's *Nicomachean Ethics*, 7.1–10: 1808–21.
11. The French phrase is *se finir soi-même*—Bergson might be thinking of *entelekheia*, which in Aristotle, who coined the term, designates the accomplishment, the actualization, even the perfection of any sort of being, in the sense that it has reached its *telos*, its end or endpoint.
12. Bergson will trace out the history of justice and at the same time show the difference in nature between two fundamental types of justice in TS, 69–81/68–81.
13. The French word rendered as "goodness" here is *honnêté*—literally, "honesty"—which in turn renders the Greek *spoudaious*, which means "(morally) good," or "excellent," as well as "serious" in the sense of being worthy of attention. The reference here is to a passage in (Pseudo-) Aristotle's *Magna Moralia* (1.9, 1187a6–7: 1877), to which Bergson turns immediately after this comment.
14. "What is helpful, or useful" and "what is advantageous," respectively. Plato uses these exact phrases in Thrasymachus's polemic challenge to Socrates to define justice in *Republic* 1, 336d: 981; Socrates takes them up in qualified form in his response at 1, 346e: 990.
15. In this and the following sentences, Bergson is translating the Greek word *epistēmē* (usually rendered in English as "knowledge") as the French word *science* (rather than as *connaissance*). However, it is possible that Bergson is using *science* because it is related to the Latin term *scientia* by which *epistēmē* is translated. His use of *science* here becomes clear in his later comparison of modern science and ancient science (177). To account for this double aspect—science as knowledge and in the sense prevalent today—this translation renders the term flexibly.
16. Socrates often raises the question of knowing whether virtue is knowledge, for example in the *Meno* (87c–89a: 887–8) and the *Protagoras* (358e–361a: 787–9).
17. Aristotle, *Nicomachean Ethics* 6.13, 1144b17 and 28: 1808.
18. Aristotle, *Eudemian Ethics* 1.5, 1216b5–10: 1925.
19. Xenophon, *Memorabilia* III.9.5: 239.
20. *Magna Moralia* 1.9, 1187a7–8: 1877. Like Barnes in this edition, few interpreters today accept that this text was written by Aristotle.
21. Aristotle, *Nicomachean Ethics*, 3.5, 1113b15: 1758. The allusion is to passages in Plato's dialogs where Socrates states the thesis, such as *Protagoras*, 345d–e: 776, and *Gorgias*, 509e: 853.
22. Pseudo-Aristotle, *Magna Moralia*, 1.9, 1187a6–8: 1877.
23. It bears repeating that this formula is *traditionally attributed* to Socrates and is not based on direct testimony, and that the *Magna Moralia* were likely not written by Aristotle.
24. Kant says this at the beginning of the first section of *Groundworks of The Metaphysics of Morals* (in *Practical Philosophy*, ed. and trans. Mary Gregor [New York: Cambridge University Press, 1996], 49/AA 4, 393).
25. This is the principle of Socratic irony; see Plato, *Apology*, 21d–e: 21.
26. That is to say, "midwifery"; see Plato, *Theaetetus*, 149b–151d: 166–8.
27. By the term "the Alexandrians," Bergson is referring, grosso modo, to the Neoplatonists; see CE, 279/322, and TS, 219–20/232–3. When he mentions Porphyry, he is referring to the

treatise *On the "Know Thyself"*; see Porphyry, *Porphyrii Philosophi Fragmenta*, ed. Andrew Smith (Stuttgart: Teubner, 1993), fragments 268–71: 295–308.

28. That is to say, Porphyry.
29. In the lecture course of the preceding year, for example, Bergson calls Plotinus a "magnifying glass" for reading the doctrines of Plato and Aristotle (see HTM, lecture on April 15, 1904, 261).
30. In *Republic* 6, 507a–509b: 1127–30.
31. The term rendered as "step" is *démarche*; see also below, 124n8.
32. Bergson is alluding to the theory of the acting subject's "intelligible character" Kant presents in the First Critique; see Kant, CPR, 535–7/A538-541/B566-569/AA 3, 366–8. The section is called "The Possibility of Causality through Freedom Unified with the Universal Law of Natural Necessity," and Bergson will refer to it several times in the final two lectures.
33. The reasoning here is truncated. Bergson seems to lean toward the idea that even if we accept that the free act in Socrates is unique (and Bergson does not accept this), Socrates is not a determinist philosopher because there are philosophers (Kant, for instance) who are on the side of freedom and also on the side of the thesis of the unique act of freedom.
34. Xenophon, *Memorabilia*, IV.2.19: 295.
35. It is, in fact, Euthydemus who answers.
36. In *Republic* 7, 514a–517d: 1132–5.

LECTURE 4
JANUARY 13, 1905

Gentlemen, I'll very briefly remind you, after this interruption of several weeks, of the [65] conclusions we reached in the last session. Moreover, it will be worthwhile to summarize these conclusions in simple common sense terms, leaving all philosophical terminology aside.

All in all, what we've said up to now is extremely simple, of elementary simplicity. The idea I've pointed out from the start, and which I developed in the first two or three lectures, is this: there's a gap, an irreducible gap, between the will, the will which is or at least appears to be free, and thought, reflection, which focuses on this freedom, which tries to grasp it, to understand it. Freedom is the real or apparent characteristic of our actions, of those at least that are not automatic, nor due to a distraction or to habit. When we think about one of our so-called voluntary actions, when we consider it not prior to it being accomplished nor after, but during, and try to make our thought coincide, as it were, with the action itself, this action will appear to us as having a certain character, an inner character. This is very clear for immediate consciousness but very obscure as soon as we try to state it in the definite terms of thought and reflection. Each of us senses very well what it means when we say that our action is free, that it emanates from our person. But if we are then compelled to explain ourselves, despite ourselves, we'll lapse into metaphors, into images that will distort the immediate intuition we had. We'll say for example that the action emanates from our will. We'll posit the action on one side, [66] the will on the other as two things distinct from one another when the will is entirely in the voluntary action. We'll say that the action emanates from us, as a way of expressing that we're free. We'll then posit our self on one side and our action on the other when the self is nothing outside of what we do.

It's as if we wanted to distinguish—I'm making this comparison but you could find other and better comparisons—it's as if we wanted to distinguish water from the source from which it springs. We might say the water flows [*jaillir*] from the source, but when we go back up to the source itself we find only water. To say that water comes from [*dériver*] the source is simply to repeat in other terms that the water flows from the source. It's the same for action. The free action posits itself, is self-sufficient; that's what freedom consists in. And when we say that the action comes from the will as from a source, we simply express in other terms and in a form that is less clear, and in a way that is a lot less true, the simple fact that the action accomplishes itself: it's self-sufficient, it posits itself, as it were, and freedom consists in that—if it exists.

I also said that reflection, as soon as it focuses on the free act, distorts it. That's because—I pointed to this idea in the first lecture, but it's helpful to return to it—it's

because reflection, and thought generally, isn't made for this use. It isn't intended for this job. To get at what is free about the action, reflection would have to grasp it as it takes place, in the present. But the essence of reflection is to consider or to think about only what has passed or what is to come. Its domain is not the present, and for a very simple reason: because thought is above all a practical faculty intended to enlighten action. No matter what theory we accept on this point, the evolutionist hypothesis or whatever other hypothesis, we'll always end up at the conclusion that reflective thought is made for representing what is entirely complete and not what is in the making [*le se faisant*], not what is happening [*en train de se faire*]. Where action, and our action in particular, is at issue, the role of reflection lies especially in preparing the action. It
[67] prepares any particular action by outlining in advance the representations, the motives, and motivations, things already made, things contained in a distinct representation, and then thought should or will be able to foresee the consequences, to represent the consequences of the action. So it places itself before or after the action, in the preparation or in the representation of the consequences, a representation that itself must enter into the preparations, but the action itself, the action being accomplished, is not an object of reflection, of reflective thought.

After all, what would be the use of reflection were it to focus on the action accomplishing itself? That is useful in one case, in a single case: when we do philosophy, and when we are concerned with freedom—but thought has not been made for that, in a general way, reflection has not been made for philosophy. I've said it many times, I've come back to this point many times: thought is capable of philosophizing but on the condition of reascending the slope of nature. It's thus generally not made for philosophizing, and in particular it's not made for philosophizing about freedom. Now, there are no other cases but this one unique case of thought philosophizing on freedom where it's useful that reflection attain the act, the action in its very accomplishment. Reflective thought turning back on action, as it were, arrives too late, the act is already accomplished when thought wants to grasp it. Thought thus arrives after, or too early before, which amounts to the same thing, it is, generally, not made for grasping action in its very accomplishment. Our thought—this is just a way of expressing the same thing—has difficulty grasping, representing to itself what is free. It is essentially analytic, it does anatomy, it's like an anatomist who dissects a corpse, who dissects only a dead person. But if you all have is a dead person, you can dissect them, but you'll never manage to think the living.

Imagine an intellect that would be nothing but intellect, a pure mind separated from the body, a pure mind that has never lived, and that consequently doesn't know what life is, what a living body is. Suppose this intellect is placed before a body that has been
[68] alive but is no longer anything but a corpse, and is asked to imagine the movement of this body. It will suppose that by putting the arms, for example, in motion, one also puts the torso in motion, which moves the legs and so on: it will certainly picture this body moving thanks to an external impulse that is communicated bit by bit. Now tell it that it's wrong, that the movement of the body does not come to it from the outside but from the inside. All well and good: this intellect will place a spring into the body, gears

engaging with each other. In both cases, it will picture a doll, the movement of a doll. Tell it that that's not how it works, that movement isn't localized at this point or that, that it's everywhere. It will multiply the springs, the gears, it will come up with all possible hypotheses except the one that's true, namely, that there's movement everywhere and nowhere. This, in reality, is the paradox that life realizes. This is what the intellect and reflection will never attain by means of recomposition. With the moral organism, it's the same as with the physical organism. When it wants to reconstitute this organism, the intellect or reflective thought will proceed by means of an interplay of springs, of gears. It will imagine strings, spiritual strings, but strings nonetheless—but the true mechanism, which is not a mechanism, which is something like the inverse of what we call a mechanism, will necessarily elude it.

So there's a gap, an irreducible gap, between the immediate consciousness we have of our freedom, of free action, and the knowledge we gain of it by means of reflection. However, when it has concerned itself with freedom, philosophy has been unable to keep itself from posing the problem, and an analysis like that, it seems, would logically carry freedom beyond philosophy's grasp. This is not at all the conclusion we came to. No, our conclusion is simply this: if, to reconstitute, to recompose freedom, we start from pure reflection, with reflection, with what is given in it and its results, then we will never reach it. Freedom is given in an intuition, in the very feeling we have of our action accomplishing itself, a feeling that is simple, not decomposed, indecomposable: if there is knowledge, if we can still use the word, of freedom, this is where it resides. Let's [69] call this kind of knowledge "intuition," if you like; we'll say that freedom is given in an intuition that is co-extensive with action; it's action grasping itself in its accomplishment. We'll never reach this intuition starting from reflection, and, picking up on a famous phrase, we can say that the one who seeks freedom will never find it, we have to start from freedom. In another sense, moreover, we can say that we wouldn't look for it if we hadn't already found it.[1] We have to place ourselves in it, we have to start from the action accomplishing itself. Then, we have to try to enlarge this intuition, which is co-extensive with the act, which is, at bottom, indistinguishable from it. That's very difficult, it requires an exceptional kind of effort, it's a victory over nature since thought does not naturally proceed that way. It's a victory, [but] a victory with no tomorrow, or rather, one whose tomorrow is necessarily a defeat because when the intuition, at a certain moment, has succeeded at reflection, we could say that the intuition suffocates itself: it can become conscious of itself, can express itself only through words intended for an entirely different usage, intended to formulate determinism. I've said it many times before: what happens is that freedom then is as if covered over and crushed by the expression that it itself has sought.[2] This is why, as soon as a theory of freedom appears, the very expressions it must make use of to communicate itself turn against it, and it ends up being crushed by opposing theories, until the day comes when the kind of hard crust that has formed on it is broken apart by a new explosion—I've used the word "explosion" before[3]—by a new intuition that seeks out freedom in the depths where it is hidden from reflection.

I said that intuitions of this kind, that these volcanic eruptions are rare in the history of philosophy, that we can count them up, and that, in general, these intuitions have not been suggested by reflection alone or by speculation alone. It's rare that the impulse didn't come from the outside, that considerations of a social and even religious kind weren't at the origin of this intuition.

[70] This is the general conclusion we reached. I added that Greek philosophy from Socrates onward presents us with an intuition of moral freedom, which took on successive, more and more complex expressions, more and more distant from the origin, in a certain sense, less and less adequate. This intuition goes back to a philosopher who is generally classed among the determinists because people have latched onto the letter of the doctrine such as his disciples have handed it down to us it much more than onto its spirit: I mean Socrates.

To be sure, Socrates didn't speak of freedom, he didn't pronounce the word, he didn't discuss the thing. We can only discuss freedom—I've said this many times already in relation to other questions—when we're face to face with determinist doctrines. Freedom only becomes aware of itself, only seeks to articulate itself when it faces doctrines that aim to deny it. Now, the question was not yet posed in Socrates's time; it's thus natural that we find in Socrates neither a discussion nor a formal exposition of freedom.

Socrates, for that matter, wasn't looking for freedom, he was concerned with something completely different. He devises a theory of action, and in devising a theory of action, he couldn't not take up action with its essential characteristics, with its characteristic, which is to be free.

In what has come down to us through his disciples, I said, Socrates bequeathed to us a conception, an implicit, and not explicit, theory of freedom. In the last lecture, I tried to articulate this theory. And in order to formulate it, I had to make things much more precise, much more than they are in the available texts, in Xenophon or Plato. This is how I presented things: for Socrates, there are, in a way, two possible determinations of human activity. We must place ourselves, by turns, between——to understand Socrates's theory, [we must place ourselves] in the following two hypotheses, which are opposite hypotheses.[4] First, let's suppose someone with perfect knowledge in the sense that Socrates gives to the word "knowledge" [*science*]. This is not about physics, knowledge
[71] [*connaissance*] of things, it's about knowledge of what concerns humans, knowledge of the human. Let's imagine someone who has this perfect knowledge. That person, then, knows perfectly what Socrates calls the Good, and the Good in the Socratic sense of the word is at once moral goodness and happiness. In the last lecture, I explained that for the Greeks in Socrates's time, goodness and happiness were but one, and this is easy to understand given the nature of ancient [Greek] society. So this person knows the Good perfectly, and in these conditions measures the value of all possible actions with perfect precision, and in each case, in each situation whatever it is, he assesses with perfect exactitude what is best. And knowing the best, that is, what he thinks is the best or the happiest, he necessarily chooses the best. So for this person who has perfect knowledge, there aren't two possible determinations. All of his actions, all that he does is foreseeable. Making use of a modern expression, this would be absolute determinism: his activity would be determined necessarily.

Now let's suppose—this is the second hypothesis—let's suppose someone who is perfectly ignorant and no longer perfectly knowledgeable, ignorance once more taken in the Socratic sense, someone who has no idea of what the Good is, who is in no way capable of assessing the value of things in general and of actions in particular. In each particular case, this person decides not on the basis of the Good but on the basis of the appearance of the Good. For he, too, is seeking happiness, he, too, is seeking the Good, but he's mistaken, or he finds the Good only by chance. Consequently, he necessarily goes for the appearance of the Good and his conduct, too, is determined, and determined necessarily, not by reality [but] by appearance—and someone who perfectly knows, I'm not saying the knowledge but the ignorance of this person, knows its nature and degree, knows its quality and quantity, can once more predict with infallible precision everything this person will do: determinism once more, the determinism of ignorance this time, while earlier it was the determinism of knowledge.

However, according to Socrates, neither the one nor the other of these two extreme [72] hypotheses is realized. Knowledge is possible and we must seek it. We don't have it naturally, we can always obtain it without going outside of ourselves because we possess this knowledge, which is not the knowledge of external things but the knowledge of internal things, human things. We possess it virtually. To acquire this knowledge, all we have to do is question ourselves, specify our ideas, as it were, consider ourselves—but we never have it completely. We are thus in a state where, being ignorant, we are nevertheless able to know. We are placed between two determinisms. But this sole fact of being in the middle, between them, allows us to oscillate, and this oscillation corresponds to what today we call free will, freedom.

Socrates would attach very little importance to this, like all the ancients would—for this will be one of the conclusions we'll take from this whole study: the ancients had an intuition of freedom, which through their philosophy became more systematic, but they attached very little importance to this freedom in the sense of free will. This is easy to understand in light of what I just said. If, all in all, being endowed with a free will consists in oscillating between good and evil, between ignorance and knowledge, then free will is an expedient. It's a means for us to elevate ourselves from ignorance to knowledge and from evil to good, but it would still be better to be good and to have knowledge of it, and not to have to get there. Consequently, free will in [ancient] thought is rather a sign of inferiority, it makes us superior to animals but, all in all, inferior to the gods. The truly wise person, who would in a way be a god, could do without free will and would be superior to those who have use of it. When we move from antiquity to modernity, we'll follow the true invention of the idea of freedom, where free will becomes a sort of creation and where this creation, insofar as it is a creation, is what really turns humans into gods, an idea that is the absolute opposite of the ancient idea. But I close this parenthesis. I opened it simply to point out to you that in Socrates's mind, undoubtedly, the fact of having chosen does not indicate a superiority. It would be better not to have [73] to choose and to be definitively and forever knowledgeable [*savant*], that is, wise.

In any case, and this is the conclusion I'd like to reach, here we have, all in all, only an intuition of human action, of the nature of human action, an intuition that is analyzed and expressed in terms of reflection, and it then ends up, in short, bringing out these two elements: knowledge [*science*] and ignorance, both elements of an intellectual nature, knowing and not knowing. Free will, if it has a place in this theory—and I believe it does—is something nonintellectual and nonintelligible by the very fact that it is placed between knowledge and ignorance. It is, in a word, a *je ne sais quoi* that enables us to opt between the two and to elevate ourselves from ignorance to knowledge—it's a residue. When we look at action, when we bring out all that is intellectual and intelligible in it, [we see that] there are two extreme limits, knowledge and nonknowledge. Then, between the two, there is what's not intellectual, which, when analyzed, might even turn out to be nonintelligible: this is what we for our part, we today, call free will, freedom.

So this is what we found in Socrates. Everything concerning freedom we're going to find in the ancients is going to flow naturally from this implicit conception—for it's not explicit in Socrates—of freedom. We're going to find in Plato, in Xenophon, and especially in Plotinus, who is the most interesting of the ancients in this regard. We're going to find ourselves face to face with beautiful and great philosophical constructions, and thereby an explicitation, if we can say this, of the intuition of freedom, but there's nothing more than that. There's a lot more on the surface but nothing more in the depth, perhaps less; I say "perhaps," because we don't know exactly what Socrates's thinking was on this point. Socrates wrote nothing, and that, incidentally, is one of the characteristics of philosophies of intuition. Philosophers of intuition are recognized by certain particular characteristics and especially by this: they write little, sometimes they write nothing. They like better to talk. The spoken word is suggestive, it suggests. The written word expresses better what has been thought in terms of reflection, it's a lot less capable of communicating an intuition, it's less suggestive.

[74] As far as we can tell from what's been published and especially from the power of the impulse that was produced, it's thus possible—I'm not saying "probable"—it's possible that there was still more in Socratic teaching concerning the fundamental nature of action, a lot more than we find in his successors, at a greater depth—we'll find all the more, in turn, on the surface. We'll find this teaching analyzed in the terms of reflection first in Plato, and it's Plato we're going to concern ourselves with today and in the next lecture as well.

First, what does Plato think about freedom? There's a large number of passages, and if we don't adopt a guiding thread—I'm going to propose one—we'll end up concluding that Plato contradicts himself not once but many times. Moreover, historians of philosophy are far from agreeing about Plato as a theorist of freedom. For some, Plato is clearly determinist. Plato does not accept freedom. This is the thesis put forward by a very talented author, Thomas-Henri Martin, in his *Studies on the Timeaeus*. In the second volume of these *Studies*, you'll find, in regard to what he calls Plato's "fatalism," a chapter presenting the reasons that would make Plato a determinist in the full modern sense of the word.[5] This is also the opinion of Teichmüller in his well-known work, *Studies on the History of Concepts*.[6] In the middle of that volume, too, you'll find a certain number of passages and arguments in favor of the thesis of Plato's determinism. In his work on Plato's philosophy, Fouillée is inclined toward this conclusion without, however, presenting it in as radical a way, and attenuating it.[7]

On the other hand, in Zeller's *History of Greek Philosophy*, you find the exact opposite thesis.[8] Zeller transforms Plato into a philosopher of freedom. He adds, to be sure, that there are Platonic texts that say the opposite. Zeller often frames his conclusions in this way.

All in all, I believe that both theses are in Plato, and that they are not irreconcilable. [75]
We indeed find determinism in Plato, that's certain. I'd even go further than those who defend this thesis: we find in Plato not one determinism but two. And precisely because there are two of them, an oscillation is possible. Then, between these two kinds of fatalism, in the middle, freedom can have its place. In that sense, Plato can be said to be a theoretician of freedom.

First of all, one thing is certain: in Plato's as in Socrates's thought, a pure intellect wouldn't need free will, it wouldn't need to choose, it would always and necessarily go for the best.

We find in the *Protagoras*, an early dialogue[9] that goes back to the time when Plato was still more or less under the sway of Socrates's ideas, we find in the *Protagoras* not just an allusion to but the development of a kind of arithmetic of the Good, as Bentham would say, or, rather, an arithmetic of pleasures.[10] When Plato was writing this dialogue, he had not yet worked out his theory of the threefold division of the soul.[11] He probably accepted, like Socrates did, the idea of the [pure] soul, of the pure intellect. Here's how he expresses it in this passage. The issue is an arithmetic of pleasures. In a general way, pleasure in this passage designates all the motivations of our activity. Pleasure is the motivation we base our activity on. Here's what a truly wise or knowledgeable person, in a word, a pure intellect would do:

> Weighing is a good analogy; you put the pleasures together and the pains together, both the near and the remote, on the balance scale, and then say which of the two is more. For if you weigh pleasant things against pleasant, the greater and the more must always be taken; if painful things against painful, the fewer and the smaller.[12]

In this whole passage, the activity of an intelligent person, who would be a pure intellect, is thus compared to the mechanism of the scale, which necessarily tilts in the direction of the greater weight.

It's in this passage from the *Protagoras*, incidentally, that we find the first example of [76]
this comparison of the will to a scale, which was to prove so successful that there is no later determinist theory that didn't compare the will to a scale. It's Plato's *Protagoras* this comparison goes back to.

This, then, is how someone who's a pure intellect would act. Now, for a whole series of reasons that I won't go into right now, Plato was led to consider the soul as a thing that is not simple. The human soul, according to Plato, is a composite. It is composed of three parts, and this tripartite division of the soul is due to its descent into a body. This, at least, is the definitive doctrine that Plato developed no further and that we find in the *Timaeus*;

for in the *Phaedrus*, a transition dialogue, we find that prior to birth, souls already have heart and appetite as much as they have intellect.[13] But Plato's definitive teaching on this point is indeed that the soul becomes divided when it enters the body. As long as the soul is not in a body, it remains simple, probably a pure intellect; but in relation to the soul, the body, or space, if you will, plays the role that in physics we attribute to a prism in the division of light: a reflection happens, a division. On the intellect, which subsists, which is what remains of the soul in its original state, two other parts come to be superposed, the heart and the appetite, that is, more or less violent passion. In fact, *epithymia*, passion, appetite, is what belongs par excellence to the body. *Thymos*, the heart, is indeed a mediator that is there because of what the soul becomes when it descends, but [a mediator] that rather looks on high while being on the ground. These are the three parts of the soul.

Once Plato has come to this tripartite structure of the soul, he imagines what someone who was only appetite, only *epithymia*, would be like, and in Plato's final dialogues, we find a clear indication of a second kind of determinism completely different from the first, the determinism to which a soul would be subject that completely delivers itself
[77] over to this inferior part of itself, to *epithymia*. In the *Timaeus*, for example, you will find a physiological description—very fanciful because the physiology of those times was hardly advanced, but very precise in its terms, of a precision that could be compared to the descriptions of current neuropathologists—the description of a mechanism by which the movement of certain humors in the body determines the formation, the birth, and the direction of our passions and our desires.[14] Besides, in a lot of passages, or at least in several, Plato distinguishes between the moral error that comes from ignorance—*agnoia*, which he calls "moral error"—and the error that consists in an illness, *nosos*, in a madness—he uses the word *mōria*—this one located in the lower part of the soul, which is like a revolt of this lower part and a revolt whose cause is corporeal, whose cause is physiological, as we'd say today.

In summary, if we were pure intellects, we would do only what is reasonable. If we were plunged into matter, entirely made of matter, we would do only what is unreasonable. And in both cases, our actions would be determined necessarily, with the determination being absolutely rational in the first case, and absolutely irrational in the second. It would be two kinds of determination.

There are indeed two kinds of determinism here, and Plato was perfectly aware of it, since, in several passages in the *Timaeus*, he distinguishes in a very clear way the two forms of determinism, the two forms of necessity, we would say today. The first is a reasonable necessity, it's—how do I put this—determination by the Good, it's the determination by the weight of the best motives, it's what Leibniz will call moral necessity. "Happy necessity," he says![15] This necessity can be defined by the attraction of the best. Then there's the other necessity, a mechanical necessity that consists in movement being determined by another movement, by a necessary mechanical, physical impulse.

[78] For example, we find in the *Timaeus*: "this ordered world is of mixed birth: it is an offspring of a union of Necessity and Intellect." Further on: "We must distinguish two forms of cause, the necessary [*anankē*]"—this, for the ancients, is the bad necessity,

the one that they like to identify with randomness, blind necessity—and "the divine."[16] Moreover, we could also cite a passage from the *Timaeus* in which mechanical necessity is clearly distinguished from intelligent causality, which is considered to be the true causality, to be higher than the former.

So, two kinds of necessity—though Plato doesn't call them both "necessity," the word *anankē* in Greek has too strict a meaning for that—two kinds of determination, two possible determinisms, the determinism of the Good and mechanical determinism, the determinism of randomness. The soul, if it were entirely intellect and purely intellect, would be given over to the first; if it were entirely appetite (*epithymia*), entirely embodied, as Plato would say, purely materialized, it would be given over to the second determinism, the determinism of blind necessity. But we are both at once, and then, in the intermediary region between thought and appetite, the region which according to Plato is that of the heart (*thymos*), freedom, in the sense of free will, would be possible. In fact, Plato conceived of his *thymos* in this way: it's an intermediary faculty between the high and the low that can occupy all the degrees one might like between the high and the low. Consequently, to choose is to choose a place between the high and the low, and choice is possible in this intermediary region.

It is possible, but does it really exist? There are certain turns of phrase by Plato that would lead us to suppose so. I'll cite in particular *The Laws*, one of Plato's last dialogues. In this text, Plato shows us that humans are, precisely, tugged between the high and the [79]
low. The high is what he calls virtue (*aretē*), and the low is what he calls *kakia* (evil or vice); they are tugged as by ropes and strings. Plato then wonders—for he is above all a philosopher, that is, he is devoted to explaining things—he wonders what causes us to incline more often to one side than to the other, as we go up or down, to lean toward *noēsis*, toward thought, or toward *epithymia*, toward passion.[17] It's clear that the more we ask these questions, the more we tend toward what we call determinism. In fact, if we have the choice between two extreme sides, and if we decide more or less for one or the other, then there must, it seems, be a reason for doing so, because we're made that way, because our character's made that way. In fact, we'll find passages in Plato where he says that it's by virtue of our character, by virtue of the character that we bear already made at birth, that we choose a place between, as it were, the two extremes. I'm quoting a well-known passage from the *Timaeus*: "No one is voluntarily bad, but the bad become bad by reason of a corrupt condition of his body and an uneducated upbringing." A little further, "In such cases, the begetters are to blame far more than the begotten, the nurturers far more than the nurtured,"[18] in other words, the parents far more than the children.

We're face to face with a fact here that is constant in the history of philosophy: as we want to grasp it, free will retreats. Free will cannot be on high in the domain of pure thought: this is necessity; it cannot be below in the domain of passion: this too is necessity; but it can be in the middle, and it consists in the oscillation between the two, and that is where we tend to place it. But the moment we're about to grasp it, we say to ourselves that now free will must be explained, that if we choose, we do so for a reason and for something. Then, as we articulate the choice, we see it vanish into thin [80] air. I said—I've already used this comparison—that free will is like smoke we're trying to catch.[19] We close our fist, and it always slips away. Expelled from above, expelled from below, free will seeks refuge in the middle, but when we want to articulate it, it vanishes into thin air. Yet Plato doesn't give up on it. Here we come to the essential point of Plato's theory of freedom: free will exists all the same. It does exist in an intermediary region, but it doesn't appear there, in this intermediary region. We do find free will, but we find it in its effects and not in the depths of its cause. The region of free will, the place where we choose the Good, is a mythical, mythological place: it's not in time, nor is it in space, it's in the world where the soul resides before its fall into a body.

You remember the myth: the souls are presented as being in a perfect state when they follow Zeus's chariot, they had wings then, but they lost the wings and they fell, they tumbled through space until the day they met with the body that was prepared for them.[20]

In book 10 of the *Republic*, a later dialogue, we find another myth, the myth of Ur, in which Plato articulates things and expresses his thought more clearly. And, I should add, Plato's myths are of the highest importance. I've said many times that Plato expresses in the form of myths what cannot be expressed in terms of reflection, of thought. Everything we call—how do I put this—pure reflection, he expresses in terms of dialectic. He expresses through myth what reflection cannot grasp. In the final book of his *Republic*, Plato shows us the souls coming before the Fates, in particular before Lachesis, one of the three Fates. I'm translating: "Here is the message of Lachesis, the maiden daughter of Necessity: 'Ephemeral souls, this is the beginning of another cycle that will end in
[81] death. Your daemon will not be assigned to you by lots.'" The "daemon" means at once character and destiny; in short, it's the destiny that will accompany you throughout your life: "You will be the one to choose your daemon. The [soul] who has the first lot will be first to choose its life, the life to which she will then be irrevocably bound. Virtue is something free"—virtue knows no master—"each [soul] will benefit from it more or less, depending on how much she esteems it. She is responsible for her choice, the god is blameless."[21]

After this passage, we find the nice, quite humorous description of the choices that the different souls make of their respective bodies and the destiny that awaits them later in their earthly existence.

There you have the Platonic conception of freedom, gentlemen. Choice seems to withdraw more and more, to the point where it is expelled into the higher world. Free will is thus localized. In modern terms, we would say that life, life in space and time, is only the development in space and time of an act, of a single timeless act by which we have set our place in the series of beings and thereby have chosen our destiny. There you have the sketch, both material and spiritual, of the Platonic conception of freedom.

We'd find a host of ideas here that have passed into modern philosophy, since we live for the most part on an ancient core of Platonism. I'll just point out the main ideas. There is, first, the idea of a distinction between physical determination, mechanical determination, the efficient cause, and moral determinism, what we call, since Aristotle, the final cause. First point, the main one. Second, there's the idea of the fall of the souls, the idea that the soul has fallen into a body and that the current life is a degradation. Then, third, the idea, which is very close to the last one, a close relative, that everything we do, everything that constitutes our acts, our conduct, our destiny, all of that only develops in time—the way a symphony develops a theme—all of that only develops in time a single action, a choice that Plato declares to come before this existence, but which modern philosophers will say comes neither before nor after, but is timeless, outside of [82] time.[22] These ideas are of utmost importance for the history of philosophy.

How did they come into being? How was Plato led to them? At first glance, these ideas, and especially the last one, strike us as a *deus ex machina*. But in reality, if we start from the Socratic conception of human action, we are quite naturally led to—on the condition that we've been gifted, it goes without saying, with the Platonic genius—we are led to this. Plato's theory emerged quite naturally, by means of a very simple mechanism, from the Socratic conception of human action. This is what I'll try to show in the next lecture. The importance of the ideas of Plato's we've just identified in the history of philosophy is so great that it's important to show how a genius like Plato had to be naturally, and had to be necessarily led to them by the Socratic conception of human action. That is what I'll demonstrate in the next lecture.

Notes

1. Compare Blaise Pascal, *Pensées*, ed. and trans. Roger Ariew (Indianapolis: Hackett, 2005), 276: "Console yourself; you would not seek me"—that is to say, Jesus—"if you had not found me."
2. In particular, see TFW, xxiii–xxiv/VII–VIII.
3. Bergson might be thinking of the first lecture of this course. Yet as early as 1888, he wrote: "It is the deep-seated self rushing up to the surface. It is the outer crust exploding, suddenly giving way to an irresistible thrust" (TFW, 169/127).
4. Bergson's remark is methodological: to understand Socrates's theory, in which freedom appears as an oscillation between two opposing states, two hypotheses, namely perfect knowledge and perfect ignorance, we must place ourselves in their respective points of view.
5. Thomas-Henri Martin (1813–84), a Catholic philosopher and scholar of Greek, author of *Études sur le Timée de Platon*, 2 vols. (Paris: Ladrange, 1841). "Fatalisme de Platon" is the second section in the one-hundred-ninety-sixth of what Martin calls "Notes" (vol. 2: 365–72).
6. Gustav Teichmüller (1832–88), a German philosopher and historian of philosophy noted for his work on Aristotle and on the history of concepts, was the author of *Studien zur Geschichte der Begriffe* (Berlin: Weidmann, 1874) and of *Neue Studien zur Geschichte der Begriffe*, 3 vols. (Gotha: Perthes, 1876–9). Bergson seems to be referring to the essay "Platon: Von der Unsterblichkeit der Seele," 107–225 in the *Studien* of 1874, specifically §4.1: "Freiheit und Böses" (146–51).
7. Alfred Fouillée, *La philosophie de Platon: Exposition, histoire et critique de la théorie des Idées*, 2 vols. (Paris: Ladrange, 1869). On freedom, see pt. 1, bk. 8, ch. 1 in vol. 1, 380–423.

8. An important historian of ancient philosophy, Eduard Zeller was the author of *Die Philosophie der Griechen in ihrer geschichtlichen Entwicklung*, first published from 1844 to 1852 and revised several times, and translated into French by Émile Boutroux and Émile Belot with the title *La philosophie des Grecs considérée dans son développement historique*, 3 vols. (Paris: Hachette, 1877–84). The relevant volume (vol. 2, pt. 2, sec. 2 of the third edition of 1875) was translated into English by Sarah Frances Alleyne and Alfred Goodwin as *Plato and the Older Academy*, 1876, new ed. (London: Longman's, Green, and Co, 1888). On the point Bergson is making, see the discussion of free will there, in ch. 9, 419–21.
9. Bergson here adopts the chronology of Plato's dialogues developed in several works by Polish philosopher Wincenty Lutosławski (1863–1954); see, especially, the major work, *The Origin and Growth of Plato's Logic, with an Account of Plato's Style and the Chronology of his Writings* (London: Longmans, Green, and Co., 1897).
10. Bergson is alluding to the English utilitarian philosopher, Jeremy Bentham (1748–1832), who, although he never uses the term, develops an "arithmetic of pleasures" (also known as the "felicific calculus") in chapter 4 of *An Introduction to the Principles of Morals and Legislation*, in *The Collected Works of Jeremy Bentham*, ed. J. H. Burns and H. L. A. Hart, 38–41 (Oxford: Oxford University Press, 1996).
11. The division is between the "intellect" (*nous*), the "heart" or "spirited part" (*thymos*), and the "appetite" (*epithymia*). This doctrine is developed in the *Republic* and in the *Phaedrus*.
12. Plato, *Protagoras*, 356b: 785.
13. Bergson is citing *Timaeus*, 41d–42d and 69c–71a: 1245 and 1271–2, and *Phaedrus*, 246a–249c: 524–7. The heart, or *thymos*, in Plato designates the seat of courage as well as anger.
14. Plato, *Timeaus*, 72e–76e: 1273–7.
15. As Leibniz argues throughout the *Theodicy*, God necessarily chooses the good: not because he is constrained to make this choice but because he wants to or wills it. In part 2, Leibniz speaks of "moral necessity," which is "worthy of God," as a "happy necessity which obliges wisdom to do good," and opposes it to "metaphysical and brute necessity, which occurs when the contrary implies contradiction." See Gottfried Wilhelm Leibniz, *Theodicy*, trans. E. M. Huggard (LaSalle, IL: Open Court Publishing Company, 1985), §§174–5: 236.
16. Plato, *Timaeus*, 47e–48a: 1250 and 68e: 1270 (modified).
17. Plato, *Laws*, 644d–645a: 1338.
18. Plato, *Timaeus* 86e and 87b: 1286. The English translations have been slightly modified to correspond better to Bergson's French.
19. This comparison appears in the first lecture of this course, above, 15. See also "Introduction to Metaphysics," in CM, 217/206.
20. *Phaedrus*, 248a–249b: 526–7.
21. Plato, *Republic* 10, 617d–e: 1220, modified to reflect Bergson's rendering. The unmodified passage reads: "Your daemon or guardian spirit will not be assigned to you by lot; you will choose him. The one who has the first lot will be the first to choose a life to which he will then be bound by necessity. Virtue knows no master; each will possess it to a greater or lesser degree, depending on whether he values or disdains it. The responsibility lies with the one who makes the choice; the god has none."
22. Bergson here is mainly referring to Kant's theory of the "intelligible character" (see the last two lectures of this course).

LECTURE 5
JANUARY 20, 1905

Gentlemen, at the end of the last lecture, I enumerated some of the main ideas, the most important ideas, the Platonic theory of freedom points out. The first—I'm speaking of the ideas that evolved in the history of philosophy and which passed, more or less transformed, into modern philosophy—the first of these ideas is that of a distinction between two kinds of necessity, the first [is] the one that would later be called "moral necessity" and that Plato does not name "necessity" because the meaning of the Greek word *anankē* is a lot narrower. But the first is a kind of intelligent, intellectual determination: it's this determination that results from the greater intellectuality of the motive or of the motivation. Let's suppose someone who is essentially intelligent. He'll relate all possible decisions, all the different sides he can take, he'll relate them to a certain standard we'll call, if you like, the Good. And, judging with perfect precision, perfect exactitude, he'll always decide for the greater good. Consequently, his actions will result from the intellectual circumstances, as it were, in which he's located, a little like the conclusion of a syllogism follows from the premises. It'll be a kind of determination, a kind of necessity. [83]

There's another one, the one that the moderns were to qualify as physical, a necessity that results from the material influence of one element on other elements. If we consider, for example, a hereditary defect, a hereditary vice implanted in the organism, it can become a cause of action. And in certain cases this cause is a necessitating cause, the [84] word "necessity" here having a completely different meaning, the necessity deriving from an impulse, as it were, and not from an attraction,[1] the necessity being that of force and no longer, as in the first case, that of persuasion, since the constraint of a purely intellectual kind is a sort of persuasion. So this necessity is of a completely different kind. And if we go further and picture—which the ancients didn't do—if we picture, as happens in certain modern theories,[2] all the phenomena of a moral, intellectual order, in humans, as being only the *duplicatum* of certain phenomena of a material order, if, for example, we say: all our sensations, our feelings, our ideas, our whole life, all of that is only the translation into a certain language called consciousness, the translation of what happens in the brain, a movement of molecules and atoms, then it is clear that every action, every decision will result from these physical antecedents, according to an absolute necessity, a necessity in the second sense of the word, and then what we call "moral necessity" dissolves into a physical and material necessity.

This is the modern form of the theory. In Plato, it's not this precise; mechanism itself, in Plato and, for that matter, in all the ancients, didn't take this form. The ancients didn't see, didn't understand—this is an effect of modern discoveries—didn't understand what is rational in mechanism; they didn't rise to the idea of a geometrical mechanism; they didn't see what is geometrical in the mechanism of theory. Nevertheless, we find in Plato for the first time the distinction between two causal orders. He says this very clearly in the *Timaeus*. There's a cause that is mind or, rather, intellect. There's consequently a moral, intellectual determination, if you will. Then there's *anankē*, necessity in the narrow sense this word has in the Greek language, blind, purely material, purely physical necessity.

We find the first indication of this first distinction between two kinds of determination,
[85] or, as we'd say today, two determinisms, the one physical, the other moral, in Plato's philosophy. This is the first idea I wanted to point out.

There's a second idea, that of a descent, that of an original fall of souls. This idea was very successful in the history of philosophy because, much later, it comes to join another idea of a completely different origin, and, we must say, with a completely different meaning, a completely different significance, an idea borrowed from Jewish philosophy and tradition. Bound together, amalgamated, these two ideas yielded a new, a completely new idea.

So there is in Plato this theory of a fall, of a descent of souls into bodies. In the past, the soul had wings. It lost them. In the past, the soul contemplated the pure Ideas, as Plato says, the Beautiful, the Good. It has forgotten all that. At most, it retains a reminiscence of it, which is more or less distant from what it knew before. So there we have a second element, a second idea we've extracted from the Platonic theory of freedom.

This idea itself, however, is not integral to Plato's theory of freedom. It immediately generated another idea that, for its part, is essential to Plato's theory of freedom. This third idea—and it's this idea which it behooves us to insist on because of the great importance it takes on in modernity—this third idea is that of a choice made by each soul prior to its earthly existence, in another, supersensible life, the choice each soul makes of its place on the scale of moral beings and of its complete destiny. This idea wasn't able to enter into modern philosophies in exactly this form. In its precise form, it implies a pre-existence of souls, and although this idea of a pre-existence of souls is accepted today by the majority, by a large share of humanity, it's nevertheless not one of the ideas that constitute our modern Western philosophy. The gist of Plato's theory on this point is not connected absolutely to the idea of a pre-existence of souls. The gist of the Platonic Idea is something that can, at a pinch, be extracted and separated from this
[86] hypothesis. It's the idea that the whole set of our actions such as they unfold in time, the whole set of our situations such as they are juxtaposed within duration, [that] all of that could be chosen all together [*en bloc*], in one blow, by a single act. There's no need for this single act to precede actual existence. It can be, I wouldn't say in actual existence but it could be actual existence itself, but this existence seen from the other end, seen—how do I put this—seen from its tip, from its summit, while the whole set of our actions and of our situations would be something like the base.

In other words, let me explain. It could be the case—and this is the modern form of this theory such as we find it, for example, in Kant, and we could interpret Kantianism in this way—it could be the case that each of our actions is determined necessarily by what precedes it, by our prior action, which is itself determined by a prior action, and so on indefinitely.[3] It could be the case that each of our situations, where we are located, was necessarily determined by their antecedents, which are themselves determined by their antecedents and so on indefinitely, and that each action was thus necessarily determined, each situation was determined with equal necessity, with equal fatedness and inevitability, and that, meanwhile, the totality of these actions, the totality of these situations, all of that was [free][4] in certain respects and formed an indivisible whole [*bloc*], or rather, a single act, one sole act of choice by which we choose both our character and the totality of our history.

This isn't inconceivable, it's not even unimaginable. All we'd need to do is accept that what appears to us in a certain respect, and normally, as a succession of terms in time, as an unfolding in time, that this same thing appears—seen from another side, perceived by a completely different faculty, by a completely different function of the mind—as a single moment, as an indivisible moment or rather as something external to time.

Picture, if you will, a cinematograph, something unfolding cinematographically, a scene on film, for example, a person dancing.[5] When I consider the cinematographic image, each of the positions of the dancer is explained by the one that precedes [it] [87]
and seems to be brought about, be determined by the preceding position and so on, indefinitely. I have a succession of positions that are determined by one another. That's what I see when I am before the screen onto which the cinematographic image is projected. But if I could turn around, if I entered into the cinematographic device as it were, if I managed to coincide as it were with the real cause of all that is happening—which is, in short, the unwinding of a spring that drives the movement of a clockwork, which movement moves the cinematographic film—then everything that unfolded before my eyes would fit into a single act, in one sole action which is the unwinding of the spring. The entire scene is played or isn't played depending on whether the spring decides—if it were able to do so—to remain wound up or to unwind, that is, depending on this undivided action.

Likewise, I could consider all of my actions without the existence that unfolds in time, all of my successive actions as so many cinematographic images, each action being explained by the series of prior actions. Likewise for my history, likewise for the situations through which I pass, each of them being explained by the situations that preceded it, by its antecedents. Why? Because I look before me, as it were, at the screen of time and space, and in this way I'm the audience of the cinematographic development of myself. But if I could turn around, I would see all of these juxtaposed events, and all of these successive actions, withdrawing into one another like a telescope being retracted, like a veil being pulled back, and I would have a single act, an act of choice, a decision of choice by means of which I have chosen my moral level, my moral worth, and also, if we can say this, the curve that my history will trace out in time, which curve is intimately connected to the moral place I've chosen.

There's thus nothing inconceivable, nothing unimaginable in this very modern idea of us having two faces, as it were, on the one side, the temporal face—my actions, my situations unfold in time, and from this viewpoint everything is determined, all of my existence is determined and determined necessarily by the prior moments. Then there's [88] another aspect that cannot appear to us because the very law of our existence, the law of our consciousness, is duration. This other aspect is a timeless aspect, and the act is given in a simple form, undivided, like a single act of choice. What appears to consciousness is the unfolding in time [of] the multiplicity of successive and juxtaposed moments.

This is the modern idea. I'm not saying that this idea is a good one and that it must have a place in our philosophy. We'll have to examine this idea closely later. We'll see that it's based on a certain conception of time and duration that is a lot closer than people think to the conception of the ancients and that it may not even fully agree with the modern scientific conception of time. There'll be a lot to leave behind in this doctrine, though there'll perhaps be something in it to hold on to. Nevertheless, we can't deny that this doctrine is important and that, as I just said, it is the extension, the transposition into our theory of knowledge of a Platonic doctrine according to which our entire existence, with its multiple actions, and with situations no less multiple in which these actions are accomplished, our entire life is the effect of a single act, which the moderns say is timeless, prior to actual existence, the ancients say.

Gentlemen, I'm insisting on this third idea because it's so important. In the last lecture, I said that this idea of a choice made in a prior existence and, more generally, all the theories of freedom that are connected to it, this idea, despite all it presents that, at first glance, is original and even a bit strange, this idea is very natural and very easily explained. When we delve into Socrates's theory, from which Plato drew his philosophy, it emerges quite naturally from it.

This is the point on which I would like to insist today since it gives us a chance to study in vivo the formation, I wouldn't say of a system, but of a scientific idea[6] that emerges whole from a kind of intuition, from an intuition. Let me explain. We can say that Socrates's entire
[89] doctrine orbits around this intuition of the duality of human nature. Socrates doesn't say this explicitly anywhere, but it's implicit in all he says. The human is double. In each of us, there is, first of all, the one who has been modeled by the surroundings, by tradition, by custom, the one who acts either through chance or in theory through routine, through simple routine,[7] the one, in a word, who lives, as it were, outside of himself, external to himself, without ever having thought of getting a grip on himself or of winning himself back. Then, there's the one who reconstructed or found himself, as it were, the person who never acts but intelligently, by reasoning about his conduct, by adapting it exactly to reason. It's certain that the majority of people live without ever seeking to get a grip on themselves, but doing so is possible for everyone. For that, there's no need to engage in any study, properly speaking, if by "study" we understand the observation of external things. No, the knowledge we must acquire for remaking ourselves, as it were, we draw this knowledge from ourselves, we possess it virtually, if not virtually, then at least partially. Each of us has the elements of this knowledge; each of us holds, so to speak, the end of the rope; we must make an effort to pull all the rest to ourselves. That's what knowledge [*science*], and also virtue, as Socrates understands it, consist in.

There is, then, a duality in us: there's the real person such as experience presents it immediately, then there's the possible person, the one who could reconstitute himself by force of reflection applied to moral matters.

This is the essence of Socrates's teaching. From there, gentlemen, it wasn't far to considering that this moral knowledge, all of whose elements we discover in ourselves, merely goes over, so to speak, the outlines, over the contours of a kind of dream that had been forgotten. It wasn't far, from there, to considering all explicit knowledge to be merely the complete return to consciousness of something forgotten. If I'm able, through an effort and without going outside of myself, if I'm able to find what is essential in all knowledge, it's thus because this knowledge is there, but half forgotten, like one of those dreams that we are on the verge of getting a grip on, on the verge of catching up to, but which slips away—through an effort, we manage to find it again. Knowledge is [90]
something like that. If that's it, if knowledge consists in remembering something, we can consider, we are even necessarily led to consider actual existence to be only the continuation, the extension of an earlier existence in which one would have known things forgotten today, to consider our superficial existence, the existence of a person who does not seek to know, who does not seek to get a grip on himself, to be an inferior existence, and to place above this inferior existence of the human being we call real, the existence of an ideal human from which the former would come about by a kind of fall. There was only one step [to take], and Plato looks to have very nearly taken it in one of his first dialogues—for the *Meno*, which is a dialogue from his early period, the so-called "Socratic" period, the *Meno* already presents us with the theory of reminiscence.[8] Had Plato continued down this path, which the Socratic teachings seen this way opened up, he might have come to conclusions rather different from the ones he ends up with on the nature of the human soul. But at the same time as Plato set out on this path, he developed another aspect of the Socratic teaching—and here we come upon an essential point.

There was in fact in the Socratic teachings an idea relating to a completely different object, a certain idea of knowledge in general. In Socrates's thought, knowledge is above all definition, that is, all in all, a general idea. What questions does Socrates ask in his ethics? They're questions like these: What is virtue? What is moderation? What is justice?[9] He's looking for definitions. To know [*savoir*] is to know [*connaître*] the principle of a thing, to bring it back to its essence, its essence being the general, the universal. Consequently, there is in the Socratic doctrine a distinction between the particular, the individual, what is done randomly by chance, by routine, and then the universal, the essential, what is done by virtue of a principle and of a definition.

So in Socrates, besides the moral theory whose broad strokes I've just sketched out, there's the definition of a method, a certain conception of knowledge, of knowing in general. To know is to know by a definition. Of course, this method of Socrates's applies [91]
only to moral things, it's concerned only with those. The knowledge of physical things, the knowledge of things in general, for its part, is useless and moreover impossible. But this teaching fell into the mind of a disciple who was probably already a geometer, who was at least very up to date on the geometric knowledge such as the ancient Greeks practiced it. In Plato's time, geometry was already quite advanced. Plato is not a creator, an inventor of geometry. No geometrical proposition in ancient, that is, in elementary geometry is named for him, but everything leads us to assume that Plato was very up to date about what was known of geometry in his time and that the Platonists privileged

geometry. Everyone knows the maxim: "Let no one enter here who is not a geometer."[10] Socrates's doctrine thus fell into the mind of a disciple who knew geometry and who loved it. Now, what's the gist of the geometrical method, of the mathematical method as the ancients practiced it? This method consists essentially in substituting ideal figures, purely intelligible figures, conceived by the mind, for real figures, sensible figures, those that are perceived in sight or by touch. For the real rectangle, say, the rectangle of a table, the geometer substitutes a geometrical rectangle, which differs from the real rectangle first of all by its perfection. For the real rectangle isn't a rectangle, it isn't constituted, composed of straight lines. When you look at it up close, it's composed of infinitely complex curves. Then, it's not a true surface. And then, the real rectangle is something, in any case, that has determinate dimensions and occupies a determinate place in space. The geometrical rectangle, on the contrary, is perfect. And then, well, it's no more this rectangle than it's that rectangle, it's the rectangle in general. The proofs we carry out on this rectangle are valid for any and all rectangles. So in short, geometry constitutes, beside and above the world of sensible, material figures perceived by the senses, the world of immaterial Forms, purely ideal, purely conceived by the mind, simple, immutable, and also, we can say, eternal. For once geometry has constructed an Idea
[92] of the circle, this Idea of the circle belongs to it as something that doesn't date from its construction but is of all time, or rather is superior to time, something, well, eternal. This geometrical knowledge, to be sure, applies, is appropriate only to the Forms, that is, to something stable, relatively invariable. But Socrates has now shown that even the most fleeting, the least graspable matters, human matters can be brought back to certain stable definitions, to general Ideas. Could we then not blend the Socratic method and the geometrical method together and thereby obtain a method applicable to every kind of thing, applicable to knowledge [*à la science, à la connaissance*] of all possible objects?

This is how, in Plato's mind, the Socratic method comes to join the geometrical method. And from this the Platonic world of Ideas was constituted, the world of Ideas; that is, according to Plato, to know, to possess knowledge, is to move into a world that is completely different from the sensible world in which we live. Sensible things are imperfect things: they are situated in space, each of them occupies a particular place. And precisely because they are in space, we can conceive a very large number of them, a number as large as we want, an indefinite number of the same genus, that are like a copy, the diversely situated copies of the model world.

So the sensible things are in space, disseminated in space; the sensible things are in time, they change, and why do they change? Because they develop, because they evolve. And why do they evolve? Because they're not done, they're never completed, perfect, they're always in search of themselves, they run after themselves, as it were.[11] And then, especially, they are arranged in space and time randomly, that is, according to the accidents that brought them to where they are. It's accident, it's randomness, it's what defies all knowledge. But above this world of things that our senses perceive, there are the Ideas, that is, the perfect, immutable, extra-spatial models of what changes, of what
[93] occupies space. The Idea is a model, that is, it's general, universal, it's a genus; it represents a genus, whereas the sensible things are individuals, being copies or repetitions in as

many exemplars of these simple models as you'd like. The Ideas are eternal, the Ideas are timeless, and especially in this supersensible world, in this intelligible world, they are arranged in a hierarchical order, according to their kinship, their natural filiation, according to their logical relations, whereas their imperfect copies in time and space entertain purely physical, that is, accidental relations with one another.

So there, gentlemen, we have the conclusion Plato ended up at by blending the Socratic method together with the geometrical method. In this way, he ended up constituting the supersensible, intelligible world, the world of Ideas above the sensible world.

This second period of Plato's thought corresponds to a certain number of dialogues that are the best known, the ones in which the theories of the Ideas are laid out. There's no doubt that during this whole period Plato's attention is diverted from moral problems, we can say, from human, truly human problems, in order to concentrate on problems relative to the theory of science, of knowledge, as we would say today. But there was a third period whose beginning must perhaps be postulated earlier than a recent theory says,[12] namely, it would have to begin with the *Republic*, the period during which Plato hasn't forgotten the theory of Ideas, as some have said, but in which Plato returns, in light of the theory of ideas, to those problems that have concerned him from the beginning, to the moral problems and, in addition, to the problems that have become interdependent with them, the geometrical problems. This is when, returning to the question of the human, Plato asks himself the great question, which is, all in all, an unsolvable question, given the form the Socratic doctrine has taken with the theory of ideas, an insolvable question, which is that of knowing what the human is.

What, generally, is the human? What are sensible things, things in general? You know that this is an extremely difficult question to answer within Platonism because, given the Ideas such as Plato uses them to construct the world, if the Ideas are immutable, perfect, [94]
maintaining among themselves logical relationships, then one doesn't see at all why this supersensible and perfect world would split to form a world of things that are always in search of themselves, as it were. The question above all lies in determining in what respects this world is the *duplicatum* of the preceding one and is distinct from it. These are big questions we don't have to resolve here. What is certain is that, in Plato's thought, there is, besides the Idea, a certain principle he calls necessity, *anankē*, which causes the Ideas to emerge from themselves in order to project themselves into space and into time in the form of shadows, of phantoms.

The, all in all, theoretically unsolvable question of this philosophy is that of saying what a human being is. What are we? Is the human an Idea? Is it a sensible thing? A human cannot be an Idea. A determinate human, Socrates or Plato for example, cannot be an Idea for one very simple reason, which is that the Idea is a genus, the Idea is not an individual thing. In addition, the Idea is immutable, while a human being evolves, changes, has a history. The human being thus cannot be an Idea, but neither can the human being be a sensible thing, and why? Ah, because in humans, there's the intellect, the *nous*, and what's remarkable about the intellect is that the more it gets a grip on itself, the more it enters into the world of Ideas, and at the limit our intellect would, so to speak, coincide with the Ideas. And we put a smaller or larger share of intellectuality even into our actions, into our conduct. Plotinus, developing Plato's idea in his own way, will say that the more we put intellectuality into our conduct, the more we enter into the world of pure Ideas, to the point where, at the limit, action becomes contemplation, he says, something timeless.[13]

So the human can be neither Idea nor thing. There would have been a solution, which would have been to turn the human into a double being that is an Idea from above and a thing from below, a being with its head in the heavens and its feet on the ground. This is the solution Plotinus will contribute, and which Aristotle prepared. For Plotinus, we
[95] have descended into a body, but in the superior part of ourselves we have not descended, and that's how we have in us this dual nature thanks to which it can be said of each of us that he is a sensible thing and an Idea, as you'd like, or, rather, as he would like, since the choice depends on him.[14]

To get there, it was necessary to subject Platonism to a real transformation because Plato would never have accepted individual Ideas, he would never accepted that there is the Idea of Socrates, of Plato in particular. No, the Idea represents a genus; consequently, there can be an Idea of the human in general but not the Idea of Socrates.

For Plato, there was only one side to take, which was to turn the *psychē*, the soul, into something that's neither an Idea nor a sensible thing. The soul is not an Idea, but it has lived among the Ideas, and prior to its inferior existence, it contemplated the Ideas. Yet it fell into a body, [and] in this sense, we are indeed, if you like, sensible things. But not constantly—we are on the verge of making contact again with the intelligible. We can do it if we want.

More than that: there are two viewpoints on our existence. If we consider it from the material side, everything is explained materially. What we do derives from our character; our character derives from physical circumstances; that depends on the kind of organism with which we have been born; that depends on material circumstances, the environment, education. Plato says all of that. Consequently, if we consider things from this vantage point, everything is determined, everything is materially necessary. But the body in which we are, the existence we lead, all of that has been freely chosen, since all of that derives from an act prior to current existence, an act by which we have chosen both our moral nature and our destiny.

Thus, summing everything up, we can provide a good explanation for the Platonic doctrine of a prior life and a choice prior to actual existence, provided we heed the fact that in the Socratic teaching, there were two things, two curves, two ideas that were perfectly defined in Socrates's mind but could no longer be so the moment they were dissociated, spelled out—and that was the case in Plato's philosophy. In Socrates, there
[96] was the idea of two humans in each of us; in Socrates there was, implicitly, the idea that there are in each of us two humans, the real human and the ideal human, the human dominated by custom and the human governed by knowledge, consequently, in reality, two individual humans. Then there was in Socrates the idea of an opposition between the sensible and the intelligible—or at least this is what Plato would see in Socrates.

By following the first of these ideas, one ended up turning the ideal human, the superior human, into what in Plato's teaching was called an Idea, but an Idea of an individual human. By going in the second direction, one could no longer have the individual Idea, there were none but generic Ideas anymore. The ideal human was no longer such and such a determinate ideal human, it was the human in general. Hence, by developing these two ideas, two conclusions that can no longer be reconciled to one another. Hence the necessity—how do I put this—of a myth, of an account that is not a dialectical account, to reconcile the different elements to one another, hence the myth of the pre-existence of the soul and the idea of a choice, in a prior life, of what we are and what we do in the current life.

You see how these various pieces come together and constituted Plato's doctrine.

Gentlemen, since this year we are studying the evolution of theories and doctrines, I wanted to take this example in order to show the mechanism through which a doctrine of this kind is constituted. Perhaps I concentrated more than was necessary on this first doctrine, on this first theory of freedom. I'll concentrate much less on the rest of Greek philosophy since we have to get to modern philosophy.[15] In the next lecture, I'll undertake to give a very brief sketch of the doctrine of freedom in Aristotle.

Notes

1. On the distinction, which at first is only implicit in ancient philosophy, between causality by "impulse" (descending causality) and causality by "attraction" (ascending causality), see CE, 279/322.
2. A reference to "parallelist" and "epiphenomenalist" theories, that is to say, essentially, contemporary positivist psychologies that, via eighteenth-century French materialism, are distantly based on Spinoza and Leibniz. Bergson examines them in *Matter and Memory*, in "The Brain and Thought: A Philosophical Illusion" (in ME, 231–55/191–210), and in *Creative Evolution* (CE, 304–5/353–5).
3. This is the doctrine of the "intelligible character"; see Kant, CPR, 535–7/A538–41/B566–9/AA 3, 366–9, and below, 243.
4. There is a word missing in the typescript. "Free" renders what we consider to be the most likely idea here.
5. The important image of the cinematograph will be at the heart of the fourth chapter of *Creative Evolution*, which is called "The Cinematographic Mechanism of Thought and the Mechanistic Illusion. A Glance at the History of Systems. Real Becoming and False Evolutionism" (CE, 238–316/272–370; see esp. 263–72/303–13).
6. "Scientific" in the sense of an epistemological idea, an idea that provides knowledge.
7. Like many French translators of his time, Bergson renders the Greek word *tribē* with the word "routine." In Plato, *tribē* does not necessarily mean a habit but an irregular practice, and it is thus opposed to technique (*tekhnē*) on the one hand and to knowledge (*epistemē*) on the other.
8. Plato, *Meno*, 81c–84b: 880–3.
9. The *Meno* opens with the question of virtue while the *Republic* begins with the question of justice.
10. Tradition holds that this maxim was inscribed at the entrance to the Academy, the school Plato founded.

11. CE, 276/318.
12. Bergson is once more referring to Wincenty Lutosławski, on whose work, as noted (60n9), he bases his general periodization of Plato's works.
13. Plotinus, *Enneads* in *Plotinus*, ed. and trans. Arthur H. Armstrong, rev. ed. (Cambridge, MA: Harvard University Press, 1989), here 3.8.4: 369–73. Bergson cites this passage in CM, 163/153, and TS, 221/234.
14. Plotinus, *Enneads* 4.8.4. Bergson seems to referring to this passage: "Souls, then, become, one might say, amphibious, compelled to live by turn the life There, and the life here: those which are able to be more in the company of Intellect life the life There more, but those whose normal condition is, by nature or chance, the opposite, live more the life here below" (411).
15. This may be an indication of how Bergson understood his transfer—which he requested—within the Collège de France; see above, 21n1.

LECTURE 6
JANUARY 27, 1905

Gentlemen, in today's lecture, I'm going to point out one or two features of Aristotle's theory of freedom. In fact, there is no systematic theory of freedom in Aristotle. There are very few systematic theories in Aristotle generally, and we must not think of Aristotle as a builder of systems in the modern way. There's nothing like that in this philosopher, very little synthesis, but a lot of analysis, Aristotle is a great analyst, an analyzer of ideas. His constant method consists in taking up ideas as they are found in language, in then straightening them out, in first defining them, and in then, finally, analyzing them into their elements, the development of which he pushes as far as possible. In this way, he obtains a number of viewpoints on a question. He digs into the question on a certain number of points. We don't always see how the analyses link up with one another. We might compare the impression they give to the one we have when we see, in our streets, for example, holes being dug for an underground passage, a railway line.[1] We suspect that all of that links up, but we don't have the blueprint. It's the same with Aristotle, he digs down at a whole lot of points, but we must reconstruct the blueprint of the underground passage. This blueprint had to exist in the mind of the author (probably a lot less systematic than a modern blueprint), but we must look for it, reconstruct it.[2] [97]

We really don't have to go to all this trouble, though, or at least there are in antiquity philosophers who to a certain degree spare us this trouble: these are the philosophers [98] of the Alexandrian School. I've said many times that we may consider a philosophy like that of Plotinus to be a kind of systematized Aristotelianism. Although he called himself a Platonist, and although he believed that he simply followed and developed Plato's thought, Plotinus is a lot closer to Aristotle than to Plato.[3]

If we take, for example, Aristotle's theory of freedom, there isn't one theory of freedom for freedom, but Aristotle dug into a whole lot of ideas relative to freedom: chance, randomness, contingency in general, and also deliberation, and then the theory of the soul in general and—how do I put this—the soul's meddling in the body, and the theory of the pure mind, the separated intellect. But to see how all this is connected, we need a blueprint, and perhaps Plotinus gives us the best signs, in regard to this question, for when, in the next lecture or at least in the one following it, I'll lay out Plotinus's philosophy of freedom, we'll see how all of these Aristotelian ideas are joined together in the mind of the Alexandrian philosopher.[4] So I'm not going to attempt this reconstruction today. It goes without saying that I can't do this as systematically, as imbued with the spirit of antiquity, as Plotinus did. Consequently, I'll delay this discussion until we consider Plotinus. Today, I'm going simply to point out one or two of Aristotle's essential analyses, analyses that relate to the question of freedom.

The first idea, the idea that Aristotle brought out and that he was the first in the history of philosophy to bring out explicitly, is the idea of contingency. In Aristotle, we find contingency clearly indicated for the first time—"clearly": as much as that's possible, since, as you know, the idea is obscure, so obscure that still today, after so many centuries of analyses, there are philosophers who declare that the idea of contingency is a pseudo-idea, that it corresponds to nothing, nothing in the things and perhaps even to nothing in the mind, that it's a pure nothingness.

Assuming it exists or at least assuming we can conceive of it, what is contingency?
[99] To believe in contingency is to believe that the future or at least the immediate future, especially the immediate future, is not absolutely determined by the present; it is to assume that what will happen in a moment does not emerge necessarily from what exists right this moment. To believe in contingency is to believe that in given circumstances, in determinate conditions, several events are equally possible. To believe in contingency is to accept, for example, that given a person's determinate motives, determinate motivations, determinate situations, at a determinate moment, and this person moreover having a determinate character, what he is going to do is not absolutely determined. He has a choice. Several actions are equally possible. In general, then, to accept contingency is to believe that the future does not emerge necessarily from the past.

That's what it is, but our mind has the greatest trouble accepting an idea like this. Our will accepts it, or at least it behaves as though it accepted it. We act as if we accepted contingency but as soon as our reflection focuses on the idea, the more it focuses on the idea, the more the idea becomes obscure and overall unacceptable for reflection. Our reflection thrives only within the determinate, within determinism. And the natural atmosphere of intelligence is necessity.

Why? I pointed to the profound reason for this, the ultimate reason, well, the final explanation of this fact in the first lecture, but if we don't go looking as far as that, if we take up the immediate reason for this tendency, we find it in the fact that our intellect is in a way made for mathematics.[5] That's the characteristic trait of our intellect. Descartes said: "everything in me is done mathematically."[6] We could all say the same, making due allowances, in the sense that the intellect of all of us is oriented toward mathematics, that is, toward the science of absolute and rigorous necessity, the science where always, no matter what the object with which it is concerned, if what is determined by the conditions posited is given, if the premises are given, or if the hypothesis is given, then the conclusion follows.

[100] So our intellect, basically, exists within mathematics. We can say we are all born mathematicians: not mathematicians in the sense of being inventors or creators in the field of mathematics—that goes without saying—but mathematicians in the sense that we all, if we're willing to make the necessary effort, we can understand mathematics, and that is the only field of study of which we can say as much. That isn't true of anything else. Not everyone manages to understand a literary work or a work of art even by focusing their attention as much as possible, but whoever is willing to make a sufficiently intense effort at attention can and must understand mathematics. To be sure, not everyone is able to make this effort of intense attention. Consequently, there's perhaps some

exaggeration in what I'm saying, but anyone who can make this sufficiently intense effort will come to understand, while with all effort, every intensity of effort imaginable, you won't come to understand a literary work or a work of art if you don't have taste. To speak like Pascal, we can say that "the geometrical spirit" is innate in everyone.[7] We can thus indeed say that we are naturally mathematicians, and, I would add—it's basically the same thing—we are naturally physicists, in the sense that this word has taken on since the time of Galileo, physics being something quite close to mathematics, a science that restores constant relations, mathematical relations between quantitative variations of phenomena that are functions of one another. We let a stone drop in free fall. At a determinate moment of the fall and when a determinate space has been traversed, the stone's speed is determined as well, determinable according to the time or according to the space traversed. The conditions being given, the phenomenon is given. That is absolutely necessary, the relation between the fact and its conditions is a necessary one.[8]

We understand this perfectly, adequately. We are naturally physicists in this sense, in the mathematical sense of the word, just as we are naturally mathematicians.

If contingency exists in the universe, the mathematical-physical habits of our mind are going to collide with something unexpected, something that frustrates them. The logic of our minds is fixed on the pattern of mathematics, and consequently our mind [101]
always expects necessity. Our mind expects to find that what happens is determined necessarily by the conditions [or by the set of circumstances in which the phenomenon happens].[9] That's what the logic of our minds says.

I'm not claiming that, if there is contingency in the world, and consequently possible freedom, at least in humans, I'm not claiming that freedom is for that reason an absurd thing, an illogical thing. Rather, it will certainly not be illogical, but extra-logical. We must always endow our logic with a suppleness, an elasticity it isn't used to and for which, all in all, it isn't made.[10]

Aristotle is the first philosopher who clearly understood this, and when you get right down to it, his theory of contingency, his assertion of contingency at its core is nothing other than that. Aristotle didn't say it in this form. First, physics such as I just defined it didn't exist in his time, only in the last three or four centuries has physics come to exist in this way. As for mathematics, it was already quite advanced in Aristotle's time, but not enough, it was still too superficial and lacked the depth to be able to take account of the very deep roots of mathematics in the human mind. Aristotle thus didn't present things in this form, he presented them in the form in which he had to, in which he was able to present them. He took logic such as it existed in his time, logic such as he basically created it himself. He took the problem of contingency from the angle where it was able to shock this logic, in other words, he posed the question as the philosophers of the Megarian School posed it to him.[11] These philosophers said that out of two propositions relative to the future one is necessarily true—that out of two opposite propositions relative to the future one is necessarily true—from which it can be concluded that there is no contingency and that the future is determined.[12]

Let me explain this point. In general, when we take two propositions of which the one affirms what the other denies, one of the two is true. This is obvious. When I say, [102]

"This table is black. This table is not black," we have two propositions of which the one affirms what the other denies. With complete necessity one of the two must be true. When I say, "Two plus two makes four. Two plus two does not make four," one of these two propositions is true with complete necessity. When I say, "Yesterday at some such time, let's say, at four o'clock, I went for a walk. Yesterday at four o'clock I did not go for a walk," one of the two propositions is necessarily true.

Thus, in general, out of two propositions of which the one affirms what the other denies, one of these is true.

Let's take a proposition relative to the future and more specifically to my own future, this one for example: "Tomorrow at four o'clock I'll decide to go for a walk, I'll go for a walk." Then let's take a proposition that denies what this one affirms: "Tomorrow at four o'clock I won't go for a walk." If we accept that out of the two propositions of which one affirms what the other denies, one is necessarily true, then one of the two propositions: "I'll go for a walk tomorrow. I won't go for a walk tomorrow," one of the two propositions is true, true right now. I cannot know which of the two is true. It's possible that no one knows which is true. But if out of the two propositions one is necessarily true, then from this moment right now one of the two must be true. Tomorrow at four o'clock, if I go for a walk, it will have been the proposition "I'll go for a walk tomorrow" that was the true proposition. If I decide not to go for a walk tomorrow, it will have been the proposition "I won't go for a walk tomorrow" that was the true one. But in any case, one of the two propositions will have been true. So now what'll happen? Because tomorrow, when the moment will have come, I will ask myself, "Will I go out? Won't I go out?" I will hesitate. I will deliberate. All of that is an appearance, and a psychological appearance, but from the moment one of the two propositions was necessarily true, it's the one that was true that is realized.

This is the Megarian argumentation as Aristotle presents it. If we accept that out of two propositions of which one affirms what the other denies one is necessarily true, even
[103] when these are propositions relative to the future, then from this moment on the future is determined, determined for all eternity, and then the appearance of things or, more generally, contingency vanishes.

Gentlemen, Aristotle refutes this argument in the ninth chapter, the famous, well-known chapter of *Peri hermēneias, On Interpretation.*[13] Aristotle poses the question: is it true that out of two propositions relative to the future, of which one denies what the other affirms, is it true that one is necessarily true? He answers no: the principle is true for all other propositions but not for propositions that relate to the future, and the reasons he provides for this are reasons coming from simple good sense, reasons of common sense, or rather reasons coming from experience. If that were true, as he says, there wouldn't be any chance in the universe, no randomness, no *tukhē*, no *automaton*,[14] and, above all, there'd be no choice in our actions. We wouldn't be able to choose, in other words, there'd be no freedom. Yet all of those things exist; therefore, it's not true that the future is determined; therefore, it's not true that out of two contradictory propositions relative to the future, one is necessarily true. What is true from this moment on is neither the proposition "I'll go for a walk tomorrow" nor the proposition, "I won't go for a walk tomorrow," it's the proposition "I'll go for a walk or I won't go for a walk tomorrow," the disjunctive proposition, the one that poses the alternative. Or to take up Aristotle's very words: what is true right now is neither the proposition "Tomorrow there will be a sea battle" nor the proposition "tomorrow there will be no sea battle," it's the proposition: "Tomorrow there will be or there will not be a sea battle."[15]

This is how Aristotle settles the question. Placed between the strict logic of the mind, between the strict logic that, it seems, wants the principle stated by the Megarians to be legitimate and universal, and experience or common sense, he opts for common sense, and he's correct to do so, I think. But perhaps we must look for other reasons, reasons that weren't simply reasons of experience and common sense. Gentlemen, I ask your leave to insist on this point because the argument just examined and dismissed by [104]
Aristotle is incredibly important.

Certainly, when we think about this Megarian argumentation—out of two propositions relative to the future, of which one denies what the other affirms, one is necessarily true—it looks like simply one of those logical quibbles the Greek mind enjoyed. But it's something completely different, it's very important, in my view, I'll have occasion to show that and return to it. There is no other argument than this one against freedom. There's no other argument. All possible arguments, all possible objections raised against human freedom lead back to or can be led back to this one. These objections can take extremely sophisticated forms, present themselves in the language of our mathematics or our physics or our psychology, but at its core, every argumentation against freedom consists—this is the essential point—in not taking time into account, in considering truth to be timeless, in dealing with the future by moving there in thought and considering it only as being outside of time. There's really only one possible objection against freedom, and that's the one. This is the form Aristotle gives it in *On Interpretation*. This is, all in all, the simplest form, the one in which the sophism is most obvious. Still, we must account for this sophism, and to do that, we're going to look for where the real flaw of this argumentation lies.

The argumentation, in short, consists in saying the following: an assertion, whatever it be, is true or false. There's no middle ground: an assertion is true or false. Consequently, when I take an assertion relative to what I will do later, it's true or false. When I take the assertion, "Tomorrow at four o'clock I'll go for a walk," either it's true or it's false. If it's true, then it's determined, decided that tomorrow I'll go for a walk. It's possible that no one knows it, that I myself know nothing about it, that no one can know anything about it, but it's somehow written in the book of logic that I will go for a walk tomorrow. On the contrary, if I don't go for a walk tomorrow, it will be the case that the proposition, "I'll go for a walk tomorrow," was false. And so, from the fact that a proposition is necessarily [105]
true or false, I can conclude that the proposition, "I'll go for a walk tomorrow," is true or false, and consequently that from this moment on its content is determined.

An assertion is true or false. What are we to think of this argumentation? Is it certain, is it even acceptable? Gentlemen, we must define what we mean by "true" and "false." What is a true assertion, what is a false assertion? A true assertion is one that conforms to what exists, conforms to reality; it's false when it does not conform to reality.

When I say, "Right now I am talking philosophy," we have a proposition that is true because it conforms to what exists. When I say, "Yesterday at four o'clock I went for a walk," admitting that I went for a walk at four o'clock, we have an assertion that is true because it conforms to what exists. For the past exists, it's even what exists the most, it's the only thing in the world that is irrevocable, indestructible.[16] The present is never entirely accomplished but the past is definitively over and done with. So when I say, "Yesterday at four o'clock I went for a walk," the assertion is true because it conforms to what is. The assertion is true because it conforms to what is, it would be false if it didn't conform to what is. But when I say, "Tomorrow at four o'clock I'll go for a walk," is the proposition true or false? Tomorrow does not exist; nothing of what will happen tomorrow exists. Consequently, to ask whether the proposition, "I'll for a walk tomorrow," is true or false is to pose a question that makes no sense because it amounts to asking whether this proposition conforms to what exists [when] tomorrow doesn't exist yet, doesn't exist now. Consequently, the words "truth," "error" lose any kind of signification, and a proposition relative to tomorrow cannot be true nor can it be false, because truth and error are the conformity or nonconformity to what exists—and the future does not exist.

But it will exist, and the proposition, "Tomorrow at four o'clock I'll go for a walk," will become true or false. If I go for a walk at four o'clock, I will be able to say, that evening
[106] or the next day, that the proposition became true. If I don't go for a walk, it will become false. Still, we will have to change its form, since what will have become true or false is not the proposition, "I'll go for a walk tomorrow," it will be the proposition, "I went for a walk today" or "yesterday." So the proposition, "I'll go for a walk tomorrow," can be neither true nor false now, but it will become so.

It's just that, and here is the origin of the illusion, I today move, by means of thought, I move to the moment when it will have become true or false, and on the basis of it having become, tomorrow evening or the day after tomorrow, either true or false, I believe I can conclude that today it is true or false. This, then, is the origin of the illusion. As one of the two propositions will have become true, I conclude that from this moment on one of the two propositions is true. That's the sophism, that's the origin of the error.

Why is this error so natural to our mind? Here we come to an essential point in the problem of freedom. Well, it's because the truth appears to us to have no date, appears to us as independent of time. The truth appears to us to be timeless.[17] The proposition, "I'll go for a walk tomorrow at four o'clock," will become true or false only tomorrow evening. Let's assume it will have become true: it will then seem to us that it has been true from all eternity. The fact is that, from the moment when it will have become true, it will be true always, eternally true, nothing will be able to prevent this act from having been accomplished. It will thus be an eternal truth, but eternal from the moment when the act is accomplished, eternal going forward, eternal a parte ante.[18] However, this eternity goes back, so to speak, it spreads like wildfire. We are loath to accept a semi-eternity, an eternity that begins at a given moment. If a proposition remains eternally true from this moment forward, it seems to us—we don't reason about this, it's unconscious in our minds, as it were—it seems to us that this eternity, which is only a semi-eternity, is not enough, it seems to us that the proposition, which became true, has been true for all eternity. It's one of the characteristics of truth, as soon as it appears to us as truth, to leap [107] outside of time and to appear to us as timeless.

Why does this happen and what is the root of the illusion? It has to do, gentlemen, with what I pointed out earlier, with the essentially mathematical character of our minds. I said that we are at ease only in mathematics. The characteristic of mathematical truths is precisely to be timeless, to be independent of time.

When I say, "10 times 100 make 1000," that is true from all eternity, that has always been true. When I say, "The sum of the three angles of a triangle is equal to two right angles," that is true from all eternity. When I take a proposition like this one, "I went for a walk yesterday," this proposition, which is a proposition of fact, is undoubtedly not an eternally true proposition like a mathematical proposition. However, it has this in common with mathematical propositions: that, from the moment it is true, from the moment it has become true, it remains eternally true, and then this proposition is as if lifted up, so to speak, by the attraction the mathematical truth exerts on it, and its semi-eternity, which only begins at this moment, is converted into a total eternity. In other words, it seems to us that the very epitome of truth is mathematical truth, all the more so since there's also this resemblance between the mathematical truths and the others, which is that mathematical truth, too, appears to have begun at a certain moment. The proposition, "The sum of three angles of a triangle is equal to two right angles," this proposition was discovered by someone, at a determinate moment in history. It's not always been known.

The other proposition, "10 times 100 make 1000," it, too, came to be known. It's not certain that humans have always known how to count up to 1000, this fact must have a date in the history of humanity. However, what's remarkable about mathematical truths is that, although they were discovered on a certain date, their eternity goes back, behind the date, infinitely. The proposition about triangles, "The sum of the three angles of a triangle is equal to two right angles," this truth, although it was discovered at a [108] determinate moment, is an eternal truth that has gone back: it's true from all eternity, it was true well before it was discovered. What's remarkable about mathematical truths is thus that, although they have begun to be *de facto* at a given moment, they have always existed *de jure*. It seems to us that every truth has come to this, and truths, even factual truths like the one I was discussing, "I went for a walk yesterday," this truth, although it becomes eternal only at a given moment and although its eternity does not have the right to go back, it seems to us that its eternity goes back all the same, that its truth has the same nature as mathematical truth.

I have to insist on this point, gentlemen, since here we come to the very root of every determinist illusion. There is—I'll try to show this, the discussion will not always be as subtle and abstract—I'll try to show that in every determinism, there is, I wouldn't say an illusion but a conception a priori, arbitrary, something arbitrary, which in short is the negation of time, the negation of [the reality of] time.[19] It's in the primitive form of determinism, such as Aristotle examined it, that we can best see this illusion for what it is. That's why I've insisted on this point.

Aristotle—I'm returning to Aristotle in closing this long parenthesis—Aristotle, I said, simply dismisses the argument in the name of experience and in the name of common sense. He posits contingency, he believes in contingency. He posits it, it's from this contingency thus laid as the basis that freedom, as Aristotle understands it, will arise.

Before I say something about this conception of freedom, I must specify that in Aristotle's mind, contingency is not at all what it is for us today. When we accept the idea of contingency, we always do so with the thought in the back of our minds that we're talking about human freedom, admitting human freedom. When we accept freedom and contingency, freedom for us is an advantage humans have, something good, something excellent, and the contingency that is to serve as the substratum of freedom is itself
[109] something good, something higher. That isn't Aristotle's idea at all. The contingency that exists in the world has to do with evil . . . Aristotle doesn't go as far as saying "evil," but contingency has to do with matter, *hylē*, that is, with a lower principle, with a principle of indetermination.[20] Not to belabor this point, I'll simply say that contingency, in a philosophy like ours, modern philosophy in general, contingency is more of a good, and in Aristotle's philosophy, it's more of an evil. The reason for this is that for modern philosophers, for those who believe in contingency, contingency is not found everywhere in nature. There are very few who believe in contingency in general. Contingency is found especially in human actions, freedom being a privilege of the human.

I won't, I'll say that immediately, restrict freedom to such an extent. In the second part of this course, in the dogmatic conclusion I'll present, I'm going to try and establish that contingency doesn't exist in humans alone, [nor][21] in the whole of nature, but exists in living beings, in organic beings [*êtres organisés*]. Undoubtedly, if by "freedom" we mean the faculty of choosing, with full knowledge of the facts, after deliberation, and after reflection—rational [*raisonnable*] freedom—then this freedom is found only in humans. But if by "freedom" we mean the creation of certain absolutely unforeseeable actions, of actions that add something to the conditions in which they are given, then this indetermination is found everywhere where there is consciousness, and de jure, at least de jure, everywhere where there is organic life [*organisation*].[22] For the conclusion I'm going to propose is this: organic life, life, in short, is consciousness;[23] organic life appears in the world at the same time as consciousness; and the raison d'être of organic life, like the raison d'être of consciousness, is choice, that is, the creation of something.[24] If there's choice, there's creation, since with the elements of reflection we cannot say a priori what will happen. What will happen adds something to the elements; consequently, there is genuine creation.

I'll try to establish that if we consider the material world in general insofar as it is material, there is no contingency. Everyone admits as much: matter is subject to absolute
[110] necessity, to unchangeable physical laws, and if the conditions in which physical facts occur are given, then these conditions determine the phenomenon absolutely. So matter, by itself, is the seat of necessity, it presupposes a force, a cause, a will, if you'd like, a will that enters into this matter, [or,] rather, a *je ne sais quoi* that wants to obtain with this matter actions that introduce something absolutely new into the world, something absolutely unforeseeable. This force, this *je ne sais quoi*, will have to enact a true

paradox. It will have to construct machines, mechanisms whose goal is to slip, as it were, through the meshes of universal necessity,[25] contingency machines, and as it were anti-mechanical machines. A living organism, basically, seen from our viewpoint, a living organism is always something like that. This is why wherever there's life, organic life, there's also indetermination, contingency, which can be quite inferior to freedom—nevertheless, even in this conception of freedom, contingency is, of course, restricted to a well-determined domain in nature. It's restricted to life, to living beings. And all in all, it's a privilege, it's a conquest, it's a victory, it's a conquest gained from the determinism of nature.

But, for Aristotle—and this is the essential point—for Aristotle, contingency is everywhere, it's in nature in its entirety, and consequently it doesn't count as a conquest of nature. It's not something added on to nature, on the contrary, it's something [nature] is missing: contingency is a defect in the etymological sense of the word, a deficiency of nature.[26] Nature should be subject to a reasonable necessity, everything should take place reasonably, but an element intervenes that degrades it. What diminishes it is *hylē*, as Aristotle says, what he calls "matter," matter being the diminishing of the Idea. The result is that things are not absolutely determined by their conditions; the result is that we must allow, within things, for a place for chance, randomness, the indeterminate, in a word, for what Aristotle calls "accident" or "contingency."

It seems that Aristotle would have had to conclude that freedom is a bad thing— [111]
that's not his conclusion at all, quite the contrary: deliberation, independence, *to eph'hēmin*,[27] all these he turns into privileges, into, in short, privileges of the human. Is there a contradiction here? We don't have the time now to examine this, but at the beginning of the next lecture, I'll show very briefly that Aristotle, who, in keeping with the very principle of his doctrine, is led to turn contingency into an insufficiency of nature, nonetheless can and must, without contradiction, consider freedom in humans as a rather good thing, as a privilege. The two theses, at least to a certain extent, can be reconciled.

Notes

1. This is not a farfetched example but evokes a common sight throughout the city at the time: construction work on the Paris Métro network begins in 1898 and continues, with almost no interruptions, until the Second World War.
2. These lines are very similar to almost contemporary ones found in the essay on Ravaisson, CM, 263–4/255–6.
3. TS, 219/232.
4. In fact, this will not happen until the March 3, 1905, lecture.
5. CE, 47/45: "We are born geometers."
6. "Tout se fait chez moi mathématiquement." Descartes makes this famous comment in the letter to Mersenne of March 11, 1640, AT III: 36n; only an excerpt of the letter, without this comment, is included in PW III, 145.

7. Bergson is referring to Pascal's distinction between the *esprit de géométrie* and the *esprit de finesse*. Ariew translates "the geometric and the intuitive mind" (S670/L512: 207–8); other translations of *Pensées* render this distinction as "the mathematical and the intuitive mind."
8. On Galileo, see CM, 228/217–18, and CE, 288–9/333–5.
9. The typescript here contains a rather obscure phrase, *où le choix est une circonstance dans laquelle le phénomène se produit*, "where the choice is a circumstance in which the phenomenon happens."
10. On supple concepts, see CM, 31–2/23, 198/188, and 207/196–7.
11. In the history of philosophy, the Megarians were a philosophical school founded around 390 BCE by Euclid of Megara, a disciple of Socrates. They are known especially through Plato's and Aristotle's objections (in particular in the text to which Bergson is about to refer). Their philosophy is obviously inspired by the Eleatics (the negation of movement); in its dialectical argumentation, it is also a very technical philosophy.
12. This is the ancient formulation of the logical principle of the excluded middle, applied here within the framework of spatiotemporal reality. It results in a specific problem often called the problem of future contingents.
13. Aristotle, *De Interpretatione*, 9: 28–30.
14. Most commonly translated in the Aristotelian context as "chance" and "accident," these two Greek terms in Bergson's mind refer to the double idea still to be analyzed by him, "chance" and "randomness."
15. This is the famous example Aristotle uses in *De Interpretatione* 9, 19a30–33, 30.
16. This is one of the main theses of *Matter and Memory* (MM, 191–4/165–7).
17. Bergson will develop this question—often in formulas very similar to what we see here—in the first Introduction to *The Creative Mind* under the heading "retrograde movement of the true," a text he wrote in 1922 but only published, in that volume, in 1934.
18. From the viewpoint of what preceded, as opposed to a parte post, from the viewpoint of what follows.
19. The typescript here says *de l'éternité du temps*, "of the eternity of time," which does not seem right.
20. On *hylē* in Aristotle see CE, 274/316.
21. The typescript here contains the parallel but illogical construction, *non pas seulement dans la nature entière*, "not in all of nature alone."
22. See MM, 330–2/279–80. Bergson uses the terms *organisé / organisation* to mean both "organic / organic life" and "organized / organization." They are rendered flexibly here.
23. See ME, 11/8. Life as consciousness will be one of the major theses of *Creative Evolution*.
24. CE, 166/186 and 232/266.
25. The image of the "meshes" is also found in MM, 278/236 and 332/280.
26. The French word here rendered as "defect" is *défaut*, which comes from the verb *défaillir*, "to fail."
27. The expression—variously rendered as "what is up to us," "depending on us," or "in our power"—goes back at least to Aristotle (see below, 92n31); it was made famous by the Stoic Epictetus, who, at the beginning of his *Encheiridion* (or *Handbook*), distinguishes between "what is not up to us" (the world) and "what is up to us" (the representation we have of the world). See Epictetus, *Encheiridion*, in *Discourses, Books 3–4. Fragments. The Encheiridion*, trans. W. A. Oldfather (Cambridge, MA: Harvard University Press, 1928), ch. 1, 483.

LECTURE 7
FEBRUARY 3, 1905

Gentlemen, first of all, I'd like to return to one or two points from the last lecture that I [113] consider important and whose development I had to cut short for lack of time.

In the last lecture, I talked about the idea of contingency in Aristotle. I defined this contingency. I began to show the difference of opinion between the ancients and the moderns on the subject of contingency. In general, I said, to believe in contingency is to believe that not everything in the universe is absolutely determined; that in certain cases, at least, the effect adds something to the causes that produced it; that in given conditions, in determinate circumstances, several events can be possible; that, consequently, the same person, in given conditions, facing a determinate situation, with equally determinate motives, motivations, can make several equally possible decisions.

I thus defined contingency as an indetermination, if not total but at least partial, in relation to the causes. I said that there's a radical divergence of opinion between the ancients and the moderns about this indetermination, about contingency, about its value in general. For the ancients, at least for those among them who believe in contingency—not all of them believe in it, and I'll insist on this point in the next lecture—but for those among them who believed in contingency, contingency is always an evil. It's an imperfection in things. It exists but it would be better if it didn't. It's a deficiency in things, a defect.

In contrast, for the moderns, or at least for those among them who have believed [114] in contingency—and there's not a lot of them—contingency is an excellent thing, it's something higher, something better that enters the world of necessity. This is the difference I pointed out in the last lecture, and I began to show the reasons for this difference. To a large extent, it has to do with the limitation of the field of contingency in those modern philosophers who've granted a place to contingency. Among the ancients, those who accept contingency put it everywhere in nature. Among the moderns, in contrast, and this is the point I wanted to return to, to avoid any misunderstandings, contingency, when they accept it, is limited to human actions. At least that's the most widespread opinion among those philosophers who believe in a partial indetermination in things. Contingency is a term co-extensive with freedom, and freedom is something that belongs solely and exclusively to humans.

I announced that the thesis I'll present in the second part of the course will be a bit different and that I'll try to extend this field of indetermination and contingency, not to the whole of nature, but to living nature. Where life begins, I believe, the field of contingency begins as well. Contingency thus means novelty, production, creation of something new, unforeseeable, and of such a nature that if the conditions in which a thing happens are given, the thing taking place adds something new, absolutely new to the conditions in which it takes place.

Suppose a nature in which there are no living beings, a nature devoid of organisms. This nature is probably subject to an absolute necessity, to the laws of necessity that govern the movement of atoms or of the ultimate elements, whatever they may be, of which matter is composed. To say that it is subject to absolute necessity is to say that nothing new happens there, absolutely nothing. Suppose a superhuman intellect that at a given moment would know the position, the direction, and the speed of all the
[115] atoms making up this material universe.[1] It would be able to predict with mathematical certainty all that will happen at any given moment of duration. Consequently, what will happen will tell it nothing: it had noticed all of it virtually in advance. For this intellect, there'll thus be nothing new in the world. Everything will be given all at once, and for this intellect everything will be as if it didn't exist.[2] In this universe, in short, nothing new, nothing unexpected happens.

Now, insert organisms into this nature, living beings, however simple they may be. The thesis I'm arguing here is that with organic life, contingency, indetermination is introduced, and that organic life has no other raison d'être. As I said the other day, the organism is a contingency machine, a mechanism put together to produce anti-mechanical, extra-mechanical actions. It's a machine for producing the unforeseeable.[3]

Note that we mustn't go too far down this path. And, to respond right away to an objection that has been made, this thesis in no way implies the negation of scientific determinism in general and, in particular, of the biological determinism Claude Bernard spoke of—which he did not confuse, as certain of his successors do, with purely physical determinism, but which, in the end, is a determinism nonetheless.[4] To say that indetermination begins with life is not at all to say that all of the phenomena that occur in living beings are contingent phenomena. Who would argue that respiration, circulation, or digestion in humans, to take that example, who would argue that these phenomena are not strictly determined by their conditions? It's quite clear that if there is indetermination, if there is contingency somewhere here, this contingency is strictly limited to the phenomena this living being attributes to itself, more particularly, when it becomes conscious of itself, that is, those that take place in the nervous system and, more particularly, at certain determinate points in the nervous system, at certain determinate points in the brain. This thesis does not imply contingency everywhere in living beings; instead, it puts contingency everywhere where there are living beings, which is completely different.

[116] When we go down the scale of animals—we can even reach the simplest system, or one of the simplest systems, since it's not the simplest: the infusoria[5]—no one will argue that nutrition, the reproduction of infusoria are phenomena that elude all determinism, no. But when infusoria move by means of their cilia, these movements are not, perhaps, strictly determinable even when we know all of the conditions. This will also be true, perhaps, of amoeba projecting out their pseudopodic filaments in a drop of water.[6] As soon as life appears, we must grant indetermination its share. What share? Exactly the same, I think, as the share we grant to consciousness, to sensation. Exactly the same,

since either consciousness has no raison d'être; or sensation has no raison d'être; or it's a kind of question posed to living beings they cannot answer,[7] a problem they cannot solve, unless there is a certain latitude for them to decide, to choose. Consciousness is thus a choice. What really proves this, simple good sense says it, is that in our actions, when we observe ourselves, consciousness is all the more intense the more difficult the problem to solve is and the more obviously it is a matter of deciding and choosing. In contrast, consciousness tends to vanish or disappear, as if it had become useless, the more we give up choosing and our actions become automatic.[8] Simple good sense thus seems to suggest that consciousness, sensation, are above all conditions of choice—how do I put this—organs of choice, organs of freedom. Consequently, if all actions accomplished by living beings were automatic, determined at least by the conditions in which they are made, then consciousness, it seems, would long have disappeared from this world—like all that is useless—having atrophied as an effect of its uselessness.

All in all, the testimony of consciousness indeed appears to show that things happen this way. This is our immediate feeling. Now, against this immediate feeling, people will invoke reasons that at first glance might appear more scientific. People will say: atoms [117] are governed by deterministic laws [*lois fatales*]. That's what physics shows. That's what chemistry shows. And when we get to biological phenomena, it's the same thing, the same atoms governed by equally deterministic laws. Why would there be an exception to this law in living beings?

This is a plausible way of reasoning, but saying that this is a more scientific way of reasoning than the other one is another matter. It's certain that determinism is strict in physics, because physics manages to rigorously determine effects in relation to causes. That it is strict in chemistry is no less certain. That it is strict in biological phenomena other than those in which the apparent sensation and consciousness of freedom intervene is very probable, we can even say it's certain. But where consciousness truly intervenes, science is powerless to determine the effect of a given cause: we cannot define the determinism,[9] we cannot determine a priori the nature of the conscious reaction to a given excitation. So science, experience don't show the determinism here. And when we expand determinism to [include] these cases, we expand the givens of experience, we extend them beyond what experience shows, which is permitted, after all, but it's no longer science, it's philosophy. We can oppose to this philosophy, which, in short, leaves the domain of experience, and leaves it completely, we can oppose another philosophy that claims to remain within the domain of experience all the more by taking an experience into account that, while it's less precise than direct and visual experience, nevertheless has its value, that is, an internal experience, the feeling of consciousness, an experience that testifies in favor of an at least apparent contingency. Those who opt for this contingency thus are consistent with experience, and it's up to those who deny [contingency] to prove their point.

That, gentlemen, is all I wanted to say, it's also, incidentally, all I'll be saying in the second part of this course. Indetermination begins with life, it seems to me, which doesn't mean—this would go far beyond our thinking—that indetermination is in all the [118] phenomena of life. Life can be considered as something huge, like a pyramid if you like, whose base is necessity. Contingency, if it exists, will be located at the point at the top of the pyramid, a simple mathematical point. But perhaps the base is made to support the whole pyramid, including what's at the top.[10] That is all I'll be saying.

In a theory like this one—which probably restricts contingency less than the other one—nonetheless, even in such a theory, contingency is still something, how do I put this, excellent or superior entering the world. Contingency is a victory won over necessity, and even more so is freedom properly speaking. For it goes without saying that freedom such as it exists in humans is something completely different from the pure contingency that can exist in beings in general: it is a contingency coupled with reason, with reflection. When the issue is this freedom or more generally contingency, we can always say that there's something higher than mechanism there.

I'll summarize what I just said: contingency and freedom, in short, all of that means creation. For me, freedom is creation, a creation analogous to the one we observe, that we believe we observe in action. I've already made this comparison, but I'm going to return to it often: freedom is a creation in the sense in which we use this word when we say that there's creation in a work of art. What do we mean by that? We don't mean by it that the work of art is a production ex nihilo, that it's made from nothing. We mean by it that, the conditions that have contributed to the production of the work being given, the work, if it is truly the work of an artist, adds to these conditions something absolutely new, absolutely unforeseeable.

Take a work of art that phantasy, it seems, ought to be most absent from, take a portrait, provided it's a portrait painted by a true master. You know the model. You know where and how the model was sitting for it, with what lighting. You know the painter, you may have seen a lot of portraits by the same painter. You can be sure that the portrait
[119] he's going to make will resemble the model and in certain ways is going to resemble the style of the painter. But what will this portrait be? You can't foresee it, and when it does appear on the canvas, it will add something, we'll see something new spring up that you could have neither expected nor foreseen.[11] I know of course that, the work produced being given, it will appear to you quite natural and you'll say that, given the model and given the painter's usual style, the portrait had to be what it is—yes, we'll say that after, but we'd never have been able to foresee it before, because the very act, the operation by which the painter makes this portrait, adds something to all the givens, and something absolutely unforeseen, absolutely unforeseeable.

The illusion of criticism, though, the eternal illusion of criticism, art criticism or literary criticism, is to believe that, because a work can be explained, perhaps, once it is produced, by its antecedents, these antecedents have produced the portrait and were sufficient to produce it. Just as the eternal illusion of philosophy is to believe that because an action, I mean a truly free action, because an action, once produced, is explained entirely, sufficiently, by all the antecedents that have brought it about, by the situation, the motives, the motivations, the character of the person, this action could have been foreseen, given all the conditions, given the motives, the motivations, the character—as if, for that matter, this very word didn't imply an absurdity: how in fact could a character be given in advance, since the character of the person who acts is modified, and is

modified by the very action which is being carried out?[12] Character is not something already made. I mentioned a moment ago a painter's style. If the painter hasn't frozen his talent, as it were, if his style isn't stereotyped, then the reason why we cannot foresee exactly the portrait he's going to make is that this portrait itself as it were modifies his style, progresses beyond what he's made earlier. It's the same thing for character. The reason why it's absurd to say that an action could be foreseen, a free action, if we knew the conditions and the character perfectly, is that we cannot know the character perfectly—for the very simple reason that it does not yet exist such as it will at the moment the [120]
decision is made, this decision being part of the character, modifying it, and something like a moment of its evolution.

So there is indeed a creation of the act by the agent in the same sense, or almost, as we say that a work of art is a creation of the artist. All the elements are given and yet what will be made, produced, with these elements will add something new.

I borrowed a comparison from the art of painting. Staying with the same kind of idea, let's consider a drawing, a student who is learning to draw.[13] The student has finished his sketch, the sketch is done. The teacher who appears, let's assume it's a great master, only has to add one imperceptible jot with the pencil to transform the whole: everything is transfigured. At the moment it's made, the free decision adds to the elements this imperceptible jot of the pencil, a nothing, but a nothing that is everything because, depending on whether it is this or that, the decision will be different.[14] Whatever decision is made, once it's made, it will be explained by its antecedents. The action is explained by its antecedents when it's accomplished, and a different action would be explained in the same way—hence the illusion that we could have foreseen the action. We explain it after the fact, it's something foreseeable after the fact, as it were, but never before, even for someone who knew all of the conditions—or, rather, this hypothesis is absurd because to know all the conditions is to accomplish the very action, the action being part of the conditions that seem to determine it.[15]

Gentlemen, this digression was worthwhile because it's important to stress that freedom, as I understand it, is the introduction of something superior into the universal mechanism. And when I speak of superiority, of excellence, I'm not making use of a vague term, and it's not a term to be taken in the moral sense—always hard to define—no, I'm taking this word "superior" in the sense it is commonly used when we speak of a superior and an inferior, the superior being the one who commands, the one who employs the agents. Contingency or freedom thus understood makes use of the mechanism as a [121]
superior makes use of the inferior, using him as an instrument.

That's all I wanted to say, but it's enough to reverse the viewpoint of the ancients completely, to invert the viewpoint of the ancients on this question. For the ancients—and here I'm returning to the specific object of this course, of this part of the course—for the ancients in general and for Aristotle in particular, things look completely different. The viewpoint on contingency is radically different. When we speak of the ancients, we must never lose sight of the fact that for them, the excellent, the superior, is above all the immutable, the immobile. To change, for an ancient philosopher, to change is to seek something, something we don't have. Consequently, if we change, it's because we're imperfect, if we change, it's because we want to be something else, something better, better than what we are. To change is as it were to run after oneself, not to be oneself entirely. Hence change is an imperfection, and what is entirely excellent and the best possible is immutable and does not leave, as it were, the immutability of its essence.[16]

This is the first point we must consider when we talk about the ancients or ancient philosophy. Then, there's a second viewpoint: for the ancients, excellence, perfection always resides in the purely rational, and for the ancients, that is rational which is logical and which most resembles mathematics or at least geometry. Now, logical relations, geometrical relations are necessary relations. When we're looking for the explanation of something, we can explain this thing with contingent conditions, with—how do I put this—relations of space and time. But to the mind of the ancients that's not truly scientific, that doesn't entirely satisfy the mind. Something is explained only when it's connected, by a necessary relation, to something else, to some timeless existence.

Let's take something familiar, this table for example. We could measure the two diagonals. I'm assuming this measurement shows us that the two diagonals are equal.
[122] There are two ways to explain this equality: the first, the simplest, will be to say that the diagonals are equal because the worker made the table this way, he produced it this way, such that the diagonals are equal. However, we will ask why the worker made the table this way. The answer will be: because he copied another table, the one he has in his workshop. "Why did he have it in his workshop?" we'll keep asking. Because on such and such day at such and such hour, he purchased it at such and such place, and so on. If we go down this path, reason will never be satisfied because one thing is assigned another thing as its reason, both being contingent, and to this a third, and so on, indefinitely.

Now there's another explanation, another way to explain why the two diagonals are equal, which is simply to say that the table is a rectangle, or nearly so, and that every rectangle—and that in a rectangle the two diagonals are equal because [they are] the hypotenuse[s] of two equal right triangles, because[17] two right triangles are equal when, respectively, the sides of the right angles are equal. We thus have a second explanation of the equality of two diagonals. This one is wholly different: it consists in immediately moving outside of time, we can even say out of space, in a sense, in considering the rectangle in general, and with this rectangle in general we explained what happens with this table in particular.

That, gentlemen, is Plato's idea, which is that any explanation worthy of the name is an explanation of this kind. Plato even goes a lot further, at least, it seems, at the beginning, at the origin of his theory of Ideas, for, he probably, little by little, moves closer to the real, to sensible reality. But in the pure theory of Ideas, the very existence of the things that we call real, sensible, individual things, with the phenomena they present in space and time, this existence is a kind of scandal.[18] These things ought not to exist, what ought to be, what truly is, are the pure essences, extra-spatial and timeless, the pure Ideas, that is, models that are to the things we call real what pure geometrical figures are to their imitations in material objects.

[123] This was probably Plato's view at the beginning, and that of Aristotle is not really very different. There is, however, this difference that for Aristotle, the world of Ideas does not

exist like the Platonic world. There's a rather big difference: [for Aristotle,] the Platonic world of Ideas does not exist, but it could exist; it's always on the verge of existing, but there's something that impedes its existence, something that compresses it, tightens it, as it were, like a spring that wants to unwind, a certain principle that, moreover, is completely negative, which Aristotle calls *hylē*, a word we translate by "matter." It's a shame we have no other word to name the thing: *hylē* is a principle of indetermination, something that impedes the Platonic Ideas. This matter, this *hylē*, is, all in all, the true cause, the true reason that, in the first place, makes it such that there are individual things in space and time, instead of there being simply universal and timeless genera. It's also the true cause that makes it such that there is change and—this is the point we're interested in—contingency in the world. And here's how: for Aristotle, a being, for example, an animal, is born, grows, reaches its full development, generates another, and dies, etc. What does that mean? It means only that this being senses that it is not completely itself. If it were completely itself, if it were a pure Form, as Aristotle says, a pure Idea, if it were completely itself, it wouldn't have to change. It changes because it's looking for itself. It develops, and when it has reached the fullness of its development, it generates another being that is like it, and so on, indefinitely. There is a *circulus*, a circle. The being would like to leap beyond itself, as it were, and reach its Idea, its *Eidos*,[19] but it cannot reach it because of matter, which represents the gap between itself and its pure Idea. It thus doesn't reach it, and it's forced indefinitely to imitate, in time and space, the immutability of its Form or its Idea by a kind of *circulus*, a kind of circular movement.[20] If an animal multiplies into an indefinite number of exemplars, this multiplication, which constitutes all the individuals of the genus, this multiplication means precisely, and shows, that the being does not completely attain its eternal and invariable Form. So matter is really [124]
the cause of the multiplicity of individuals, and it's also the cause of change, for if the being coincided with its Idea, it would no longer have any reason to change, it would be immutable, it would be eternal. And it's change that entails contingency for the very simple reason that, the moment beings change as an effect of their materiality, they are subjected in space and time to all the accidents of a spatial and temporal nature, not to mention that they constantly infringe on one another and that none of them manages to develop only what it is: hence the mistakes of nature, mistakes that make it such that nature pursuing one goal attains a different one; hence chance, randomness, in a word, contingency in all its forms. Contingency, change, and in general—not always, as we're going to see—in general, individuality, all of this is thus the effect of an evil principle, as it were, although Aristotle does not treat the principle in this way. He does, however, in one or two passages talk about what makes it evil.[21] All of this has to do with an evil principle that refracts the unity and the indivisibility of the Form.

Let's suppose for a moment that matter disappeared from Aristotle's theory, let's make *hylē* vanish. What's going to happen? First of all, if we take an example, a dog, let's say, a horse, a species, we're going to see the individuals merge: we're no longer going to have anything but the Form, what Plato called the Idea, the Idea of horse, the Idea of dog. All the developments in time of the different individuals corresponding to these species are going to merge like a fan being closed, and there'll no longer be anything but the immutability of the essence. In short, we've nearly reached the Platonic myth of the Ideas, nearly but not entirely. And this brings me to the essential point, since this is what is of interest to Aristotle's theory of freedom.

We don't have the time to cite texts. I indicated the supporting passages in a Saturday course I taught here two years ago.[22] If we take into account some passages we can draw attention to in Aristotle, this is the conclusion we end up with: if we suppress matter,
[125] if we suppress the *hylē* for animals in general —for dogs, say, for horses—then what I just said is perfectly true: all of them merge, there'll no longer be anything but the unity of the Form or of the Platonic Idea. But this will not be true for the human being. The human being is a being apart, because the human being is not only like the animal. It not only has a body and a soul. For Aristotle, the soul is closely united with the body, body and soul are two aspects of the same thing, but in the human, there's something more, in humans, in addition, there's the principle Aristotle calls *nous*, a word we translate by "intellect," and which in Greek has an intermediary meaning between what we call today "intellect" and what we call more generally "mind"[23]—in a word, the mind, *nous*, is something that enters into humans at the moment of birth and survives them, it's the eternal part of ourselves.[24]

This *nous* has two parts. There's one that Aristotle calls *nous poiētikos*, which is the main part, which is everything, even, the part of the mind we're not conscious of at all. It's [this part] that does everything, as Aristotle says.[25] Then the other part of the intellect, which we are conscious of, is the development of this part of the mind within time, it's what Aristotle calls *dianoia*, discursive intellect. It's something that, through its movement in time, imitates the immutability of the true mind, of the Idea, like the circular movement of the celestial sphere imitates divine immutability.

What is this *nous*, and where does it come from? Ah! that's a hard question to answer, since we don't have anything in Aristotle to shed light on it. Some have claimed that this *nous* is God himself, Aristotle's God entering, as it were, the human soul.[26] No, Aristotle's God—who has not gone beyond himself, according to what Aristotle says, and who is always, eternally enclosed in himself[27]—Aristotle's God is clearly not that. But there's something of that.

The *nous*—I can only hypothesize on this, but we must take inspiration, when we interpret these texts, it's not forbidden to take inspiration from the Alexandrians—this *nous* could indeed be the link between God and the soul. In Aristotle, God is enclosed
[126] in himself, but even so, in the end, he's a light, as the Alexandrians will say, he's the sun, if you like. God may well remain within himself, there are beams of light that stream into the various souls.[28] The *nous* for each of us would be one of these beams of light, it would be—how do I put this—a possible vision of God.[29] We must suppose that human souls are different from other souls in that they are capable, as the Alexandrians will say, of turning back or converting toward God.[30] And this vision of God will become possible for the various souls located in various places. Perhaps this is what Aristotle means by "mind"—or, rather, it's doubtful that he asked himself the question, doubtful that he was looking for the relation between the *nous* and the divine nature. But if we want to systematize his teaching, since he hasn't done it himself, this is the conclusion

we'd reach as the only one able to establish a connection between the stages of the system.

So if we suppress *hylē*, the principle of all contingency, the principle, too, of all division, the individualities of the various beings disappear, but undoubtedly not the human individualities, they subsist; it's something that enters into each of us at the moment of birth and that survives the body, that is, in short, what is truly human in us.

I said that from the viewpoint of the theory of freedom this is of the utmost importance, for it allows us to understand how, for Aristotle, contingency, which in general is an evil in itself since matter is its cause, contingency in humans, however, from a certain angle, becomes a good. For there's no doubt possible on this subject. In the *Nicomachean Ethics*, book 3, freedom or, as Aristotle says, independence, *to eph' hēmin*, is considered, all in all, a privilege of the human. The same in the second book of the *Physics*.[31] I already told you the other day that Aristotle clearly opposed choice to chance, which are the ordinary and as it were natural manifestations of contingency.

What, then, is this particular mark of contingency in humans that turns human freedom into something, I wouldn't say good, but relatively good? For Aristotle, human action, virtuous action leads humans back toward the state of pure mind. You remember [127] that for Aristotle, the virtue par excellence is contemplation,[32] and consequently being perfectly good would be to become pure intellect, pure mind once more. And what, for lack of this superior virtue, is the average virtue for Aristotle? It's moderation, measure, regularity. I would almost say that circularity in movement is an imitation, in the domain of movement, of the immutability in the domain of pure thought. Consequently, for Aristotle, to be virtuous is to return to the immutability of pure thought without matter. This allows us to understand the mark specific to contingency in the human. Alone among all beings, the human is capable of as it were reversing the direction of the movement of nature. In all the other beings, contingency is solely a descent, since matter is what degrades the Form. But the human alone is capable of getting a grip on itself, of reascending the slope of nature, of returning to the Ideas, to pure thoughts.[33] If there were no contingency, humans would be incapable of doing this. Consequently, contingency in the world, by making freedom possible, makes it such that virtue and, in short, the return are possible. In this sense, freedom is a good, but, as you can see, this good is only the corrective of an evil. It would have been better not to descend, then we wouldn't have to go back up, but it's through freedom that we go back up. If there were no contingency in the world, there would be no matter, no materiality, nothing would have descended. Consequently, contingency is, in short, a kind of evil, but given that this evil exists, the human is a privileged being insofar as it is able to go back up the slope. Consequently, in the human, contingency, while it is an evil, is a lesser evil. It's the means of correcting as much as possible the evil there is in nature.

Since we're dealing with texts by Aristotle—I already said this the other day—we have to systematize Aristotle's thinking, we have to make it a lot more systematic than it is. He has left us analyses, and we're trying, as much as possible, to synthesize. But when we make this synthesis, we notice that Aristotle's thought doesn't contain the contradiction we thought we'd find there. So at first glance, contingency in the world is

[128] an evil, it's an effect of materiality. In the human, and probably thanks to the fact that the *nous* enters the soul, a return is possible, a movement that allows us to go back up the slope. And if there were no contingency in the world, this movement undoubtedly wouldn't be possible. Thereby, freedom is a good, but if there were no contingency in the world, freedom wouldn't be necessary either. All things considered, contingency is an evil.

It was necessary, I think, to dot all the i's, and really to show in what ways the idea of contingency such as we'll have occasion to define it in this course contrasts with the idea of contingency such as the ancients accepted it.

To have done with the Greek philosophers, we still have to talk about the theory of necessity that has always developed alongside the theory of freedom and take up this theory in the relatively perfect form that the Stoics gave it. That's what we'll do in the next lecture, and there we'll have an example, an application of the law which I've been pointing out since the beginning of this course, of the general law: we'll see how the Stoics not only presented in very precise terms a theory of universal necessity but also tried at a certain moment to resorb human freedom into this universal necessity by giving a definition of freedom that makes it coincide with necessity. Such was the work of the most remarkable philosopher of the Stoic school, a veritable work of genius, the work of Chrysippus. I'll say a few words about this work in the next lecture.

Notes

1. For this fiction, known as "Laplace's demon" after French polymath Pierre-Simon Laplace (1749–1827), see CE, 40–1/37–8, and below, esp. 219–20.
2. The "it" in this sentence probably refers to the new.
3. Compare the ending of *Two Sources* (TS, 317/338).
4. Bergson's 1913 paper on Bernard (CM, 238–47/229–37) aims to demonstrate these points in detail.
5. "Infusoria" designated an order of the kingdom of protozoa (both taxons are no longer in use) whose members are characterized by the presence of cilia. It derives from the fact that these microorganisms can develop in infusions of vegetal matter.
6. "Amoeba" is a generic term for several kinds of single-cell organisms that project out of themselves temporary filaments, so-called pseudopodia (lit. "false feet") by means of which they move about and feed themselves.
7. Each perception is thus "an elementary question to my motor activity" (MM, 41/43).
8. Here Bergson is inspired by Félix Ravaisson's analysis of habit. See CM, 274–5/266–7, and compare ME, 14–15/10–11.
9. In the sense of "define the way determination works here."
10. For a similar image, see ME, 194–5/160.
11. Similar passages can be found in CE, 13–14/6–7 and 293–4/340–1.
12. See TFW, 172–3/129–30.

13. From a different angle, Bergson considers the questions of painting and learning to draw in a nearly contemporaneous text, "The Life and Work of Ravaisson" (originally a eulogy delivered in February 1904), by way of the examples of Leonardo da Vinci and Johann Heinrich Pestalozzi (CM, 272–4/264–6 and 286/277–8).
14. The concrete realization of the picture brings with it this "unforeseeable nothing that is everything in the work of art" (CE, 293/340), this "unforeseeable nothing which changes everything" (CM, 107/99).
15. For this argument, see TFW, 183–92/137–44.
16. CE, 272/313–14.
17. This second "because" does not have the same function as the first and could be replaced by "in effect," since it brings in a supplementary presupposition that is necessary for understanding the argument just presented.
18. In the sense of something that causes offense, a metaphorical stumbling block (*skandalon*), as at 1 Corinthians 1:23 or on several occasions in Romans.
19. This Platonic-Aristotelian term means "form" or "idea."
20. For this imitation of the immutable by a circular movement, see CE, 280–1/323–5. Bergson takes this up in a moment (89), and although he is discussing Aristotle, there is a distinct echo in these passages of Plato's definition of time as the "moving image of eternity" (*Timaeus*, 37d: 1241).
21. Plato, *Physics*, 192a, 1.9: 328.
22. If Bergson is indeed referring to the academic year 1902–1903, then the text he was explaining on Saturdays is book 2 of the *Physics* (see M, 572). But we should recall that the 1903–4 course was dedicated to book 12 of the *Metaphysics* (M, 613). Which passages is he talking about? While we have no documents that would allow us to say which with certainty, Bergson, in a footnote to a discussion in *Creative Evolution* of ideas very close to those presented here, cites a passage from *On the Soul* (430a14–15, 3.5: 684, in CE, 279 note a/322n1)—a text he had already used in the other course he taught in 1903–4, "Histoire des théories de la mémoire." In these lectures on the history of theories of memory, he takes up the very topic that comes up in the next sentences, the Neoplatonic doctrine of the "active intellect," which is inspired by Aristotle. See HTM, especially the lectures of April 15 and 22, 1904.
23. In general, "nous" is translated into English as "thought." The term translated as "mind" is *esprit*, which also means "spirit."
24. Closely paraphrasing Aristotle, Bergson in the earlier course says that "the intellect is something that enters the soul through the door" (HTM, 265).
25. Aristotle, *On the Soul*, 430a14–15, 3.5: 684 (cited in CE, 279 note a/322n1).
26. Alexander of Aphrodisias being one of the first; on Alexander and his great importance for Bergson, see the February 17, 1905, lecture, 107.
27. In *Creative Evolution* (CE, 278 and 539n117/321), Bergson alludes to *Metaphysics*, 1074b34, 12.9: 1698.
28. CE, 278–9/321.
29. CE, 279/322.
30. An allusion to the Plotinian, and generally Neoplatonic, teaching according to which each being finds itself at the intersection of a movement of procession from God and a movement of conversion toward God.

31. See Aristotle, *Nicomachean Ethics* 3.5, 1113b19–22: 1758, and compare *Physics* 2.4–6, 195b31–198a12: 334–8; see also above, 80n27.
32. *Nicomachean Ethics*, 1177a 12–27, 10.7: 1860–1.
33. A strangely Bergsonian formulation of an idea that is hardly Bergsonian. See for example CE, 33–4/29–30, and CM, 216/206.

LECTURE 8
FEBRUARY 10, 1905

I announced in the last lecture that today I'd provide a very brief sketch of the theory of [129] universal necessity, fatalism such as we find it in those ancient philosophers who gave this doctrine its most precise and most powerful expression, that is, in the Stoics.

In a certain sense, the Stoics continue the philosophy of the first physicalists, the nature philosophers of Greece, and of Heraclitus in particular, with whom they have profound similarities. I've said it many times, the belief in necessity is a natural belief. We see it emanating from the physicalists' philosophy, even if the physicalists were not led to ask themselves the question of freedom, and the Stoics took up this belief, which continues throughout the entire history of philosophy, and gave it a systematic form. In that, they're the successors of Heraclitus and the ancient physicalists. But in another sense, they're just as much the continuators of Aristotle, since between Heraclitus and the Stoics there was Socrates, there was Plato, there was Aristotle, and the Stoics could not not have taken this great intermediary philosophy into account. I'll go even further: the Stoics are a lot closer to Aristotle than to Heraclitus, and there's hardly anything to be done to go from Aristotle to the Stoics, nothing to add, I would say, just something to cut away.

It's important, gentlemen, to dwell on this point, since we have here the first example of a fact we find throughout the entire history of philosophy. This fact is what I'd call the necessary choking of the doctrines of freedom by speculations concerning the whole of nature.

I said it in the first lecture, and I'll repeat it many times: our intellect, our reason, [130] goes from instinct to necessity. We really understand, we clearly see only necessity, the necessary determination of the effect by the conditions in which it happens. That alone is clear to our mind. We could say that the systematization of this belief in necessity is the natural philosophy of the human mind. And when some philosophers assert freedom in the sense in which we take this word, that is, the freedom that implies choice and therefore contingency, then this belief, this assertion of human freedom is quickly resorbed into the most natural and most normal philosophy, which is the philosophy of necessity. It's squeezed into necessity as into a vise, as it were. It has forced the door open, and once it has entered the normal and natural domain of speculation, it seems that, having had to force the door open, the door closes on it and it's captured and as if crushed—in fact, that's how it ends, it's always the annihilation of the belief in contingency and of the assertion of freedom.

In going from Aristotle to the Stoics, we'll have a first example, a first application of what I just said. Since we have here a very important fact, it's important to return briefly to the conclusion of our last lecture and to recall in a few words what Socrates, Plato, and Aristotle did from the viewpoint of the theory of freedom to show how, by means of a very simple transformation without an addition of any kind but rather by means of a subtraction, we can go from the last form of this philosophy, the form that Aristotle gave it, to Stoicism.

I said, gentlemen, that the belief in freedom is implicitly contained in everything Socrates says to his disciples. Without doubt, people have often talked about Socrates's determinism and about the famous formula, "No one does evil voluntarily." And it's true that for Socrates the wicked person is an ignorant person, and in this sense, if we posit ignorance, then wickedness, immorality, amorality, or the absence of morality follow. The question is whether, for Socrates, we aren't free to choose between knowledge and ignorance. Yet there can be no doubt on this point: all of Socrates's conversations with
[131] his disciples converge on this point, which is that we have the choice, the choice between remaining what we are naturally, remaining what we are by accident, chance, and upbringing, remaining humans who obey a routine or what the circumstances suggest—or, in contrast, we get a grip on ourselves, we truly become ourselves again, and do so thanks to a clear awareness of what the Good is, an awareness we can acquire on our own or thanks to a teacher who teaches you nothing, who teaches you simply to look inside yourself. So the implicit belief in freedom is indeed there in Socrates, and it cannot not be there, given that what this philosopher really cares about is action, action alone; he doesn't worry about speculations, or he speculates only about action.

This is the starting point of what there is of a belief in freedom in Plato and Aristotle. Plato's and Aristotle's doctrines on this point are a lot more similar than one would think at first. That's quite natural since they derive from a common inspiration. At first glance, the distance [between them] can appear considerable. They do not have the same formulas, they do not have the same theses. For Plato, as we've seen, freedom—in the sense that we ourselves give to this word today: a choice—freedom resides above all in an act prior to actual existence, an act by which each soul chooses what today we would call its character or its destiny. The soul has lived in a higher world, and it has chosen, by means of a truly voluntary act, the place it will occupy once it is plunged into a body, the place it will occupy in the series of beings. So there's an act prior to actual existence, an act prior to birth.

I'm not saying that we wouldn't find a lot of passages in Plato that seem to indicate that even in actual existence, there is a certain choice to be made among several options. But looking closely at these passages, we see in them—and this has been shown clearly by historians of philosophy[1]—we see in them all of the elements of what today we'd call psychological determinism, the act being necessarily conditioned by the circumstances in which it happens, in particular, the conditions, the particular circumstances of birth,
[132] and of upbringing as well.[2] Such that this freedom of choice that Plato may have been trying to put into actions, into the acts of normal life, this freedom ascends necessarily, the more closely Plato follows it, it ascends necessarily higher and higher. Having tried to put it on earth, he's compelled to bring it back to the heavens, as it were, and it's by means of an act of will prior to life properly speaking that we choose all that happens to us and all that we are.

With Aristotle, the thesis of freedom appears in a rather different form. In effect, Aristotle rejects the Platonic myths. For Aristotle, freedom, independence, as he says, is a characteristic of the soul (to which mind, intellect, is added), of the soul in the body. Moreover, Aristotle doesn't localize freedom in a single act, an act that would then be refracted as it were in space and time. No, he places freedom in ordinary action, everyday action, action that repeats, that ends up constituting a habit. But when we look at this closely, we see that on this point Aristotle is extremely close to Plato and that he barely avoids the Platonic myths. At its core, what in fact is freedom for Aristotle? Aristotle pictures the soul as interdependent with the body: in short, he defines the soul properly speaking as the form of the body, as the entelechy of the living body.[3] To be sure, something extra enters into the human soul: in the human soul, there's the *nous*, there's thought, whose best part, the superior part, is not conscious. We don't know this best part of thought, the *nous poiētikos*, the truly creative intellect, the one that makes everything, that puts everything else into motion. We do not know it. Where is it? It's behind the part of the intellect that we do know, and that part is a movement in time.

In what region can the best part of the intellect have its seat? It's not divinity, for although some people have interpreted Aristotle's doctrine in this way, it seems that this interpretation is inadmissible.[4] It's not divinity, but I said that it's something like that and that we have to picture the active but unconscious part as a kind of link between humanity and God such as Aristotle conceives of him. The region is thus, in short, [133]
pure thought, it's that part of ourselves that's at the same external, the part of us that hasn't descended, Plotinus would say.[5] There's but a slight difference between this kind of doctrine and a doctrine like Plato's, which shows us the soul in the heavens, in the world of Ideas, and descending. When we discuss the Neoplatonic doctrine in the next lecture, we'll see how these two doctrines, Plato's and Aristotle's, nearly coincide on this point.[6]

What is freedom for Aristotle? It is, in short, the faculty we have to reascend as high as possible toward the pure thought that's in us, without it, properly speaking, being us if we understand our self to be the soul as locked up in a body. According to Aristotle, it's the faculty we have that allows us to give ourselves over to pure contemplation, it's the supreme virtue. Or, if we can't attain it, it's doing something that is its imitation, for the virtue we practice in everyday life, which is of a more bourgeois nature, this virtue that consists in living a regular life, in living moderately, in practicing moderation in all things, is like an imitation, in the sphere of movement, of the immutability of pure thought.

So to distinguish precisely between the two doctrines of Plato and Aristotle, I would say that for Plato freedom is above all a descent, freedom is the act by which we choose, insofar as we descend into a body, the place that we'll occupy in the series of beings, while for Aristotle, freedom above all lies in the ascension, in the re-ascension. But in both cases, there is a certain hypothesis, which hypothesis is the same in both doctrines, and it's this hypothesis that makes freedom possible, that is the very essence of Platonism and Aristotelianism insofar as their systems grant a place to freedom.

What is this hypothesis? In short, it's the distinction between two different worlds: the sensible world, the world that our senses perceive, the world of change, of movement, of becoming, and then the intelligible world, the world of pure Ideas or, as Aristotle says, the world of Forms, the world in which the essences superior to space and time are
[134] arranged according to their profound relations, their logical relations, instead of being dispersed in space and time by accidental causes. This is the distinction of two worlds, the one that is known immediately by perception and the one to which we raise ourselves by conception, by knowledge. For Aristotle as for Plato, this second world is the true world—I'm not saying real; if this is not the one that is, it's the one that should be. Plato tells us: this is the one that is. Aristotle tells us that it is, but that it's prevented from being completely what it would like to be. There's a *je ne sais quoi*, a share of unreality, as it were, that mixes with the Ideas, with the Forms. We can use these two terms interchangeably: *Eidos* means "Form" or "Idea."[7] This share of unreality mixing with *Eidos* makes it such that the Idea is scattered about, multiplies itself in individual repetitions, and, on the other hand, it generates becoming instead of remaining in its immutability. It's a negation, as it were, that is added to what is positive in the Idea, and this negative demeans it. *Hylē*, matter, is a negation. We have to think of *hylē* as a kind of zero. If I take the number one, then, depending on whether I leave it as it is or whether I add to it, on its right side, one, two, three, or four zeros, I either abandon it to its unity or I multiply it indefinitely. Aristotelian matter is something like a zero placed to the right of the number one: it's nothing, as it were, but this nothing multiplies the Idea and demeans it.[8]

So in Aristotle's doctrine we have Forms, Ideas, that exist theoretically, that constitute the world of knowledge; then we have the principle that Aristotle calls "matter" mixing with these Ideas, a negative principle, which demeans the Ideas. At its core, this is the same hypothesis as Plato's; in both cases, we see the distinction between de jure and de facto [*le droit et le fait*]: de facto is what we perceive; de jure is the world of Forms or Ideas, arranged in the order demanded by knowledge.

There is thus a duality of the sensible and the intelligible, there is, to use the metaphor I used earlier, there are, as it were, the earth and the heavens. For Aristotle and for Plato, freedom exists entirely in the interval between the earth and the heavens, between what exists for knowledge [*science*] and what exists for the understanding [*entendement*],
[135] between perceptible existence and existence as it is known. Freedom is in this interval. If things were absolutely what they must be, there would be no place for contingency, no place for freedom. Everything would be perfectly rational, everything would hold together logically. But there is a gap between what is from the sensible viewpoint, between what does exist in time and space, and what should exist. And it's this gap that measures out contingency, it's thanks to this gap that contingency is possible. Freedom is situated in this intermediary region. For Plato, freedom consists in choosing one's place in the intermediary region. For Aristotle, it consists, not in choosing one's place once and for all, but in accomplishing an indefinite series of actions that, all the same, end up creating habits and setting a place.

For both, freedom is particular to humanity, for the very simple reason that the human is the sole being to participate in both worlds at once, in the sensible and in the intelligible. There's the heavens and there's the earth, and then, there's a scale extended between the two: the human is, as it were, this scale, or, rather, humans choose their place on the degrees of this scale.

Implicitly, Socrates said something like this: he said that for each of us there is a choice to make, as it were, on this scale that separates the person who is absolutely ignorant from the person absolutely knowing, knowing from virtue's viewpoint, from the viewpoint of the Good. Plato's and Aristotle's doctrines are speculations that started from this observation, and as happens to philosophers who really are speculative philosophers, they went over the limit, the two limits Socrates had defined, the top and the bottom of the scale. There was the sensible world and the intelligible world, and hence these learned constructions in which freedom finds a place, no doubt, but not a place larger than it already had, implicitly, in Socrates's teachings.

We've had to proceed by reconstitution, by reconstruction. This is what freedom was for Plato and for Aristotle. To go from this doctrine of freedom to the assertion of universal necessity, there was no need to add anything, just to take something away. It sufficed to take these two worlds, the sensible world and the intelligible world and— [136]
since freedom was possible only thanks to the gap that exists between the two worlds—bring them together in such a way that they end up coinciding. I said that freedom is between the heavens and earth: it was necessary to take the heavens, take the earth, and make them move toward each other in such a way that there was no longer any gap, nor any play, as it were, between the two. Freedom then was truly caught in a vise and crushed. There was no longer any place for it. This is what Stoicism did. Stoicism is nothing but this.

This doctrine is among those whose true character has been most misunderstood. Generally, when we talk about the Stoics, we picture the Stoics as pure moralists, philosophers who were concerned solely with morality, especially with morality, who added physics, and metaphysics itself, to this morality simply to satisfy the basic duty of philosophers. That's not it. It's possible, it's certain even that these were the characteristics of Roman Stoicism. Because the Romans were hardly philosophers. The Romans never understood anything about philosophy except ethics in its exclusively practical and applied aspects, but they hardly understood the principles posited by the Greeks. And since it so happens that we judge Stoicism above all through Roman Stoicism, the opinion that the Stoics were above all moralists is naturally given credence. If morality had been the Stoics' exclusive, or even just their main object, they probably would have made room for contingency, for freedom, for they would have started with action. When we heave the lead in the world of action, we pull freedom back up with it. When a doctrine is absolutely determinist, absolutely fatalist, we can say, a priori, as it were, that it doesn't originate from speculation about action as such but about the whole of nature, where it is indeed difficult to find a place for freedom. I've said many times that we encounter freedom only if we start from it. We don't find it along the way, we must start from it.

So the Stoics aren't simply moralists. On the contrary, the texts we still have from the Greek Stoics, the founders of Stoicism, really bring out the speculative character of this [137] philosophy, which is above all mathematical and physical. The Stoics, then, are neither exclusively nor mainly moralists; they are, properly speaking, physicalists.

At the beginning of this lecture, I said that in certain respects they are the successors of the Ionian School, and of Heraclitus in particular. I added that between Heraclitus and the Stoics there was the whole philosophy of Ideas, there was Aristotle. The Stoics are very close to Aristotle and, if I had to characterize their philosophy, I'd say that it is an attempt, it seems, to simplify Aristotle, to turn Aristotle's philosophy into something simpler, more accessible for everyone and more popular, as it were. The Stoics are the philosophers of antiquity who have sought—grant me the modern expression—to "democratize" philosophy, to make it accessible to everyone. Platonic-Aristotelian philosophy was an aristocratic philosophy, an artistic philosophy.[9] The conceptions that comprised it were extremely subtle and hard to follow. The Idea or the Form, *eidos*, this Idea that is something eternal, timeless, immutable, and is really true; then this undefinable *je ne sais quoi* being added to it that, being added to it, takes something away from it, making it such that everything falls and everything degrades—[all] this was difficult to follow and to grasp. The Stoics quite simply sought to melt these two principles, Idea and matter, into a single one.

The great difficulty lay in grasping this duality of *eidos* and *hylē*, of Idea or Form and matter. The Stoics sought to make this duality disappear and to melt the two principles into a single one. In this way, they came up with—and this took a certain creative genius—they came up with an intermediary principle that participates in both, which they defined in many ways. But if among the terms they bequeathed to us we had to choose the one that's the most expressive and provides the most complete idea of the doctrine—the term truly opposed to the *eidos*—it's the term *logos* that we'd have to retain.

The Stoics talked about the *logos spermatikos*, and this *logos* was very successful after
[138] Stoicism. I'm not talking about the special meaning this word took on a lot later, I'm talking about the meaning it has in Plotinus, which is very close to the meaning it has in Stoicism.[10] It's important to know the meaning of the word *logos*, since this meaning will give us the key to the doctrine of necessity in the Stoics, I'd even say to a lot of the doctrines of necessity, even several modern doctrines, even as it allows us to understand the relation between Stoicism and what preceded it.

What is this *logos*? The Greek word *logos* has many significations, and we don't find a word in French to translate it by.[11] For the Greeks, this word is brimming with things. The literal and precise meaning of *logos* is speech [*parole*], discourse. What is discourse, speech, a sentence? A sentence, that's words, syllables following one another, that are juxtaposed in time and even in space, since sound is something material: in whatever way we picture it, even if we are not familiar with the modern theory, it occupies space.[12] A discourse, a sentence is thus a series of articulated sounds that are juxtaposed, but at the same time as it's sound, it's an idea, it's a thought that expresses itself through the words, and this thought is not distinct from the words that express it, since, for the Greeks, thought and speech are inseparable. We only speak with words, and thought is inherent to the words that express it.

So let's consider a sentence we hear. These words, these syllables we hear are something juxtaposed, something diffuse, as it were, in space and time, and yet all these syllables taken together yield a meaning, any idea you like, something absolutely indivisible, I'd even say—the Stoics wouldn't have said this—I, for my part, would say, something immaterial.

So here we have one and the same thing that, when considered as diffuse and as it were slack, extended, is material and, when considered as concentrated, as taut, is, as we would say today—which the Stoics didn't say—something immaterial.

This is the first meaning of the word *logos*, a discourse that is multiple from one angle, and one from another; diffuse, diluted from one angle, and concentrated from another.

The word *logos* also means: reason, sense of reasoning. It's discursive reasoning, [139]
the reasoning that takes time, that is composed of parts. *Logos* is thereby quite distinct from *noesis*, which then is pure thought, the one that can fit into an intuition, in the intuition of an instant. So *logos* is a kind of reasoning. What is reasoning? It's a series of propositions that follow on one another, that are juxtaposed, that take time. To be sure, when we consider not each proposition one after the other but the totality of propositions, we have the impression that it's absolutely one, something indivisible, whatever the intention of the person who lined up the propositions and the reasoning, since, in the thinking of the one who reasons, all the propositions are but one. They want to prove something, they have an intention. This intention subdivides in the person's mind into a series of propositions, which, understood by us and admitted into our mind, are going to reconstitute and reproduce the idea, the original intention of the person who spoke. We thus have an intention in the one who reasons, an intention, that is, something simple, indivisible, undivided, concentrated, something that is then scattered into a series of propositions, which represent the same thing in a diffuse state and that, when they are heard and understood by the person who is looking to be convinced, merge, concentrate themselves again, and reproduce the original unity of the intention from which they emerged.

Thus reasoning is again something that from one angle is simple, undivided, and taut, in a state of intention, and seen from another is multiple, divided, slack, in a state of extension. In this second sense, *logos* no longer represents speech but reasoning. And in this second case as in the first, we have in reality something double-sided, one and multiple, concentrated and diluted, taut and slack.

There is a third meaning, which is less known and thus less important. For the Greeks, *logos* also means role, the role of an actor. This is one of the meanings of the word: the role of the actor considered in the sentences he utters, in the scenes he acts, in the situations through which he passes, something like the role of an actor. Consequently, it's indeed [140]
something extended, as it were, in time and even in space, but seen from the other side, it's something unified and stable. The actor who acts well is the one who has global vision, as it were, of the totality of his role, a vision that holds in one sole instant, in a simple impression. This, incidentally, is how great actors differ from mediocre ones. They manage, to use a common expression, to "compose" their role. What is composing a role? It amounts to seeing it, despite its complications, as something absolutely simple, such

that the endpoint of the role is contained in its beginning and in the middle. The actor who composes his role is one who merges all of its parts; then, after having composed it, the actor "exposes" it, that is, he works things out in such a way as to reproduce, by the reciprocal penetration of all of his role's parts, to reproduce, by the reciprocal interpenetration he achieves in our mind, the one and simple impression he himself had of the role. The role of the actor is, while he is acting, the unrolling of something that was rolled up in his mind. The word "role," moreover, expresses the idea of a scroll quite well. I'm not saying that the origin of the word might not be a bit different, it's possible that the word refers to the scroll upon which the role of the actor was written, but in either case, whether or not we assign an as it were material origin to this word, in either case, the role of an actor is something rolled up for him, unrolled for us. There's this double-sidedness, extension and distension in space and time, tension and concentration in thought.

So there we have two meanings of the word *logos*, but at their core all are identical. The word *logos* in the mind of a Greek arouses the idea or image of a double-sided reality, concentrated on one side, diluted on the other, taut on one side and slack on the other, and, as we would say today, corporeal on one side and spiritual on the other—even if certain Stoics declared that all reality is corporeal; [but here,] we'd have to agree what [141] meaning they gave the word *sōma*.[13] In any case, *logos* indeed implies the representation of a reality that presents these two sides successively or even simultaneously.

To go from Plato and Aristotle's philosophy to the philosophy of the Stoics, all we have to do is substitute *logos* for *eidos*. When we take *eidos*, the Idea, it's something immutable, eternal. We must add to it, to explain reality, which is fleeting, which is multiple, which is corporeal, we must add a second principle to it, such as matter, *hylē*. We will then have that duality that is so difficult to think. With *logos*, we don't have this duality. We can imagine an explanation of the universe such that from one angle, seen from a certain angle, the universe would be multiple, distended, then, considered from a different side, it would be something unified, simple, concentrated. This is a much simpler conception, borrowed from a more popular order of ideas, for notice that *eidos* is an image borrowed from the plastic arts. What is *eidos*? It's the particular idea a sculptor has when he makes his statue. He wants to express something: he thinks of Jupiter, Minerva, or Venus. Then he has to realize this idea. To realize it, he'll have to call upon another principle, a material principle: he'll take some clay, he'll start to mold it. He must add something to his idea to turn it into a reality, and what he adds to the idea is a diminishment, something that diminishes it, for no matter how much the artist mold and remold his clay, he will never manage to express completely what he had in mind. The relationship between idea and sensible reality in a philosophy like that of Plato and Aristotle is a relationship of this kind: there is the Idea, then there is its sensible representation by a principle that entails the diminishment of the Idea and thereby its representation. But this is something difficult, subtle to grasp, while *logos* is an image borrowed from a much more popular art, the art that all the Greeks practiced instinctually, the art of speaking, for the Greeks are great conversationalists. *Logos* is a metaphor borrowed from the art of oratory. When we speak, we line up words, something material, but all these words combined yield a meaning. This meaning is something simple, indivisible. We thus have an image or an idea, if you will, that allows us to grasp more simply the difference or the relationship [142] between what today we call the spiritual and the corporeal, or if you prefer, between the sensible and the intelligible, a much simpler image. The Stoics are going to explain the world in general with this image. The world is the unrolling of something that is rolled up, it's the extension, the slackening of something taut.

It's likely, for that matter, that the Stoics wouldn't have been able to apply this idea of *logos* to the explanation of the world if they hadn't gone through an intermediary, through the consideration of living beings, since *logos spermatikos*, as they call it, is the explanative reason for living beings. Take a living being, a plant for example: the plant goes through successive phases, it evolves, as we'd say today—notice the term *evolvere*[14]—the plant evolves, there's the stem, the leaves, the flowers, the fruit, etc. But all of that conforms to a rational law, to an order settled in advance, and all of these phases, according to the Stoics, according to the ancients, were contained already in the seed. Consequently, the seed provides us, in a concentrated state, with what is then going to be diluted, going to slacken into space and time. That's what *logos spermatikos* is. We generally translate this expression by "seminal reason." This translation does not provide a precise idea of *logos spermatikos*. The literal meaning of this word is the role inherent to the germ, inherent to the grain. There is *logos spermatikos*, there is a role that will be unrolled: we'd thus have to translate by "inherent role of the germ," or, if we want to keep the word "reason," we could translate as "generative reason." It is the reason that generates, that develops in reasoning in space and time.

There we have it, gentlemen, the *logos* as something all ready to explain the universe in general through the intermediary of the living being to which it's been applied. Only in the next lecture will I very briefly show how, with this idea of *logos* and yet other ideas, ideas connected to this one, the Stoics managed to present, in a form entirely clear and precise, the clearest and most precise that antiquity has bequeathed to us, the idea of universal necessity, and how one of them, the greatest among them, Chrysippus, believed that necessity so understood could still be called, in the case of humans, [143] freedom, freedom being defined in so subtle and, in certain respects, so profound a way that it coincides with necessity.

This part of the Stoic teachings is what particularly interests us, since what we find of this kind of thing in the moderns comes from there and was directly inspired by Stoicism.

Notes

1. Bergson is referring to Thomas-Henri Martin, Fouillée, and Teichmüller. See the January 13, 1905, lecture above, 55, and 59–60n5–8.
2. The January 13 lecture suggests that Bergson is referring to Plato, *Timaeus* 87b: 1286.
3. Aristotle, *On the Soul*, 412a27, 2.1: 657. This definition is quoted in CE, 300–1/349.
4. See the preceding lecture, 88.

5. Plotinus, *Enneads* 4.8. See also the January 20, 1905, lecture above, 86.
6. He won't actually present the argument until the March 3, 1905, lecture.
7. See CE, 272–3/314, for more on the meaning of the word *eidos*.
8. For this whole process of the degradation of the Forms, which results from the competition between immutable ideas and nothingness, see CE, 273–4/315–16.
9. CE, 298/346.
10. Bergson will later (101) give and explain the—according to him—right translation for this expression. Generally, the expression *logos spermatikos* or "seminal reason" refers to the thesis that there is something rational, discursive, or linguistic in the concrete generation of a being—and likewise, inversely, that there is something vital and processual in every logical production.
11. The same is true for English.
12. Bergson, it seems, is referring to electromagnetic theory.
13. By *sōma*, literally, "body," the Stoics in fact meant "everything." In establishing a parallel between the material and the bodily, the corporeal, Bergson implicitly aligns the immaterial and the incorporeal, thereby defining the Stoic notion of incorporeality in nonmaterialist terms.
14. *Evolvere* literally means "to unfurl a scroll."

LECTURE 9
FEBRUARY 17, 1905

Gentlemen, today I must complete the sketch of Stoic philosophy as a fatalist philosophy [145] I began in the last lecture. The Stoics, I said, are the ones, among ancient philosophers, who have the clearest and also the most self-conscious conception of universal determinism, of the doctrine of fatalism. They caught sight of all its consequences. They sought to find out how one could, within the hypothesis of universal necessity, explain the feeling of freedom, and even preserve the word "freedom," and with it, to some extent, the thing. And in this sense, among the philosophers of antiquity, they are the ones who posed the problem of freedom. People before them had talked about necessity; people before them had talked about freedom; but it's starting with them that freedom, from the philosophical point of view, is a problem.

I said that this philosophy is above all a metaphysics, or, as the Stoics said, a physics. It's a certain conception of the universe, and this conception of the universe is a conception whose primary objective seems to have been to place philosophy within the reach of everybody, as it were. The philosophy of someone like Plato, like Aristotle is something extremely subtle because of the duality of principles this philosophy accepts: matter and form, *eidos* and *hylē*. The objective of the Stoics, first of all, is to replace this duality of principles, which generates countless complications and which is the cause of so many subtleties, with one single principle that will necessarily be located halfway between the two. The Stoics gave different names to this single principle, but I said that the word that [146]
best expresses it is the word *logos*.

At the end of the last lecture, I enumerated the ideas included in the comprehension of this word. This Greek word is a word that contains a host of things. The *logos*, I said, is discourse, speech, that is, the juxtaposition of words, of syllables that take up a place in time, and even, since sound in short is something material, in space as well, it's a juxtaposition in space and time. Speech is something material, but something like a spiritual current passes through it in the sense that, when I take a sentence, even when I take the whole discourse, it has but one meaning, which, as meaning, is, in short, unified and indivisible. So discourse is reason materialized, if we can express it this way, or even—and this will be more Stoic—it is rational matter, intellectual and even intelligent matter.

I also said that *logos* is a reasoning, it's discursive reason. It's a series of propositions that follow one another, that are diverse, multiple, juxtaposed, but all the propositions converge on the demonstration of something, on the establishment of a point, on the genesis of a conviction. In the mind of the reasoner, this conviction splits up, as it were, into multiple propositions aimed at developing it, and these same propositions, received by the listener, recompose in his mind, if he accepts them, into a simple conviction. So discursive reasoning is indeed a unified multiplicity, if you will, or a multiple unity, as some would say; it's a double-sided reality.

I also added—this is the third point—that *logos* designates equally well the role of an actor, that is, something conceived by the actor himself as simple, for he has a conception of his role, and undoubtedly he has an undivided vision of this role. But for the spectator, this role subdivides, unrolls in multiple scenes, in actions, in situations, in sentences, in juxtaposed words. We thus have something, I said, rolled up in the mind of the actor,
[147] which is unrolled for the spectator, and which is rolled up again in the mind of the spectator when the spectator turns all the aspects of the actor's role into the simple idea that the actor wanted him to receive.

In short, the word *logos* has multiple meanings, but all of these meanings converge on the same point. In the idea of *logos*, from whichever side we consider it, there's always this: a double-sided reality, something that as multiple, as unrolled, as slackened, or as extended, is material, and that, when considered as one, as taut in itself, as undivided, is something rational, intellectual, and even intelligent.

Let's suppose for a moment that the universe is a kind of *logos*, a kind of discourse. This universe, then, considered from a certain side, is the extended universe, distended into the space and time that our senses perceive, it's the universe we call material properly speaking. But this doesn't prevent this universe, seen from a different side, from being something unified, simple, I wouldn't say "spiritual," since the Stoics wouldn't have accepted this word, but something absolutely indivisible and taut in itself. The universe thus presents the two aspects of a discourse, multiple insofar as it is made up of a juxtaposition of syllables, and unified insofar as it is only one and the same signification.

This is the conception, a bit simplified perhaps, but in the end this is the Stoic conception of the universe. For the Stoics, in short, the universe is at once matter and intelligence, without the two things necessarily excluding one another; on the contrary, they penetrate each other and even, in their mind, they're mixed together. The universe is corporeal and it is intelligent. The Stoics insisted on this point: the universe is corporeal. Everything that is is corporeal; everything that is is a body, *sōma*, they said, and on this point they took up Heraclitus's idea that what explains all things are the transformations to infinity of this same corporeal, material principle, fire, the creative fire [*feu artiste*] of which Heraclitus had spoken.[1] In one sense, everything is thus corporeal, but at the same time everything is rational and everything is intelligent. The Stoics insisted on this point, too. For them, the universe was something animate, they said, and intelligent. They also called this world-soul God. God, they said, is not in the heavens, he is throughout all
[148] things, he circulates throughout all things, he moves throughout everything. Was this, as some have said, as is sometimes said today, a materialist doctrine?[2] It all depends on what we mean by the word. But one thing is certain and that's that the Stoics encouraged ambiguity on this point by insisting on the materiality or, rather, on the corporeality of their principle. But there's no doubt that when they insisted on this point, they especially aimed to distinguish themselves from the Peripatetics,[3] to distinguish their philosophy from that of Aristotle. When they insist on the corporeality of their principle, they do

so to point out that the principle of things is not the Idea of Plato or the Idea, the Form of Aristotle.[4]

So the Stoics themselves encouraged equivocality on this point, but what's certain is that the God of the Stoics is really the universe, but the universe viewed from the side that we today don't call "corporeal": God is the universe seen from the side of tension, from the side of unity, and, I would almost say, from the side of spirit.

We must always think back to the comparison of the universe with *logos*, with discourse. For the ancient Greeks, the speech of a discourse expresses the meaning of this discourse, and the idea, the meaning is inseparable from the word that expresses it. When we have juxtaposed words with words, we undoubtedly have something material, something multiple, and nevertheless, all these juxtaposed elements, reunited, are equivalent to the undivided unity of the meaning they express. God, the God of the Stoics, is to the universe, considered as corporeal, what the meaning of the discourse is to the discourse itself. I'd actually say that God for the Stoics is the signification of the world. The result of this—this is an immediate consequence of the principle asserted—is that if the God of the Stoics is something a lot closer to the bodies, to the material universe, than Aristotle's God, then inversely, the world of bodies, the material universe is something—how do I put this—less material, less corporeal, in the modern sense of the word, than Aristotle's material universe. The Stoics said that matter is continuous; they said that bodies can be totally penetrated by one another. Continuous matter, penetrable matter is something that resembles, in certain respects, the existence that today we call psychological existence, for psychological life, [149] too, is the continuity of interpenetrating terms. To speak of the continuity, the indefinite penetrability of matter, is indeed to attribute a quasi-psychical nature to matter.[5] Moreover, the Stoics insisted—and this is important in regard to their theory of necessity—on what they called "universal sympathy." By this, they understood the absolute interdependence of all the parts of the world with one another. They said that the world as a whole is conspiring with and sympathetic to itself. They also said that all things are intertwined with each other. There's thus universal interdependence, universal sympathy.[6]

Chrysippus said that a drop of water that falls into the sea changes not only the whole ocean but also the whole universe, and there is no object, no phenomenon of the universe in which we cannot read, as in a book, what is happening in the universe as a whole. This idea of a co-penetration of all things, and of the presence of the whole in each of its parts, this idea also concurred with psychological existence.[7]

So, as you can see, there's a lot to say about the materialism of the Stoics. What's certain is that while they made God enter profoundly into the world and, all in all, spirit into matter, they in return made matter go halfway toward what we call spirit and even divinity.

These premises, these preliminary explanations were necessary, gentlemen, so as to be able to characterize the Stoic idea of necessity. From this conception of the universe, and also of divinity, the Stoics concluded universal and, as they said, absolute necessity. That is obvious.

How, in fact, did this doctrine essentially extricate itself from Aristotle's doctrine? And what, in short, led Aristotle to preserve freedom, the free will whose idea, incidentally,

had been conveyed to him by Plato? In short, when we get to the bottom of things, the Stoics and Aristotle would agree, and I think all the ancients would agree on this point, which is that necessity should exist in the universe. The universe should, in all of
[150] its parts and in all of its changes, be subject to laws that are absolutely intelligent and reasonable. The universe should be reasonable, and of course, if everything is reasonable, if everything is rational, there's no place for indetermination, nor for contingency, for things will be exactly what they must be. On this point, then, there's no divergence among ancient philosophers, they all, basically, agree on this point: if things were absolutely reasonable, rational, there would be no place for contingency, for indetermination, nor, consequently, in humans, for freedom.

If Aristotle accepts human freedom, and contingency in nature in general, it's simply because things aren't absolutely as they should be, because things don't entirely conform to reason. And why aren't things absolutely as they should be? What proves that the universe is not absolutely rational? According to Aristotle, according to Plato, the proof is evident, the thing is obvious, as it were. What proves that things are not as they should be is that there's movement, that there's change in the universe. Movement, for Aristotelian and Platonic philosophy, movement is the tangible proof of the imperfection of things. If the world entirely conformed to reason, to intelligence, there would only be Ideas, immutable Forms; the universe would be something like the geometer's world, whose essences rest on their immutability. But there is movement, there is change, there is becoming, things are perpetually transforming. And this proves that things are not what they should be and that there's a gap between what is and what should be. And it's this gap, this interval that brings about contingency in the world. This gap can be measured by contingency. Undoubtedly, for Aristotle, the freedom of the human isn't randomness, isn't chance. But it does have the same principle as randomness and chance, in the sense that it's the radical contingency of things that makes human freedom possible, the function of our will being to put things back in place, as much as that's possible, and to make it such, in regard to what we're concerned with, that things are what they should be.

[151] So it's because things are not what they should be that there's contingency in the universe, indetermination in things and freedom in humans—but for the Stoics, and this is the big difference, for the Stoics, things are what they must be for the very simple reason that for the Stoics, change, movement is not an imperfection, since they look for their explanatory principle in something that has the same nature as discourse. Discourse is something essentially mobile. Discourse isn't like the Form, like the Idea, *eidos*, something we contemplate in its immutability. No, discourse is a thing that unrolls, that goes here and there, and that reaches an endpoint via all kinds of detours, no doubt—but a single idea gives birth to all this, there's a single meaning, a single signification. Consequently, the Stoics' principle is one that's intelligent, rational, and yet mobile, in movement; hence there's no longer any reason to consider that movement realizes a gap between what is and what should be. The world is exactly what it should be, and hence everything is rational, everything is intelligent, everything is philosophically explainable, which amounts to saying that there's no place in the universe for contingency, nor, consequently, any place for freedom in humans.

So universal necessity follows from Stoicism's very principle. The Stoics expressed this principle in many ways, and we're spoiled for choice among the texts from Greek Stoicism that have survived, although only relatively few and fragmentary texts have done so. I'm going to limit myself to the most precise formulation, a passage from Alexander of Aphrodisias in his *Peri heimarmenes*, in his treatise *On Fate*.[8] Alexander of Aphrodisias is refuting the Stoics and Chrysippus in particular: "Nothing is without a cause; it might as well be said that something can come from nothing."[9] To say that something can come about without a cause is to maintain that something can come from nothing. So nothing comes about without a cause, and he concludes that the same causes always produce the same effects: "in the presence of identical causes . . . there is every necessity that the same [152]
things should happen." This is a passage from Nemesius, *De natura homini*.[10]

This is, stated in different terms, the same principle contemporary determinism formulates: the same causes have the same effects. This is the principle that governs all of nature. Nature is subjected to ineluctable laws because the conditions being determined, what happens is determined.

John Stuart Mill, in particular, draws on this principle: the same causes produce the same effects, the negation of human freedom, the negation of free will in humans.[11] As soon as the same causes have the same effects—given the same conditions, given the same situation, the same motives, the same motivations—the same action will happen, and consequently, our activity is subjected to ineluctable laws, like the rest of nature.

When we come to this argumentation, we have to wonder whether the same causes can ever recur in the psychological world.[12] I'm willing to grant that the same causes always produce the same effects, but I wonder whether the same causes ever recur. Does the same situation ever recur, the same external situation and the same internal situation, the same external situation and the same state of mind? Ah! Yes, if the same situation recurred exactly, we'd end up with the same thing, but the two things would be but one, the two situations would be but one, and as soon as they are distinct, they cannot be similar. Consequently, we could at a pinch grant this principle, but this in no way entails the necessary negation of human freedom. But I close this parenthesis.

So there we have the exact assertion of universal necessity. We could find other Stoic texts that further characterize this necessity, but, this time, by the sympathy of everything with everything, that is, by the absolute interdependence of things, or, as we'd say today, of the phenomena of the universe among themselves. What characterizes universal necessity, that by which it can be defined, is precisely that nothing happens in [153]
one point of the universe that doesn't have an impact somewhere else.

Note that physical determinism today proffers as its principle, as its own formulation, the law of the conservation of energy. This law means that when a change occurs somewhere, there must be another change, complementary to it, somewhere else.[13] This is a necessity of the same kind, as it were, as the Stoic's sympathy, but, and this goes without saying, it's something a lot more precise in the sense that the law of determinism thus formulated makes the phenomena calculable, it's something mathematical, whereas the interdependence the Stoics spoke of is something more anthropomorphic and as it were more organic. They think about the universe—this was one of their images—as being a kind of immense animal, such that if we prick one part of the animal, the entire body feels it. There's a Stoic text that says exactly that.[14] Nevertheless, in the mind of the Stoics as in the mind of modern determinism, universal necessity is above all the perfect interconnection of all the parts of the world, a connection of such a kind that nothing can happen somewhere without having an impact somewhere else and, in the end, everywhere, for we can always repeat, step by step, the same line of argument and say that a change that occurs in turn presupposes another, and so on indefinitely.

In short, and to summarize everything, I'd say that if we grant contingency and therefore freedom, we thereby accept that there are closed systems in the universe.[15] And we accept, consequently, that there are changes of the closed systems, for example, represented by human beings or living beings, the changes being connected to their actions—whereas to assert universal determinism, universal necessity is to say that there are no changes within the nature of these closed, independent systems and that the entire universe forms a single closed system.[16] The Stoics very clearly said that the universe is this kind of closed system, and in this sense they provided a formula of universal
[154] necessity as precise and as rigorous as was possible in their time.

It's obvious that this principle of universal necessity entails, in particular, the negation of free will in humans, and the Stoics said so, too, with the greatest precision. They stated that the *logos*, or the soul, of the world—the *logos spermatikos* insofar as it is considered, if you like, in the entire universe—that the world-soul is the same thing as fate. And since fate rules the phenomena of nature at the same time as human actions, there's one single law that governs not only nature but also, in humans, everything that has been, everything that is, and everything that will be.

The Stoics thus deduced the negation of free will as an immediate consequence from the principle of their system, but they confirmed this principle with other reasons as well. In the Stoics texts we have, we find the a posteriori demonstration, as it were, of the necessary determination of our actions.

First of all, the Stoics took up the Megarians' argument I've presented at length in this course, the argument according to which one of two opposite propositions relative to the future is necessarily true. Aristotle refuted this argument.[17] The Stoics refuted this refutation. How? We don't know, no texts on the subject have been preserved. But what's certain is that the Stoics considered Aristotle's refutation, which I presented here, to be invalid. It's not certain, for that matter, that all of the Stoics, on this point, took up the Megarians' idea. We'd undoubtedly have to mark some reservations, especially where Chrysippus is concerned. But another a posteriori proof, which all of the Stoics accepted, was the proof drawn from predictions, from divination.

Divination was held in great honor in antiquity. On this point the Stoics accepted the widely held, popular beliefs. According to them, the future can be predicted. Oracles, augurs predict the future. Yet if the future can be predicted, that's because it's
[155] predetermined. There we have an experiential [*expérimental*] proof of what today we call determinism, the fatedness of human actions. Calling it "experiential" might be saying too much, since one might have wondered whether the prediction of human actions was really possible and whether divination was something serious. But it's remarkable—we'll

have to come back to this point—that, in all ages of history, people have considered what is only a theoretical construction to be an experiential truth. I'm not saying that this is the case with all so-called experiential truths, but there is no a priori construction that doesn't take on the appearance, the illusory form of an experiential truth. The possible prediction of the future among the ancients, then, was one of these kinds of constructions. It's certain that there is, I wouldn't say experiential, but at least empirical evidence of determinism accepted today that at its core consists only of a priori hypotheses or mental constructions, that will, perhaps, have the same effect on our descendants as the proof of the fatedness of human actions the ancients drew from divination has on us.

Be that as it may, this was one of the Stoics' arguments against human freedom. Then, there was a more serious argument: the refutation of commonly accepted ordinary ideas and in particular Aristotle's ideas on the subject of chance and randomness. For, among the ancients, the idea of free will, of free choice, was intimately tied in with—this goes without saying—the idea of contingency—and here, the ancients were right. And the idea of contingency, for its part, was tied to the idea of chance, to that of randomness. Although Aristotle clearly opposed, in the texts we talked about, choice to randomness and to chance, nevertheless, if choice is possible, it's because there's contingency in nature and because this contingency present in nature generates, according to Aristotle, chance and randomness.[18] The Stoics were the first to maintain in a completely rigorous way that randomness was not a reality, that the notion of randomness is, as we would say today, completely subjective, that randomness is a word we use to cover up our ignorance of the true causes, the determinant causes.

Such, gentlemen, were the Stoics' arguments against free will. But here the fact appears that I already announced several times in this course: we're face to face with a [156] fatalist theory, a theory that absolutely denies free will in humans. It's the essence of such a theory to aim to agree with common sense and above all to aim to absorb into itself, to resorb, I said, the previously accepted theory of human freedom.

Unfortunately, the treatise by Chrysippus hasn't been preserved,[19] who, as I said, is the most important member of the school, the genius of the Stoic school. But from the fragments by Chrysippus that have come down to us, we can glean not that he was looking for something intermediary between the doctrine of necessity and that of freedom, as some have claimed[20]—no, he believed in the absolute necessity of all things—we can glean that he aimed to show that freedom is preserved in a fatalist theory like the one he advocated, that the belief in freedom is preserved as such in the doctrine of absolute necessity. And it's very intriguing to see that he goes about demonstrating this exactly as modern philosophers had to go about it, as Leibniz in particular did, to demonstrate that his determinism is equivalent to freedom.

As far as we can tell based on the texts that have come down to us and which are insufficient, as far as we can tell by means of a reconstruction, Chrysippus must have said something like this: to believe in freedom, to assert freedom is to assert three different things. First, when we act, when we accomplish an action, another action was possible. This is the first thing: to believe ourselves free is to believe that, when we act, another action was possible. Second, to believe in freedom is to believe that, when we act, we're the author of our action. In fact, to believe in freedom is just that, it's to believe that we've produced our action ourselves, that we're its author. Finally, to believe in freedom is to believe that we deserve praise or blame based on whether we acted in a good way or in a bad way.

It's thus to believe these three things. But according to Chrysippus, judging by what
[157] has come down to us, these three assertions subsist as such, just as correct, just as legitimate, just as true, in the theory that asserts universal necessity.

Let's begin with the first of these assertions. Chrysippus's argumentation on this point appears to have been extremely subtle, but no more subtle than Leibniz's. He wrote a treatise on the possible, in four chapters. In this work, he defined the possible: that which happens when nothing prevents it from happening. We call "possible," he says, that which happens when nothing prevents it from happening, and he appears to have understood by that rather something like this: we call possible that which could have happened when we see no impediment to it having happened. Thus, when we act, our action undoubtedly is absolutely determined, it is fated. Nevertheless, there are other actions of which we perceive clearly, rightly or wrongly, that they could have happened if there'd been no impediment to them happening. So our action is contingent. We must call "contingent" that which happens in such a way that another thing would be possible. Possibility consists in the fact that we perceive no impediment to it happening.

The response to him was: but this contingency is only an appearance. As soon as your action happens necessarily, another action could not have happened and was prevented from happening. You believe that there was no impediment, but there was one as soon as what you did was actually done.

Chrysippus replied to this in an extremely subtle way by providing a definition, now, of necessity. He said: what is necessary, what in fact excludes the belief in free will is that which is true for all eternity, for example, "two plus three equals five." So there we have something necessary; what is expressed by an eternally true proposition is necessary. But an action I do today, which is expressed, for example, by this proposition, "Here's what I did today," this proposition has begun to be true today. It has thus not been eternally true, and in this sense it's not necessary.

In short, Chrysippus's argumentation probably amounted to saying this: there are
[158] absolute necessities. But when we're speaking about our freedom, we thereby understand that we are not subject to an absolute necessity. We're right, in the sense that absolute necessity is a logical necessity, like the necessity of this proposition, "two plus three equals five." Yet we're not subject to that sort of necessity. If we are subject to some sort of necessity, it's an entirely different kind of necessity, which consists in a proposition that begins to be true only when the action is accomplished.

Gentlemen, this appears very subtle, but it's exactly what Leibniz said in his *Theodicy* and elsewhere when he claimed that his doctrine, which is an absolutely determinist doctrine, didn't change anything about everything admitted on the subject of freedom. In paragraph 52 of part one of the *Theodicy*, he puts it as follows:

> All is therefore certain and determined beforehand in man, as everywhere else, and the human soul is a kind of spiritual automaton, although contingent actions

> in general and free action in particular are not on that account necessary with an absolute necessity, which would be truly incompatible with contingency.[21]

So it's the same thesis: everything is determined, everything is certain in advance. Everything we must do is determined in advance and nonetheless the actions we call free and contingent aren't for all that necessary, aren't of an absolute necessity.

I'm not going to provide a lengthy presentation of Leibniz's proof, but in short it amounts to this: what we call absolute necessity is a geometrical necessity like two plus two equals four, since when we take a factual proposition, I'll randomly take this one: "I went for a walk today," it's not a proposition that presents such absolute necessity. It wouldn't be absurd that I didn't go for a walk today. We call possible that whose contrary is not absurd. The contrary of what I did today is not absurd. It was thus possible, even though what I did today was necessarily and fatalistically determined by the sympathy—here I'm using the Stoics' expression on purpose—by the sympathy of all the parts of the world with one another, since in order for what I did today not to have been done, the whole world, from beginning to end and including even the [159] smallest details, would have had to be radically different from what it is. Everything is thus determined and nonetheless the actions that we call free really are free actions in the sense that these are actions whose contrary is possible—provided the contrary does not imply an absurdity or a contradiction, as the contrary of the proposition "two plus two equals four" does. This, in short, is Chrysippus's argumentation, as far as we're able to reconstitute it.

We come now to the second point. The issue is to establish that in such a theory, the actions that we call free are indeed actions of which we believe ourselves to be the authors. On this point, the Stoics' proof was very simple. What does it mean to be the author of an action? It is to feel that this action emerged naturally from the sensible and intellectual states in which we are placed, so much so that being the author of an action is to feel that this action has emerged from an inclination we find ourselves having, and from the decision we made, from a choice we made, or, as the Stoics said, from the assent we've given. So, in the case of the actions I call free, there was an inclination on one side, spontaneity of the senses, and there was also the consent of the intellect. The action I call free has thus indeed emerged from my will, since it emerged from what composed my will, inclination and reason. Now, the inclination had to be what it was; the consent had to be what it was; it was fated that I had this inclination, fated that I made this judgment, fated that the action emerged naturally from this judgment and this inclination—yet, by definition, we call those actions "voluntary" that seem to conform to our will, we call "free" the actions emanating from us, the actions that conform to our consent.

There are thus, to talk like the Stoics, there are fatalities and cofatalities, *fatalia* and *confatalia*.[22] There are things fated and things co-fated. Let's suppose that only the act, all alone, were fated—ah! I wouldn't feel free. But since it's not only my act that is fated but also my inclination and my consent, which are connected to this fatedness by means of a cofatedness—ah! I am free, my freedom being, precisely, the concurrence of these elements, which are all necessary.

[160] Here again, we'd find the same argumentation in Leibniz, in paragraph 55 of that same part one; having formulated his determinism, he says:

> This consideration demolishes at the same time what the ancients called the "Lazy Sophism" which ended in a decision to do nothing: for (people would say) if what I ask is to happen it will happen even though I should do nothing; and if it is not to happen it will never happen, no matter what trouble I take to achieve it. . . . But the answer is quite ready: the effect being certain, the cause that shall produce it is certain also; and if the effect comes about it will be by virtue of a proportionate cause. Thus your laziness perchance will bring it about that you will obtain naught of what you desire, and that you will fall into those misfortunes you would by acting with care have avoided. We see, therefore, that the *connexion of causes with effects*, far from causing an unendurable fatality, provides rather a means of obviating it.[23]

Thus, if I do nothing, what will happen will be the effect of my laziness—but my laziness was fated, as are the consequences of my laziness. The very role of will and freedom is thus defined by a series of cofatalities, as it were.

Finally, the remaining third point: we act as though praise and blame subsisted, according to the Stoics. In fact, we praise what is good, we censure what is bad, just as we admire or do not admire a good or a bad painting; these are as it were aesthetic qualifications.

According to an argument preserved by Alexander of Aphrodisias, the Stoics said something like this: we honor the gods and we praise them, we consider them as those among all beings who are the most praiseworthy, and yet they don't have to choose between good and evil, they can only do what is good. Praise and blame thus address acts, behaviors, and beings in whom choice and will are not necessarily found.[24]

It's a very intriguing thing that we find this reasoning in all of the modern determinists. We'd find more than one passage in Leibniz going in this direction, but the passage—
[161] unfortunately we don't have time to read it completely—the passage that presents the most intriguing parallel is perhaps this passage from [John] Stuart Mill's *The Philosophy of Hamilton*, in chapter 26, which is entitled "Freedom of the Will." He puts it like this—it's likely that he wasn't familiar with the Stoics' texts, yet he makes exactly the same hypothesis:

> Suppose that there were two peculiar breeds of human beings,—one of them so constituted from the beginning, that however educated or treated, nothing could prevent them from always feeling and acting so as to be a blessing to all whom they approached; another, of such original perversity of nature that neither education nor punishment could inspire them with a feeling of duty, or prevent them from being active in evil doing. Neither of these races of human beings would have free-will; yet the former would be honored as demigods, while the latter would be regarded and treated as noxious beasts.[25]

It's always the same idea, that praise and blame do not imply free will.

Gentlemen, I wanted to insist on this Stoic doctrine because of its importance in the history of philosophy. To finish up on the philosophy of the ancients, we still have to lay out very briefly Plotinus's very interesting views on freedom. That will be the subject of the next lecture.

Notes

1. Heraclitus, fragments D85–7 in "Heraclitus," *Early Greek Philosophy*, ed. and trans. André Laks and Glenn W. Most, vol. 3, *Early Ionian thinkers, Part 2*, 114–337 (Cambridge, MA: Harvard University Press, 2016), 179.
2. This is still the commonly accepted interpretation today. Recall, however, that Bergson in the preceding lecture (100 and 102n13) tends toward a slightly different interpretation, which he further develops in this and the following paragraphs, based on the Stoic distinction between "corporeals" and "incorporeals." One of the great French texts on this question was written at this exact time by one of Bergson's students, Émile Bréhier, who may have attended these lectures. See Bréhier, *La Théorie des incorporels dans l'ancien stoïcisme* (Paris: Picard, 1908).
3. That is, from the disciples of Aristotle.
4. The typescript reads "Aristotle's Idea of Form."
5. Bergson laid out this argument already in TFW, 88–90/65–7.
6. It is worth recalling, perhaps, that both the Greek prefix *sym*– and the Latin prefix *con*– mean "with"—*sympatheia* is "feeling with" and *conspirare* means "to be in harmony with."
7. The verb Bergson uses, *concourir à* (in the sense of "to contribute to," "to work toward"), should probably be conjugated in the present, since the theory he is discussing is not explicitly stated by the Stoics.
8. Alexander of Aphrodisias (approximately 150–215 CE) was an Aristotelian renowned for his commentaries on Aristotle. Bergson devoted the Saturday course in 1900–1 to explicating Alexander's treatise *On Fate* (see M, 438).
9. Bergson seems to be referring to chapter 22 of *On Fate*; the translation here is from Bergson's French, but the text is available in English. See *Alexander of Aphrodisias On Fate*, trans. R. W. Sharples (London: Ducksworth, 1983), XXII, 192.9–16, 70–1.
10. Nemesius, bishop of Emesa, was a Christian theologian of the fourth to fifth centuries CE. The section Bergson is referring to, entitled "On Fate," targets the Stoic doctrines in particular; see *On the Nature of Man*, ed. and trans. R. W. Sharples and Philip J. van der Eijk (Liverpool: Liverpool University Press, 2008), 184–6. The quote is from sec. 35, p. 185.
11. John Stuart Mill, *A System of Logic: Ratiocinative and Inductive*, III.5 and VI.2, in *Collected Works of John Stuart Mill*, ed. J. M. Robson et al., 32 vols. (Toronto: University of Toronto Press, 1963–91), 7: 306–69 and 8: 836–43.
12. This is an argument made in TFW, 199–201/149–51.
13. Bergson will return to the law of the conservation of energy in the March 24, 1905, lecture, 165–6; for more on his interpretation of it, see CE, 213–14/242–3.
14. Bergson is probably referring to Alexander of Aphrodisias's treatise *De mixtione*, in which Alexander critically reconstructs a line of argument in the Stoics. See *Alexander*

of Aphrodisias on Stoic Physics: A Study of the De Mixtione with Preliminary Essays, Text, Translation and Commentary, ed. Robert B. Todd (Leiden: Brill, 1976).

15. "Closed off by nature" and not artificially closed, which does not prevent them from being open in the sense that there is metabolic exchange with what lies outside them (CE, 18–27/12–23).
16. For Bergson, in contrast, the universe is indeed, like living beings, a system "closed off by nature," albeit one that is in "progressive growth" (CE, 14–18/12–23 and 296/343).
17. See the January 27, 1905, lecture above, 73–7.
18. This is in the second book of Aristotle's *Physics*.
19. Bergson is probably referring to Chrysippus's *On Fate*, of which only a few fragments survive, for instance in citations by Cicero (see next note).
20. Bergson seems to be referring to chapter 17 of Cicero's *On Fate*. See Cicero, *On the Orator, Book III, On Fate, Stoics Paradoxes, Divisions of Oratory*, trans. H. Rackham (Cambridge, MA: Harvard University Press, 2004), xvii: 235–7. Leibniz contests this interpretation in a text Bergson himself comments on approvingly in the April 14, 1905, lecture; see below, 207–8.
21. Leibniz, *Theodicy*, I.§52: 151.
22. See, for example, Cicero, *On Fate*, which mentions Chrysippus in this context (xiii: 225–7).
23. Leibniz, *Theodicy*, I.§55: 153, Leibniz's emphasis.
24. See *Alexander of Aphrodisias On Fate*, sec. 37, 91–2.
25. John Stuart Mill, *An Examination of Sir William Hamilton's Philosophy, and of The Principal Philosophical Questions Discussed in His Writings*, ed. J. M. Robson, *Collected Works of John Stuart Mill* 9, ch. 26: 456. The proximity of the French to the English text—and its divergence from the published translation by Émile Cazelles, *La Philosophie de Hamilton* (Paris: Baillière, 1869), 560—suggests that Bergson translated the passage himself.

LECTURE 10
FEBRUARY 24, 1905

Gentlemen, before we take on the Neoplatonic theory of freedom, which will conclude [163] the history of ancient philosophy portion of the course and after which we'll move on to the moderns, we must say a few words, as I announced the other day, about the Epicurean theory of freedom and of necessity, since both are found in Epicurus.[1] Even at first glance, it would be hard to overstate the importance of Epicurean philosophy in relation to the theories of freedom and necessity, since the Epicureans provided—following Democritus, by rather diluting the force of his doctrine—a theory of necessity that, looking at it from the outside and taking it externally, seems to come quite close to certain modern and even contemporary theories.[2] On the subject of freedom, too, in relation to contingency, they put forward views so radical that, to find something equivalent, we'd have to clear an interval of twenty centuries after Epicurus and reach, I'm not simply saying the moderns but, even, our contemporaries. Concerning necessity, Epicurus, following Democritus, laid out the thesis we today call the thesis of mechanical necessity. He, too, sees the material universe as a series of mathematical points that act and react on one another in such a way that these reciprocal actions and reactions are the exclusive [consequence] of the respective positions of these points in relation to one another.[3] This is the very formula of mechanical necessity: a universe composed of points subjected to forces that are a function of distances, as we would say with more precision today.[4] Neither Epicurus nor Democritus said these things with such precision, but there [164] is in both of them the same kind of doctrine.

I'll add that they gave a schema of this mechanical necessity to which the universe would be subject, a representation that comes quite close to those of modern science. As it is for the moderns, the material universe for Epicurus, and for Democritus as well, is composed of discontinuous elements separated by empty intervals, each of which is indestructible and unchanging, capable of moving in such a way that through connections [*rapprochements*], through combinations of atoms with each other, through the variation of their relative positions, different phenomena, diverse manifestations of matter are generated.

When viewed from the outside, this atomism is analogous to that of the moderns. It goes without saying that the atom of the modern physicist and especially that of the modern chemist is an atom endowed with much more specific properties. We've endowed the atom with everything necessary, for example, for its properties to explain all the modalities of chemical combination. We also assume attractive and repulsive actions between the atoms that the ancients did not assume. For that matter, had they made such a hypothesis, they would have been unable to do anything with it, given the

state of their mathematics. There are thus profound differences between this atomism and that of current science, or at least that of science a few years ago, for, as you know, the theory about the constitution of matter is undergoing a transformation that might be quite profound.[5] Nevertheless, if we consider ancient atomism and the atomism of almost current science from the outside, there are clear analogies. The main one is that on this particular point of mechanical necessity, these two schemas are rather similar. The idea of mechanical necessity is in Democritus and in Epicurus, and then—this goes without saying—it reappears in modern philosophy. I said the other day that the Stoics presented a conception of universal necessity, but this isn't a purely mechanical necessity like that one.[6] For the Stoics, the necessity of natural phenomena
[165] is due solely to the interdependence of all the parts of the universe among themselves. It's because each part of the universe is indissolubly connected to the whole that it is absolutely determined both in what it is and in what it does. For them, the world is an animal, a living being, a huge animal, and just as we cannot jab one specific spot in an animal without the whole body feeling the prick, so in the material universe we cannot disturb one part, however small it may be, without the totality of the universe being upset by it. But this interdependence is an organic one. I'll add that it is a rational interdependence. The universe is a discourse in which everything fits together and whose meaning, whose signification, is simple. And because the universe, in its totality, considered across space and across time, has an absolutely determinate meaning, a determinate signification, we couldn't modify one little part of it without disturbing the whole, since the whole would [then] no longer have the same meaning. In a perfectly composed discourse, one that would be perfection itself, given the meaning of the discourse, the signification, the idea to be established, all the sentences would follow from one another, and in each sentence each word, and in each word each syllable, each letter, each stress. We couldn't disturb one stress without the meaning of the whole being changed.[7] In a doctrine like that of the Stoics, necessity descends from the whole to the parts: because the indivisible meaning of the whole is given, each part must itself be determined.

Necessity of the Epicurean kind and mechanical necessity generally are entirely different, the opposite. Here, necessity does not descend from the whole to the elements, it ascends: it ascends from the elements to the whole. There's no signification, there's no meaning of the whole, there's, consequently, no idea determined by the discourse. No, there are only letters, the letters of the alphabet; they are thrown across space; they meet; we will be able to read what results from their meeting, yes, all of that can yield a meaning, but that's simply random, and what's necessary, in short, are the elements.

We thus have a radical difference between these two kinds of necessity. In the Stoic doctrine of necessity, necessity is the determination of the whole, considered as
[166] something simple and undivided, and this necessity descends to the elements, which are to the whole as the letters of the alphabet are to the whole discourse; whereas in the Epicurean doctrine, in Democritus's much more than in Epicurus's, necessity is based on the elements and in the course they take,[8] and the necessity of the whole is only the sum, as it were, of these elementary necessities. There's no question that of the

two conceptions of necessity, the one of Democritus and Epicurus is a lot closer to our modern conception than [that of the Stoics].

To be sure, gentlemen, in Epicurus, as far as we can judge from texts that have come down to us, the doctrine of mechanical necessity doesn't have the purity we find in Democritus's theory. You know the modifications to which Epicurus subjected this theory: to the necessary movements of atoms Democritus spoke of, he adds contingent, whimsical movements that allow the atoms to veer to the right, or to the left, to swerve from the path that, as Lucretius says, destiny has set out for them, such that historians of philosophy were able to say that Epicurus's doctrine isn't a doctrine of necessity but a doctrine of randomness.[9] That would be to exaggerate things a lot, and it would even be to not characterize Epicurus's doctrine exactly. There is in Epicurus—as far as we can tell from the texts—there's a doctrine of contingency, but it's added onto the doctrine of necessity: it's a doctrine based on necessity. In all likelihood, Epicurus made use of the swerve of atoms, of this whimsical force that atoms possess, only to explain, first, the formation of the world in general, but [also] the details, to explain the actions of human beings and of living beings in general.[10] For everything that belongs to the explanation of physical phenomena, in all likelihood, he didn't take the swerve into account. He would consider a material object to be composed of atoms that possess, besides their fated and necessary movement, a power of swerving whose whimsical movements balance each other out such that [the swerving] does not appear in the whole, in the total object.

When we look at Lucretius's poem—Lucretius being the disciple par excellence of Epicurus—from beginning to end, [we see] that Epicurus[11] insists on fatedness, on the [167]
absolute necessity of the phenomena of nature. This is the very leitmotif of his poem; there's a certain number of verses or groups of verses that recur rather often, with slight modifications, and express this idea: "Certum ac dispositum est," "It is determined, it is fixed once and for all."[12] And when he explains the objective of his poem, he says, "Doceo dictis quo quoeque creata / Foedere sint, in eo quam sit durare necessum," "What I am teaching is certain: it is necessary that each thing continues to be what it was at the moment of its formation."[13]

The text is much more formal: "foedus" is a treaty. By a kind of treaty, nature has committed itself to preserve things as they are. We also read: I teach "what can be produced, what cannot be produced and how each thing has a determinate power and a determination which has its deep roots," "Quid possit oriri, / Quid nequeat, finita potestas denique cuique / Quanam sit ratione atque alte terminus haerens."[14]

This is thus really a theory of determination, of the necessity of the course of nature. Granted, Lucretius accentuated "necessity" more than Epicurus did. But Lucretius is a faithful disciple of Epicurus, and in the very texts by Epicurus that have come down to us, we'll find the expression of the belief in necessity, in particular, the statement of the principle at the origin of every kind of mechanism and every kind of determinism: nothing comes from nothing.[15]

Gentlemen, the doctrine of necessity is thus indeed at the basis of Epicurus's philosophy. But superposed on this doctrine of necessity, there is, as I announced a moment ago, the doctrine of freedom and, more generally, of contingency in nature. In

fact, if the atom is subject to laws that govern its natural movement, it can, according to Epicurus, at a certain moment, veer off, carry out a transversal movement, *paregklinein*—"para" indicates transversality—it can deviate very slightly from the line it's supposed to follow, and this deviation happens without any reason, it's a whim of the atom. It can bear right, left, deviate from the path that destiny assigns it: this is the *paregklisis*. The
[168] Greek word has been translated as *déclinaison*. This swerve is a phenomenon that some scoffed at,[16] but this idea that has been scoffed at is quite understandable if we go back to the probable origins of the doctrine. Epicurus valued human reason, and he did so for reasons of a practical order: if humans are not free, they cannot choose the rule of their conduct, their ethics. Epicurus provides a kind of morality made to be adopted by people, [made] to give them peace of mind. There must therefore be freedom for humans to be able to choose their rule of conduct. Animals, with which humanity shares many characteristics, must also be free. If humans, if animals are free, then—since they are made of atoms, of the same elements as nearly all of nature—freedom, or at least contingency, must be found in the elements in general.[17] For Epicurus, the human soul, like bodies, is made of atoms, it's a body. For him, the human soul is a composite of atoms that are more mobile than others, but in the end it's made of atoms. States of mind, ideas, feelings, representations, all of those are certain groupings of atoms; when the groupings change, the states of mind change, too, just as when we turn a kaleidoscope, there are different images obtained from different groupings of pieces of glass. So the soul is made of atoms, like bodies, and if we grant the soul the faculty of choice, then it's because the atoms that compose it are not subject to absolutely fatal laws, because they have the faculty to veer off slightly, to deviate slightly from the course that mechanical necessity sets out for them. If the atoms of the soul have this property, all the atoms possess it; hence the *paregklisis*, the sideward movement, becomes a general property of the atoms composing nature, the universe.

This very briefly summarizes the theory of contingency in Epicurus's physics. As I said at the beginning, to find something like it, we'd need to cross twenty centuries after Epicurus and reach modern philosophy, Cartesian philosophy, for it's in Descartes that we find necessity also at the base of the universe. The universe is subjected to mechanical laws, to the laws that Descartes has formulated. Nevertheless, human freedom exists, freedom in the sense of choice; it is superposed onto this necessity. To be sure, Descartes
[169] didn't say, as the Epicureans did, that this freedom suppresses natural necessity. No, Descartes believed, rightly or wrongly, that this freedom could be superposed onto the mechanism of nature without suppressing it.

To be sure—and this is another very important difference—Descartes confined, limited this freedom to the movements carried out by humans. There are thus profound differences, and if we wanted to find, on this point, doctrines that are closer to Epicurus's doctrine, we'd have to, as I said earlier, reach the contemporaries, reach the philosophers who believe in contingency being present everywhere in nature, in a radical contingency inherent to the elements.[18]

Very interesting theories have appeared in our time that tend to compare the laws of physics, the most precise laws governing nature, to the laws the statisticians present to us, which express regularities underneath which there are irregularities, but irregularities that compensate for one another, that balance one another out. When we consider people who cross the same bridge every day, when we count them up, we find that every day, with few exceptions, every day more or less the same number of people cross the same bridge. So here we have an original law, a regularity. However, none of these people in particular was obliged to cross the bridge and their crossing the bridge has something accidental to it; it's a contingency. Each person was able to cross the bridge on a whim, but all the whims of all the people who cross the bridge are compensated by [the whims] of those who do not cross the bridge, such that in the end we have an average that is always more or less the same. The laws of nature would be something like this. When we take a material object, however small it might be, it's a world: it's composed of an enormous number of parts. When we take a phenomenon occurring in this object, however short-lived it might be, it fills an enormous interval from the viewpoint of nature, in the sense that, during the smallest fraction of a second that we spend perceiving it, billions of billions of vibrations of elementary phenomena have occurred.[19] We perceive only the exterior of things, just as what we perceive of the states of mind of the people who cross a bridge is the exterior. We perceive—how do I [170] put this—phenomena only in bulk, as it were. It could be, it's possible, it's probable even, as some people say, that if we considered the phenomena that are strictly elementary, we would find inclination,[20] contingency, but all these indeterminations compensate for one another. In short, we're dealing with a nature that grosso modo, seen through our senses—which consider only enormous masses—we're dealing with an absolutely regular nature, subject to an absolutely necessary law.

As you can see, this doctrine came out of Epicurus's doctrine, since Epicurus put contingency into the elementary movements. Epicurus also—this is at least probable—understood the necessity of phenomena to result from all the whims and from all these elementary indeterminations, in a way, compensating for each other.

This is why, gentlemen, we can say, as I said at the beginning, that of all the doctrines of antiquity, the Epicurean doctrine concerning the questions of necessity and freedom, if we consider only its outside, its external appearance, is the one closest to our own. And yet, a very intriguing phenomenon occurred: first, that Epicureanism has played no role in the genesis, in the appearance, and in the development of the modern doctrines I was just talking about, and then, that Epicurean physics has had almost no influence on the course of ideas both in antiquity and in modernity. I just opened a parenthesis on Epicureanism in this lecture; I'm going to close it. We'll no longer be concerned with this doctrine except to mention it here and there when it makes a sporadic reappearance in philosophy. Epicurus's ideas on the subject of freedom and necessity did not evolve.[21] They didn't produce anything, while ideas less close [to our own] that our science and our philosophy were to come to, less precise ideas, evolved and exercised a considerable influence. When we take the Stoic doctrine of necessity, which we talked about earlier, a necessity much less precise, less mechanical than the necessity that regulates the atoms of Democritus and Epicurus, when we take Stoic teaching as it appears in Neoplatonism— [171] despite Plotinus who constantly fought against it but was under its influence—this teaching, contributed by the Neoplatonists, reaches the moderns and plays a role in the evolution of the conceptions of necessity. Just as, when we take the theory of freedom in Plato and in Aristotle, this theory that spells out necessity in a less precise, less radical form than Epicureanism, this theory, again thanks to the Neoplatonists, crossed the Middle Ages and reached modernity. Still today, with the profound modifications I'll talk about, these ideas are part of the intellectual substance on which we are living.

We might thus wonder—this would lead us to a more general question—we might thus wonder why theories like that of Epicurus on the problem of freedom and on the problem of necessity remained sterile while others evolved. I repeat, this is a very general point, but paying attention to it is worthwhile. What we might find, perhaps, is that the destiny of an idea, its force of evolution, that is, the influence it exerts or that it possesses over minds, this force has a lot less to do with the content of the idea, with what I would call its "materiality," than with the primary impulse with which it was endowed, with the impetus[22] with which it entered the world. We could say—here I'm borrowing an image from a body in motion, from ballistics[23]—we could say that there are ideas that are like projectiles: what's in the idea itself is less important than the force of projection, than the initial speed. There's not a lot of difference between the bullets of our sophisticated rifles, at least the bullets we still used a few years ago, and the bullets used in the slings of antiquity: they were pieces of lead. The difference, rather, lies in the initial speed as they leave the weapon. It's the same with ideas. The materiality of ideas, what they contain, what we see of the idea, is perhaps less important than what we don't see, that is, the impulse [*impulsion*] the one who made it enter into the world of ideas endowed it with.[24] The word "impulse," to be sure, is something very vague, and we'd have to look for a way
[172] to define it in a general way, which would be rather hard to do. Yet, in the particular case we're concerned with, that's not difficult: we're dealing with a theory of necessity that didn't evolve and with a theory of freedom that had no influence either. What is this due to?

I said at the beginning of this course, gentlemen, that the raison d'être of the theories of necessity is that they can satisfy the demands of reflective thought. The intellect that reasons, the intellect in the strict sense, needs to picture things within a framework of necessity, and this is because it needs, as I said, to form pairs, to consider each thing as necessarily connected to the condition, to the situation in which it occurs.[25] When we take a modern conception of mechanical necessity, we see that it satisfies this need fully and completely. And why? Because it comes about, it emerges from the very discoveries of science. Our conception of mechanical necessity, of universal mechanism, our very conception of the universe as composed of discontinuous points, of material points subject to forces that are a function of distances, this conception was suggested by modern mechanics. And this mechanics itself emerged from the scientific discoveries of the Renaissance, from Kepler's law, from Galileo's law, as well as, later, from Newton's laws.[26] So this mechanism expresses this mechanics, which itself expresses these fundamental laws. And this allows us to understand the very character of the schema by which we pictured matter until recently, that is, as composed of points that act and react on one another, more or less the way the sun and planets reciprocally influence each other in our solar system. Our conception of matter is largely astronomical.[27] The conception of mechanical necessity such as we find it in modern science is nothing other than the generalization of certain laws that were discovered at the beginning of our science, and that are, in short, the expression of certain very general facts. This mechanism is an explanatory mechanism: with this schema of mechanical necessity we can account for determinate phenomena.

When we take mechanical necessity as we find it in the Epicurean doctrine, on the [173] contrary, [we see that] it doesn't explain anything. It can't be applied to any determinate fact, and, all things considered, when we place ourselves in the viewpoint of the ancients, this conception of necessity is less scientific than the Stoic conception of necessity. To someone in antiquity, the Stoic conception of necessity allowed at least for giving explanations of different phenomena that weren't very precise, anthropomorphic explanations, granted, but they were explanations, and in any case this doctrine accounted for the appearances. The universe does in effect look like an organism in which everything fits together. In contrast, the Epicurean doctrine of necessity didn't account for the appearances since no one has ever seen the movements of atoms, and it also couldn't explain any determinate fact. It was thus, for its time, less scientific than the Stoic conception of necessity.

And what about the doctrine of freedom? What is the raison d'être of a doctrine of freedom? I said, also at the beginning of the course, that while the raison d'être of a doctrine of necessity is to satisfy the demands of reflective thought, a doctrine of freedom must satisfy what I call "immediate consciousness." It must respond to the givens of immediate consciousness. It must, to a larger or smaller degree, be the work of intuition. And if the theory of freedom we find in Plato and in Aristotle has borne fruit, if it has evolved, it's because it's retained something, I said, of Socratic inspiration and because something of the profound inner life of someone like Socrates passed into their theories of freedom. When we look at the doctrine of freedom in Epicurean physics, we find that there's nothing inward about it; it's been constructed from the outside. Why does Epicurus believe in the contingency of the movements of atoms? Because he believed in human freedom. But why does he believe in human freedom? Because humans must be free to choose their rule of conduct. Epicurus never appeals to the inner life, never. His disciples learned certain formulas by heart.[28] There's thus nothing intuitive in the [174] origins of this doctrine, just as there's nothing explanatory in the Epicurean doctrine of necessity.

It's thus, of the two doctrines, the one of necessity, the other of freedom, it's thus because the first has nothing explanatory, the second nothing intuitive, that neither the one nor the other has evolved, the history of philosophy showing us that a doctrine of necessity owes its force to its explanatory power and a doctrine of freedom to the power of impulse, as it were, it was given in the inner life.

Now I come to the more general question I stated earlier: in a general way, what makes it such that a philosophical idea has or doesn't have a certain impetus at its origin, that it has a force of penetration or not, that it has vitality or that it lacks this vitality? Gentlemen, undoubtedly, a lot could be said on this point, but perhaps this is what's essential: a philosophical idea, in short, develops, evolves, and influences minds in proportion to what I'd call its "degree of positivity," I mean in proportion to the affirmation it contains. In contrast, it's sterile, it's impotent, it's inert in proportion to the negation it contains. A critique that's nothing but critique, a negation that's nothing but negation, is, from the philosophical viewpoint, struck with sterility and impotency. When we study the history of doctrines, we're amazed to see how little of all that is critique remains. Critique is what makes the biggest impression at the moment it occurs. A critique is something that can always be formulated in a way that is more precise and more scientific, and it's pertinent in the moment, but then hardly anything remains of it. When we read the polemics between philosophers, objections and responses, we see that nothing or nearly nothing has remained of these polemics. If something does remain, it's because they have mixed dogmatic affirmations into the critiques and polemics. In a critique in general, what subsists is the dogmatic part the critique contains in a virtual way.[29]

When we take the most significant critical work in the history of philosophy, Kant's critique, which is the most formidable attack on metaphysics ever imagined, what emerged from it? The boldest metaphysics emerged from it, Hegel's philosophy emerged from it, etc., that is to say, they looked for the metaphysical seed in Kant's critique, not [the seed] of critique but of dogmatism that this critique contained, and that is the seed that evolved. In philosophy, and even almost everywhere, critique is what takes hold immediately; but what subsists are the dogmatic elements this critique contained, if it contained any, otherwise very little of it remains. An idea can be criticized in detail, it's no worse off: it will subsist as long as no other positive, dogmatic idea has replaced it. This seems to be a general law in the history of philosophy, and that's very easily understood: the mind lives on affirmations and not on negations. Negation is always clear-cut, a lot more clear-cut than affirmation. There are no degrees in negation, while there are degrees in affirmation. This is why negation always appears in a form a lot more precise, a lot more clear-cut and clear than affirmation, but it's struck with sterility and impotency.

The historians of philosophy get this right, and they instinctually guess the character of an idea. If this idea is an idea with a purely critical and negative origin, its form may well be affirmative, the idea does not evolve, it cannot evolve; just like an idea with an affirmative origin: the form may well be negative, this idea evolves all the same. When we take Epicurus's doctrine, we find an application of this law. Following Democritus, Epicurus affirms the fundamental necessity of the laws of nature, the necessity of the movements of atoms, as the substrate at least of the phenomenon of the swerve. But what is this affirmation for Epicurus? In his thought, it's nothing other than the negation of the intervention of the gods in nature. Epicurus's mechanism means nothing other than that. Epicurus wants to grant humans freedom by freeing them from the fear of the gods. For him, the issue is to show that the gods do not intervene in the course of nature, and this will be proven if it's established that nature is subject to laws, or, as we'd say today,
[176] subject to purely internal forces. Epicurus granted physics importance only insofar as it was capable of delivering us from superstition.[30] Although this doctrine of necessity thus

may well appear in the form of an affirmation, it's only a negation, and [the historians] got that right.

When we take Epicurus's doctrine of freedom, in short, the doctrine of contingency, it's the same thing. Why does Epicurus affirm that humans are free? We find the reason in one of Epicurus's texts preserved by Diogenes Laertius: "It were better, indeed, to accept the legends of the gods than to bow beneath that yoke of necessity which the natural philosophers have imposed."[31] In other words, once Epicurus posits necessity in nature to banish the gods from it, he affirms the contingency of the movements of atoms and human freedom to banish from nature the fatalism that the physicalists were able to find in it. And since this doctrine of necessity is but a negation of the gods' interventions, I'd say that the doctrine of freedom is but a negation of this negation, the negation of the necessity that had thus made its way into nature. So, at least from the viewpoint of its physics—I'm not talking about its ethics, which is of great importance and had a great influence—but, from the viewpoint of its physics, it's a doctrine of pure negation, and that is probably why this doctrine had so little influence and why it hardly evolved, and, even, didn't evolve at all, while, in contrast, doctrines that were objectively less true, doctrines that were more distant from the results modern science was to lead to, have had a very great destiny.

Gentlemen, it was perhaps worthwhile, precisely because there is an application of a general law here, to insist a little too much on Epicurus's physics, on Epicurus's doctrine of necessity and freedom. To conclude, we still have to present a sketch of the theory of freedom in the philosophy that is like a synthesis of all of ancient thought, Neoplatonist philosophy. That will be the subject of the next lecture.

Notes

1. Bergson may have made this announcement informally before or after an earlier lecture.
2. Less famous than Epicurus and their later disciple, the Roman Lucretius, Democritus of Abdera (ca. 460–370 BCE) and Leucippus were among the founders of ancient atomism.
3. Since the construction in the typescript, "are exclusive of the respective positions," does not make sense, the sentence is likely missing a noun.
4. In Newtonian physics, a body exerts on another body a gravitational force that varies not only by virtue of its mass but also by virtue of the distance that separates them, namely in inverse proportion to the square of this distance.
5. An allusion to the first developments of quantum mechanics. Almost immediately and thanks to first-hand knowledge of Max Planck's articles on black body radiation of 1900–1 and Einstein's breakthrough series of articles of 1905, Bergson had a sense of the potential of quantum mechanics for the renewal of physics as a whole. The "science of a few years ago" alludes to the physics of James Clerk Maxwell and, especially, of William Thomson (Lord Kelvin) and Michael Faraday, according to which atoms are principally "centers of force"; see TFW, 206/155; MM, 264–6/224–6; and CE, 181–2/204–5.
6. A reference to the earlier lectures of February 10 and 17, 1905.
7. Compare the example of the musical phrase in TFW, 100–101/75.

8. The typescript says *démarche*—approach, steps (to be) taken—which the French edition amends to *marche*—march, progress, operation.

9. Lucretius (*c.* 99–55 BCE) was a Roman poet and philosopher, a distant disciple of Epicurus, and one of the main authors by whom Epicureanism is known to us. Bergson is referring to his famous poem, *On the Nature of Things*; see Lucretius, *De rerum natura*, trans. W. H. D. Rouse, rev. Martin F. Smith (Cambridge, MA: Harvard University Press, 1924), 2.216–93: 113–19.

   "Historians" refers above all to Jean-Marie Guyau, author of *La Morale d'Épicure et ses rapports avec les doctrines contemporaines* (Paris: Ballière, 1878).

10. What Bergson here calls *déclinaison*, or "swerve," is the *clinamen*, the central doctrine of ancient atomism, introduced by Epicurus and taken up by Lucretius. Bergson's first explanation of the *clinamen* appears in the sentences that follow; he will develop it later (e.g., 118).

11. Read: "Lucretius."

12. Lucretius, *De rerum natura* 3, verse 787; see also verses 794–5. The translation in the text renders Bergson's own. The full Latin text is: "certum ac dispositum est, ubi quicquid crescat et insit." In Rouse's translation: "It is fixed and arranged where each thing is to grow and have its being" (249). Bergson's development of his point here follows rather closely the one in a very early text of his, the *Extraits de Lucrèce: Avec commentaire, études et notes* of 1883 (in M).

13. *De rerum natura* 5, verses 55–7: "Cuius ego ingressus vestigial dum rationes / persequor ac doceo dictis, quo quaeque creata / in eo quam sit durare necessum." Rouse: "His footsteps I tread, his reasonings I follow, whilst I teach in my discourse by what law all things were made, how bound they are to abide in it" (383).

14. Lucretius, *De rerum natura* 1, verses 594–6. Rouse: "what could arise and what could not, in a word, in what way each thing has its power limited and its deep-set boundary mark" (49).

15. See Epicurus's letter to Herodotus in Diogenes Laertius, *Lives* 10.38–39: 567–9. The Epicurus texts that have survived are three letters (to Herodotus, to Pythocles, and to Menoeceus) as well as a number of maxims and sayings.

16. It was ridiculed from the very first time it was stated, for example by Cicero in *On Fate* (sect. 20: 243–5).

17. The "nearly" (*presque*) in the sentence does not mean that certain zones of nature contain something other than atoms (according to Epicurus, even the gods are composed of atoms) but rather that at least some of the atoms that constitute humans and animals are, because of their round and smooth shape, much more mobile than other atoms.

18. Bergson seems to be thinking of Émile Boutroux, the author of the 1874 book, *De la contingence des lois de la nature*, English translation: *The Contingency of the Laws of Nature*, trans. Fred Rothwell (Chicago, IL: Open Court, 1920). Bergson alludes to this book on the last page of *Matter and Memory*. But, like some of the statements at the beginning of the lecture, the considerations that follow refer to theories that are a lot more recent, namely, to the initial developments of quantum mechanics.

19. In *Matter and Memory*, Bergson provides the example of red light, which vibrates four hundred billion times per second (400–480 THz, in fact), while our eye grasps it only as a stable quality—the color red (MM, 272–3/230–1).

20. Given the context, it is possible that this *inclinaison* should read *déclinaison*, "swerve."

21. In the sense that, in the history of life, certain species have crossed the ages in their original form.
22. This "impetus" is the *élan* made famous by its role in *Creative Evolution*.
23. From Greek *ballein*, "to throw."
24. Bergson uses similar imagery to illustrate the evolution of life in *Creative Evolution*, 93–4/99–100.
25. He is referring to the first lecture of the course on December 6, 1904, esp. 13–14 and 15–16.
26. CE, 289–90/333–5.
27. CE, 34/30.
28. See book 10 in Diogenes Laertius, *Lives*, 528–677.
29. Compare ME, 77/62–3.
30. See Epicurus's letter to Pythocles in Diogenes Laertius, *Lives* 10.85-87: 615–17.
31. This passage is from the letter to Menoeceus, preserved in Diogenes Laertius, *Lives of the Eminent Philosophers* 10.134: 659.

LECTURE 11
MARCH 3, 1905

Gentlemen, we must complete this very quick examination of the problem of freedom [177] in the ancients by discussing, as I announced the other day, the Neoplatonists and, in particular, the head of the school, Plotinus. Plotinus's doctrine of freedom is by far the most complete, the most highly constructed of what the ancients have bequeathed to us on this question. Overall, Plotinus's philosophy appears as the most systematic that the ancients have handed down to us. As I've already said,[1] we must make an effort at reconstruction if we want to think, for example, Plato's philosophy as a unified philosophy. And there are many ways we can get it wrong, since there's no evidence that Plato conceived his philosophy with this systematic unity. Similarly, when we study Aristotle we realize that we're dealing with analyses that bear on a very large number of ideas, but as for the synthesis, it hasn't been done, it's up to us to do, and there's no evidence that we won't go, when we attempt this unification, much further than Aristotle wanted to go. But when it comes to Plotinus, it's entirely different.

Plotinus constructed his doctrine not once but as many times as he wrote treatises, and he wrote fifty-four of them. His work has reached us intact. There is hardly a book of the *Enneads* that is not a view on the whole of the system.[2] It's thus one great construction, perfectly coherent, perfectly unified.

I'll add that this philosophy, at the same time as it appears in a synthetic form, as a synthesis of itself, is also a synthesis of all Greek philosophy.[3] This is what Plotinus [178] wanted to do, and we mustn't be mistaken about the nature, nor about the objective of Plotinus's work. Plotinus lived in the third century CE in Alexandria, in an environment where all the religious and philosophical doctrines of the East were able to meet, but he wasn't much under their influence. We might perhaps find traces of this influence in the tone in which he expresses himself, a tone of inspiration, a semi-religious tone, very distant from that of someone like Plato or Aristotle. But that's about all, and if we consider the materiality of his doctrine, we see that we are really dealing with Greek, and exclusively Greek, thought. Plotinus wanted to be Greek. Plotinus's idea is that the doctrines that tend to supplant those of the Greek philosophers are barbaric doctrines; that there is reason to look for a certain number of ideas, well-known ideas, in all philosophers of classical antiquity; that these must be unified into a whole; and that a seawall, so to speak, must thus be built to counter the rising tide of new ideas.

Plotinus thus started from the idea that there is a Greek philosophy and that this philosophy has a unity. The thought in the back of his mind[4] is that the truth is found in Plato and that Aristotle only repeats Plato, deforming Plato. That's why Plotinus's teaching is so close to Aristotle's, to such a point that when we read him, we are hard-pressed to say whether we're dealing with Aristotelianism or Platonism. Plotinus thus started from the idea that Plato and Aristotle said more or less the same thing. As for those who came before Plato and Aristotle, they had a sense of what Plato and Aristotle were going to say. Those who came after, in the beautiful things they said, repeated and developed Plato and Aristotle. As for the Epicureans and the Stoics, Plotinus leaves them aside or, rather, considers them to be deviations from Greek philosophy—he constantly fought the Stoics—but, in a word, his idea is that there's a great current of Greek thought, that it must be grasped and its direction clearly marked.

This, then, is the fundamental idea of Plotinus's philosophy. We misunderstand his
[179] philosophy when we consider it to be a kind of eclecticism. It's certain that we find in Plotinus nearly all of the ideas of the Greek philosophers, but does that make his philosophy an eclecticism? It would be eclecticism if we had a juxtaposition of ideas, but in Plotinus, the ideas borrowed from his predecessors are not juxtaposed, they are blended, and all this forms an absolutely coherent and systematic unity. We don't have theories placed end to end, as it were, along an indefinite line. No, we have to picture a circle and the radiuses of a circle—but radiuses that are not complete, that do not reach the center. Plotinus conceived the different Greek philosophers as having placed themselves on different points of the circumference and having aimed at the center. Each of them thus followed a radius, as it were, but without reaching the end.[5] Through an effort of thought and reflection, Plotinus follows each of these radiuses to the end, he reaches the center, and he thereby obtains an idea that, for him, is the quintessence of Greek philosophy. This is why Plotinus's philosophy is so instructive for anyone who wants to understand antiquity, and even modernity. When we have an idea, even just a vague one, of Plato and Aristotle, then when we read Plotinus, we'll understand Aristotle and Plato much better. We must then return to Plato and Aristotle, and we realize that, thanks to Plotinus, we've gone very far along lines whose direction they simply indicated. That is why studying Plotinus is so useful for understanding Greek philosophy.[6]

Gentlemen, in regard more particularly to the problem of freedom we're currently concerned with, the study of Plotinus's philosophy is doubly interesting. First, for the very reason I just pointed out to you: Plotinus allows us to understand everything that's essential in the ancient philosophers as an intuition, properly speaking, of freedom. We find hardly anything in him but what's in Plato and Aristotle, but it's much more systematic, it's more coherent. And precisely for this reason, in him, we see the difficulties that the ancient theory of freedom raises much better. Plotinus made an effort to resolve these difficulties. He didn't always succeed, but at least he highlighted them, and he posed the problem in its most precise and, as it were, most acute form.

[180] Then, this study has another advantage, precisely because it allows us to identify the quintessence of the Greek ideas on the subject of freedom. We see the contrast with certain ideas contemporaneous with them, which we'll have to talk about next time and which prepared the modern doctrine of freedom.

Christianity overcame Neoplatonism, but having vanquished it, it absorbed certain essential elements of this philosophy, by transforming them, incidentally, and by transfiguring them as an intermediary. This philosophy exerted a profound influence on our modern philosophy. Plotinus will allow us to determine with precision the ways in which this new conception of freedom differed from the ancient conception.

From this double viewpoint, the study of Plotinus's philosophy in general and of his theory of freedom in particular is of great interest. Seeing how little time we have, I can unfortunately only present a very brief and very insufficient sketch of this theory. Let's say simply that we'd have to focus our examination on three essential points.

The first point is this: Plotinus, I said earlier, fought the Stoics, and the Stoics' fatalism in particular, but he was also under their influence, he couldn't not be under their influence. He was under their influence in the sense that, despite everything and as if despite himself, he believes, with the Stoics, in a perfect regularity of the course of nature, in the unity of nature. The Stoics introduced this idea into Greek philosophy, and it wasn't possible not to take it into account. In Plotinus, we find a large number of passages where this unity of nature, this interdependence of all of its parts, this regularity of its course are fully brought to light.

I'll cite only a couple of texts, those that are quite characteristic of and essential to the theory of freedom. For example, in the fourth Ennead, paragraph 32, we read: "We must posit that our universe is a living being"—here we have an image borrowed from the Stoics—"a living and single being that encompasses all the others within it. This universe is thus sympathetic to itself, and what is distant is close"—that is, what is distant in space [181] is close sympathetically—"the way that in an individual animal, the nail, the horn, the fingers and all the organs, which nonetheless do not touch one another, are close."[7]

Plotinus thus has a Stoic image in mind here. He conceives the unity of nature like that of an organism whose parts are separated in space but are contiguous, as it were, by means of the influence they exert over the others and by their reciprocal interdependence.

Elsewhere, in the third Ennead, we find other images that express the same thing. Perhaps the first we'd have to cite is the passage in which Plotinus compares the material universe to a dance.[8] In a dance, he says, there's a multitude of movements, movements of the arms, the legs, the body. Each of these movements is made up of an infinity of movements of the muscles, of the joints, and if we wanted to explain one of these movements by means of other movements, we'd undoubtedly manage to do so, since all of it hangs together, but we'd never see the end of it. There's a complete, a possible explanation of the whole, which would have to be conveyed in the idea of the one who dances. The one who dances is not conscious of all of his movements, he is simply conscious of one thing: he wants to dance. This simple idea then divides into an indefinite multiplicity of movements. What we call the multiplicity of these movements is, in short, nothing other than the unity of the intention.

Among these many passages, there are thus several in which Plotinus compares the organism of things to a dance. Plotinus insists on this point: the sympathy of the parts with one another arises simply from that it divides them, as it were, it divides the unity of the intention.

Then we have a passage that might be good to read because it expresses the same thing but in a different way. Here, the universe is compared to a drama, a play. This point is essential from the viewpoint of the comparison between Plotinus's teachings and

those that were to supplant Neoplatonism. In regard to this comparison, Plotinus tells
[182] us that the things of this world are not serious, that all of that has the importance of a play, the importance, the regularity, and the well played order of a play: "The battles that mortal humans wage against one another in a well-regulated order like those humans who have fun dancing a Pyrrhic dance indeed show us that the affairs which humans find serious are only the play of children." And a little later: "Murders, deaths of all kinds, the storming and pillaging of cities, all of that we must consider as we consider, at the theatre, the change of scenery and costumes with all the theatrical imitations of cries of suffering and sorrow."[9] So we always see in these different images—the image of a drama, the image of a dance, the image of an organism in which everything fits together—so we always find the same thought, that of a well-regulated unity that is constitutive of the course of nature.

Once this unity of nature is established, Plotinus wonders how it's compatible with human freedom. He poses this question with the greatest precision. The problem is posed in the third Ennead. I'll translate the sentence word for word. "It suffices to find a solution that, on the one hand, preserves the principle of causality"—literally: will leave nothing without a cause, that preserves the sequence and the order of things—"and that, on the other hand, will allow us to be something."[10] The issue thus is to find a solution that, on the one hand, preserves the order and the sequence of nature, the unity of nature; that leaves nothing without a cause; that fully satisfies the principle of causality; that nonetheless does not absorb the self, as we would say today, into nature but allows the self to be something.

The problem of freedom had never been stated with such precision, and we can say that still today we wouldn't be able to formulate it in other terms nor with more precision.
[183] This is indeed the question: there's a unified nature, it seems, in which everything is regulated, in which there are laws that govern in a necessary way the connection of causes and effects, and nonetheless we believe that we are something—each of us believes himself to be something and even to be someone. How are we to remain something and nonetheless preserve the unity and perfect coherence of nature? Plotinus stated the problem; I am not saying that he solved it. The solution of the problem, for that matter, is inseparable from the solution of another problem.

I come to the second point, which is even more essential than the first in Plotinus's philosophy. The big question—if the issue truly is to make humans something or someone and, nonetheless, not to break the structure of the natural laws for that purpose—the question is what the relation is between the human being considered as thought, as will, in a word, as mind, and the human being considered as a body, as acting in space and time.

If we opt for the fatalist solution, like that of the Stoics, if, in a word, we opt generally for what today we call determinism, the question doesn't even arise. There are material elements that act and react on each other. In certain particular situations these material elements organize themselves into living beings. But the independence of these living beings is purely relative: it's only an appearance and there are, in short, only absolutely necessary reciprocal actions and reactions of all the material elements on one another.

But if the human truly is something, as Plotinus says, and if nevertheless the human is inserted into the course of nature, then the issue is to explain how it's possible that from one angle the human obeys natural laws and from another angle the human is distinct from them. In other words, the big problem is to explain life.

In a purely determinist and, at its core, purely materialist doctrine, life enters into the category of the other phenomena.[11] But when we accept the idea of an at least relative independence of the human from nature, we thereby attribute a certain kind of special origin to life, one that differs from that of pure composite matter. The theory of freedom, in other words, is complete only if it presents a theory of the origin of life, of the origin [184] of organic life.

Plato and Aristotle had already conceived this theory, but not in this form. It's not a theory of organic life they propose but, well, a theory—how do I put this—of the entry of the individual into the body that represents this individual from the viewpoint of nature.

We find this theory in Plato. You recall that for Plato the sensible world contains bodies. The body is part of the sensible world. Then, there's the soul, which has descended into the body. This soul was living in the world of Ideas, it was contemplating the Ideas, then it fell and forgot what it saw, because of the very effect of its fall into the body. The soul thus enters into the body. When and how? Plato doesn't tell us and, truth be told, this Platonic teaching is only a myth, a symbol, an allegory. What's underneath the myth? It's really difficult to say. Given his distinction between the sensible world and the intelligible world, Plato wouldn't be able to tell us either what a soul is or how it enters into a body with any precision. The soul cannot be an idea, nor is it a body; it's something in between, it's a mixture. What mixture? Plato doesn't tell us with any precision, no more than he tells us precisely how the soul's entry into a body is possible.

Aristotle abandoned this myth, but at its core, his conception is not very far from Plato's. To be sure, what he calls the soul is something a lot closer [*voisin*] to the body: it's the very exaggeration[12] of the body, it's the form of the body, it's what's truly human in each of us.[13] It's not the soul properly speaking, it's thought, it's intellect. Plotinus expressly tells us in these very terms that thought comes from the outside. It enters through the door at the moment of birth, it enters into the soul and then into the body. He doesn't tell us that it forgets what it's seen, but it amounts to nearly the same thing, since thought, which is knowledge, by its entry into the soul no longer has anything but the simple power of the knowledge of all things.[14] But a doctrine of this kind is very close [185] to the one that says that the soul at an earlier time knew all things, and once it entered the body, it forgot them.

Aristotle doesn't tell us with precision, no more than Plato did, where the *nous* comes from, where thought comes from, and how its entry into the soul and then into the body works. The problem is thus the same. The terms are different, but it's really the same problem that both Plato and Aristotle state and that Plotinus tries to solve. For it's in Plotinus, and only in Plotinus, that we find an attempt to solve this problem: What is the human? How does it come to be here? What did it come here to do? Where does it come from and what has it come to do?[15] This, then, is the second point worth examining in Plotinus's philosophy.

There's a third. Let's accept that the human has a certain independence from nature. Let's accept this idea of human freedom. Let's accept that on a certain point the human can—Plotinus didn't manage to shed light on this part of the problem—but let's accept that to some extent, the human can force the mechanism of nature and that that is its freedom: What's the value of this freedom? Up to what point does it make sense to use it? Isn't there a better way to use it? This is a problem quite characteristic of ancient thought. Let's say we can choose between different actions in space and time: is there reason to use this faculty of choice, or wouldn't it be better to choose to no longer choose, as it were, that is, to withdraw, to detach ourselves from this existence in space and time to reach a higher life, a superior life? Here we have a third problem; the central problem, as I said earlier, is the second one.

In many passages, Plotinus has provided us with the elements of an explanation—oh! a very complex, very subtle one—of what he calls the descent of the soul into the body, of the soul taking on of a body. Let's try to extract what's essential from this doctrine. When we consider a living body, an organism, we find that it's composed of different parts juxtaposed in space but perfectly coordinated to each other, working harmoniously
[186] together, in such a way that each part reverberates, as it were, with all that's happening in the others. As Plotinus says, they're distant in one sense and close in another. In space, they're distant, but they act as if they penetrated each other, each being a part of what's happening somewhere else. Thus, on the one hand, separation in space and yet, on the other, reciprocal interlocking and as if mutual penetration. Let's say that this unity of organization [*unité d'organisation*] is the soul, let's agree to call "soul" this something that puts all of the parts of the body together and ensures the harmonious functioning of all of the parts and their mutual agreement. We'll thus say that there is a soul in the body, or rather, since this will be more precise, we'll say that the body is in a soul. It's not the soul that's in the body, Plotinus says, it's the body that's in the soul.[16] There is a unity and then, inside of this unity, a diversity.

That said, given that what we see in space as an organized body is a divided unity, a complex unity, a multiple unity, can't we move, in thought, to a point where all these divided parts, all these elements separated from one another, meet and, so to speak, coincide? According to Plotinus, we must picture—it's a very subtle idea—we must picture the body, and also the soul—consequently the vegetative[17] soul, the organizing soul of the body—we must picture this body and this soul as a slackening of something, something that, in the state of being taut and concentrated, would seem to us to be united in a single point but yet, in souls and bodies properly speaking, is separated by intervals.[18] This point from which the soul starts, where everything that, in the body, is a systematically organized diversity is represented as a unity—this coherence and this systematization coming from this very unity—this [point] is what Plotinus calls the Intelligible or the Idea. In other words: the souls have their summit in what Plato called the world of Ideas, in what Plotinus, like him, still calls the world of Intelligibles, yet with the difference that the Platonic Ideas are never individual Ideas, while, for Plotinus, each individual has its Idea. There's Socrates in the flesh and blood who walks about in space
[187] and time; that's Socrates distended, as it were, into space and into time. Then there's

the concentration of Socrates, something indivisible, that in its unity expresses what the living Socrates expresses in its diversity. And this Idea of Socrates, which the living Socrates hangs on, so to speak, this Idea is in the intelligible world, the Platonic world of Ideas.

There's a very Neoplatonic image, which will perhaps make more sense of this thought Plotinus has. Picture a point of light and then, starting from this point of light, a cone of light made up of beams of light leaving between them, wherever there are no beams, an interval of darkness.[19] For Plotinus, the soul and the body are this cone of light seen from a certain distance from the summit: the beams of light are the soul, the set of beams of light, that's the soul. The darkness that separates the beams from one another is what Plotinus calls "matter." It's nothing, it's nothingness, but it's this nothingness that makes it such that the beams of light are separated from one another. If we want to abstract from this blackness, from this nothing, we must move to the summit of the cone, to the point of light where there's no longer anything but light. This is what Plotinus calls the Idea, the Intelligible, the starting point of the soul and thereby of the body: a very subtle but also very profound Idea intended to dispel all the difficulties of Plato's as well as Aristotle's teaching on this point. When Plato tells us: the soul descends into the body at the moment of birth, Plotinus accepts this idea. But this descent is not a historical fact, it doesn't happen at such and such a moment, it's always happening, at every instant, we are up high and we are also down below. Aristotle tells us: thought, the Idea, enters into the soul and consequently into the body. Plotinus accepts this doctrine of Aristotle's, since what he calls idea, *noētos*, is indeed thought, it's the *nous*, since each of the *noēta* contains the whole *nous*. He, too, says that thought enters into the soul and thereby into the body, but that happens at every instant. At every instant, our nature is double; at every instant, we are, seen from a certain angle, body and soul, and, seen from a different angle, pure Intelligibles.

This is Plotinus's viewpoint. I hasten to add that, in Plotinus's thought, this is not a construction. Undoubtedly, the doctrine is above all constructed, but at the same time, [188]
Plotinus claims that he's doing a work of intuition, and he draws this theory of the nature of the soul and its relation to the body—if I dare express it this way—he presents it as an experiential fact. According to Plotinus, if the body and consequently the soul as well are a kind of distention of what is our very essence—a distraction in the etymological sense of the word, "dis-traction," *dis-traere*, to pull from different sides—then we can, by means of an intense effort, by gathering ourselves up into ourselves, place ourselves back into the pure Intelligible, into this Idea of ourselves which is the essence of our self. And there, we become conscious of what we are in reality in a concentrated state, while usually, we know ourselves only in the distended and dispersed state.[20]

And, according to Plotinus, we can go even further, for the operation by which we go from our distracted self, distended into body and soul, to a concentrated self, which is no longer anything but a pure Intelligible, this operation can continue further and higher. For we must recognize that, for Plotinus, the different Intelligibles that make [up] such and such an individual, which are the source of different individualities, these different Intelligibles are, in short, only visions of an entirely superior unity. This is what

Plotinus calls the One or God, a being superior to Being: it is more than being, more than thought, more than Idea. All Intelligibles are only visions, so many visions of this superior unity.

Here again, according to Plotinus, the thing can be observed by a kind of internal experience, and this is what he called *exstasis*. It's a state in which, by means of an absolute simplification, the soul goes from the state of division in which it generally exists, first to a state of concentration, which is the state of the Intelligible, in order, from there, to overcome the Intelligible and reach what is more than thought.

We mustn't exaggerate, as some do at times, the irrational element in the ecstasy as Plotinus described it for us. His ecstasy, all in all, is quite close to the state of a soul that thinks the Intelligible. This is not something absolutely irrational. When we read Plotinus's *Enneads*, it's very difficult to determine which passages relate to the ecstasy
[189] and which relate to this move into the Intelligible, that is, into the intermediate region. Even if he often expresses himself in a way that suggests the opposite, it's probable that, for Plotinus, this passage from the first state to the second takes place through an imperceptible transition.

But here's a passage that gives us an idea of the matter—we'd have to read Plotinus himself to understand what he understands by these different states—that gives us, I'm saying, an idea of the method, not only of the method but also of the impression we undergo when we place ourselves in this higher state, or rather when we leave it, for it is easier to define this when we leave it than when we enter it. I'm talking about the beginning of book 8 of the fourth Ennead: "Often waking myself from my body"—Plotinus doesn't say, "waking myself from the sleep of my body," but "waking myself from my body," so for him, the body is sleep, it's sleep, it's the soul asleep—"often waking myself from my body and becoming external to the other things, internal to myself, contemplating a marvelously great beauty, having lived the best life, having coincided with the divine"—it's quite difficult to say whether this is about God, what Plotinus calls "the One," or about the Intelligibles, because the Intelligibles, too, are divine—"having coincided with the divine, having set myself up [*édifié*] in it, and having reached this activity of life up there, having set myself up [*installé*] above all the other Intelligibles, after this stay in the divine, having redescended into the intellect, into intuition by reasoning"—that is to say, having left the sphere of the Intelligible for that of the development of the Intelligible in time—"I wonder how I could indeed redescend, how my soul could indeed become internal to this body."[21]

Plotinus thus tells us there's a certain state . . . it's quite difficult to tell from this passage whether he's speaking of the ecstasy or the intermediary process, it's probably both. He says that it happens to him that he places himself in the divine and then when he redescends, it becomes a problem for him to know how he can indeed have a body. The problem is solved, so to speak, by the fact alone that he ascends, that he sheds the
[190] sleep of the body, but the problem arises in an insolvable way as soon as he redescends. Plotinus thus presents this observation of the existence of a point fixed, as it were, in the Intelligible, where the very source of corporeal and also animated existence would be, as a fact of intuition, and of a very special intuition.

This point being established, we have to wonder whether it's possible to give a rational explanation of the descent of the soul into the body. Plotinus asks himself the question in the following form: the body that lives in space and time is a body generated by a certain process and this process appears to us as a process of nature, a natural process. How is this natural generation of the body compatible with the adoption of a certain body by the soul or—if you prefer—by the pure Intelligible, which is above the soul? In a certain sense, we make our body, Plotinus will tell us, but in another sense, nature makes our body.[22]

I would have liked to present to you today the solution of this problem such as Plotinus gives it to us in a very interesting form, but I see I don't have the time for it. I'll thus postpone, gentlemen, the description of this part of Plotinus's doctrine until the beginning of the next lecture, and Plotinus's conclusion on the theory of freedom as well. In the next lecture, I'll set up a comparison between this conception of freedom and the one that develops in its full scope during the same period and was to replace this first one. Our next lecture will probably be the last before the series on modern philosophy. Immediately after that, we'll get to Descartes.

Notes

1. See, for instance, the opening of the January 27, 1905, lecture above, 71.
2. Porphyry, a disciple of his, collected and organized the fifty-four treatises Plotinus wrote into six "enneads" or "groups of nine."
3. CM, 227–8/217.
4. This "thought in the back of his mind" recalls Pascal's *pensée de derrière la tête* (*Pensées*, S650/L797: 196).
5. For this conception of the intellect, see, for instance, Plotinus, *Enneads* 6.9.8.
6. See also above, 44 and 48n29.
7. Bergson provides his own translations of Plotinus. Here he is citing *Enneads* 4.4.32; Armstrong's translation is on page 235 of the Loeb edition. The quotation inside this quotation comes from Plato's *Timaeus*, 30d3–31a1: 1236.

   In *Creative Evolution*, Bergson specifically refers to this very passage when he speaks of "the very unity of life, which is, to use an expression from an ancient philosopher, a whole that is sympathetic with itself" (CE, 151/168).
8. This passage is actually found in *Enneads* 4.4.33: 239.
9. Both of these passages are from *Enneads* 3.2.15; Armstrong's translations on pages 91 and 93.
10. Bergson quotes the very first lines of the paragraph, *Enneads* 3.1.8, Armstrong, 31.
11. That is to say, the same category as all other phenomena.
12. By *exagération*, does Bergson mean the realization, the concretion of the body? Whatever the term he pronounced, it should be a gloss on the Aristotelian idea of "entelechy."
13. CE, 300–1/349.
14. "Knowledge" here renders *connaissance*. The reference is to Plotinus, *Enneads* 4.8.4: 411.

15. ME, 71–3/58: “Whence do we come? What are we doing here? Whither are we bound? If philosophy could really offer no answer to these questions of vital interest, . . . we could well indeed say,—to adopt a phrase of Pascal,—that the whole of philosophy is not worth an hour’s trouble.” The reference is to Pascal’s *Pensées,* S118/L84: 25.
16. Here, Bergson is likely thinking of certain formulas in *Enneads* 4.3 he makes use of in his own work; see CE, 187n/211n1.
17. The typescript here has *indicative*; an alternative, though less likely, reading would be *intellective.*
18. In *Creative Evolution* (CE, 187n/211n1), Bergson attributes such a doctrine to *Enneads* 3.6.17–18: 277–85 and 4.3.9–11: 63–73.
19. Among the many occurrences of this image in Plotinus and in his successors, Bergson may be thinking of *Enneads* 1.7.1: 271.
20. For a similar description, see CE, 178/201–2.
21. Bergson’s translation of *Enneads* 4.8.1; Armstrong’s version is on page 397.
22. See *Enneads* 6.7.5–7: 101–9. Bergson invokes these passages in “Dreams” (ME, 117–18/96–7).

LECTURE 12
MARCH 10, 1905

Gentlemen, first, I'm going to finish quickly the presentation I began of Plotinus's theory of freedom. [191]

I divided the problem into three questions. First question: Can the human will break the order of nature, which Plotinus—with the Stoics, even though he fights against them—considers to be a regular order, the effects being tied to their causes? This is the first question.

The second is this: How does the soul take on a body or, rather, how does the intellect split itself into a soul and a body? This is the essential question in Plotinus's philosophy, since we are inserted into nature by the body, and consequently, the big question is to what extent we are what nature has made us and to what extent we are what we want to be.

Finally, the third question was this: If we suppose that our will can break the series of causes and effects and in this way force, as it were, the course of nature, is it desirable that we use this power? Or does true freedom not consist, on the contrary, in detaching ourselves from nature and in returning to what Plotinus calls the Intelligible?

Of these three questions, I said, the most important or at least the one that Plotinus discussed the most copiously is the second, the question of what *ensōmatōsis* is, that is, the soul taking on a body.[1] And I added that according to Plotinus, if we want to understand this operation, we must move to the Intelligible. The body appears to us as [192]
included in a soul, and the soul itself is like the distention or the dilation in space and time of an Idea, of an intelligible essence. This is what Plotinus calls the *noēton*, that is, the Platonic Idea, but this Idea has become that of an individual, no longer that of a genus.

So we elevate ourselves to this Intelligible. In this Intelligible, we find the root of the soul, and consequently of the body, which is but a kind of Intelligible. Moreover, we're going to encounter all the other Intelligibles: in the Intelligible, there's the Idea of Socrates, then the Idea of all the other individuals, in short, the Idea of all things, because when we particularize nature as we should, we find not so much things as beings. To each soul corresponds its Intelligible such that, in short, above nature, above the things scattered in space and time, we have the Intelligibles, of which the things, in a way, are but the relaxation and diminishment. These Intelligibles, taken together, constitute the intelligible world, *kosmos noētos*, or what Plotinus calls "the Intellect," the Intellect being the seat of the Intelligibles.[2] What characterizes these Intelligibles residing in the Intellect is that they aren't separate and distinct from one another, as things in space and time are. What we perceive in space and time are things that are juxtaposed or that succeed one another, distinct and consequently separated from one another, but [there,] there's space and time that cause this separation. There's necessarily reciprocal penetration, counter-penetration of all Intelligibles of one another, and thus each of them reflects all the others at the same time as it reflects the Intellect that is their seat.[3]

In a certain sense, the Intellect is the sum, the whole of the Intelligibles, but in another sense each Intelligible is all of the Intellect. In fact, all Intelligibles, according to Plotinus, are only viewpoints, as it were, on something that surpasses them all, viewpoints on what Plotinus calls the One, God, in a word, the absolute unity, which is more than Intelligible and more than Being.

Picturing things this way requires viewpoints or views of one and the same thing. Let's imagine, for example, a town situated in a valley and surrounded by an absolutely continuous string of hills.[4] From each of the hilltops, we have a view of the town. There'll be as many views of this town as there are hilltops, and, if we suppose there to be an infinity of them, there'll be an infinity of possible views. It's always the same town, and yet all the views differ from one another and each of them, in a certain sense, contains the others. Now, if we want to picture the Intellect, each of these views will be one of the Intelligibles. To obtain what Plotinus calls the Intellect, we'd have to suppose that, by means of a movement so fast as to be instantaneous, we could place ourselves in all the viewpoints at once, that we could bring them all together by means of a movement so fast that, all at once, we'd have the as it were global vision of all that appears, of all these successive viewpoints. We would then have the Intellect.

The Intellect is thus the set of Intelligibles, but the Intelligibles are, in a different sense, all of the Intellect, since in this global vision of the town seen from all sides at once there is nothing more than this same town that one can view from a single point. This, then, is the relation of the Intelligibles to the Intellect according to Plotinus.

That being established, the process of *ensōmatōsis* such as Plotinus pictures it appears rather clearly: we must picture all of nature, all of nature in space and time, as a body, as a huge organized[5] body, and this body is contained in what Plotinus calls the world-soul, the soul of the whole, *pantos psychē*. Every body is contained in a soul, and if everything is likened to one soul, this whole is the World-Soul.

What is this World-Soul? It's none other than the development of the Intellect in space and time. If we take this Intellect, the seat of the Intelligibles, this Intellect, while remaining where it is, can descend through a part of itself, just as beams of light start out from a point of light without the point of light being diminished in any way. For the
[194] Intellect to proceed in this way, for it to become a soul and consequently a body, it doesn't need to add anything to itself; it's not an addition, on the contrary, it's a diminishment. Just as, to draw beams from a point of light, there's nothing to be added except empty space, some sort of shadowy space all around, so that beams of light emerge from it—for it to radiate, we add nothing [*du rien*], as it were—so there's nothing to be added to the Intellect for it to become a soul and consequently a body and nature: on the contrary, a principle of diminishment, a shadowy principle must join it. This is what Plotinus calls "matter," something purely negative. This, then, is the Intellect that has proceeded in the form of a Soul and consequently in the form of nature.[6] What will this nature produce?

Being only the expression and the expansion of the Intellect, which is the set of the Intelligibles, it goes without saying that this nature will produce bodies that, considered by themselves, considered as parts of the whole, will reciprocally, as it were, correspond to the Intelligibles located in the Intellect.

Nature will thus produce Socrates's body through the usual process of generation. But what is Socrates's body? It's something that will have its corresponding Socrates in the Intelligible, since nature, which is the development of the Intellect through the effect of the Soul of nature, presents parts that correspond, each of them, to parts of the Intelligible. Nature will thus produce Socrates's body through its usual process, but there's an intelligible Socrates, the true Socrates, who at the same time, thanks to the same causes, will descend, will proceed, will seek to give itself a body. Just as the entire Intellect proceeds into the World-Soul and consequently into nature, so each Intelligible proceeds into an individual soul and consequently into an individual body. If nature didn't make the body, [the individual soul] would. Plotinus tells us that if it were alone, each individual soul could make all of nature, could reconstruct all of nature.

This is easily understood: from the moment that each Intelligible virtually contains all of the Intellect, each individual soul could do everything that the Soul of the whole does. But it doesn't have to do it, since at the moment when it would do it, as it were, it finds that the thing is done. The Soul of the whole, the universal Soul, which is, we could say, the older sister of the individual soul, the universal Soul blossoms into nature, and [195] in this nature, then, are the organic bodies in space and time in the form of individual souls.

In a sense, then, our body is the product of nature, of what today we would call "organic forces," which, according to a lot of people, are reducible to physical and chemical forces. But nature, Plotinus tells us, only sketches the individual body and soul, which would have produced it itself if the universal Soul wasn't there.[7] The individual soul is inserted into the body, it finds this body all prepared to receive it.

Plotinus returns to this point in many passages, and he expresses this idea in many images, often in the form of myths. He'll tell us, for example, that the soul first resided in its Intelligible up above. Then it was seduced, it contemplated itself in a mirror, in the mirror of Dionysus, he says, in the mirror of Bacchus. In effect, the soul sees its own image in matter, since the body nature sketches is the image of a soul situated in the Intelligible: [the body] reflects all of [the soul's] dispositions, all of its inclinations.[8]

The soul thus believes it perceives itself in this mirror: it's attracted—it's seduced—it falls. And from that moment on, it's captured in the body, it becomes its prisoner. This is just a way of speaking. When Plotinus presents the basis of his thinking on this point, he does it in a form that's a lot more precise and more scientific. We could find many passages; I'll refer to a particularly instructive passage from the sixth Ennead. We don't have the time to read it in detail. Plotinus tells us in this passage that the World-Soul could indeed produce a sketch: "What would prevent," he says, "the Soul of the whole from making a preliminary sketch, the Soul that is the universal *logos*, that contains all the *logoi*, before the individual souls settle in it, and what prevents this sketch from being a preliminary illumination of matter?" And then: "The soul that carries out the work"—this is the individual soul now—"going over these traces once more, articulating them piece by piece, makes the body and becomes itself that to which it has added itself, conforming itself to it."[9]

[196] Plotinus's language here is a bit obscure, but the idea is clear. This is what Plotinus means: he compares nature to an immense carpet, a carpet with lines going in all directions. By paying attention, I can separate out certain shapes on this multicolored carpet where the lines go in all directions, let's say a geometrical shape, a pentagon. Was this pentagon drawn on the carpet? Yes and no. No, in the sense that what was drawn on the carpet were the lines going in all directions, but what nature did not will—if it was nature that produced this carpet—is the pentagon. What creates this pentagon anew and brings it to life, as it were, is my attention, by focusing on this point and by organizing the lines in a certain way. Nature produces organic bodies, just as the one who produced this carpet draws certain shapes without drawing them, without willing them. For the body to truly organize, the individual soul must, furthermore, insert itself, by a kind of focusing, into the shape that it has separated out from the infinitely complex shape[s] of the carpet.

So this is indeed the idea I pointed to earlier: nature sketching the body but the body awaiting the insertion of a soul in order to become entirely what it must be; a soul, moreover, that would have produced the body if nature hadn't taken care of producing it.

This solution is very interesting, we may even say, very profound, and our philosophy may perhaps have an interest in transposing it into the language of modern science.[10] The solution, in short, amounts to this: we are part of nature. What we do and what we are comes from nature. But perhaps nature is still us, in the sense that perhaps nature as a whole is only the manifestation of something simple of which we're a part, for the simple, as Plotinus says, can, in a certain sense, be decomposed. In this case, what we call our "place in nature" is only the projection, as it were, onto the plane of space and time of the place we occupy in the intelligible, in the incorporeal, and in the extra-spatial.

This, then, is the solution to the second question according to Plotinus. If we looked
[197] at it more closely, we'd see, moreover, that Plotinus only pushed to the extreme, only exacerbated, as it were, the ideas of Plato and Aristotle, of Aristotle especially, on this subject.

We must now conclude very quickly. First, as far as the first question is concerned, can this soul inserted into a body or, rather, this soul containing a body occasionally break the mechanical circle of nature? Can we influence nature in such a way as to triumph over and vanquish the regularity of the laws of nature? Plotinus would say so; he would say so to remain faithful to the tradition of Plato and Aristotle. Twice he says that we have this power, in particular in the fourth book of the fourth Ennead, to which I refer you because we don't have the time to read this passage.[11] Plotinus says that we must take the reciprocal influences into account that may work on one another; he's fighting against Stoic determinism. The two or three passages we can cite in support of indeterminism of the will in Plotinus are all polemics against the Stoics, who are not named, but who are clearly at issue.

Plotinus thus lays out this view only to fight against Stoicism. He is visibly at a loss for an explanation of this indetermination of the will. In fact, there's a consequence that's incompatible with the premises of his doctrine: if all that happens in nature, if all of nature is only the projection of the Intellect into space and time, if consequently our body and all our body does is the projection into space and time of the Intelligible corresponding to our soul, then consequently everything that happens in space and time is only the projection of something given, something given all at once in the incorporeal and in the eternal. I don't see how indetermination in time can find its place here. The truth is that a doctrine of this kind, if it's self-consistent, ends up in something like Leibniz's preestablished harmony,[12] all the bodies of nature being perfectly ordered and coordinated in relation to one another for the very simple reason that they are the multiple manifestation of one single thing, perfectly unified and undivided in itself.

Moreover, we mustn't forget, we mustn't close our eyes to the fact that Leibniz's pre- [198] established harmony is something Leibniz borrows from Plotinus. I stressed this point some years ago.[13] Leibniz's monads are Plotinus's Intelligibles, each individual being a viewpoint on the whole; the relations between the Intelligibles, between the *noēta*, are entirely analogous to the relations that Leibniz later was to establish among the monads.

So in regard to this first question, Plotinus tries to solve it in the direction of indeterminism. It's clear that he manages to do so only with great difficulty and even that he wouldn't have managed to do it had he remained entirely in agreement with his principles. Here again, Plotinus is very instructive because he shows us that philosophers who were famous, Plato and Aristotle, that is, the philosophers whose teachings he follows, and whose ideas, as I said, he exacerbates—how these philosophers had introduced freedom, a bit like contraband, into their essentially intellectualist system, which lent itself to that only with some difficulty. It probably took reasons of a moral order to make them grant this place to freedom. However, there were other reasons, the belief in randomness, the ancient belief in the *automaton*.

That, then, is Plotinus's implicit response to this second question. This leaves the third: is it desirable that we be able to force the mechanism of nature? Is it desirable that our actions be able to pass through the meshes of necessity? If that were not desirable, the question we just asked, the question of learning whether freedom is really possible, would lose some of its importance, since if it's not desirable, there's no need to force the principles and the postulates of the system to establish its possibility. For this question, we have a very clear, very precise response from Plotinus. We have to go to book 8 of the sixth Ennead, which, incidentally, in terms of form, is one of the most beautiful Plotinus wrote. Its title is: "On Free Will and the Will of the One." In this book Plotinus asks himself this question—this is chapter five of the eighth book: do true freedom, true independence not consist, reside in action?[14] He answers: no. First, we are not masters of [199] the action, and this is what solves, in a rather precise way, the question whether Plotinus accepts or does not accept indeterminism. We are not masters of the action, of the accomplishment of our actions. Consequently, if freedom exists somewhere, it isn't in the accomplishment of the act. Where then must we put it? The last sentence of paragraph 5 tells us: "Freedom does not reside in action but in the intellect"—verbatim—"which is tranquil in relation to action, that is, in the intellect, which is not interested in action."[15] A little later, in the sixth paragraph, he will tell us that freedom and independence do not refer to the exterior but to the interior of thought and speculation.[16]

We'd find the commentary on this sentence, incidentally, in the eighth book of the third Ennead, which I explained here at length some years ago,[17] the book in which Plotinus establishes that what is above everything, and at the origin of everything, is contemplation, speculation, that all the rest, all that isn't contemplation, is but a diminishment of contemplation. We'd need to read several paragraphs from this book at length. I'll limit myself to quoting one or two sentences, for example, from paragraph 4: "Humans produce action when they are too weak for contemplation, action being only the shadow of contemplation. It's because they cannot see, and yet desire to see, that they act and that they produce."[18] Thus, the goal, the very foundation of life, what must be our goal, is to contemplate, to see the temple of the true. Those who act, those who produce, are those who cannot have this vision, who seek it, who want to fabricate, as it were, something that will give them an image of it, a necessarily imperfect and
[200] faded image. It would be better not to produce, not to act, and simply contemplate: "But everywhere we find that action and production are only the weakening of contemplation or its accessory,"[19] that is, its accompaniment, today we'd say its "epiphenomenon," it's its epiphenomenon. And here's the proof: "Witness the infants slow of mind who, incapable of science and speculation, turn toward the arts and crafts."[20] Thus, to act, to produce is an inability to contemplate, it's the inability to contemplate, and, in a general way—it's really a bit stronger—Plotinus will define action and production as a diminishment of contemplation. Let's suppose a being devoted to contemplation, let's suppose the contemplation growing dark, this becomes action, this becomes production, which is entirely in keeping with the premises of his system. How does the Intelligible become soul and body in space? By diminishing itself through an addition of materiality and obscurity. Consequently, to become entirely ourselves again, if we want to turn our freedom into the object that we should turn it into, if we want to recover ourselves, we must reascend the current by which we descended into space and time. We proceeded in the form of soul and body; we must reascend from the body and the soul to the pure Intellect.[21] By thus entering into pure speculation, we use our freedom in the truest way.

This is Plotinus's conclusion. Here again, Plotinus only presents the ideas of his predecessors and allows us to understand them. He allows us to understand them much more clearly by, as it were, taking the limit, as mathematicians say, for we find the idea that action and production are things inferior to contemplation in Plato, we find it especially in Aristotle, but much less systematized. Although it's an implicit postulate of his doctrine, Aristotle never went so far as to say that acting and producing consist in
[201] speculating badly, as it were, speculating imperfectly; he doesn't go so far as to identify action and production with a lesser speculation—that's what Plotinus does.

We're finished with Plotinus, we're done with ancient philosophy, we must now move to modern philosophy and to Descartes, which we'll do in the next lecture. We're going to take an abrupt leap. We have so few sessions available that the course is necessarily discontinuous. The point is not a complete history of the problem of freedom; the point is to highlight a certain number of important solutions to the problem by showing how they are connected to one another. However, we can't leave Plotinus without showing very briefly not what explains the transition but what explains the reversal of the viewpoint.

I just said that the last word of ancient philosophy is this: action and production are a weakness of contemplation. In the philosophy we'll consider the next time, Descartes's philosophy, we're face to face with the absolutely opposite idea. Where the question of freedom is concerned, this is one of the great ideas of modern philosophy. There are others, but this is one of the great directions and perhaps the main one: this idea is that on the contrary, action prevails over speculation, that the will is superior to the intellect in the sense that the intellect can be considered a creation of the will. In Descartes, we'll find the theory that it's the divine will that creates both things and reality, and even the truth. Descartes applies certain restrictions to this idea, but, in the end, it's in Descartes. God creates not only reality but the truth: in this sense, the understanding, like all truth, proceeds from the will. Undoubtedly, this infinite will, according to Descartes, is in God alone, not only de jure but de facto. In humans, the will is limited de facto because humans find before them nature already created and truth already created, but de jure, the human will, the soul is infinite, unlimited, and it could create everything, it can will anything. This is thus the reverse of the ancients' viewpoint on this question, the will taking first place and with the will, action in general.

The origins of this theory, it's been said many times, must be sought in Duns Scotus.[22] [202]
We don't know through what intermediary it reached Descartes, but very probably, whether he was aware of it or not, he owes the gist of this theory to Duns Scotus.[23] In fact, the idea that the will prevails over the understanding is very clearly expressed in Duns Scotus. But when we go to Duns Scotus's texts themselves, we see that Duns Scotus considers this idea to be a lot older, to go back to the very origins of Christianity. The influence of Christianity on modern philosophy is undeniable. When we refer to Duns Scotus's text—there are a lot of them, but the main passages are in his great work *Distinctiones et quaestiones*—we would have to go to the forty-ninth distinction.[24] Here, Duns Scotus examines with the greatest precision—he does this in a lot of other passages—Saint Thomas's idea, Saint Thomas's thesis that the intellect prevails over the will: *intellectus nobilius voluntate*.[25] He fights against this thesis with seven arguments. The Scholastic doctors are in the habit of numbering the arguments; there are seven, corresponding symmetrically to Aquinas's reasons.[26] The most striking of the reasons [Duns Scotus] gives is certainly the second, which can be summarized like this: if the intellect were above the will, there would be something higher than charity, *caritate melius* or *nobilor*.[27] Yet nothing can be above charity since charity is the first of the gifts. Duns Scotus cites Saint Paul on this point; he takes shelter under Saint Paul's authority. Indeed, in the First Letter to the Corinthians, there is this sentence that charity is the first of the gifts.

When we look at this letter, we in fact find something like what Duns Scotus says, there's this sentence in particular: "Even if I have all knowledge [*science*], complete knowledge, even if I surpass all other humans, if I don't have charity, I am nothing."[28] So it does seems that there is an allusion here to the doctrine according to which we owe,

not only what we have—the text doesn't say *outhen ekhō*, it says *outhen eimi*[29]—not only
[203] what we have[30] but what we are, to this source of existence that is, above all, charity and thus will—for the word "charity," *agapē* in Greek, has a wider meaning than our modern word: "charity" is indeed a form of the divine will.

In Saint Paul's Letters, we'd find another word whose meaning it would perhaps be useful to define, it's the word *kardia*, that is, the "heart." In the literal sense, this word designates rather more of an affective faculty, the faculty of choosing voluntarily. For example, one will say . . .[31] We'll find that "God's love" belongs to the heart, is in the heart.[32] It's a rather remarkable fact that this same word "heart" designates a purely intellectual faculty. We'll find this, for instance: "the law," the moral law, "is written on their hearts."[33] So there really is—it thus seems that Duns Scotus's version is justified on this point—there really is a sort of implicit psychology (even if the Letters do not aim to develop a psychology), certain features of which clash with the psychology of Greek philosophy. For the idea that the intellect is an intellectual faculty that can derive, as it were, from a faculty whose essence is individual and voluntary even as it participates in the intellect, this idea would have scandalized the Greek philosophers. We find many different psychologies in the Greek philosophers, but all agree in considering sensibility and the will as diminishments of the intellect or in any case as species of which the intellect is the genus. Whereas here, the order of the faculties is reversed: the intellect, as well as the species, fall[s] under the genus of something that is affective and voluntary—or something of that nature, since it is probable, it is likely, that *kardia* designates, in this language, something that transcends what we call "will" and what we call "sensibility" but that is, nevertheless, a lot closer to them than it is to the pure intellect.

We don't have to resolve this question here, which exclusively concerns theology and the history of religions, the question of whether this Scotist tendency is or isn't
[204] the fundamental tendency of Christianity. But from the viewpoint of the history of philosophy, that is, from the viewpoint of the question that interests us, the real question isn't that one at all. The question is which of the particular tendencies called "Scotist" or "Thomist" is in sharp contrast with the tendency of the ancient philosophers, the Greek philosophers. If the question is posed in this way, then there's no doubt about the answer. The idea that the will prevails over the understanding, the idea of the primacy of the will, as Schopenhauer will say, this idea would have been rejected as shocking by the ancient philosophers,[34] whereas it is one of the dominant ideas of modern philosophy.

There's another one as well, one that, for that matter, caused modern philosophy—which accepted it—very great difficulties. This is what I'd call the idea of the primacy of the will not only in relation to the intellect but in relation to nature. Jewish theology accepted creation, it's one of the essential ideas of this theology: the divine will created the world. Now, the idea of creation is absolutely absent, as you know, from Greek philosophy: when God intervenes in the world, he does so to arrange the world,[35] he doesn't create things, whereas in Jewish theology, there's the idea that God created the world. So the order of nature is the work of the will. Once this order has been created, the divine will can still intervene to break what has been established, and the idea of miracles is essentially tied to the idea of creation. We find nothing of the sort in the ancients, nothing of creation. Truth be told, their conception of the order of nature, as I pointed out, was less rigid, less rigorous, less geometrical, than that of the moderns, but they already had this idea of the regularity of nature. They believed that nature is rational, that it complies [*se conformer*] with reason. As I said earlier, when Plato and Aristotle introduce a certain indetermination into things, they do so against their will: it would be better if there were no contingency, no indetermination, and contingency, indetermination come from irrational elements being mixed in with things. In contrast, in Jewish theology, as I said, we find the idea that the indetermination that makes miracles [205] possible can on the contrary be the sign of something excellent: the divine will at least is something higher than nature. As for the human will, we find hardly any indications on this point in the Old Testament, but the effect of Christianity was certainly to establish a more intimate relation between humanity and God, a relation of filiation as it were. Humans fell away from God because of sin, but they can return to God, in certain cases they return through regeneration.[36] Humans thus are extremely close to God, to the point of participating to some extent in the divine power, God acting in certain cases in humans and through humans.[37] The idea of a quasi-infinite material power immanent to moral force, an idea we don't find in the ancients, the idea that there's a power of explosion in justice, goodness, charity, an infinite explosive force, as it were, capable of pulverizing the greatest material obstacles, this idea was very far from the thought of the ancients. We find it latent in modern philosophy, and, as I said, it has been the source of really big problems for philosophy because in modern philosophy the necessity of the course of nature becomes something much more rigorous than it was for the ancients. Science will place in nature an order that is not only regular but geometrical; hence the urgent character the problem of freedom and the relation between the moral order and the physical order will take on.

Be that as it may, and this is what I'll conclude with: immanent to modern philosophy, there's the idea of the primacy of the will not only in relation to the intellect but even, if not de facto at least de jure, in relation to nature, in relation to facts of nature. If we looked for the psychological origin of these two ideas, the idea of the double primacy, we'd find it undoubtedly in the fact of psychological observation that the will is indeed something amazing, something that from certain angles, in certain aspects at least, partakes of the miraculous. The will is indeed a force capable of increasing indefinitely in itself.[38] A natural force is something given, given not only in quality but even in magnitude; but a moral force, in a word, the force of willing, is something whose magnitude is not given, [206] in the sense that with a little we can do a lot or, rather, there is neither a little nor a lot: we can will to will, will to give ourselves will-power.[39]

From the physical viewpoint, there's a paradox, but this paradox is a moral truth, a truth of moral observation: the will is capable of multiplying itself; it creates itself, and in certain cases it creates the intellect; through a kind of calling forth of force, the will can grow and as if illuminate the intellect. It's been said many times: a darkened intellect can be illuminated by a bout of enthusiasm, that is, thanks to the will reaching an acute state. So there's something like an indefinite reservoir of energy, and of an energy as it were transformable into intellect. What's remarkable is that this power of the will

is due above all to the direction. The forces of nature are forces whose intensity isn't a function of their direction, doesn't depend on the direction we give them. But the force of the will comes to it from its direction; we could even define moral force, insofar as it distinguishes itself from physical force, in this way: a force whose intensity comes to it from its direction. If the will adopts a direction randomly, its force will be neutralized; there is one direction, and only one, the direction we call the right direction, where, on the contrary, its force will multiply indefinitely. We have here a psychological truth that the ancients didn't perceive or that they perceived only very vaguely, and that is what we call "psychological intuition." Now, philosophy on the one hand and theology on the other will have their interpretations of this, and we'll see how these interpretations varied, but the tendency of modern philosophers in general, and of Descartes in particular, has been to very quickly make the participation of the human will stop at this infinite something, and straight away to see the intervention of something, or of someone, infinitely superior to the human. The discussion, all in all, bears on this, on the intervention. But above all the discussion there's this fact, which we can say is a fact of psychological observation. This, it seems, is one of the essential points, one of the
[207] essential ideas that passed into modern philosophy and that explain the reversal of the viewpoint on the question of freedom.

We'll talk about this reversal in more detail in the next session, gentlemen, where we'll take on the study of the problem of freedom in Descartes.

Notes

1. The typescript says *ensomatone*. It's difficult to tell what Greek terms Bergson pronounced since the Corcos brothers, who were the stenographers for this course, did not know Greek. The term suggested here, *ensōmatōsis*, literally "embodiment" or "incarnation," has the meaning Bergson indicates, the soul taking on a body. Clement of Alexandria and Stobaeus both use it; Plotinus, however, does not.
2. In fact, numerous occurrences of the expression, *kosmos noētos*, can be found in Plotinus, for example, the "intelligible universe" of *Enneads* 5.9.9: 309. There are none in Plato.
3. On the basis of the reciprocal penetration of the states of consciousness in duration, each of them also reflects all the others (although this is not an "Intelligible"). That is why Bergson can write that "the whole personality is in a single one of them, provided that we know how to choose it" (TFW, 165/124).
4. A similar example appears in "Introduction to Metaphysics" (CM, 189/179–80).
5. Bergson's term is *organisé*; compare 80n22 above.
6. "Proceed" in the technical Neoplatonic sense of separating from, of descending from a principle.
7. In keeping with what he says in the preceding paragraphs, Bergson seems to mean that the individual soul would itself have produced the individual body had the universal soul not already done so.
8. Bergson is quite fond of these passages in *Enneads* 6.7.5–7: 101–9. The section he is referring to here (as he is also, as noted, in ME, 117–18/96–7) is 6.7.5: 101.

9. The translation of these passages from *Enneads* 6.7.5–7 is based on Bergson's French translation but also incorporates some phrases from the Armstrong translation (107).
10. As Bergson does in the second chapter of *Matter and Memory*: the brain, by means of imitative movements, "sketches" the memory to be recalled; the nature of this memory, however, is "past in general," and it contrasts with the mechanical process.
11. Bergson is probably thinking (as above, 129) of *Enneads* 4.4.34: 243–5. Another passage he may have in mind is from the third Ennead, in particular *Enneads* 3.1.7: 29–31, which targets the Stoics' necessitarian doctrine and which he already used in his high school teaching. We might also add *Enneads* 2.3: 53–101 and *Enneads* 6.1, whose last part, starting at 6.1.25: 89, critically examines the different Stoic categories one by one.
12. On Leibniz, see the April 7 and 14, 1905, lectures below, 196 and 202. The kinship between Plotinus and Leibniz is one of Bergson's favorite theses. He asserts it again in *Creative Evolution* (CE, 303/353), but he had already insisted on the similarities between Leibnizian monads and Plotinian Intelligibles in the first course he gave at the Collège de France in 1897–8 as Charles Lévêque's replacement. See M, 413, and above, 21n1.
13. Again, he is probably referring to the two courses from 1897–8 (M, 413).
14. *Enneads* 6.8.5: 239, in the opening sentence of the paragraph.
15. *Enneads* 6.8.5; the English here follows Bergson's French rendering. Armstrong's translation of the passage can be found on p. 243.
16. See *Enneads* 6.8.5: 243–5.
17. We have no way of knowing what lectures Bergson is talking about here, but it cannot be the 1897–98 lectures, since these concerned the fourth Ennead (M, 413).
18. Plotinus, *Enneads* 3.8.4; compare the Armstrong translation, 371–3. Bergson cites these exact lines (in translation and in Greek) in *The Two Sources* (TS, 221/234 and 221n1/234n1).
19. This sentence comes a little later in the same paragraph, *Enneads* 3.8.4. Bergson cites this sentence (in Greek) in "The Perception of Change" (CM, 153/163; Andison translates the Greek into English).
20. Bergson shows himself to be against this conception in the Second Introduction to *The Creative Mind* (CM, 100/92).
21. "Proceeded" once more in the Neoplatonic sense of the word, where "procession" is opposed to "conversion"; see above, 138 and 146n6.
22. For example, Wilhelm Kahl in his *Die Lehre vom Primat des Willens bei Augustinus, Duns Scotus und Descartes* (Strasbourg: Trübner, 1886).
23. John Duns Scotus (1265–1308), who was Scottish, was one of the most important philosophers and theologians at the end of the Middle Ages. He tied his teachings, especially those of his Parisian period, in with Franciscan doctrine. The Franciscans were one of the two most powerful mendicant orders of the Middle Ages. The most illustrious philosophical figure of their rivals, the Dominicans, was Thomas Aquinas (the Saint Thomas mentioned in a moment).
24. Now more commonly known under the titles *Opus Oxoniense* or *Ordinatio*. See Duns Scotus, *Ordinatio*, in *Opera Omnia*, ed. Commissio Scotistica, vols. 1–14 (Vatican City: Vatican Press, 2013); the passage Bergson cites—book 4, distinction 49, part 1, question 4—can be found in 335–56 of volume 14 of this edition.
25. Literally, "the intellect is nobler than the will."

26. Aquinas makes the argument in several texts. In the *Ordinatio* passage Bergson is discussing here, Duns Scotus cites (on pages 334 and 335) *Sentences* IV, d49, q1, a1, qc 2 (on page 349); *Summa Theologiae* I, q82, a3; and (on page 351) *Sentences* IV, d49, q1, a1, qc 3, and *Summa Theologiae* I, q82, a1. Scotus in *Ordinatio* proffers three arguments (the second of which Bergson will turn to in a moment); the seven arguments Bergson mentions can be found in the *Lectura in librum secundum sententiarum* (also known as *Reportata parisiensia*) II, d39, in *Opera Omnia*, vol. 19, 377–87.
27. "Better than charity," "nobler" than charity; see *Ordinatio* 4, d 49, p 1, q 4: 346–9. Note that the "charity" at issue here—which can also be rendered as "love"—is the *agapē* Saint Paul discusses in chapter 13 of his First Letter to the Corinthians, to which Duns Scotus responds directly here. The "gifts" Bergson refers to in the next sentence are the "spiritual gifts" Paul introduces in the preceding chapter, 1 Cor 12.
28. 1 Cor 13:2. In the New Revised Standard Version, the passage reads: "And if I have prophetic powers, and understand all mysteries and all knowledge, and if I have all faith, so as to remove mountains, but do not have love, I am nothing."
29. "I have nothing," "I am nothing."
30. Here and just before, rather than *ce que nous avons*, "what we have," the typescript says *ce que nous savons*, "what we know," which is a possible reading.
31. There is a gap in the typescript here, though it seems very likely that only a few words in ancient Greek, which the stenographers were not familiar with, are missing.
32. Romans 5:5.
33. Romans 2:15.
34. Schopenhauer, "The Primacy of the Will in Self-consciousness," ch. 19 in *The World as Will and Representation 2*, 212–57.
35. This is what Plato's demiurge does in the *Timaeus* (28a: 1234–5).
36. In the Christian conception, a conversion prompts the regeneration of the soul: the baptized are "born again" and their sins are remitted.
37. Bergson will evoke this Paulinian teaching again in *The Two Sources* (TS, 232–3/246).
38. See ME, 38–9/31.
39. See TFW, 157/119.

LECTURE 13
MARCH 17, 1905

Gentlemen, today and in the next lecture, we're going to be concerned with Descartes's [209] theory of freedom. I'll briefly recapitulate one of the conclusions on this subject from my last lecture. I said that one of the essential ideas of Jewish theology, an idea that, moreover, passed as such into Christianity, is that of God's omnipotence, which, according to this theology, is concentrated in his will. God created the world. He can intervene in the world such as he created it by means of miracles. God's will asserts itself, and asserts itself by means of actions.

I said that this idea was not only foreign to classical philosophy, to ancient Greek metaphysics, but also was in absolute contradiction to them. Not only is the idea of creation absent from Greek philosophy, but also this entire philosophy is averse to the idea of a God who would intervene by means of actions, the idea of an acting God, in a word, of a willful God. And that's because for the Greek philosophers—in regard to this point I demonstrated the continuity of this tradition all the way up to and including Plotinus—for the Greek philosophers, action is a diminishment of thought, a diminishment of contemplation. The true reality, Plotinus concludes, is thought, it's the Idea. Consequently, it's the absolute immutability of being, enclosed in itself, whose activity, if activity there be, is an activity turned toward itself, turned to the inside of itself, in reality simple contemplation, simple self-vision. A being who acts is a being who is not complete, is a being who's seeking itself, who runs, as it were—I've already said this several times—after itself in time and also, in certain cases, in space. It's thus incomplete. [210]
It needs to realize something because it doesn't see clearly, perfectly. If it saw perfectly, it would be content with seeing. But it sees obscurely, and thus it seeks to construct, in space and time, the things which will bring to it a clearer image of what it sees vaguely.[1] But being things, they remain necessarily vague, for what is clear is the Idea, the pure intelligible.

We devoted part of the last lecture to this point. Plotinus bequeathed to us the quintessence of ancient thought. He showed us sensible reality in space and time, that is, bodies and also souls: for the soul is something that contains the bodies, regardless of whether we're talking about the individual soul or the world-Soul, the individual body or the world-body. So body and soul represent a descent into space and into time. If we want to find the principle of which bodies and souls are diminishments, that is, the principle of action without degradation,[2] we have to reascend to what Plotinus calls the Intelligibles situated in the Intellect, the Intellect being nothing other than the totality of co-penetrating Intelligibles, of Intelligibles penetrating each other. We must thus reascend to the pure Intelligible, and this pure Intelligible is the perfect being, the true being. For Plotinus, are these Intelligibles God himself? Not yet. God, he'll say, is more than Intelligible, more than the Intellect. Why? Would it be because Plotinus put something above the Intellect properly speaking? No. When we look at it closely, we see that, for Plotinus, the Intelligibles aren't, as it were, truly intellectual enough to be God himself. Pure intellectuality would be absolute, true unity. In the Intellect, there are Intelligibles. Undoubtedly, the Intelligibles are mutually penetrating, nonetheless, that isn't the absolute unity: there's still a duality, Plotinus tells us, of what beholds and what is beheld, whereas God is absolute and complete unity.

So Plotinus's doctrine is really the most absolute intellectualism, a super-intellectualism, intellectualism pushed as far as it can be pushed. And in presenting this
[211] doctrine to us, Plotinus believed he simply reproduced the ancient tradition. And, as I've said several times, he wasn't absolutely wrong: he went further than his predecessors, he exacerbated their ideas by pushing them all the way, but in doing so, he made their ideas all the clearer. What Plotinus has given us in the *Enneads*, in short, is the key idea of the entire tradition of ancient philosophy since Socrates and Plato.

Gentlemen, this idea is absolutely the opposite of the one I stated a moment ago: the essence of being is not will, is not action, but contemplation. Opposing the idea that the essence of being is the intellect or supraintellect, which is still more intellectual than the intellect, opposing this idea is the one I stated in the last lecture and recapitulated a moment ago, the idea that the very root of being is the will, that the intellect, the idea itself, is a manifestation of the will. Undoubtedly, we find this idea already in Jewish theology, but, I said, we [also] find it in Christianity. It's one of the currents of Christianity, a current that leads to transforming God into the being that is above all will, the divine intellect being prevailed over, as it were, by the will of God, being something like an act, a manifestation of his will.

Gentlemen, this is the current I pointed out in the last lecture and which is, as I said, the current opposed to that of the traditional philosophy of ancient Greece. Well, this is the current, it seems, that Descartes's philosophy harnessed. The influence of Christianity on this philosophy is incontestable, it's very profound. We have too much of a tendency to consider this philosophy to have emerged from nothing. It was Chasles who said about Descartes's metaphysics and analytic geometry that it springs up one fine day without any antecedents, ready-made, like a child born without a mother, born having no mother, *proles sine matre creata*.[3]

Is that true of his geometry? That's not certain, it's not even absolutely probable, but it's certainly not true of his philosophy: it has antecedents, and it has very deep roots in Christianity. We must not forget that Descartes was taught at La Flèche by the Jesuits,
[212] whose teaching was extremely eclectic.[4] It's very hard to believe that Duns Scotus's ideas, for example, along with many others, didn't reach him, perhaps not with the name Duns Scotus on them, but it's very hard to believe, I'm saying, that these ideas didn't reach him in one form or another via either the philosophical or the religious education he received. And even if we supposed they didn't come up at La Flèche, Descartes like every person in his time lived in an atmosphere saturated with Christianity. He couldn't have conversed, read, thought, without gathering up, as something in the air, ideas that were,

all in all, the ideas of one of the greatest doctors of Scholasticism, that, moreover, as I showed the other day, may have been formulated by Duns Scotus with more precision and in an exacerbated way but nevertheless represent, in their exacerbation, an already very old current that can be considered one of the directions of originary Christianity.

So a priori, there's no doubt that Descartes's philosophy was under the influence of Christianity in general. And when we find analogies so striking, so complete as the ones that exist between Descartes's theory of freedom and of the will in humans and in God, and this same theory in Duns Scotus, it's very hard to believe that there isn't a certain kinship between them.

Leaving this historical point aside, let's recapitulate very briefly—these things are well known—let's recapitulate Descartes's theory relative to the will and freedom in God and in humans.

In God the will is infinite. God creates the truth and reality. God creates the truth: God could have made it such that what is true was false and what is false was true; he could have made it such that geometry didn't exist or that our geometry was false, that the radiuses of the circle were not equal to one another.

There'd be several texts to quote in this regard. I'll limit myself to recapitulating the best known of these. This is one of the letters to Mersenne: "Indeed to say that these truths are independent of God is to talk of him as if he were Jupiter or Saturn . . . Please do not hesitate to assert and proclaim everywhere that it is God who has laid down these laws in nature just as a king lays down laws in his kingdom."[5]

This is quite a radical thesis. God creates the truth. He could make it such that the true would be false. To be sure, Descartes somewhat attenuates this thesis in some other passages in his writings. He'll tell us, for example, that God cannot change the truth once he has established it.[6] Here we already have a restriction applied to God's omnipotence in relation to the creation of truth. He'll also tell us—and then this is more interesting and more awkward—he'll tell us that God cannot not have willed the best, that which is the best. In the Fourth Meditation, Descartes presents the idea in this way:

> It also occurs to me that whenever we are inquiring whether the works of God are perfect, we ought to look at the whole universe, not just at one created thing on its own. For what would perhaps rightly appear very imperfect if it existed on its own is quite perfect when its function as a part of the universe is considered.[7]

Descartes in this passage expresses himself exactly as Leibniz will express himself, namely, when we consider the whole universe, all in it is for the best, but when we take an isolated, separated part, we'll be able to judge that it is not so. But we must take the whole into account, and then all is the best possible. Had Descartes really accepted this theory, he wouldn't have considered the divine to be creating the truth and reality by an absolutely free, that is, contingent decree. Nonetheless, we must take into account that in this passage and in others we could interpret in the same way, Descartes simply wants to say this: God created the truth. God, in short, created the good. When we judge his work, if we want to declare it good or evil, we must apply the criterion of good and evil, and

we must apply this criterion such as God made it. God created the criterion by means of
[214] which we are called to judge his work. When we're called to judge his work, we find that he has made everything for the best, but it's God himself who created the rule to which we refer and according to which we judge his work. There is thus no contradiction, as some have thought, between passages like this one and those where Descartes asserts that God creates the true, creates even the good by a decree of his free will.

In addition, we have a quite conclusive text on this point, a passage from a conversation between Descartes and a young student, Burman, the text of which was discovered—probably the text was taken down in shorthand—that was discovered, I'm saying, a few years ago in a manuscript at Göttingen.[8] In this very intriguing conversation—because Descartes is probably having a meal with the student in question, chatting about all sorts of things, especially about metaphysics, and responding to the objections made to him, to the requests for clarification being addressed to him, without any ulterior motive to attenuate his doctrine, often going all the way to the limit of his idea, which simplifies it and clarifies it a lot—in this conversation, the interlocutor asks him: "But does it follow from this that God could have commanded a creature to hate him," him being God, "and thereby made this a good thing to do?" Descartes answers him: "God could not now do this." He ordained that it would be otherwise, and we know that God doesn't change. But wouldn't he have been able to? We have no idea. And why wouldn't he have been able, after all, to command a creature to do this?[9]

Thus, according to this text, God did indeed arbitrarily set what is true and false, and not only what is true or false but also what is good and evil. God is the creator of the truth; he is also the creator of reality. He created the world; and not only did he create it, but he still creates it constantly. Recall the famous theory of continuous creation.[10] Without God's constantly renewed creative act, the world would not subsist for one single instant; God must resume the creative act at each moment of duration.

What is intriguing and instructive for us is that Descartes responds to the objections that Gassendi made to him on the subject of continuous creation: "But that's the opinion
[215] of all theologians."[11] That's not certain, but it shows us that Descartes himself wasn't unaware of the close connection between some of his essential doctrines and those of theology.

So much for freedom and will in God. God's freedom and will are infinite, and God is the creator of existences and essences, of realities as much as of possibilities.

Let's turn to the human. In humans, the will is infinite as well. Descartes put forward the idea, one of the essential ideas of his philosophy, that the human will is infinite like the divine will. We could quote many texts on this subject, here's that of the Fourth Meditation:

> It is only the will or freedom of choice, which I experience within me to be so great that the idea of any greater faculty is beyond my grasp; so much so that it is above all in virtue of the will that I understand myself to bear in some way the image and likeness of God. For although God's will is incomparably greater than mine, both in virtue of the knowledge and power that accompany it and

> make it more firm and efficacious, and also by virtue of its object, in that it ranges over a greater number of items, nevertheless it does not seem any greater than mine when considered as will in the essential and strict sense. This is because the will simply consists in our ability to do or not to do something (that is, to affirm or deny, to pursue or avoid).[12]

Descartes's thought is thus quite clear, and he clarifies it still more in other texts.[13] Our will is infinite in the sense that we can will everything, that at any time, we can decide between yes and no. The faculty of choice is absolute, it's an absolute and consequently an infinite, since the infinite is not what is very large, the infinite is what defies all measure, what does not admit of more or less, what is given entirely or not at all. Well, that's the will, it's given entirely or it isn't given at all. If it exists, it's an absolute, it's an infinite, and we experience this absolute in ourselves, in the sense that, according to Descartes, we experience, first, that we cannot do anything, then, that in all circumstances we can opt between one [216] decision and the opposite decision, and even in deciding we have the feeling that our will infinitely surpasses, overflows the decision taken and could do something else.

Our will is thus infinite like the divine will. However, there's the difference between our will and the divine will that God creates the truth, he creates the good, while humans find before them a truth, a good, things as well, an already created world, already made. Thus, de jure, they can undoubtedly will anything, but de facto it's really difficult for them not to will what appears to their intellect as the best. For their intellect is there, which considers things, which looks at them, which weighs the value of the different parties, and according to the judgment that the intellect will have made, the will in general will come to a decision—with certain restrictions, to be sure, the restriction that the will could, when it comes to that, decide differently and that in many cases, it does decide differently simply, Descartes tells us, to prove its free will to itself.[14] Nevertheless, if the will comes to decide in favor of what the intellect judges to be best, freedom, it seems, will be subject to rather severe restrictions.

In fact, there are passages in Descartes that could be interpreted in the sense of a rigorous determinism. We don't have the time to quote all these passages, but in the "Reply to the Sixth Set of Objections," Descartes puts it like this: "But as for man"—he has just spoken of God—

> since he finds that the nature of all goodness and every truth is already determined by God, and that his will cannot tend toward anything else, it is evident that he will embrace what is good and the true all the more willingly, and hence also more freely, in proportion as he sees it more clearly. He is never indifferent except when he does not know which of the two alternatives is the better or truer, or at least when he does not see this clearly enough to rule out any possibility of doubt.[15]

This passages implies—and we'd find other passages in this sense that are more explicit[16]—that when Descartes considers the relation of the human will to its intellect, it seems—this is only a semblance—it seems to lean toward determinism, humans deciding as it [217] were necessarily in favor of what their understanding presents to them as being or as appearing to be best.

I'm saying it's only a semblance because we mustn't forget Descartes's theory of judgment.[17] For Descartes, judgment is not the work of pure intellect, judgment is the work of the will. Judging, saying that something is good or bad, that it is true or false, is an act of will because it is choosing. Judging is opting between two contrary assertions, for example. It's thus willing, it's the will that judges. So when we act, we undoubtedly decide in favor of what our intellect judges to be best, but this judgment of the intellect is still the will, and in the judgment of the intellect that determines the will, there's only a ricochet, as it were, of the will itself.

This is a very interesting theory, one we could compare, in certain aspects, to current psychological theories, for example, to the theory of belief and of conviction.[18] More and more, we tend to consider belief and conviction and even judgment in general to be works of the will as much as works of the intellect. The two faculties, moreover, aren't as separate as an abstract psychology might have us believe. They aren't separated by an impenetrable barrier. They undoubtedly would be if reasons appeared in abstracto, if then the will followed the judgment made by the pure intellect. Left to its own devices, the intellect would present to us what to it would appear to conform most with the good and with the useful, and then we would choose it necessarily. But that's not how things happen. In fact, the intellect decides by placing itself in the viewpoint of the moral good or in the viewpoint of the useful, but the will is there, with its preferences, and it determines the intellect not to consider certain reasons, to skate over this or that reason and to pay more attention to others, and so. When the will comes to a decision according to the intellect's indications, it comes to a decision, to a large extent, according to its own natural impulse.

Too often we consider deliberation and action to be separate states, distinct from the
[218] voluntary act: on the side of deliberation, there would be motives, motivations reviewed and weighed, then the action would follow the deliberation. Sometimes, things happen like that, but often they happen completely differently: the action that will take place, the action that aspires to be, presides over the deliberation; invisible, no doubt, but it does preside over the deliberation by allowing certain reasons to speak, by cutting others off, and in short, when the deliberation comes to an end, it results in what the will desired. I'll add that this second case, which is an extreme case, is as rare as the first, and that in general, the deliberation doesn't derive from the action, nor does the action absolutely orient the course of the deliberation. Rather, there's something of both, there's reciprocal action and reaction, there's reciprocal influence of the deliberation on the action that will happen and of the action that would like to happen on the deliberation taking place. And in short, the final action is the synthesis of these two tendencies, a variable synthesis depending on the person, a synthesis, moreover, that is never dull and that is a characteristic phenomenon of the exercise of human freedom.[19]

As you can see, the seed of the psychology I think we're tending toward [today] can be found in Descartes: there are passages where Descartes says that in the course of deliberation we can if we like turn our attention away from this or that reason, which we

do.[20] This passage, by the way, astonishingly resembles one in Duns Scotus, in which he says almost the exact same thing.[21] We thus find the seed of this psychology in Descartes and even earlier than Descartes. Nevertheless, it's not exactly in that sense that we'd have to orient Descartes's thought, since in his theory of the human will in its relations with the intellect, he seems to be preoccupied with something else entirely. Descartes's idea, in short, is that left to itself, left to its own devices, the intellect would probably end up coming to a decision all the same, and perhaps it wouldn't need the cooperation of the will. It would end up coming to a decision when everything has been completely, perfectly clarified, when it sees beyond a doubt that the good is there. Then the good would be accomplished necessarily. However, the intellect would need time, a lot of time. In many cases, it would need an infinite time, as the mathematicians say, that is, in [219]
practice, it would never reach the end. But the action is there, which can't wait. Then the will intervenes. The will cuts, it slices through the knot that the intellect doesn't manage to undo, to untie.[22] It can get it right but it can also get it wrong. Error, in short, comes from this disproportion between the will and the intellect, the intellect being finite, needing time to progress, and the will being infinite, being fully in each of its acts, fully in the present moment and not waiting;[23] but so does judgment more generally, insofar as it's immediate, insofar as it presents complete clarity.

If we now looked, at the basis of this theory, for Descartes's very intention, we'd undoubtedly find, as I said earlier, that it's not a psychological intention but a theological intention. Descartes is concerned with explaining the error, the evil that exists in the world, without tracing responsibility for it back to God—since, after all, God created all things, it seems that he's responsible for error and evil. Descartes's solution, then, consists in this: we'll say that God created the human intellect, which is a good and is only a good. He also created the human will, which is an infinite good, which is even closer to God than the human intellect. He created only these two things. As for evil and error, they are due to the coexistence of these two goods and as it were express the gap between them.

The human intellect is, if you like, a small circumference. The human will is an immense circumference concentric with the first [which it] exceeds infinitely. And then the zone of judgment, of choice, and consequently of error and evil is the space, the ring, if you like, that separates the two circumferences from one another: it's an empty ring, it's emptiness. God could not make emptiness, he makes only fullness. But this interval of emptiness is the region of judgment, of willing, of the true and the false, of human good and evil, such that good and evil exist without God having willed them in any way. In short, this theory is still a continuation of a very ancient principle, the Scholastics' [220]
principle: evil is a deficient and not an efficient cause.[24]

Thus, we're always led back to concerns that are analogous to those of the theologians and to solutions that, all in all, are rather close to theological solutions. That's one aspect, at least, of Descartes's metaphysics. There is another that I can only point to here at the end, but it might be interesting to pursue this aspect more deeply. It's very remarkable to see what emerges from this Cartesian metaphysics of the divine will and the human will and the relation between them. It's a theory, it seems, that pushes human freedom to its extreme limits, this freedom being something analogous to divine freedom, so it's freedom granted the human as much as it's possible to grant the human freedom. And yet, what's going to emerge from this metaphysics are doctrines that absorb the human will into the divine will, absolute metaphysical determinisms like Spinoza's, for example, and even Malebranche's, which is very close, in certain respects at least, to Leibniz's doctrine. This is very remarkable, and it would be worthwhile to look for why this radical determinism emerged from a doctrine that, it seems, is a doctrine of extreme freedom.[25]

If we explored this more deeply, we'd see that Descartes, without having wanted it, without having sought it, and explicitly saying the opposite, is rubbing shoulders with the doctrines that emerge from his. He's very close to them, and that has to do with the enormous, not to say insurmountable, difficulty of understanding the coexistence of several infinities. The human will is an infinity, the divine will is an infinity as well. How can the infinite divine will be distinguished from the human will which, too, is infinite? Where and how does the separation exist? It cannot consist in a difference of place and of time. Space and time are principles of separation, undoubtedly, for sensible things: two things can be identical and nevertheless be distinct insofar as they occupy different
[221] places in space and time. Such is not the case with the will if we consider it to be infinite, since, as infinite, it's not in space, nor in time.

We can still think that things not in space and time are distinguished by their qualities, but the human will and the divine will, as wills, have the same quality or, rather, have no quality: it's an absolute power of arbitrating, of deciding between yes and no. It's thus already very difficult to see how these wills, how in this kind of doctrine the human will can be distinguished from the divine will. But I'm going further, and there are, it seems, certain essential doctrines in Descartes's philosophy that are of major, fundamental importance, that can gain all their force and take up their complete significance only if we orient Descartes's philosophy of the will in this direction, although, I repeat, Descartes never did so himself; we won't find any decisive texts to support this interpretation. However, I don't think that certain of Descartes's doctrines can be conceived, understood in their full force—and without being completely consistent—if we don't push the interpretation in this direction. I'm only speaking of Descartes's fundamental way of proceeding and of the means by which he establishes the substantial existence of his own thought.

You remember that, after having doubted everything, after having produced an absolute emptiness in his thought, Descartes is face to face with his thought itself. He has dismissed everything: thought, at least, remains.[26] "I think" is the affirmation he cannot escape: "If I think, I exist." But I exist as thought, or rather as instantaneous act of thought. At the moment I think, I am sure I exist as thought, but it's an evanescent thought and an evanescent existence. My existence is going to end with the act by which I think my thought, begin again with the following act, and I am not truly certain of the substantiality of my person. How is Descartes going to get out of the instantaneous? He tells us: I find in my thought, in my intellect, the idea of God, the idea of the perfect being, the idea of infinity. Then he establishes, through the reasoning you're familiar
[222] with, that if we think God, he exists. Now, if God exists, he cannot have wanted to deceive me. All the intellectual faculties I had placed under suspicion, the senses, reason,

and especially memory: I am justified in having full confidence in these faculties. I can then affirm the existence of my ego, of my person, not only in the instantaneous but in time and even as a genuine substance.

This is what's been called the Cartesian circle, that is, the circular reasoning by which Descartes establishes his own substantiality.[27] But there's a problem that hasn't been noticed enough, it seems. Descartes finds in himself the idea of the infinite, the idea of the perfect being; however, he had emptied everything from his mind. What, then, can this infinite be that he comes into contact with? It can only be something that as it were supports his thought itself, the substratum of his thought. But we know that this substratum is the will [*la volonté*], for below thought, supporting it, intervening in each of its manifestations, there is the will [*le vouloir*], and we know that the will is infinite. Well, wouldn't this infinite will be what Descartes finds in his thought? And when he tells us that in his as it were emptied thought, he still finds God, how are we to interpret things if not by supposing that the willing of a human being is like the contact—I am not saying that it's God himself—but the contact with God?

Descartes never said this, but it seems that his doctrine of certainty tends toward an affirmation of this kind. And if that's how we interpret the Cartesian circle, as it's being called, the reasoning by which Descartes proves his own substantiality to himself, and the existence of things, this reasoning becomes much less complicated and, in short, less subtle, and, frankly—since we really have to use this word—it becomes less artificial, since the reasoning will simply mean this: I think, and in the instantaneous act of thought I grasp my existence. But that's only a pulsation of thought, as it were, I place myself in this pulsation of thought and I descend all the way down to the principle of vitality that is the source of this phenomenon. I stand this instantaneous existence I grasp in the act of thought, a fleeting existence, [I stand it] up against something eternal, against an eternity that is its substrate, and this eternity, that's the point of contact between me and God. This point of contact is the will, willing, but this willing is like the extension of the [223] divine willing.

I repeat, there is nothing like all this in Descartes's texts, but what has emerged from Descartes's philosophy does seem to indicate that this is the spirit of his doctrine. There's of course a lot to say on this point, as also on the determinism at which Descartes at certain moments ended up, by following this—if I dare put it like that—unconscious interpretation of his doctrine. At the beginning of the next lecture, I'll quote two passages in Descartes that are absolutely determinist and even, if I may say so, fatalist. We'll see that behind these assertions by Descartes, there's this latent interpretation. This will only be the beginning of the next lecture. We'll have to examine a point that's very important for us, and more interesting than the one we studied today. Today, I showed the doctrine of human freedom and human will in Descartes, such as they relate to divine freedom and the divine will. We still have to seek out what the relation of the will to nature is in Descartes's philosophy, and how the freedom that Descartes attributes to himself is compatible with the invariable order of the world such as Descartes conceives it. This question, much more relevant today than the previous one, is the one that will be the object of my next lecture.

Notes

1. Bergson is echoing 1 Cor 13:12, from the chapter he discussed in the previous lecture, 143–4.
2. The phrase is obscure. It might mean "the principle of action insofar as it has not yet suffered degradation."
3. Michel Chasles, *Aperçu historique sur l'origine et le développement des méthodes en géométrie* (Brussels: Hayez, 1837), vol. 1, 94. This statement about Descartes seems to have enjoyed a certain degree of fame. The Latin phrase—"a child born without a mother"—comes from Ovid (*Metamorphoses: Volume I: Books 1-8*, trans. Frank Justus Miller, rev. G. P. Goold [Cambridge, MA: Harvard University Press, 1916], 2.553: 98–9). Chasles (1793–1880), a mathematician and historian of mathematics, is referring to Montesquieu, who uses the Latin phrase as the epigraph for the first volume of *L'Esprit des lois*.
4. Bergson is referring to the Jesuit *collège* in the town of La Flèche, halfway between Angers and Le Mans.
5. This is from the famous letter to Mersenne of April 15, 1630, PW III, 20–5/AT I, 135–50, here 23/145. The truths at issue are mathematical truths.
6. This appears most clearly in Descartes's reply to the fifth set of objections, PW II, 261/AT VII, 380.
7. Descartes, *Meditations*, PW II, 39/AT VII, 55–6 (this is the Latin version of the *Meditations*; the French version can be found in AT IX).
8. Discovered in 1895 in Göttingen and published by Charles Adam as "Manuscrit de Gœttingen" in the *Revue bourguignonne de l'Enseignement supérieur* the following year, "Descartes's Conversation with Burman" (PW III, 332–54/AT V, 144–79) is a text whose authenticity and significance have long been a subject of debate among commentators.
9. "Descartes's Conversation with Burman," PW III, 343/AT V, 160.
10. This idea is developed in *The Principles of Philosophy* I.21 (PW I, 200/AT VIIIA, 13).
11. More precisely, in the section of his fifth set of replies concerned with "Objections raised against the Third Meditation," Descartes speaks of "something which all metaphysicians affirm as a manifest truth" (PW II, 254–5/AT VII, 369–71).
12. Descartes, *Meditations*, PW II, 40/AT VII, 57.
13. We can think of Descartes's letters to Mesland of May 2, 1644, and February 9, 1645; see PW III, 231–6 and 244–6/AT IV, 111–20 and 172–5.
14. This is an obvious allusion to the February 9, 1645 letter to Mesland: "For it is always open to us to hold back from pursuing a clearly known good, or from admitting a clearly perceived truth, provided that we consider it a good thing to demonstrate the freedom of our will by doing so" (PW III, 235/AT IV, 173).
15. Descartes, Sixth Set of Replies, PW II, 292/AT VII, 432–3.
16. For example, in the Fourth Meditation (PW II, 40/AT VII, 57) and the May 2, 1644, letter to Mesland (PW III, 233–4/AT IV, 115–16).
17. This theory is presented in the Fourth Meditation.
18. Bergson is probably thinking of William James, with whom he was friends. James's *The Will to Believe* was published in 1897 and translated into French in 1916. See William James, *The Will to Believe and Other Essays in Popular Philosophy*, in *The Works of William James*, ed. Frederick Burkhardt, Ignas K. Skrupskelis, and Fredson Bowers (Cambridge, MA: Harvard

University Press, 1979). In this very general context, we might also think of Alfred Fouillée and his *Psychologie des idées-forces* (Paris: Alcan, 1893).

19. Here Bergson is summarizing several analyses from *Time and Free Will* (TFW, 157–8/118–19 and 169–70/127–8).
20. See, for example, the February 9, 1645 letter to Mesland (PW III, 245/AT IV, 173).
21. See the passages from the *Ordinatio* and the *Reportata parisiensis* cited above, 147n24 and 148n26–27.
22. Compare this description to what Bergson says in *Time and Free Will*: "The abrupt intervention of the will is a kind of coup d'état which our mind foresees and which it tries to legitimate beforehand by a formal deliberation" (TFW, 158/119).
23. Here Bergson is presenting Descartes's theory exactly as we find it in the Fourth Meditation.
24. This theory comes from book 12 of Augustine's *City of God*, trans. Philip Levine, vol. 4 (Cambridge, MA: Harvard University Press, 1966), 35–7.
25. Bergson will ask this same question, which to his mind is of the utmost historical and philosophical importance, in *Creative Evolution* (CE, 298/346).
26. Bergson in this paragraph is summarizing the first three Meditations.
27. It seems that the Jansenist theologian Antoine Arnauld, in his objections to Descartes's *Meditations*, was the first to refer to this reasoning as a "circle"; see the "Fourth Set of Objections" in PW II, 150/AT VII, 214.

LECTURE 14
MARCH 24, 1905

Gentlemen, today we're going to examine what I called the second aspect of the theory of freedom in Descartes's philosophy. In the last lecture, we were concerned with the relations, according to Descartes, between human freedom and the divine will. Today, as I announced, we must examine what, according to Descartes, the relations between human freedom and the general order of nature are. [225]

If we wanted to treat it thoroughly, this second question, like the first, would entail rather long developments. We'd have to examine Descartes's theory from a variety of perspectives. I'll limit myself today to very briefly pointing out the main ones, especially from the viewpoint of lessons to be learned, the dogmatic conclusions to be drawn from this part of the history of philosophy.

The first lesson to be drawn from it would concern what I'd call the psychology of the theories of freedom or, rather, the psychology of the theoreticians of freedom. I've said—this is an idea that has already come back several times and could serve as the leitmotif of this course—I've said that freedom understood in the sense of free will, in the sense of intuition, can be given only in the immediate feeling that we have of ourselves.[1] It's a matter of intuition, it's an intuition we must, undoubtedly, try to render as rational as possible, subject it, if possible, to analysis. But the analysis will never see the end of it, we'll have to push the resolution of this intuition into rational elements very far, we'll never exhaust this analysis, because between the faculties of intuition and the faculties of analysis [226] there is, if we can put it like that, an incommensurability. Or, to use a different image: intuition gives us a feeling of ourselves that is something fleeting, fluid, and analysis is an instrument that cannot make contact with this fluid reality without congealing it at least partially. We must thus constantly take this contact with intuition back up: an extremely difficult operation, this, to analyze an object with a tool that deforms and denatures it. In any case, this resolution of the intuition into rational elements, by means of analysis, can be pushed very far, but it goes without saying that we'll never manage to resolve an intuition like that of freedom into mathematically precise elements.

Reflection, on the contrary, is a faculty that is essentially mathematical. I mean that the more precise it becomes, the more it takes on a mathematical form. I think I've already pointed out that we are naturally mathematicians.[2] Even if we don't understand mathematics, even if we think we don't understand it: the geometrical form is nevertheless the form of our mind and, not understanding the technicalities of mathematics, when we reason about things in general, our reasonings nonetheless are such that the more we push them, the more we strip away the vagueness that comes from our inexperience or our ignorance, the more these reasonings will tend to take a mathematical form. They are, if we can say this, virtually mathematical. Quite naturally, we're brought to mathematics and—this follows from the last claim—we're naturally brought to a mechanistic conception of things: it's the most natural conception, it's the one that presents itself by itself to our mind.

Mathematics was the first science to be constituted. When philosophy, in turn, was constituted, it was on the model of geometry, and we ourselves, when each of us starts to philosophize on the whole set of things, we quite naturally end up at a more or less vague, more or less confused mechanism. We are instinctually mechanistic and each of
[227] us, if left to ourselves, as it were discovers a mechanism. It seems to cast a spell on us, a sort of mechanistic drunkenness sets in. Things appear so simple when we look at them from this viewpoint!

So reflection is instinctually mechanistic and mathematical, and it's placed over and against an intuition that's difficult to grasp and still more difficult to resolve into rational elements, that in any case will never be resolved into rational elements so precise that they'd be mathematical elements properly speaking.

There we have the double tendency of the mind. We find these two tendencies united in Descartes, and that is something very interesting and very instructive for us.

The tendency toward geometry and mathematics was stronger in Descartes than it ever was in anyone else. Descartes is essentially a geometer, and he made the most beautiful discoveries in mathematics that have ever been made. Descartes was thus a great geometer and, had he wanted to, he could have been a great physicist. What he did in physics shows us that he could have been a great physicist had he wanted to, but he didn't want to. He no doubt didn't attach enough importance to physical facts as physical facts, and when he did research in physics, it was, it seems, above all, with an eye to confirming his general philosophy of nature, which philosophy, in his mind, was to supplant Aristotle's—he could have been a physicist like he was a geometer.

We can thus foresee that, in Descartes, mechanism will take its most precise and most radical form, and in fact, the mechanism Descartes constructed has remained the model mechanism: every mechanistic doctrine will tend, to the extent that it becomes more precise, to take the form of Descartes's mechanism.[3]

We thus find the mechanistic tendency in Descartes—this is a commonplace—to be as pronounced as it can be. But Descartes, and this is also interesting for us, Descartes was at the same time, in quite an extraordinary phenomenon, a person endowed with intuition, I mean, a man who believed in feeling, in what I call the immediate givens of consciousness. He didn't talk about this a lot, but it's evident.

[228] What I said the other day about his metaphysics in general could serve as a confirmation of this thesis. If we went through Descartes's correspondence, for example, in the letters where he discusses morality, especially the letters to Princess Elizabeth, we'd see that we're dealing with a person who is, at the same time as being a mathematician, at the same time as being a geometer, a moralist who has a very lively and very clear feeling of internal things. In Descartes, we even find the touch of mysticism I pointed to—this is a rather intriguing coincidence, perhaps it's only a coincidence—in most of the philosophers who affirmed free will, who believed in freedom.

Let's not forget that Descartes believed that his great discovery in mathematics was revealed to him in a dream. During the night of November 10, 1619, when he had three successive dreams, supernatural voices revealed to him, he says, the rules of the true method, the one that led him to his mathematical invention.[4]

So we find in Descartes, again very pronounced—although the first appears a lot more clearly, it goes without saying, than the second—the mathematical tendency, the mechanistic tendency, as well as the tendency toward intuition, toward pure intuition. This explains why Descartes, who constructed a mechanistic doctrine, in its principles the most complete and the most perfect we can imagine, nevertheless subjected it to attenuations.[5] At first glance, this mechanism seems to be as radical as a mechanism can be. It comprises everything in nature, and living beings, which for Descartes are mechanisms like the others, living beings work like a clock.[6] It even encompasses the apparently intelligent actions that animals perform. For Descartes, animals are automata, they are machines. This mechanism engulfs everything except the actions that consciousness shows us. Where consciousness shows us our free activity, ah! that's where Descartes stops. He stops at the exact moment when consciousness intervenes, and he concludes, from our having immediate consciousness of our freedom, of the action of our mind on our body, as he says, that this action is real and efficacious, that it slips through the meshes of natural necessity, and that the mechanism will adapt as best it [229]
can, that, in any case, the inner feeling is right.[7]

This is the first point, the first conclusion to be drawn. There's a second, which is the verification of another law that is correlative to the first and that I've already stated several times. I said that it's possible to bring the givens of pure reflection and those of intuition together in one philosophy, but that these two kinds of givens are hard to reconcile with one another.[8] They don't get along. Sooner or later one of the two tendencies wins out over the other—it goes without saying that reflective thought always prevails.

Intuition is something unstable by nature, something hard to pin down, something, consequently, that's hard to defend, that lacks equilibrium. Reflection, insofar as it aims at rational elements, analytic reflection always ends up triumphing over intuition. This is what happened with Descartes's philosophy. We see that right after this philosopher, his disciples, even the ones who come immediately after Descartes, will lean in the direction of determinism, in the direction of a mechanism without any restriction.

The two elements, reflective analysis and intuition, were juxtaposed in Descartes. One of the two, the second,[9] took up ever more space and finally, and very quickly, took up all of it. This happened very quickly, and it happened in two different directions. It happened through the metaphysicians and through the physicists. I'll talk about the first, the metaphysicians, those whom today we call psychologists.[10] I'll talk about them in the next lecture and the two that follow it. I'll show that, based on the relations Descartes admitted between human freedom and the divine will, someone like Spinoza, like Leibniz will end up at what they, for their part, consider a theory of freedom. When determinism absorbs the theory of freedom, it always considers itself a theory of freedom.[11] We'll see how these philosophers end up at a fatalism, at an absolute, radical determinism, or, if we want to call freedom the kind of activity that concerns us, we'd have to say that freedom excludes any and all contingency and variety of indetermination.

[230] The transformation of the doctrine of freedom into a doctrine of necessary determination is thus accomplished by the metaphysicians. It's also accomplished by those whom we call more particularly scientists, and we'll see—we already saw this last year, for that matter, in relation to the theory of memory[12]—that, first in the seventeenth century, but above all in the eighteenth century, through physician-philosophers, Descartes's theory of human activity was diminished to the point of becoming a radical determinism, an absolute mechanism. Via continuous intermediaries, we can go from Descartes's doctrine of the relations between freedom and nature to a theory like that, for example, of the machine man we find in the eighteenth century.[13] Descartes had already spoken of machine animals, machine beasts. This was an extension of Descartes's theory, not only of Descartes's theory of machine animals, but of Descartes's conception of nature in general. Up to the beginning of the nineteenth century, there was thus a continuous development of the Cartesian doctrine, and this continuous movement of the Cartesian doctrine was toward a radical mechanism that entered science and, what's more, remained there. Still today, when scientists affirm the thesis of a radical mechanism encompassing all human actions—it's far from being the case that every scientist supports this thesis, it's far from being the case, moreover, that all the scientists who engage with these questions declare that [when they do so,] they're doing scientific work—but when a scientist reduces human activity to a kind of automatism, he is taking his inspiration more or less consciously from Cartesianism.[14] They'll show us, for example, that certain movements, great agitations happen in certain cerebral centers in relation to sensations; they'll suppose that other phenomena of the same kind happen on the occasion of memories or are the source of the memory; that others of these movements are the source of ideation; that all these phenomena, all these movements compensating each other can in certain cases result in a voluntary decision; that all of this happens automatically; that consciousness may be unaware of all these processes but joins them
[231] like an epiphenomenon. Although this view is based on observation, on experience, it's probable, it's infinitely probable that no psychological act takes place without a cerebral counterpart. But it's a very long way from here to asserting that mechanism is absolute, that within this series of phenomena, which to a certain extent condition one another, there is no fissure, no discontinuity, no space [*vide*] where freedom and contingency can enter.

When we make this *saltus*,[15] when we thus take the leap from the entirely incomplete givens of observation, of experience to an assertion so precise and so radical, then we're clearly taking our inspiration from a general conception of nature, [a nature] likened to an immense machine where everything meshes, where everything happens through springs and cogs. This amounts to saying that we unconsciously take Cartesianism as our model and that we unconsciously take our inspiration from it; we unconsciously and thereby excessively take our inspiration from it.

Descartes was well aware that mechanism in general, the likening of nature to a single big machine, was, all in all, something hypothetical. And it's because he understood

that this was a hypothesis that he wasn't afraid to correct this hypothesis with another hypothesis, which was that of human freedom, all the more since this hypothesis had, all in all, an experience on its side, the testimony of immediate consciousness. The philosophers who today profess, for example, mechanism are far from attenuating their views in such a way, and they cannot do so because as scientists [*savants*], not always, but, well, as scientists, they're not aware of the metaphysical character of their thesis. They take this thesis as a given of observation, as a given of experience. I tried to expose this error just last Saturday by studying Spencer's *First Principles*,[16] the chapter entitled "The Persistence of Force," where Spencer doesn't draw as his conclusion the assertion of determinism—no, in this part of his book at least, that question doesn't interest him and, for that matter, it never interested him much, he reasons about this point with a view to other conclusions—nevertheless it's very striking and very instructive to see that Spencer imagines that this law of the persistence of force is a given of experience, a given [232]
of science.[17] According to him, science teaches us that there is always one and the same, always constant quantity of force present in the universe that passes through a multitude of states, like a body that would by turns transform into a host of phantoms but in all these transformations remains identical with itself. According to him, this doctrine is a given of experience, and probably, as I said the other day, it's because science does in fact formulate a certain law of the conservation of energy that Spencer believed that by speaking of the conservation of force in general in the universe, he was doing scientific work. But when science speaks to us of the conservation of energy, is this really what it's telling us? Scientists apply this law of the conservation of energy only to well-determined systems, closed systems, and more particularly to the systems that physics and chemistry study, systems that, as everyone agrees, don't leave any room for contingency, for indetermination, nor—this goes without saying—for freedom. In addition, there's an understanding that this law applies to systems assumed to be isolated, assumed to be closed, and that we are not justified in likening the universe in its totality to this kind of system, [that] at least this hypothesis is entirely arbitrary. Then, finally and above all, science is never about a thing that is conserved or conserves itself [*se conserver*] in the diversity of its manifestations, about I don't know what fluid force passing from one reservoir into another. That's not it at all. What's conserved in a system when we speak of the conservation of energy is a certain number that remains constant, nothing else, a number that's the sum of two parts, the sum of two terms, the one representing the energy of the movements, the actual energy of the system, the other representing the internal energy, the different forms of internal energy.[18] What remains constant, then, is a number, and a number that is a measurement, like all numbers, and that, being a measurement, necessarily implies that we obtain it through considerations that are to a large extent conventional. The convention is always the same when the first part is at issue, the first term of the sum, as the function of mass and speed. But for the second term, the convention varies according to whether it's caloric energy, electric energy, [233]
etc.; it's not absolutely a convention.[19] It's easy to see that this convention is grounded in nature and that there's a share of convention in all nature. What's maintained is not a thing, it's a number. But going from these entirely restrained and limited givens of science

to a law of the persistence of force that encompasses the entire universe and, moreover, affirms the conservation of a thing that always remains the same in the diversity of its manifestations, that's no longer doing science, that's doing metaphysics.

Whoever accepts this law of the persistence of force not realizing that it's a metaphysical law and thinking that it's a scientific law, won't attenuate it as the philosopher will be able to do, who, taking inspiration from inner experience—which, after all, is important, too—will understand that this generalization is a hypothetical generalization that, in short, implies metaphysics.

Descartes's theory of the relations of freedom with nature in general is thus instructive from this second viewpoint. The restrictions that Descartes applies to this mechanism are instructive. We see, for example, that the radical mechanism taken at its source considers itself a metaphysics and consequently has no fear of attenuating, of applying certain restrictions, certain reservations, when it's facing facts of inner experience that are not compatible with radical mechanism.

Gentlemen, it was perhaps useful to engage in these preliminary considerations because [what], above all, we're looking for this year in the history of philosophy is a dogmatic teaching [*enseignement dogmatique*], dogmatic conclusions. It's important, however, to summarize with precision Descartes's ideas on these two viewpoints, his ideas on the mechanism of nature and his ideas on the restrictions, the reservations we ought to apply to it.

I'll only cite the very principles of the mechanism of nature according to Descartes. We find them formulated in the second part of *The Principles of Philosophy*, paragraph
[234] 36 and following. Descartes states the law that, according to him, is the fundamental law of the mechanism of nature, the law of the conservation of movement: in nature, always the same quantity of movement is preserved. I'm reading the passage:

> Admittedly motion is simply a mode of the matter which is moved. But nevertheless it has a certain determinate quantity; and this, we easily understand, may be constant in the universe as a whole while varying in any given part. Thus if one part of matter moves twice as fast as another which is twice as large, we must consider that there is the same quantity of motion in each part; and if one part slows down, we must suppose that some other part of equal size speeds up by the same amount.

Movement is preserved in nature in such a way that, if there's more of it at one point, there's less of it at another, but there's always compensation: "For we understand that God's perfection involves not only his being immutable in himself, but also his operating in a manner that is always utterly constant and immutable."[20] This is a very remarkable thesis. Descartes states the principle that always the same quantity of movement is preserved in nature, and what does he base himself on, what is this principle based on? On the stability of divine decrees. God created a determinate quantity of movement. This quantity could be modified only if God wanted to take something away from or add something to it, but that would be contrary to the usual stability, to God's usual constancy. That's why there's always the same quantity of movement in the universe. This argumentation undoubtedly appears to us today to be hardly scientific, but is the law to be established a scientific law? I'm not talking about the inexactitude of the law. You know that soon after Descartes, people realized that there can be no conservation of the same quantity of movement in the universe. They substituted force for movement.[21] And the idea of energy, moreover, [235] became progressively more complicated. It took on its definitive form only with the constitution of the mechanical theory of heat. It has also been much enhanced these last few years.[22] So I'm not alluding to what might be wrong in the statement of this law. I accept that the law, insofar as it is a generalization of a scientific truth, is correctly stated. I even accept that, in the end, this is what Spencer calls "the law of the persistence of force." Is the law of the conservation of energy extended to the totality of the universe a scientific law? No, I just said that science only ever speaks of the conservation of energy in a certain sense, within a certain limit. A generalization as vast, as enormous as that, on the contrary, is a generalization that is not scientific. In any case, linking a nonscientific law, an extrascientific law, to nonscientific, ultrascientific considerations is, all in all, more scientific than passing off as scientific a law that is only a hypothetical and, in short, a priori generalization of certain very restricted results given in experience. So let's not hurry too much to criticize Descartes's argumentation; let's say instead that in Descartes, we cannot change the metaphysical character of the doctrine.

This character exists just as much in a doctrine like Spencer's. I've already tried to show this: to speak of the law of the persistence of force in Spencer's sense is to do metaphysics; all in all, it's not, as Descartes did, linking this law solely to the will but linking it to a kind of necessity, of *anankē*, that would hang over things. Things as a whole must conform to this law. It's not theology, but it's—I'm exaggerating things on purpose—to a certain extent it's mythology, it's necessity accepted at the origin of things, hanging over things. And this without taking experience into account, this appearance in experience that is the inner feeling of our freedom, the feeling that should lead us, at least in this case, to make an exception.

Thus, this argumentation of Descartes's is instructive in that it shows us that Descartes was fully aware of the hypothetical character of the principle, and he expressed this [236] hypothetical character by linking this principle to a metaphysical hypothesis.

This, then, is the law of persistence or conservation of movement. If we accepted this law of the conservation of movement in all of its rigor, the result, it seems, would be that everything in the universe is calculable. A superhuman intellect that would, at a given moment, know the location, the speed, and the direction of all the particles of matter would be able to foresee, predict—if it was endowed with an infinite mathematical aptitude—everything that would happen.[23] There's no question that a principle of conservation, regardless of whether we call it the principle of conservation of movement or of energy, if it applies to the totality of things, must permit this calculation and thereby render impossible the discontinuity of the universe and the formation, at certain points, of centers of indetermination and thereby of certain free activities. Descartes, however, did not draw this conclusion, and according to him, human activity can slip through the meshes of this necessity.

A little later, in paragraph 41 of the second part of the *Principles*, we find this assertion: "The first part of this rule is proved by the fact that there is a difference between the movement of a thing and its determination in a certain direction; for the determination of the direction can be altered, while the movement remains constant."[24] Here's what that means: Descartes believes that the quantity of movement is constant in the universe. It doesn't follow that the direction of each movement is necessarily determined: provided that the quantity of movement persists, it's not necessary that the direction be considered as determinate. Is it with an eye to human freedom and to explain how our freedom is possible that Descartes applies this restriction to this principle or at least that he interprets it this way? That's not absolutely certain, though it's highly probable, it's at least
[237] possible, since in the sentence that immediately precedes this one we read:

> All the particular causes of the changes which bodies undergo are covered by this third law—or at least the law covers all changes which are themselves corporeal. I am not here inquiring into the existence or nature of any power to move bodies which may be possessed by human minds, or the minds of angels, since I am reserving this topic for a treatise *On Man*.[25]

So in this passage at least, Descartes is thinking of freedom. He doesn't say that this indetermination of direction has to do with our freedom or that it makes our freedom possible, he mentions it immediately after having spoken of freedom. So it's indeed possible that to Descartes's mind, human freedom is compatible with the mechanism of nature, since, this mechanism being entirely in the law of the conservation of movement and this law not entailing the absolute determination of the direction of all movements, we can conceive that certain movements are indeterminate, and it's this indetermination that our freedom would take advantage of. That is possible, and if Descartes reasoned this way, he obviously made a mistake, which, for that matter, people will notice very quickly after him.[26] They had no difficulty showing that if the same quantity of movement is conserved in the universe, it's impossible to assume that partial movements have a determinate direction, given that to modify the determination of these movements, other movements must obviously be added to it—and we'll certainly always see a force intervene, a force that will be compensated for by the previous force. Which amounts to saying that one is introducing something into the system.

So if this is what Descartes meant, he made a mistake, from this point of view. It's possible however—this is a simple conjecture I'm making—it's possible that Descartes intended to reconcile human freedom with the mechanism of nature in a different way, or at least that he intended to apply another restriction, another reservation to the universal mechanism.

Let's now ask how today still, how today especially, we would conceive the possibility of an intervention of freedom in a world that would be subject to a more or less universal
[238] mechanism. It's clear that in such a world the phenomena we'd be dealing with would be phenomena to which in general we could apply the law of the conservation of energy. On what conditions would it be possible for freedom to slip through the meshes of this web?

We'd have to suppose that in certain cases, for example in the case of cerebral phenomena, something like accumulations of reserves of energy, systems of potential energy, occur at certain points that, to become actual, are just waiting for a signal, for the trigger to go off, so to speak.[27] We'd have to imagine—this is a simple metaphor—explosive materials that are simply waiting for someone to pull the trigger. The force used to pull the trigger to get the explosion going can be extremely small, nearly nothing compared to the force stored up only waiting for the chance to explode—it could be something of the sort. What we call freedom would be considered from the material side as a certain power and also as a certain triggering potential. This, it seems, is how we could picture, provisionally, in an enormously simplified form undoubtedly, the conservation of freedom in the midst of nature's mechanism.

It's possible that Descartes had a conception of this kind, for how does he picture the action of the soul on the body? We don't have the time to enter into all the details, nor to read the texts. On this subject, I'll remind you of things you know well: for Descartes, when we carry out a voluntary movement, it's our will that acts. When we carry out a voluntary movement, this is because animal spirits—a very subtle matter—the animal spirits contained in the brain are launched along the nerves to the muscles and dilate or contract the muscles.[28] The movements of the muscles are thus due solely to the force launched into these muscles in the form of animal spirits. Descartes in one particular passage compares the soul when it acts on the animal spirits via the pineal gland, compares the soul to a fountain keeper.[29] The brain with the animal spirits is a spring and the animal spirits fly from this spring. The role of the soul is to open this or that canal, this or that nerve, for these animal spirits, just as a fountain keeper opens [239]
up this or that tube—since the nerves, for Descartes, are tubes—this or that tube for the water shooting out. That amounts to saying that the soul opens or closes faucets, it squeezes triggers; it is thus essentially a force of triggering. So it does seem—this is a latent thought of Descartes's—that he had, I'm not saying the idea of reconciling freedom with mechanism this way, but of applying in this form a restriction—and this restriction, while slight, is no less serious—a restriction on universal mechanism.

So this, gentlemen, is the second point on which we should insist if we had the time. Descartes thinks that human freedom is compatible with determinism such as he understands it, be it because this mechanism includes a certain indetermination due to the fact that the direction of all the movements is not necessarily determinate even though the quantity of movement is determinate, be it, on the contrary, because he supposes that the soul is capable—acting on the body with a very minimal, nearly null, force of triggering—is capable of occasioning movements that can intrinsically testify to an expenditure, as great as we'd like, of force.

There is now a third point to consider, which is the mechanism of the action of the soul on this pineal gland via which the action of our will on the animal spirits in general takes place. You know that Descartes didn't discuss this action of the soul, on the body in general but also on the pineal gland in particular, where it is specifically located, Descartes didn't discuss this action or, rather, he tells us, in two or three passages that very much accord with each other that there's no need to discuss it. On this subject, we should read a letter to Arnauld:

> That the mind, which is incorporeal, can set the body in motion is something which is shown to us not by reasoning or comparison with other matters, but by the surest and plainest everyday experience. It is one of those self-evident things which we only make more obscure when we try to explain them in terms of other things.[30]

[240] But there's an even more intriguing passage in a letter to Princess Elizabeth:

> That is why[31] people who never philosophize and use only their senses have no doubt that the soul moves the body, and that the body acts on the soul. They regard both of them as a single thing, that is to say, they conceive their union; because to conceive the union between two things is to conceive them as one single thing. Metaphysical thoughts, which exercise the pure intellect, help to familiarize us with the notion of the soul; and the study of mathematics, which exercises mainly the imagination in the consideration of shapes and motions, accustoms us to form very distinct notions of the body.[32]

Thus, if we want to have as distinct a notion as possible of the soul, we must turn to metaphysics; if we want to have a distinct notion of the body, we must turn to mathematics. But what must we do to know how the soul is united with the body? "It is the ordinary course of life and conversation, and abstention from meditation and from the study of things which exercise the imagination, that teaches us how to conceive the union of the soul and the body."[33] Now that's very remarkable. If we want to conceive the soul we have to turn to metaphysics, to conceive the body to geometry, but for the union of the soul and the body, we mustn't study, we must simply let ourselves live. We draw the conception of the action of the soul on the body immediately from the feeling we have of our concrete life. This is extremely instructive, and it shows us the role that intuition, the inner immediate feeling, plays in Descartes's philosophy. It's true that having the immediate feeling of this union is no reason for it being absolutely incomprehensible and beyond theoretical explanation, but that's what Descartes believes he must demonstrate.[34] It's not surprising that Descartes accepted this,[35] for in his philosophy, given his conception of the soul and the body, there could be no contact, no communication between the body
[241] and the soul, such that the relations of the soul and the body became a simple fact that must be noted and that isn't open to analysis. It's hard for the mind to resign itself to accepting that, to accepting in such conditions an intuition, even a very strong one, even a very lively one. An intuition can never be completely resolved into rational ideas; still, it must be resolved indefinitely. We thus understand that, after Descartes, philosophy did not resign itself to accepting things in this form. It would have been natural, it seems, by accepting intuition, to try to find out how Descartes's theory of the soul and the body would have to be modified for their relation, their communication, not to be entirely beyond explanation, not entirely unintelligible. That was the path to be followed; it was not the one that was taken. No, on the contrary, people accepted Descartes's definition of the body and the soul because it was completely clear, because these were the two clear and distinct ideas that Descartes naturally contributed.[36]

Accepting these two ideas, reasoning about them, people came to conclude that any sort of relation between the body and the mind thus defined is impossible, as is any reciprocal action, from which it follows that freedom, the action of the soul on the body, was sacrificed. The intuition aspect we usually reach was limited and we ended up with radical determinism.

In the next two or three lectures, I'll show what kind of determinism was reached, via two quite different paths. In the next lecture, we'll be concerned more particularly with metaphysical determinism.

Notes

1. This was the starting point of the first lecture.
2. In the sixth lecture; see above, 72–3.
3. In *Duration and Simultaneity*, Bergson repeats this assertion in almost the same form to justify his favorable reception of Einstein's thought (DS, 124/181).
4. Baillet recounts this episode in his 1691 *La Vie de M. Descartes*, 2 vols. (Paris: Horthemels, 1691), 1.1.2: 81–4, https://gallica.bnf.fr/ark:/12148/bpt6k75559n/f155.item
5. On the tension between these two orientations of thought, which Bergson thinks are constitutive of Descartes's philosophy, see CE, 297/344–5.
6. See, for example, the letter of November 23, 1646, to the Marquess of Newcastle (PW III, 304/AT IV, 575).
7. Here, Bergson is taking up the theory Descartes lays out in *The Principles of Philosophy* I.39 (PW I, 205–6/AT VIIIA, 19–20).
8. See the first lecture of this course, December 6, 1904, p. 16.
9. Read: "the first."
10. This reading—*psychologues*—is uncertain. Did Bergson say "philosophers"—*philosophes*—instead, as opposed to the "scientists," the *savants* mentioned in the next paragraph? Yet "psychologists" would be justified by the argument that the "metaphysicians" evoked here (Spinoza and Leibniz) make pronouncements on the nature of the mind and that their theories of thinking, which go in the direction of a rigorous determinism, are extended by nineteenth-century scientific psychology (an argument Bergson first makes, in very general terms, in *Matter and Memory*).
11. According to a very strange process that Bergson thinks occurs regularly in the history of philosophy; see above, 20–21 and 109.
12. See the concluding lecture of May 13, 1904, in HTM.
13. Bergson is alluding to *L'Homme machine* by French medical doctor and materialist philosopher Julien Offray de La Mettrie (1709–51), first published in 1747; see *Machine Man and Other Writings*, ed. and trans. Ann Thomson (New York: Cambridge University Press, 2008). Bergson discusses La Mettrie in more detail in the lecture mentioned in the previous note (HTM, 327–30).
14. See CE, 305/355; ME, 47–51/38–41 and 232–4/192–4.
15. Latin for "leap."
16. This is the text to which Bergson dedicated his Saturday course that and the following year (see above, 22n2). Published in 1862 and subsequently reworked several times, *The First*

Principles, considered by many Spencer's most important book, exerted a major influence over the young Bergson. He would later break away from Spencer and, in *Creative Evolution*, seek to substitute "the true evolutionism" for "the false evolutionism" developed in *First Principles* (CE, 5–6/x).

17. For Bergson's view on the law of the conservation of energy (or of "force," a term widely used by Spencerians), see TFW, 143–55/107–17, and CE, 213–14/242–3, as well as above, 107–8.

18. The "energy of movements" refers to kinetic energy, "internal energy" to potential energy. For more on this, see CE, 213–14/242–3. Bergson's analysis is inspired by a book published in the same year as this lecture, Pierre Duhem's *L'Évolution de la mécanique*. Bergson explicitly cites (CE, 213 note b/243n1) the first chapter of the second part, entitled "The Physics of Quality"; see Duhem, *The Evolution of Mechanics*, trans. Michael Cole (Alphen aan den Rijn: Sijthoff and Noordhoff, 1980), 105–15.

19. That is to say: the energies at issue are energies of different *qualities* that, according to Bergson and Duhem, we arbitrarily try to merge into a single quantitative value, a "convention."

20. Descartes, *Principles*, II.36 (PW I, 240/AT VIIIA, 61).

21. This is an allusion to Leibniz and to his critique of Descartes's laws of movement, first articulated in the *Brevis demonstratio erroris memorabilis Cartesii* of 1686; see "A Brief Demonstration of a Notable Error of Descartes and Others concerning a Natural Law," text 34 in PPL, 296–302. See also "Discourse on Metaphysics," in PE, 35–68, here §17: 49–51.

22. Bergson is referring to the foundation of thermodynamics at the beginning of the nineteenth century, inaugurated in particular by Sadi Carnot's 1824 *Reflections on the Motive Power of Fire*, ed. E. Mendoza (Mineola, NY: Dover, 1988), and the advances made by Ruldolf Clausius and, especially, Ludwig Boltzmann; see CE, 214–15/243–5.

23. Compare CE, 40/38: "Everything is given"; see also above, 82 and 90n1, and below 178–9 and, especially, 219–20.

24. Descartes, *Principles*, II.41 (PW I, 242–3/AT VIIIA, 65). "This rule" refers to the statement in the preceding paragraph: "if a body collides with another body that is stronger than itself, it loses none of its motion; but if it collides with a weaker body, it loses a quantity of motion equal to that which it imparts to the other body" (II.40, PW I, 242/AT VIIIA, 65).

25. Descartes, *Principles*, II.40 (PW I, 242/AT VIIIA, 65). The law in question is the rule just stated concerning a body colliding with other, stronger or weaker, bodies. Descartes never wrote the "treatise" he mentions here, which should not be confused with the *Treatise of Man* of 1633.

26. See, for instance, Leibniz, *Theodicy*, I.§61: 156–7, or Spinoza, *Ethics* IIIP2: 494–7.

27. Bergson articulates this theory in the first chapter of *Matter and Memory* and, at length, in *Creative Evolution* (esp. CE, 107–9/116–17).

28. See, for example, Descartes, *The Passions of the Soul*, I.7–11, PW I, 330–2/AT XI, 331–6.

29. This passage is found in an early text, the *Treatise on Man*; see PW I, 100–1/AT XI, 131–2. According to Cartesian physiology, the pineal gland is the point of contact, in the brain, between the soul and the bodily functions.

30. This letter dates from July 29, 1648; see PW III, 358/AT V, 222.

31. The transition appears just as abrupt in the French, but it is not so on the level of content: like Bergson, Descartes has just explained that the union of the soul and body is "known only obscurely by the intellect" but "known very clearly by the senses."

32. Descartes to Princess Elizabeth, June 28, 1643, in PW III, 226–9, here 227/AT III, 690–7 here 692.
33. This, too, is from the July 28, 1643, letter to Elizabeth, PW III, 227/AT III, 692.
34. Instead of *croit avoir à démontrer*, "believes he must demonstrate," an alternative reading would be *croyait avoir démontré*, "believed he had demonstrated."
35. "This" being the incomprehensibility of the immediate feeling of the union of soul and body.
36. CE, 297–9/345–7.

LECTURE 15
MARCH 31, 1905

Gentlemen, in the last two lectures, I showed the mixture, in Descartes, of rational, purely rational elements, and elements borrowed from what I called intuition, the immediate testimony of consciousness. All the principles of a pure intellectualism are there, but Descartes never pushes the development of his principles all the way: he stops at the exact moment when he would go against the testimony of what I've called consciousness, the inner feeling. [243]

Now I must show—this will be the objective of this lecture and the next two—how the rational elements of this doctrine came out on top, how they developed, how they took up all the space and stifled the other elements, by absorbing them, according to a law confirmed, I said, throughout the history of philosophy. We thereby end up with the most radical determinism, with the doctrine of absolute necessity.

Let me say immediately that while I tried to show how considerable Christianity's influence on Descartes's philosophy was, it's no longer the same, or at least it's much less true, for Descartes's successors, for those who pushed his doctrine in the purely intellectualist direction. Philosophies like that of Spinoza, like that of Leibniz, are clearly—it seems to me at least—partial returns to ancient philosophy, to the philosophy of someone like Aristotle, like Plotinus. These doctrines are forms of Cartesianism, granted, but Cartesianism seen through Aristotle or seen through Plotinus.[1]

I'm not saying that this return to the ancients, to Greek philosophy, was deliberate, voluntary, well considered. It's even possible that simply by pushing intellectualism all the way, simply by claiming to provide an absolutely unified and simple, consistent and logical explanation of the totality of things, simply by pushing intellectualism all the way, it's quite possible that we tend toward a doctrine like that of the Greek philosophers, who were essentially intellectualists. It's quite possible that simply by wanting to make Cartesianism perfectly consistent, we push it in the direction of a philosophy such as Neoplatonism, such as Plotinus's doctrine. So this could all be just coincidences. Nonetheless, the resemblances in the details are so striking, the resemblances of expression as well, between a doctrine like that of Spinoza or of Leibniz on the one hand and Greek philosophy on the other, that I cannot believe in a pure and simple coincidence. There was clear influence, influence for which we can, when it comes to Leibniz, reconstitute the intermediaries—this is a lot more difficult for Spinoza, we have to proceed by means of conjectures. Nonetheless, there seems to be no doubt that these two philosophies, which, both of them, are philosophies of necessity, are partial returns to the doctrine of an Aristotle and above all of a Plotinus, Plotinus being, as I've shown here this year, a systematized Aristotle. [244]

It's Spinoza, then, whom we're going to look at summarily today. Spinoza's objective is Aristotle's very objective, for when we open his *Treatise on the Emendation of the Intellect*, we find pointed out, on the very first pages, the goal of philosophy such as he understands it:

> Our happiness depends solely on the quality of the objects to which we cling by love, for strife will never arise on account of that which is not loved; nor will there be sadness if it perishes, nor envy if it is possessed by another, nor fear, nor hatred, in a word, no disturbance of the soul, all the things that occur in the love of perishable things, but love of an eternal and infinite thing feeds the soul with, and joy alone, a joy without any sadness.[2]

[245] Philosophy's objective is thus to tell us what we must love. And what we must love is what nourishes our soul with a joy without sadness and without mixture, an infinite, that is, the love of an eternal and infinite thing, as Spinoza says.

This is exactly what Aristotle was telling us in book 10 of the *Nicomachean Ethics*: philosophy's goal is just this, it's, "so far as we can, making ourselves immortal."[3] The word *athanatizein* is untranslatable, it means: making immortality for oneself [*se fabriquer de l'immortalité*], we must make immortality for ourselves. This is exactly the objective of philosophy such as Spinoza understands it.

If we take Plotinus instead of Aristotle, we'll find analogies of expression that are even more striking. The goal is thus the same. I'll add that the means is the same. How would an ancient detach the soul from perishable things to attach it to eternal things? This process takes place in pure intellect. Naturally, when it goes as far as its natural consequences, our intellect encompasses the things of space and time, such as the accidents [*hasards*] of time and of place have made them. Natural knowledge grasps the accidental [*accidentel*]: science, belief, in the end all that isn't the highest kind of knowledge, all of that is attached to the accidental, to what exists at a certain point in time, in a certain location in space, thanks to chance, accident, and to what is connected with other things by purely accidental relations. What does a wise man do? What does a philosopher do? He substitutes essential relations for these accidental ones. He goes from accident to essence. He moves from the things that are given in space and time, and arranged in an accidental order, to purely intelligible objects situated in a higher world where they solely maintain relations among themselves, which are profound, essential, relations of true kinship. By detaching ourselves from the superficial knowledge of the accident to attach ourselves to this profound knowledge of the essence, we manage to escape what passes away, what changes, to place ourselves back in eternity. This is exactly what Spinoza says in *The Treatise on the Emendation of the Intellect*. The goal of
[246] philosophy is this: to see things not as they are accidentally but as they are essentially, to see them, as he will say especially in the *Ethics*, to see them in God.[4]

In a certain sense, the objective and the means are the same, as you can see, gentlemen, as the objective and the means employed by Greek philosophy. We could say that the plan is identical; the execution differs. The execution is profoundly different. For the ancients, the essential, what is really true, the essence of things is what they call "Idea" or "Form." It's what in the Middle Ages was called *universalia*, universals. The ancients believed that what passes, what's contingent, what's accidental, is the individual, but the genus is what subsists—I'm saying "the ancients," not all the ancients, for Plotinus asserts that alongside the eternal genera there are eternal individuals, individual Ideas as well—but in the end, the tendency of the ancients is that, what's essential, what's eternal is the genus. Spinoza, for his part, comes on the scene after Kepler, after Galileo, after Descartes, after people who transformed the very idea of science. To know scientifically, for the ancients, was to move from the individuals we see in space and time to intelligible genera or essences located in a supersensible world. For a Kepler, for a Galileo, for a Descartes, to know scientifically is something entirely different: it's to establish a law. It isn't to move to a genus or to an essence, it's to move to a law.[5]

What is a law? It's a stable relation between objects or phenomena situated in space and time. A law is a constant relation between variable terms, the very terms of our experiences. From this, it follows that for modern science, to elevate ourselves to what is independent of time, to go to the eternal, isn't to leave the world we live in, it's simply to discover in this world itself stable, eternal relations that are like the very framework of the phenomena.[6] There's thus no need to move to a supersensible world to look there for what is superior to space, time, and accident, it's enough, staying in this world itself, to discover stable relations, relations by means of which the phenomena that pass away are [247]
as it were stood up against something eternal.

This is the guiding idea of modern science, an idea that's very different from that of ancient science.[7] For ancient science, the object of knowledge is the genera, the universals. For modern science, the object of knowledge is laws. And while for an ancient philosopher, elevating ourselves to the imperishable, elevating ourselves to the eternal consists in leaving the world such as we immediately know it, a modern philosopher on the contrary will be able to say that, without leaving this world, we discover the eternal by looking at things from the right angle. All we have to do is look at the things that change from a certain side, to take them from a certain bias, and to see them from a certain angle. So the difference is considerable.

Spinoza couldn't not have taken these givens into account. I'm not saying that he knew the science of a Kepler or of a Galileo, but he knew Descartes who, for his part, had a very clear conception of scientific laws such as the moderns in general understand them. Given that, we can say that Spinoza had no other objective than to start anew, working with modern science, with the modern conception of laws, the very work that Aristotle and especially Plotinus had done with the frameworks of ancient science as their subject.[8] So it's the same kind of enterprise: to go from the perishable to the eternal by means of the intellect, to detach oneself from what perishes in order to attach oneself to the eternal. There's this difference from the ancients that for Spinoza, this eternity is not transcendent to the things, it's not exterior to them, it's immanent to them. It's enough to take things from a certain side, to see them from a certain angle, to go, without changing anything objectively in them, as they said in the seventeenth century, without changing anything in their materiality, from what perishes to what outlives itself or, rather, to go to what is eternal.[9]

In these conditions, what transformation did Spinoza make Cartesianism undergo? There can be no question here of summarizing Spinoza's entire *Ethics*, gentlemen, not even the first two parts, which from the viewpoint of the question that concerns us
[248] would be the most interesting to examine. I'd simply like to show how, on which points, Spinoza transformed, modified Descartes's doctrine, thereby transforming it from the doctrine of freedom that it was into a doctrine of necessity, and of the most radical and the least flexible necessity that has ever been formulated.

You recall, gentlemen, that for Descartes material things are extended things. Matter is extended, things are portions of extension. The modifications of things are modes of extension. And precisely because the very essence of material things is extension, it follows that matter can be treated geometrically: matter obeys purely mathematical laws. In Descartes's doctrine, to be sure, there are restrictions, reservations, and he, in short, attenuates the doctrine. And in my last lecture, I showed how Descartes, by accepting the influence of the soul on the body, by asserting that souls act on bodies, Descartes thereby establishes a certain discontinuity within universal mechanism. It's no longer an absolute, radical mechanism. On the contrary, there are ruptures[10] if, every now and then, there are human bodies with souls in these bodies that act, and act freely, choosing their decisions and executing them.

Spinoza will erase this discontinuity because his goal is to reestablish the complete unity of Cartesianism, his "proximate" goal. I just defined the other for what he writes, I just defined the other goal.[11] So the issue, for Spinoza, is to reestablish the complete unity of Cartesianism and erase any trace of discontinuity. Spinoza will tell us that bodies are modes of extension, that each mode of extension is explained by other modes of extension, and that this is true for all modes of extension. This amounts to saying that, if we translate this idea into our current language, that the modes—that the world is composed of bodies that act and react on each other mechanically and according to absolutely necessary laws, which are the very laws of mechanics. For example, all that happens in the current state of the world is explained by what preceded, and all that will follow is explained by what currently exists in the state of the universe. Consequently, an infinite intellect, a mathematician who'd have an infinite, superhuman intellect, would
[249] read in the present state of the universe all the states to come and all the past states,[12] for if the material universe constitutes one single machine, in which everything is joined to everything, then everything happens mechanically and everything can be calculated or could be calculated mathematically.

So all the successive states of the universe are contained in any one among them. We see things that follow things, states that follow states, states of the universe that follow other states of the universe—in any one of these states, all the others could be read.

Let's go further: if we can read all the other states in any one of these states, then that amounts to saying that all past, present, and future states of the universe are given all together [*tous ensemble, en bloc*]. We see these states from a certain angle, from a certain side, as following on one another. We think that an infinite intellect perceives them from a different aspect, and as given all at once, for if the present adds nothing to the past, if the present is only a new perfectly foreseeable state given in the past, then there's never anything absolutely new in the universe, never anything added to it in an absolute way, and we can say that everything is given, everything at once. Consequently, seen from below, if we can say it like that, seen from below, the states of the universe appear to us as given one after another, there's an indefinite series of them, and each of them is composed of an indefinite number of parts, but seen from above, all this would appear all at once. It's clear that it wouldn't be in this form, but all this would appear all at once, very much like the mathematician with an infinite intellect I talked about earlier could represent the totality of past, present, and future things in one single formula: this formula would appear to him in a simple and indivisible form, and it would present to him, in this form, the indefinite series of changes that succeed one another in space and time.

I just paraphrased Spinoza's idea, but basically, this is indeed the one he lays out in the first two parts of the *Ethics*. Concerning bodies, there are two ways of looking at them. Seen from below, as I said earlier, bodies are modes of extension that follow on modes of extension, and their series is indefinite in time and their number indefinite in space. But seen from above all this would appear all at once in a simple, indivisible form, [250]
in the form of what Spinoza calls extension, extension as such, extension as attribute [*l'extension attribut*]. The relation of extension as attribute to extension as mode, to the modes of extension, this relation is thus the relation of the simple and indivisible formula to the indefinite developments that can be drawn from it.

We mustn't, when we read the *Ethics*, think that the modes of extension designate parts of extension. To give rise to the modes of extension, extension as an attribute isn't cut up into modes. No, we might as well believe that to get the change of a banknote, it's cut up into little bits of paper. Little fragments of banknotes are no more the change of the note than fragments of extension, if we were able to divide it—and it is indivisible[13]—would be the change of extension. Between the extension as attribute (extension as such [*tout court*]) and all the modes of extension, there is, for Spinoza—I'm making a comparison that seems to me quite in the spirit of the doctrine—there is the same relation as between a banknote, here representing an infinite amount, and the change, representing this amount, which would have to be counted indefinitely and whose count would never be exhausted.[14]

So Spinoza restored the complete unity in Descartes's mechanism. We'll say that the material universe is simple undivided extension, expressing itself in multiple forms by an indefinite number of modes that follow one another and are juxtaposed. That's it for bodies.

Let's now move on to minds, to souls. It'll be the same thing. Descartes had said that there are human souls created by God; it's God who creates them and who preserves them. We thus have a multiplicity of terms given together and successively. These souls are as it were disseminated in the universe.[15] All this is discontinuity, it's not the unity, the simple unity we're looking for. It's discontinuity, consequently, for a Spinoza, it's unintelligibility, it's not entirely clear for the intellect. The issue is to get unity. For that, we won't need to go beyond Cartesianism's own terms.

[251] What is a soul for Descartes? It's thought: states of mind are forms or modes of thought. Spinoza will limit himself to observing that souls are, as we would say today, states of mind that succeed each other in thought. Consequently, souls are modes of thought. Souls are not like islands in the ocean, as it were, islands placed here and there in an ocean. No, we must picture an ocean of thought, [picture] thought; then, in this thought, regions comprising modes of thought, and these different regions, these series of modes of thought, will respectively be Peter, Paul, etc. So souls are modes of thought, and modes of thought that symmetrically correspond to modes of extension.

Descartes said something like this, since he did say that states of our soul correspond to the states of our body. To be sure, he didn't state the reciprocal proposition, and he didn't say that a determinate state of the body necessarily corresponds to every thought. But Spinoza goes all the way. For him, a soul joined to a body is a series of modes of thought that correspond symmetrically to as many modes of extension. The correspondence is perfect, so much so that we can say that the soul, to use Spinoza's language, the soul is the idea of its body. We call "soul" the idea of the body.[16]

This being established, being given that the soul is the idea of the body, that the soul is a series of modes of thought that correspond to modes of extension, I can repeat for thought all I said for extension: since all modes of extension, if we could see them all together—which is impossible, it's an infinity—but, in any case, since all modes of extension, if we could add them up, would yield something absolutely simple and indivisible, which is extension, so all modes of thought, if we could see them all, if there were no contradiction in supposing this, all the modes of thought, if we could add them up, would yield thought, nothing more than thought, thought, too, being something absolutely indivisible, something that will be to the series of the modes of thought—I can
[252] in fact repeat the comparison indefinitely—what the banknote would be to the change that we can get for it. So we have thought as attribute in which all possible present, past, and future modes of thought merge.

So, gentlemen, here we are, we've reached extension on the one hand, thought on the other. Where do they come from? Descartes had said: they are creations of God. It's God who created extension and thought by an act of will. It's God who establishes a communication between the two, a communication that is, moreover, unintelligible. Spinoza will reject a theory like this for the same reasons that made him reject the theory of souls separated from bodies and relatively independent of one another. No, extension and thought aren't creations,[17] since according to what I just said, extension and thought are absolutely simple, absolutely indivisible, absolutely infinite. They are the infinite, both of them, for we call "infinite" what contains in a simple and indivisible form elements whose enumeration would never come to an end.[18] So they're infinites; they're eternal things as well: thought and extension are given from all eternity. They are, consequently, expressions of God, for God is infinite, eternal. Moreover, he cannot not be, he posits himself simply because he is possible.

Gentlemen, I cannot go into all the details of this demonstration, but for Spinoza, a proposition like this one: "God exists," is a proposition having the same nature as this one: "2 × 2 = 4" or "A = A."[19] When did "A = A" begin to be and what makes it such

that "A = A"? "A = A" posits itself by itself. We could suppress all the things we see in the universe and the idea "A = A" would subsist. It's eternal. It's self-sufficient. It's self-causing. It's in this sense that Spinoza will tell us that God is the cause of himself.[20] By means of a certain number of theorems, Spinoza establishes that a proposition that consisted, basically, in saying that God is not, is a contradictory proposition.[21] The infinite, by its infinite substance alone, the substance of God, simply because it is possible, exists and necessarily posits itself. God being posited, both extension and thought are posited with him [*du même coup*], necessarily, being divine attributes, that [253]
is, things that express God. They are expressions of God, the word "expression" having to be taken in the mathematical sense—this is a point I already had the opportunity to treat here a few years ago[22]—for I really believe that Spinoza, in this doctrine, takes his inspiration from the key idea of Cartesian geometry.

Descartes is the creator of analytic geometry; it's even his most beautiful creation. What is the method of this geometry? It consists in expressing geometrical things in algebraic terms, for example, the pure idea of circumference. Descartes's geometry shows us that this idea of circumference can be expressed in two ways. It can be expressed by a circle, that is, a round figure on the board, a geometric circumference. Then, this same idea can be expressed by an algebraic equation. Both the circle figure and the algebraic equation completely express the idea of the circle. All that is contained in the idea of the circle will be discovered by means of a series of deliberations on the figure, and everything that is contained in the idea of the circle will be in a series of transformations of the equation as well. So much so that, although the equation bears no resemblance to the figure—there's no kind of resemblance between the figure and the equation—nonetheless, the figure and the equation say exactly the same thing, provide the translation of one and the same truth in two different languages. That is what Spinoza calls extension as attribute and what he calls thought as attribute. These two terms are to substance, as he says, that is, to God, exactly what the circle figure and the quadratic equation are to the idea of the circle. Posit the idea of the circle—it posits itself, no one ever created circumference—posit the idea of the circle and you necessarily posit the circle as figure and the circle as equation, and, undoubtedly, a host of other possible expressions that we don't have, that we'll never have. Well, posit the divine substance—it posits itself, it can no more not be than a geometrical figure, and the impossibility is even greater when it concerns God than when it concerns a geometrical figure—posit God and you necessarily posit all possible expressions of God,[23] consequently, the expression as attribute, the expression [254]
as thought, and infinities of other attributes that we don't know, that we'll never know. So thought and extension are two expressions of the essence of substance. I'm quoting the very terms Spinoza uses in the sixth definition at the beginning of the *Ethics*, where he defines God. He ends this definition by saying that God possesses an infinity of infinite attributes, each of which expresses the essence of substance.[24] So we have expressions of the divine substance in extension as attribute and in thought as attribute. This itself will make us understand the soul's relation to the body.

Descartes said—and this is the nerve of his theory of freedom insofar as it's opposed to universal mechanism, as I showed the other day[25]—Descartes said that the soul acts on the body, that the soul is capable of moving the body. But for Spinoza, this is something unintelligible, and doubly unintelligible: first because we don't understand that thought communicates with extension and extension with thought;[26] and then because supposing such an action to intervene in the universal mechanism means breaking the unity of the whole.[27] So the soul doesn't act on the body, nor the body on the soul. It's as though there were reciprocal action—and it must be so, for what is the body? It's a series of modes of extension. What is the soul? A series of modes of thought. What are the modes of extension? They develop all the content of extension. What are the modes of thought? They develop all the content of thought. Yet thought and extension say the same thing, express the same thing. So each of all the developments of thought will correspond to all the developments of extension, and subsequently a mode of extension will correspond to each mode of thought, and reciprocally.

Let's suppose a poem like the *Iliad* or the *Odyssey* is translated into French and into German.[28] If the translation is absolutely word for word, a German word of the German translation will correspond to each French word of the French translation. Someone who doesn't know that there is a Greek *Iliad* and that these are two translations might
[255] think that the German term has determined the French term or that the French term has determined the German term. But the truth is that neither has the French influenced the German nor has the German influenced the French, but that the two poems, French and German, translate the same thing. It's the same for extension and thought, the mode of extension and the mode of thought being two translations, two expressions of one and the same thing, in such a way that the parts correspond to each other one by one. It's as though the mode of extension determined the mode of thought and reciprocally, but there is only correspondence and parallelism.

There you have a much simplified synopsis. But for the subject that concerns us, we have to simplify. We're looking for the main features of Spinozism, insofar as Spinoza is, in this first part at least, Cartesianism pushed all the way. There you have Spinoza's doctrine, its main features, as we find it in the first two parts of the *Ethics*.

It goes without saying that Cartesianism is not interpreted here: it's the doctrine of absolute necessity.[29] I won't quote all the texts; there would be too many of them. Spinoza couldn't have more contempt, more scorn for those who believe in contingency in the universe, for those who believe in free will. "Those . . . who believe," he says in the third part of the *Ethics*, at the end of proposition 2, "those . . . who believe that they either speak or are silent, or do anything from a free decision of the Mind, dream with open eyes."[30] And elsewhere, he'll explain to us what the illusion of contingency and free will is based on. In reality, he says, there are only two kinds of things, those that are necessary and those that are impossible. The thing that happens is the necessary thing. The thing that doesn't happen is the impossible thing. To believe in freedom, to believe in free will at least, to believe in contingency is to imagine that there's something intermediary between necessity and impossibility. This simply has to do with our being misinformed, with our not seeing clearly what's necessary and clearly what's impossible. In this case,
[256] we place ourselves between the two: we consider several hypotheses as to be equally possible, to be plausible. The truth is that what was possible has been realized, that what

is possible is being realized, that all that has not been realized is impossible, and that there is no middle ground between the impossible and the necessary. That's Spinoza's doctrine.[31]

This doctrine, too, results necessarily from the premises posited. God posits himself. He is the cause of himself. *He* is necessary. God positing himself posits his attributes, that is, all possible expressions of his essence. He cannot not posit them. They are posited at the same time as himself, just as all the possible expressions of the circle are posited with the idea of the circle. Then, the attributes being posited, you cannot not posit the modes that are their small change, that express in the form of a multiplicity what the attributes express in the form of an indivisible unity. Thus bodies and minds are given with all their modes.

There you have the doctrine of absolute necessity, rigorous, inflexible, the doctrine presented in the first two parts of the *Ethics*.

We would now have to examine—but that would go beyond our goal, it's not what we have to do, we're dealing with theories of freedom and of necessity—we'd have to examine the other three parts of the *Ethics*, which in Spinoza's thought are the main ones since all that's been said up to here is only the means: the point is to reach the goal. The goal is to define beatitude, what Spinoza calls true freedom, emancipation [*affranchissement*], for Spinoza does not believe in free will, but he does believe in what he calls freedom.[32] We know—I've said this before[33]—that that has been the claim of all the doctrines that have denied free will, to claim nonetheless that they're doctrines of freedom and that freedom can be defined in terms of necessity.

What will this freedom be? Freedom will be for humans what it is for God. For although everything God does, everything he is, is absolutely necessary, although by positing God we posit all that he is, just as by positing the triangle we posit all the properties of the triangle, Spinoza will tell us nonetheless that God is free, understanding by that that nothing constrains him; that God carries out exclusively the demands of his essence; that there is nothing outside of God, nothing that weighs on God.[34] God [257]
posits himself. He is entirely himself. *That's* his freedom: his freedom is a necessity that nothing external determines, it's what we call internal necessity. This is how, according to Spinoza, we must define freedom. Well, freedom for humans will consist in participating in God's freedom, that is, in placing themselves back in God. To be free is to be aware of universal necessity, to be aware of this: that seen from a certain angle, we are God himself. To be free is thus to enter back into God. That's where beatitude is; that's where eternity is as well.[35]

This is exactly what the ancients said, what Plotinus in particular said, for there'd be an extremely interesting comparison to be made between Spinoza's conclusion and the eighth book of Plotinus's sixth Ennead, which is entitled "On the Freedom and Will of the One," that is, of God.[36] In this book, Plotinus defines divine freedom exactly as Spinoza will define this freedom later. God is the cause of himself. God hypostatizes himself.[37] God's will, God's freedom coincide with his substance. For humans, freedom consists in entering back into God by taking part in the divine freedom, by taking part in his eternity. So the solution's the same as that of the ancients. However, to reach this solution, Spinoza has to fight against formidable difficulties that ancient philosophy did not know. The ancients got themselves out of trouble—this would be a very interesting thing to show, quite entertaining, I'd say, for we could take Spinoza's mechanism apart and compare its pieces to those of a philosophy like Plotinus's—the ancients, I'm saying, had the concept of *hylē*, the idea of matter, which solved a lot of difficulties.

What is the great difficulty for Spinoza, the one he grapples with in the last three books of the *Ethics*? The difficulty is to explain how there can be something outside of God, how we can be outside of God—for we are outside of God and in certain cases we enter back into God. How is this thing possible? For the ancients, it was very simple: there's a negative principle, the principle of disorder, which is called *hylē*, which in being introduced into the intelligible, into the eternal, causes them to degenerate. But Spinoza—I said this at the beginning—is not going to posit a supersensible, eternal
[258] world. No, eternity is immanent to the very things. So how can there be something in eternity that is external to God, external to itself as it were? Since for Spinoza, in the state of what he calls "servitude," slavery, we are outside of God, outside of ourselves,[38] freedom is a return to oneself, a return to God. How is this externalization in relation to God possible? I'm well aware that Spinoza declares that error and evil—all that, for him, is the same thing—that error and evil are purely negative things, they're inadequate knowledge, a knowledge that places us outside of God. It's incomplete knowledge; evil, error have nothing positive about them.[39] Nevertheless, these particular modes, which constitute our soul, have two ways of existing: in a certain sense detached from God, and in another sense seen in God. This duality was the great difficulty for Spinoza. We shouldn't be surprised that he did not manage to overcome it completely.

Be that as it may, we have with Spinoza's doctrine a very clear-cut, very clear example of what a mixed doctrine like Descartes's turns into, that is, a doctrine containing rational elements and elements of inner observation, elements of intuition, when we aim to rationalize this doctrine completely: the more we rationalize it, the more we unify it, the more we tend to dismiss contingency and, in the sense we give to this word, freedom. All in all, in fact, Spinoza's doctrine is the most perfect and the most complete expression of the most absolute determinism.

Now in the next lecture and in the ones following it, we still have to look at other forms of determinism that are a lot simpler and also a lot clearer. In the next lecture, we'll discuss, very summarily, Leibniz's determinism.

Notes

1. CE, 298–9/346–7.
2. Instead of citing it exactly, Bergson here paraphrases a passage found near the beginning of Spinoza's *Treatise on the Emendation of the Intellect* (CWS, 1: 3–45, here 9).
3. Aristotle, *Nicomachean Ethics*, 1177b33, 10.7: 1861.
4. See especially *Ethics* VP32–37: 561–8.
5. For the whole analysis that follows, see CE, 284–90/328–35.

6. CE, 303/352.
7. Compare the discussion of *science*, knowledge, in the early lectures (e.g. 42).
8. CE, 300/348.
9. That is, to see things from the viewpoint of the content of an idea, not of its form or of the stuff (thought) from which ideas are constituted.
10. Bergson here uses the intriguing expression *solution de continuité*, in which *solution* has the meaning of "dissolution."
11. "'Proximate' goal" (*but 'prochain'*) in the sense seventeenth-century philosophers speak of a "proximate cause" (see, for example, Descartes's 1647 "Comments on a Certain Broadsheet," PW I, 305/AT VIIIB: 360). The proximate cause is the cause closest to an effect as opposed to the ultimate cause or, here, the ultimate goal, the "other" goal "just defined" with *The Treatise on Emendation of the Intellect*, which is the possession of an eternal and infinite good.
12. Compare the discussion in this and the following paragraph with what Bergson says above, 82 and 90n1, 167 and 172n23, and, especially, below, 219–20.
13. Spinoza makes this important point in *Ethics* IP15S: 421–4.
14. For the image of money, see CE, 281/324–5 and 296/343; and CM, 190/180.
15. Bergson is alluding to Spinoza's rejecting the idea of "real distinction"—the idea that things are distinct—on the basis that it implies more than one substance (*Ethics* IP4: 411). Descartes asserts such a distinction in *The Principles of Philosophy*, I.60, PW I, 213–14/AT VIIIA, 28–9.
16. Spinoza, *Ethics* IIP12–13: 456–62.
17. This follows from *Ethics* IP5–6: 411–12.
18. *Ethics* IP15S: 421–4. On infinity in Spinoza generally, see Letter 12 to Meyer, CWS 1, 200–5.
19. For a similar argument, see CE, 276–7/242–3.
20. On the notion of a self-cause, see Spinoza, *Ethics* ID1: 408.
21. Here and in the sentence that follows, Bergson is thinking of Spinoza, *Ethics* IP11: 417–19.
22. It's not clear which year Bergson is referring to. None of his courses on single texts since he began teaching at the Collège de France specifically addressed this topic. The 1902–3 course, "Histoire de l'idée de temps," contains nothing like it, either. This leaves the 1900–1 course devoted to "L'idée de cause" (summarized in M, 439–41) and the 1901–2 course devoted to "L'idée de temps" (also summarized in M, 513–17). (An English translation of the lecture course on the history of the idea of time and of the summaries is forthcoming in this series.)
23. Spinoza, *Ethics* IP16: 424–5.
24. Spinoza, *Ethics* ID6: 409.
25. See the preceding lecture of March 24, 1905, esp. 169.
26. Spinoza, *Ethics* V, Preface: 543–6.
27. This breaking apart amounts to instituting "a dominion within a dominion" (Spinoza, *Ethics* III, Preface: 491).
28. "Introduction to Metaphysics," in CM, 187–90/178–80, and CE, 301–2/349–51.
29. The thrust of the sentence—*Il va sans dire que le cartésianisme n'est pas ici interprété: c'est la doctrine de la nécessité absolue*—seems to be that Spinoza, who develops a theory of absolute necessity, is not concerned with interpreting Descartes.

30. Spinoza, *Ethics* IIIP2S: 497.
31. Here, Bergson paraphrases and blends different passages from Spinoza's *Ethics*, among them IP17: 425–8; IP33: 436–9; IP36: 439; IIIP2S: 494–7; and IVD: 546–7.
32. Spinoza, *Ethics* IVP73S: 587.
33. In the first lecture of the course (20–21) as well as the preceding lecture (163).
34. Spinoza, *Ethics* IP17C2 (and everything else under this proposition): 425–8.
35. Bergson may have *Ethics* VP36: 564 in mind, a proposition he comments on in similar terms in "Philosophical Intuition" (in CM, 133–4/124).
36. On *Enneads* 6.8, see also the March 10, 1905, lecture, 141–2.
37. That is, God, outside of and so to speak below (*hypo-*) himself, produces these levels or states of reality (*-stases*) that are first the Intellect, then the Soul.
38. A reference to part IV of the *Ethics*, "Of Human Servitude." The Latin *servitudo* is sometimes rendered in English as "bondage."
39. On this doctrine, see Spinoza, *Ethics* IApp: 439–46 and IIP33–36: 472–4 (which specifically concern the question of error) and the set of letters exchanged between Spinoza and Blyenbergh, letters 18–24 and 27: 354–92 and 394–5.

LECTURE 16
APRIL 7, 1905

Gentlemen, today we must talk about the problem of freedom in Leibniz's philosophy. [259]
In reality, we'd have to lay out or summarize this entire philosophy if we wanted to have an adequate idea of freedom as Leibniz conceives it. You know how complex this philosophy is and how it must have evolved in the mind of the author, in how many different forms he presented it, how it's perhaps even more complex than it appears to us through the known and published texts, for the unpublished texts are even more numerous. There can be no question, it goes without saying, of laying his philosophy out completely. What I intend to do for Leibniz is what I already attempted for Spinoza in the last lecture, to show for this second philosopher, as for the first, how a doctrine of freedom like Descartes's evolves when only the purely rational elements are retained toward a doctrine of necessity. Like Spinoza, Leibniz, in short, sought to eliminate the elements of discontinuity from Cartesianism that were there and that are so many elements borrowed from inner immediate observation; and also like Spinoza, he was thereby led to a doctrine that is an inflexible determinism, just as, like Spinoza, he wasn't able to push Descartes in this purely intellectualist direction without thereby returning to the philosophy of the ancients, to the philosophy of a Plato, of an Aristotle, or of a Plotinus.[1]

Gentlemen, that seems to me to be the essential consideration, the guiding idea for
a study of Leibniz's philosophy. Leibniz is a pure intellectualist. No one has ever been [260]
more of an intellectualist or even as much as he was. He's more of an intellectualist than Spinoza, for Spinoza was an intellectualist by an effort of the will, and there are passages in the *Ethics*, especially in the last book, where Spinoza's intellectualism seems ready to crack, as it were, due to the effect of an inner thrust or an inner pressure.[2] But we find nothing of the kind in Leibniz. Leibniz is a philosopher who never worried. Nothing troubles him. He finds everything easy. He's convinced that reality can be fully resolved into ideas. He's convinced of the perfect harmony of things.

Descartes said, "everything in me is done mathematically."[3] Leibniz could have said, "everything in me is done musically." Somewhere he defined the pleasures of music by saying that it's an unconscious arithmetic.[4] In music, there are harmonic relations [*rapports de convenance*] between the number of vibrations, and it's these relations, it's this harmony, which perhaps is instinctive to the ear, that makes the pleasure of music. Leibniz is convinced that the universe is one big symphony and that a mathematics of this music is possible. There is, as it were, a possible mathematics of quality, and this mathematics of quality is philosophy itself.

So no one has ever been more of an intellectualist, we could even say, more of a mathematician—provided we understand this word in a very special sense—no one has ever been more of a pure intellectualist than Leibniz. But no one among the moderns has ever been on the path of ancient philosophy more than he. It's very interesting to see how, as he grows older, the seed of intellectualism, of Neoplatonism especially, planted in him since his youth, evolves and ends up absorbing everything.[5]

I said that this is the idea we constantly have to keep in mind when we study this philosophy. Not that we should disregard the great importance of the interpretation Leibniz's philosophy has been given these last few years, by Mr. Russell in England, and in France, in a more absolute, more radical form, by Mr. Couturat. According to this
[261] interpretation, Leibniz's philosophy is above all a logic, that is, the principle of sufficient reason being posited first and understood in the sense in which Leibniz understands it, that is, as a principle of pure logic, a principle that posits that the maximum of being is realized automatically, this principle being posited, the monad, and Leibniz's whole philosophy generally, follows in a necessary deduction.[6]

This point was established by a variety of considerations, in particular, by the two authors' allusions to important, albeit very short works by Leibniz, the *Discourse on Metaphysics* in particular, [and] then a still much shorter treatise of five or six pages, which Couturat published in 1903, a small treatise in Latin, which is of the greatest interest, where in fact we see Leibniz's whole philosophy unfold from the principle of sufficient reason, which philosophy thereby becomes a kind of logic.[7]

This interpretation is very important, and I'll add that it is, in a sense, the true interpretation. I mean that if Leibniz had been asked how he'd like his doctrine to be interpreted, it's likely he would have answered that it should be done in this way. And if he had been asked which of his works he'd like to see remain, assuming that only a few could remain—it's said that material for fifty volumes remains—it's likely that he would have liked to see one or the other of these two treatises survive.

Thus, if we were to ask a mathematician who discovered a very beautiful theorem what he'd prefer survive of his theorem, the sheet of paper with the demonstration or the thousand little slips of paper on which he sketched all the attempts at reaching the theorem, attempts that weren't successful but are like so many unfinished roads leading to this point, it's clear that what he'd like to see survive is the sheet of paper with the complete demonstration and not all these little slips of paper. And yet, for the historian of philosophy, these little slips of paper are extremely important, and even in regard to the personal meaning we must attribute to the discovery itself. For the discovery is the endpoint, it's the point where the mind of the author comes to a rest, as it were, but
[262] all the attempts represent the movement toward the endpoint, the internal movement of thought, and by making contact with this movement, we better understand, first, where the author arrived, but especially where he could have gone. His thought is more fertile in this moving form than it is when at rest. That's why—although this entirely logical interpretation of Leibniz's philosophy is likely the definitive interpretation at which we'll stop—nevertheless, to really understand Leibniz, we perhaps must go about it differently: we must start where he started, that is, from Cartesianism, and see how,

under the constant attraction of ancient philosophy, of Plato's, Aristotle's, and especially Plotinus's ideas, he finally arrives where he did arrive.

This, it seems, is the work we need to do. Let's recall, gentlemen, the main features of the theory of the Intelligibles and the Intellect in Plotinus. Plotinus shows us the One, as he calls it, that is God, positing himself. God is the absolute Good, the "Good" being synonymous with existence or rather with "hyperexistence," as Plotinus says.[8] The Good exists by the sole force inherent in its Idea or in its super-Idea. God posits himself. Now, once God is posited, all the essences, or, as Plotinus calls them, all the Intelligibles, are necessarily posited, being like rays, he says, emanating from this sun, or better being like visions, [like] so many visions of God,[9] each Intelligible representing something like a conversion, a turning back toward God. Each of the Intelligibles is God seen from a certain angle, and there are as many Intelligibles as there are possible visions of the One. They're all different from each other, precisely because they're not the same vision of the One, and yet each is the whole, each represents the whole. Each Intelligible represents all the other Intelligibles, given that each of them is the complete representation of the One but taken from different viewpoints.

The Intelligibles do not act on each other. There's no action, no movement in the domain of essences. All Intelligibles agree with each other since they complement one another. Each Intelligible, moreover, generates, through an extension of itself, a soul, and this soul represents a descent of the Intelligible; it's the Intelligible emitting an extension [263]
by which it falls into space and into time. Hence corporality,[10] for bodies are nothing but the materiality of the souls, matter entering into the soul, which materialized soul results from the sole fact that the Intelligible, by means of the intervention of matter, of *hylē*, descended into space and time.

These are some of the principles of the doctrine of Intelligibles in Plotinus. Well, gentlemen, as I tried to show seven or eight years ago, prior to the work that's been done on this connection, this doctrine is to a large extent Leibniz's very doctrine of the monads.[11] The monads, too, are substances composing the universe. Monads are so many representations of the whole. Each monad is representative of the universe, is a mirror of the universe. The different monads are so many representations of the same whole, but views taken from different points. Thereby, the monads are complementary to each other, as different views taken on the whole complement each other. Each of the monads is enclosed in itself, the monad has no window onto the outside. Nonetheless, all the monads agree with each other: it's a great harmony, a great symphony, for the very simple reason that, although each [monad] represents views taken from different points, these views are taken on the same plane, they complement one another and exactly fit into one another.

In the doctrine of the monads or of preestablished harmony, we thus have, in many respects, a reproduction of Plotinus's theory of the Intelligibles. There's a difference, to be sure, and it's a major one, it's what explains the raison d'être of Leibniz's philosophy.

For a philosopher like Plotinus, the Intelligibles, the essences, can generate bodies only on the condition of degrading, of descending. It's not the Intelligibles that are constitutive of the material universe, no, it's the extensions of the Intelligibles constituted by the souls, which souls exist only because there also exists a wholly negative principle that Plotinus, like all of his predecessors, called *hylē*, matter.

[264] For Leibniz, in contrast, there's no *hylē* in the sense the ancients gave to this word. In fact, Leibniz comes after Descartes, he comes after Kepler, after Galileo, after all of those who showed that the material universe is a universe subject to fixed and rational laws. In the ancients, the raison d'être of *hylē* was the belief that there is something accidental, contingent in the material world, that the world is not subject to an absolutely regular order. Since the day that modern science was constituted and that, with it, the conviction that the universe is subject to absolutely regular laws was introduced, since that day, too, the conception of *hylē*, of the principle of indetermination, was banished forever, and corporality[12] thus has to be explained completely differently. No longer is there, below the Intelligibles, a shadowy and dark space into which the Intelligibles send their extensions, which are the souls coupled with materiality. No, materiality will be in the Intelligibles themselves, in the monads themselves, in the sense that space will be in the monads, will be the confused aspect of the monads. Extension will be simply the blurry aspect that the essences take on by their multiplicity.

In other words, if you want the theory of Plotinus's Intelligibles to turn into Leibniz's theory of monads, you'll have to take space and time, which for Plotinus are below the Intelligibles, and make them ascend into the sphere of the Intelligibles as a kind of blurry cloud surrounding the Intelligibles—materiality will then be the confusion of the Intelligibles. This change would need to be made, and it would be of central importance, especially from the viewpoint we're concerned with, since in a doctrine like that of Plotinus, a certain indeterminism is possible. For Plotinus, there can be indetermination in the material world. As I showed, Plotinus insisted on this point. His conception of *hylē*, of matter, allowed him to introduce a certain amount of indetermination into the material world, and if he appears not to have done this in a very clear way, it's because he's under the influence of—while fighting against them—the Stoics, who, for their part, showed that the material universe is a coherent whole. So with *hylē*, the ancient philosophers, like Plotinus, were able to accept indetermination. But once this concept
[265] is eliminated, Leibniz finds himself face to face with his monads, like Plotinus face to face with his Intelligibles: there can be no kind of indetermination there. All monads are posited as soon as God is posited, being the whole possible representation—more or less distinct, more and less blurred—of what God sees distinctly. Consequently, everything is given all together in the absolute,[13] and there is no place for indetermination and contingency and, in the sense we give to this word, to freedom.

This, then, gentlemen, is where a very brief comparison between Plotinus and Leibniz will lead us. There'd be another, no less instructive comparison to be made, and then this would allow us to link up to the interpretation I talked about earlier, the recent interpretation of Leibniz's philosophy, there'd be another comparison to be made between this philosophy and the conception of science that we find in Plato, in Aristotle, and in Plotinus himself, but especially in Plato and Aristotle.

What is this conception of science? I've already presented it this year, but I'll very summarily recall its main features.[14] If we really want to understand it, we have to

oppose it to our own conception of science. We're used to, for some time now especially, considering science as being symbolic of reality, I'm not saying necessarily conventional but symbolic, that is, science expresses, translates into terms of the human intellect relations between things, [relations that] perhaps are artificial, perhaps are absolutely natural; but in any case, science is a translation, a symbolic expression.[15] That's what it is for us. First there are the things we perceive and then there is science, which is the translation of the things. But for the ancients, it's the exact opposite. For Plato and for Aristotle, there is science first: it's not us who make science. Science is not a human work, all we do is discover it. It's there in the things, underneath or above the things, whichever you want. Science is what is given first. First there is the system, I wouldn't say of truths, but of essences, it's this system that science must discover. So there are essences that science must reach, then there are the things in the proper sense. The things perceived by us are given after this science as diminishments, degradations of these realities that are [266]
immanent or transcendent but, in any case, superior to sensible realities. If we were able to grasp these essences, what Plato calls "Ideas," what Aristotle calls by the same Greek word *eidos*, which we sometimes translate as "Form" when we're dealing with Aristotle, if we were able to grasp these Ideas, these Forms, these "notions," as Leibniz will say, then we'd be able to draw from these notions, just by unwinding, so to speak, their content, all the truths of science. Someone who could move in one leap into the Platonic world of Ideas, or someone who could take Aristotle's *nous*—the intellect Aristotle speaks of, the intellect that enters into the soul—and [who] in that intellect, to talk like Aristotle, could make everything that is potential pass into actuality [*passer à l'acte*], someone who managed to move into the Platonic world of Ideas or into Aristotle's Intellect, for the effect would be the same, that person would have all the notions whose contents would simply need to be unwound to have all of science. Would the one who'd accomplish this know, could they know, guess, or determine a priori everything that happens in the world, in space and time? Certainly not. For a Plato and an Aristotle, the things that unfold in space and time are knowledge diminished or altered by *hylē* being mixed in, and they consequently enclose a host of accidents, a host of things that can't be drawn from the notion. But those things aren't important for knowledge, they're external to knowledge, knowledge isn't concerned with them.

When we take Leibniz's doctrine presented in its logical form—at which he arrives quite naturally by starting from the ancient conception of science and suppressing, here again, *hylē*, matter in the sense that Aristotle gave to this word—the theory presented in the *Discourse on Metaphysics* is that the notion of a thing or of a life envelops, contains, all that can happen to it.[16] If I could grasp in itself the notion of my self, of my person, I would so to speak read in that notion all that I do and will do, the words I utter at this moment and also the intonation I give them. And for one of these words to be different from what it is, the notion would have to be different from what it is: everything in me [267]
would be changed, and, moreover, [everything] in the whole universe, too, because of the interdependence of the notions among themselves.

What did Leibniz do in relation to Aristotle? He took up these notions, these *eidē* of Plato and Aristotle; he supposed that they developed without the intervention of a principle of degradation, of diminishment, like the ancient *hylē*. I'll add that he considers these notions as individuals, while in Plato the notions represent a genus, but already in Aristotle, certain notions at least are individual—I've tried to establish this point—in Aristotle, there are individual notions at least of humans, but it's straight out true of Plotinus, who, for his part, expressly says that there are individual *eidē*.[17] So on this point, Leibniz didn't have to modify ancient philosophy, but now as always he dismisses *hylē*, matter. Then, while for the ancients time is possible only through the degradation of Ideas—the degradation of notions that emerge from the Intelligible in the form of souls—for Leibniz, on the contrary, time exists in the notion itself, being the blurry aspect that the logical deduction takes, the logical evolution, the deduction, in a word, of all of that's contained in the notion.

Thus, by starting from the Aristotelian and Leibnizian conception of science and by eliminating *hylē*, we arrive more or less at the doctrine presented in the *Discourse on Metaphysics*, just as, by taking Plotinus's doctrine, his theory of the Intelligibles, and by eliminating *hylē*, we arrive at a doctrine analogous to the one presented in the *Monadology*.[18] These two doctrines, in short, are the same thing. In the *Monadology*, what's in question are monads, that is, souls or perceptions; in the *Discourse on Metaphysics* what's in question are subjects and predicates. What in the *Monadology* is called "souls" or "monads" is called "subject" in the *Discourse on Metaphysics*; what in the *Monadology* is called "perceptions" is called "predicates" in the *Discourse on Metaphysics*—these are two ways of expressing oneself, the one being more akin to Plato, the other more akin to Aristotle.

I would add—if I didn't fear to be forcing things by being too precise—I would add
[268] two viewpoints that correspond, one to extension, the other to time. When we place ourselves in the viewpoint of space, when we analyze space and extension according to Leibniz, we arrive at a system of perceptions that, at a given moment, are complementary the ones to the others in instantaneity. When, on the other hand, we analyze duration, we arrive at a series of predicates emerging from the same subject.[19] In one case, we have an analysis of extension, in the other an analysis of duration, and the two analyses are linked. I'll add that both result in the most inflexible determinism.

What do we have when we place ourselves in the viewpoint of the *Monadology*? We have, at a given moment, the states of all monads that are so complementary to one another that, given a state of all monads except one, the state of that one, of this last monad, is rigorously and absolutely determined, just as in a jigsaw puzzle, the form that one of the pieces must take is absolutely determined by the empty space produced by the combination, the complementarity as it were, of all the others. So it's an absolute determinism in the instant. If, on the contrary, we take the *Discourse on Metaphysics*—I'm exaggerating the difference, for the two works interpenetrate—we have a determinism that's just as inflexible, but one that instead is based on the consideration of time. Given a notion—and the notions are given for all eternity—given a notion, all the possible predicates of this subject are contained in the notion.[20] This again is determinism, and an inflexible determinism. So whether we start from one point or whether we start from the other, we always end up with determinism.

Gentlemen, to reach Leibniz's theory of freedom, we have to leave these generalities behind and show with more precision how Leibniz, starting from Descartes, evolves toward the viewpoint of the ancients and necessarily ends up there. Leibniz starts from Cartesianism, from Descartes's theory of extension, for example. Material objects are parts of extension. All these parts of extension jostle one another. That is a mechanism governed by necessary laws, and in particular by the law of the conservation of movement. Descartes, to be sure, introduced exceptions to this mechanism, exceptions, [269] moreover, that, as I see it, didn't compromise the generality of the laws. As we've seen,[21] he accepted that the direction of movements is not absolutely determined, that the soul acting on the body can create the direction, and thus freedom, in the sense of free will, is possible: the soul, intervening, produces certain movements of the body, which it has chosen, and thus, without violating the fundamental laws of mechanics such as Descartes understands it, freedom is possible.

Leibniz starts from a critique of this idea in Descartes. He noticed, and he had to notice, that once the principle of Cartesian mechanics is posited, it's quite difficult to accept any indetermination, any contingency in the world. He showed, to use his expressions, that it's not only the quantity of moving force that is preserved in the world but, as he says, the quantity of direction, which amounts to saying that all the phenomena of nature insofar as they are movements are rigorously determined by the conditions in which they take place.[22] So the determinism of nature is an inflexible mechanism, and in the domain of extension, a rigorous necessity is the law.

Gentlemen, the older Leibniz gets, the more he breaks away from Cartesian mechanism—he breaks away from it quite quickly, for that matter—and from the idea that material things are above all extension; quite quickly, he abandoned the idea that extension is the essence of matter. Nonetheless, space always remained for him the plane of projection, the plane imagined by us—for in itself it has nothing real about it—onto which all realities are projected, preserving at least certain of their intimate relations. Such that if the realities projected onto the plane of space appear to us as subjected to an inflexible determinism, the determinism that will govern these realities in themselves will be inflexible. Consequently, the determinism that manifests in the mechanism of the universe, considered from the metric viewpoint, is truly symbolic of the determinism that is at the very root of things.

That's the starting point. Now, we'd have to see how it evolves in Leibniz's thought, how the conception of the things themselves projected onto the plane of space evolves. [270] We have to do this if we want to know the cause, the profound reason of the determinism that manifests in space in the form of a universal mechanism.

So how did Leibniz progressively arrive at his conception of things such as he pictures them, at his conception of substance, of the monad? I said that he quite quickly rid himself of the Cartesian idea that the essence of material things is extension. That's because he was totally filled, totally impregnated with this ancient idea that what is homogeneous is not real. Reality is essentially quality and consequently heterogeneous to other realities.

At the beginning of the second book of the *New Essays*, Leibniz expressly tells us that what is uniform and all of whose parts are identically the same cannot be a reality: it's only an abstraction.[23] Well, space, extension, being conceived as something homogeneous can only be abstractions and not realities. We must reach reality and reality can only be heterogeneous to itself.

How are we going to find this reality? Extension is indefinitely divisible, and the true element, the element we want to reach, is an indivisible. It seems that Leibniz began by picturing these indivisible elements we want to reach as mathematical or, rather, dynamic points, mathematical points that would be like forces.[24] The reason he turns these mathematical points into points of force is that he noticed that bodies are in no way indifferent to movement, to which, according to Descartes, they oppose resistance. And to say "resistance" is to say "force": consequently, there is, inherent to matter, force. So these points, which are the ultimate elements of matter, are points of force, dynamic points.

Then Leibniz takes one more step: he wonders what this force is. Naturally, he finds that we know a force only by effort. Our consciousness shows us what force is by
[271] informing us of the effort we are making. Consequently, these points of force are points of effort as it were, kinds of soul, little souls.

It does seem, it's certain, even, that Leibniz began by putting the souls, all the souls, even what he calls spirits—superior souls—into mathematical points. In a letter to Father Des Bosses, he tells us, "Many years ago, when my philosophy was still too immature, I located souls in points."[25] We find analogous expressions in two letters Leibniz wrote to John Frederick, Duke of Brunswick-Hanover. There he says expressly that "minds occupy points, minds are in the points."[26] In this, too, we must see but a reminiscence of the Cartesian theory that locates the soul in a point, in the pineal gland. Consequently, the idea has nothing all that extraordinary about it.

So we have these elements of matter that have become little souls located in points, [souls] whose essence is force, effort.

Leibniz analyzes the idea of force itself. Here, we can only restore things by conjecture, but there are two or three texts that Couturat has recently quoted that seem indeed to authorize this conjecture. He arrives at the idea that effort isn't something clear, distinct. Consequently effort is nothing definitive; effort is resolved into a series of states. To say "effort" is to say "tendency"; to say "tendency" is to say "transition from one state to another"; and transition, for the philosopher who is looking for clear ideas, transition, which is movement, is something that isn't clear, for what is obscure from the intellectualist viewpoint is, precisely, transition, effort. What is clear, what is distinct, are the states themselves: consequently, the effort resolves into a series of states.[27]

Which are these states? It's perceptions, as Leibniz says, since he calls "perceptions" states of mind, states of the monad.

Having reached this point, we thus have the gist of the conception of monads. We'll say, first, that matter is composed of points, which [points], examined up close, become
[272] points of force, which [force,] seen up close, appears as effort, that is, as a series of states of mind, and finally, there's nothing but states of mind, there's nothing but perceptions. The entire material universe, at a given moment, is thus to be recomposed from perceptions, as Leibniz says.

What does that mean, and how can the whole be reconstructed from perceptions? First, we must remember that de jure, each of these souls or each of these monads, as Leibniz says, perceives the totality of things. There's no soul—whether the issue is our souls, which Leibniz calls "spirits," or souls in general, or "naked" monads[28]—there's no substance, in a word, no monad that doesn't perceive virtually the totality of the universe. That's obvious since we must take into account that the monads such as Leibniz understands them cannot influence each other, cannot act on one another. If we say that bodies are made of extension, of parts of extension, that's fine, then there can be reciprocal influence. If with Descartes we say that there are souls and bodies, we can, with him, locate the soul in the pineal gland: there'll be reciprocal influence of the soul on the body and of the body on the soul, just as of bodies on one another. But I am supposing that there are only souls, and—this is Leibniz's hypothesis—if there are only souls, there can be no reciprocal action: a soul cannot act on another soul, for every action presupposes some space across which the action is accomplished.[29] So these substances cannot influence one another. Henceforth, everything a substance perceives, it perceives in itself: perception is a kind of dream.

So the monad perceives everything it perceives in itself. Now, what can a monad perceive? It can perceive everything: de facto, it perceives only a very small part of the whole, but de jure, it would perceive everything.[30] What I will have perceived from my birth up to my death is hardly anything; but I could have gone to a host of places where I haven't been, had all sorts of experiences, travelled to the most distant lands, and everything I'd have perceived, I would necessarily have drawn it from myself, for I don't go out of myself. It's a dream I'm unfolding. I could, right now, perceive [273] anything whatsoever: it's thus because I have in me the whole universe, represented blurrily, as Leibniz says. It's the same for all monads, even monads constitutive of bodies. Consequently, each monad is a perception of the whole universe; it's just that [only] a very small part of this universe is represented there distinctly, that is, consciously, and the rest blurrily, that is, unconsciously.

How are we going to reconstitute the universe with this perception of the entire universe? Let's first try to simplify things, and in order to do that, let's represent the perception in a form less general than Leibniz did. Perceptions for him are states of mind. Let's suppose a perception of a material object, and to simplify things even more, let's suppose that it's a visual perception. The trick of the doctrine of the monads on this point is to reconstitute each part of the universe with the totality of possible perceptions of the universe.

Let me explain. There are two ways of representing bodies from the visual point of view. First, we can picture bodies as we usually do. Here we have a table, then other bodies, the walls of the room, and so on. All the bodies are parts of the universe that by their juxtaposition constitute the universe. That is the way of seeing things that common sense has adopted, and it's the way philosophers themselves, in general, see things.

Leibniz's way of picturing things is entirely different. We must picture all possible photographic, if you like, views of the universe, taken from all possible viewpoints, as existing.[31] Suppose some photographic views, but ones that reproduce the natural

dimensions of things and that preserve their colors: all these photographic views taken from all possible viewpoints of the universe are complete representations of the universe. It's just that what appears in one is disguised in another; what is distinct in one is blurred in another. This is precisely why there is no relief on any of these photographs. What would it
[274] take for us to be able to reconstitute, with these photographs, the complete relief of things? With the stereoscope, we already have a means of partially reconstituting this relief. When we put two views taken from two different viewpoints corresponding respectively to the two eyes into a stereoscope, we have the beginnings of the relief of things. We see objects in the stereoscope that begin to turn, but we can't go all the way around them.[32] If we had a marvelous, a miraculous stereoscope which allowed an infinity of plane views of the universe taken from all possible viewpoints to converge together, we'd have the very relief of things. We'd have, in short, we'd have the visual nature being absolutely identical to the real visual universe, such that, instead of considering it as formed from the juxtaposition of visible parts, we can consider this real visual nature as composed of the complementarity of all possible views we'd take of this nature if it were distinct from the views themselves.

Leibniz's monad is just that: the monad is a view of the universe. And it's the totality of these views of the universe that makes the universe. All these views are necessarily complementary with each other, and what makes them complementary with each other, or rather the effect of their complementarity with one another is the very relief of things—an effect, I said, but it's rather a cause.[33]

A moment ago, I was, in short, talking about the miraculous stereoscopic vision of all these views at once. This is the very vision that, according to Leibniz, God has of things. There's a passage in the *Discourse on Metaphysics* where he says that God, precisely, runs through all possible views of all things in an instant.[34] Leibniz's God is the very relief of things. It's by God, Leibniz tells us, that the preestablished harmony among the monads is explained, and this preestablished harmony is one of the proofs of God's existence—in fact, I think, the preestablished harmony is God himself! Moreover, Leibniz tells us, in a text from one of his letters I quoted earlier, to duke John Frederick: "the harmony of things, that is, God."[35] Thus, there are all the possible views of the universe, then
[275] God who alone is the relief of the universe, all these views being constitutive of the relief of things. Thus, you see what in a doctrine of this kind space turns into and what extension turns into. Space simply represents the points, imagined by us, in which we must place ourselves to take all these views of all things. There's no one point of view that's appropriate enough. We must picture these views as starting from certain points imagined by us, juxtaposed to one another, [and] that's what we call space. If two views are very similar, the two points we imagine will be very close together; if they are very different, the two points will be distant. Thus, space shows us, symbolically, in the form of magnitudes, purely qualitative differences, which alone are real, for the qualities are in the things. Generally, to know how we must classify these plane views I talked about earlier, to obtain the relief of things, to know how we must classify them, we must move into this space imagined by us and determine the positions of all the viewpoints corresponding to these views in relation to one another. That is what Leibniz expresses by saying that space is an order of coexistence.[36]

There you have, gentlemen, what had to be said about Leibniz's philosophy to get to his theory of freedom. I dwelled on these premises more than I wanted, but I believe it's indispensable to clarifying the conclusion. Now we still have to look at this doctrine of freedom, which is so original, which is a doctrine of necessity—an odd thing, but this phenomenon already occurred in antiquity and it reoccurs with Leibniz. Leibniz wanted to show us that his determinism is a doctrine not only of freedom but even of contingency, thereby taking up again, albeit with a lot more depth and force, Chrysippus's attempt in antiquity.[37] Like Chrysippus, Leibniz, in taking the idea of necessity in its modern form, will show us how it can become freedom, and even contingency, in terms of necessity. This will be the object of the next lecture, which will be the last of this first semester.[38]

Notes

1. CE, 298–9/346–7.
2. CE, 298/346.
3. See the January 27, 1905, lecture above, 72 and 79n6.
4. Leibniz repeats this formula—music is "a hidden exercise of arithmetic where the mind is unaware that it is counting"—many times. It first occurs, it seems, in an April 17, 1712, letter to Goldbach. The Latin text of the letter can be found in Adolph-Andrei P. Yushkevich and Yu. Kh. Kopelevich, "La correspondance de Leibniz avec Goldbach," *Studia Leibnitiana* 20, no. 2 (1988): 175–89; the letter is no. 6, 181–3, the quote is from 182.
5. Bergson, as noted (see the March 10, 1905, lecture above, 141 and 147n12) is quite fond of this thesis.
6. This interpretation attempts to lead all of Leibniz's philosophy back to strictly logical—and not, for example, mathematical—principles. It developed in the context of a quarrel about the foundations of mathematics: are these foundations entirely logical (Russell's and Couturat's position)? Or does mathematics include a certain number of principles that are irreducible to logic (the so-called "intuitionist" position of Poincaré and Brouwer)? Or does mathematics rest on a system of independent axioms that would simply need to be exhaustively presented (Hilbert's "formalist" position)? Bergson is alluding to Bertrand Russell's *A Critical Exposition of the Philosophy of Leibniz*, originally published in 1900 (London: Cambridge University Press) and translated into French in 1908, and to *La Logique de Leibniz* (Paris: Alcan, 1901) by Louis Couturat. Couturat (1868–1914) was a philosopher, a historian of philosophy, logic, and mathematics, and a proponent of symbolic logic, whom Bergson, despite their marked philosophical differences, chose to fill in for him the following year, 1905–6. See the editor's note on Couturat's opening lecture, "La logique et la philosophie contemporaine," in Couturat, *Logique, mathématiques, langue universelle: Anthologie 1893-1917*, ed. Michel Fichant (Lyon: ENS Éditions, 2018), https://books.openedition.org/enseditions/8171.
7. For an English translation of "Discourse on Metaphysics," see PE, 35–68. The shorter text is most likely the 1689 *Primae veritates*, first published in Couturat's edition of *Opuscules et fragments inédits de Leibniz* (Paris: Alcan, 1903). It is at the center of Couturat's interpretation. For an English translation, see Leibniz, "Primary Truths," also in PE, 30–4.
8. See Plotinus, *Enneads* 5.2.1: 59–61, and 6.9.3–5: 311–23. *Hyper-* because the Good, as Plato says (*Republic* 6, 509b), is *beyond* being.

9. For Bergson's use of this image, see above, the March 3, 1905, lecture 133–4.
10. The typescript contains the surprising *corporaléité*. What word did Bergson actually pronounce in the lecture? *Corporalité*? *Corporéité*? *Corporéité* at least can be found in a published work (as "corporeity" in CE, 309/360).
11. Bergson is likely referring to the lecture course of 1897–8. See M, 413, and the March 10, 1905, lecture above (142 and 147n17). As for the "work" he mentions, he is very probably thinking of Georges Rodier's now classic study, "Sur une des origines de la philosophie de Leibniz," in *Revue de métaphysique et de morale* 10, no. 5 (September–October 1902): 552–64.
12. Again *corporaléité*; see note 10 above.
13. CE, 40/38.
14. For this conception, see above, 177; CE, esp. 277–8/320, 284/328, and 303–4/353; as well as CM, 231–3/221–3.
15. As he will do in CE, 184/208 and 193–5/219–21, Bergson is carefully positioning himself in the contemporary debate around "conventionalism." Although none of these authors actually claimed the designation, it was attributed to Pierre Duhem, to Henri Poincaré, and to Bergson's own student, Edouard Le Roy.
16. See Leibniz, "Discourse on Metaphysics," §8: 40–1 and §13: 44–5.
17. For Aristotle, see above 86–9; for Plotinus, 132–3 and 137–8.
18. A text from 1714, situated at the other end of Leibniz's philosophical career. Rodier (in the article cited above, "Sur une des origines de la philosophie de Leibniz") places it at the heart of his comparison of Plotinus and Leibniz.
19. Here, Bergson probably has in mind Leibniz's double definition in his correspondence with the Newtonian Samuel Clarke: he defines space as the order of possible coexistences and time as the order of possible successive positions. See Leibniz, *The Leibniz-Clarke Correspondence*, ed. H. G. Alexander (Manchester: Manchester University Press, 1956), Leibniz's third letter, §§4–6: 25–7; fourth letter, §§8–18: 37–9 and §41:42; fifth letter, §§27–32: 63–4, §§36–3: 66–78, §§79–80: 81, and §§104–6: 89–90.
20. In the *Discourse on Metaphysics*, substance, too, is considered an essence or, more precisely, a "notion"; see Leibniz, *Discourse on Metaphysics* 8: 40–1.
21. See the March 24, 1905, lecture above, 167–9.
22. Very early on, Leibniz reflected on the laws of motion and their formulation by Descartes. See the two treatises from 1671, "The Theory of Abstract Motion" and "An Example of Demonstrations about the Nature of Corporeal Things" (combined as text 8, "Studies in Physics and the Nature of Body," in PPL, 139–45). The expressions "moving force" and the "quantity of direction" appear several times in Leibniz's works, but see, especially, the 1697 "Clarification of the Difficulties which Mr. Bayle has found in the New System of the Union of Soul and Body" (text 52 in PPL, 492–7).
23. "Things which are uniform, containing no variety, are always mere abstractions: for instance, time, space, and the other entities of pure mathematics." Leibniz, *New Essays on Human Understanding*, ed. and trans. Peter Remnant and Jonathan Bennett (New York: Cambridge University Press, 1996), 2.1.2: 110.
24. With this way of putting things, Bergson is alluding to the physics of Maxwell, Thomson, and Faraday such as he depicts it in TFW, 206/155; MM, 264–6/224–6; and CE, 181–2/204–5; see also 123n5 above.
25. April 30, 1709, letter to Des Bosses, in PPL, 596–9; the quote is from the postscript, 599. Bartholomew Des Bosses (1668–1738), to give the English variant of his first name, a Jesuit

priest, was not only a constant correspondent of Leibniz but also translated the *Theodicy* into Latin; see *Tentamina theodicææ de bonitate Dei, libertate hominis et origine mali Latine versa & notationibus* (Frankfurt: Bencard, 1719).

26. These two letters date from May 21, 1671, and October 1671; see Leibniz, *Sämtliche Schriften und Briefe,* second series, vol. 1, respectively: no. 58: 105–10, here 108 and 109, and no. 84: 159–65, here 162. Leibniz was librarian for John Frederick, Duke of Brunswick-Calenberg, in Hanover from 1676 to 1679.
27. See CM, 187–8/178.
28. For the "naked" monad, see "The Monadology," in PPL, 643–53, here §24: 645.
29. See, for example, "Discourse on Metaphysics," in PE, §§14–15: 46–8, and "The Monadology," §7: 643.
30. Compare this to ME, 95–6/77–8.
31. For this whole analysis, see CE, 301–2/350–1. Bergson is taking up turns of phrases and conceptions from his theory of perception, first developed in the opening chapter of *Matter and Memory.*
32. For this technical analysis, see CE, 302–3/351–32. Stereoscopes are devices that create an impression of three-dimensional depth—"relief"—by presenting two slightly different images to the viewer's eyes. First developed by Charles Wheatstone in the 1830s, they were widely used in experimental psychology in the mid-nineteenth century, work with which Bergson was familiar. In TFW and MM he radically disagrees with authors like Wilhelm Wundt and Théodule Ribot as to the conclusions to be drawn from such experiments. See also Jacqueline Carroy and Henning Schmidgen, "Reaktionsversuche in Leipzig, Paris und Würzburg: Die deutsch-französische Geschichte eines psychologischen Experiments, 1890–1910," *Medizinhistorisches Journal* 39, no. 1 (2004): 27–55, esp. 33 and 40.
33. Does this last sentence imply an uncertainty on Bergson's part? In the passage in *Creative Evolution* (CE, 302/351), this is indeed an *effect*, the effect of the very complementarity of the views, which is to be seen in the relief of things.
34. In fact, the passage is not in "Discourse on Metaphysics" but in "On Contingency," in PE, 28–30. The sentence to which Bergson is alluding seems to be: "But the reason"—the reason for the truth of contingent propositions analyzed to infinity—"is understood completely only by God, who alone traverses the infinite series in one stroke of mind" (28).
35. Leibniz, letter to John Frederick, October 1671.
36. See *Leibniz-Clarke Correspondence*, esp. Leibniz's fourth letter, §41: 42, and his fifth letter, §106: 90.
37. On Chrysippus, see the February 17, 1905, lecture, 109–10.
38. After the April 14 lecture, there was a two-week break.

LECTURE 17
APRIL 14, 1905

Gentlemen, in the last lecture, we saw how Leibniz, starting from the Cartesian theory [277] of extension, goes down the path that leads to a philosophy like Plotinus's. We recalled how Plotinus understands the relation between what he calls the Intellect and what he calls the Intelligibles: all the Intelligibles are different from one another, they are different essences, but each of them is the entire Intellect, the Intellect seen from a certain point, as it were, and all the different essences—which are but different views on one self-same thing—are thereby complementary, hence a harmony between them. An analogous relation, I said, exists between Leibniz's monads.

Leibniz starts from Cartesian extension: matter is extension. It's true that for Descartes, in extension there are bodies, some of which at least are capable of spontaneous acts [*démarche*] involving a certain indetermination. That is due, I said, to the fact that, for Descartes, the quantity of movement is determined, but not the quantity of direction, such that the human soul, for example, can give the movement of the body the direction it wants. Leibniz corrects this principle: according to him, the quantity of direction is just as constant as the quantity of movement. There is no possible indetermination in the domain of extension. Then, if in extension everything is determined, we can already a priori infer determination in the real, because for Leibniz, space, although it has no reality in itself, although it's only a blurry perception, space can nonetheless be considered—this is an image I used before[1]—as the plane of projection of reality, the plane on which [278] realities are projected while preserving at least some of their essential relations with one another, such that, if within this plane of space there is determination, we can infer the real determination in things.

The main thing, to be sure, remains to be done: to find out what things are and how their rigorous and absolute determination follows from the nature of things.

In the last lecture, I showed the main stages Leibniz's thought goes through. We saw how for him Cartesian extension cannot be a reality because what's homogeneous is always abstract, is only an abstraction, and is not a reality. The issue is to find the heterogeneous elements that underlie extension, as it were. For Leibniz, these elements are at first indivisible points that become dynamic points, points of force, which points of force become points of effort, force being known to us above all as effort, which effort itself, when analyzed, resolves into a series of states, the transition being obscure, and what is clear being the perception, the static state; consequently, finally, what composes material reality are the monads, in short, points of perception.

The material world, the whole universe, is thus composed of what we could call "indivisible visions" of the whole. The material world isn't made of parts external to other parts, of things external to other things. The world isn't composed of parts, I'd say, it's composed of wholes.

We have to picture—this is an image I've used many times, but it's a comparison, I believe, that's very close to reality—we have to picture stereoscopic views of the universe, plane views like all the views we see stereoscopically, stereoscopic views of the universe all different from one another although they represent the same universe, one view representing in the foreground what the other represents in the background, one showing us distinctly what the other shows us blurrily. There'll be thousands and thousands of
[279] stereoscopic views or, if you like, visions of the universe, there's an infinity of them. And then, what we call the universe itself is the vision in relief, the stereoscopic vision of the whole. This stereoscopic vision of the whole, this vision in relief, is, basically, nothing other than the totality of stereoscopic views taken together, since all these views taken together will be the very relief of things. The universe is thus made not of parts but of wholes, each of which is indivisible, for we mustn't forget that these views of the universe are perceptions, states of consciousness, states of mind, therefore something undivided.

What we call the "universe," is, in short, the totality of these stereoscopic views. What we call the "preestablished harmony" between the monads is nothing other than this very relief of things. What we call "space" is something simply imagined by us, a blurry perception; that is, when we consider all these views of the universe, we relate each of them to a viewpoint—there are no viewpoints in reality, there are only views, but we can, we must, even, consider each view as taken from a viewpoint, and the totality of these viewpoints will be space. These viewpoints are simply imagined, and the totality of these viewpoints will be simply imagined. Space thus exists only in relation to us, and as the vague perception of the ranking of the monads. The ranking of the stereoscopic views in order to reproduce the relief is a qualitative order. This qualitative order is expressed quantitatively by the positions in space that we imagine. If two views are similar, we relate them to points that are close together; if dissimilar, to points distant from one another. Space symbolizes, translated into quantities, into magnitudes, the qualitative differences found in real substances. That is all that is real in space.[2]

As for Leibniz's God, his role is absolutely the role of Plotinus's Intellect in relation to the Intelligibles. Plotinus shows us the Intellect looking over all the Intelligibles; he uses the Greek verb *diexerkhesthai*, "to pass in review."[3] The Intellect goes over the Intelligibles in an as it were immobile and thereby eternal movement. There's a complete vision, the
[280] vision in relief as it were of all the Intelligibles. In the *Discourse on Metaphysics*, Leibniz uses a completely analogous expression to indicate God's relation to the monads: he looks over all the monads in an instantaneous, immobile movement.[4] All the monads are related by us to viewpoints. God is at all the viewpoints at the same time, or rather, he's at none of them; we must define it precisely this way: God is the monad that has no viewpoint. This is how we must define Leibniz's God.

The relation of Leibniz's God to the monads is thus completely analogous to the relation of Plotinus's Intellect to the Intelligibles. The resemblance is striking.

I also pointed out a big difference between the two doctrines, which is of capital importance: to pass from Plotinus's Intelligibles to corporeal realities, the Intelligibles must, by extending themselves, go out of themselves, extend themselves into souls, which are coupled with matter, with *hylē*, and thereby distended into space and into time. The Intelligibles must thus let something of themselves go. They're not constitutive of the reality we have before our eyes, whereas Leibniz's monads are constitutive of a reality immanent to things, and that for a very simple and very important reason, for the whole secret of the transition from the ancients to the moderns—to those among the moderns who are in the tradition of the ancients—is found here.[5] This reason is that Leibniz no longer has *hylē* at his disposal, the irrational principle of the ancients. This principle disappeared the day scientists, and Descartes among them, showed that nature is rational and subject to a mathematical plan. From that moment on, there was no place for *hylē* in things anymore. And consequently, the monads, in order to give us things in space and time, do not have to descend, all they have to do is stay where they are. As for space, it's nothing other than the blurry aspect of the coexistence of substances and the human way of representing, of symbolizing, the very multiplicity of the monads—but above all the order of the relation between the monads.

Thus, gentlemen, with the analysis of Cartesian extension, Leibniz is on the path to a doctrine very close to that of Plotinus. This is where we left off the last time. I'll add [281] now—and this is still more important for the theory of freedom—that Leibniz, analyzing no longer simply extension but duration, is thereby led to a conception of science that is extremely close to Aristotle's. I'm alluding especially to the numerous passages you'll find in the correspondence between Leibniz and Arnauld and also in the *Discourse on Metaphysics*, which this correspondence centers on. There's a passage that seems to me to be quite essential in this regard. Leibniz puts it like this:

> Let there be a straight line ABC representing a certain time. And let there be an individual substance, for example, I, enduring or subsisting during that time. Let us first take me subsisting during time AB, and then me subsisting during time BC. Then, since the assumption is that it is the same individual substance that endures throughout, or rather that it is I who subsists in time AB, being then in Paris, and that it is still I who subsists in time BC, being then in Germany, there must necessarily be a reason allowing us truly to say that we endure, that is to say that I, who was in Paris, am now in Germany. For if there were no such reason, we would have as much right to say that it is someone else.

Thus there must be a reason that authorizes us to say that it's the same self that was in Paris and that now is in Germany:

> It is true that my internal experience convinces me a posteriori of this identity; but there must also be an a priori reason. Now, it is not possible to find any reason but the fact that both my attributes in the preceding time and state and my attributes in the succeeding time and state are predicates of the same subject—they are in the same subject.

Thus the reason for which it's the same self that endures during time AB and during time BC is that the series of states that unfolded during time AB and the series of states that unfolded during time BC are predicates, attributes of the same subject:

> Now, what is it to say that the predicate is in the subject, except that the notion
> [282] of the predicate is in some way included in the notion of the subject? And since, once I began existing, it was possible truly to say of me that this or that would happen to me, it must be admitted that these predicates were laws included in the subject or in my complete notion, which constitutes what is called I, which is the foundation of the connection of all my different states and which God has known perfectly from all eternity.[6]

Thus there's a subject that is called "I" and that contains, as predicates that are inherent to it, all that I do and all that happens to me across time.

This, moreover, becomes a lot clearer in light of the text of the *Discourse on Metaphysics* itself, of which we here[, in the letters,] have only a commentary. "We have said that the notion of an individual substance"—that is, the notion of Peter, Paul, or Jack—"includes once and for all everything that can ever happen to it and that, by considering this notion, one can see there everything that can truly be said of it, just as we can see in the nature of a circle all the properties that can be deduced from it." Thus in the notion of Peter, Paul, or Jack I could see all that happens to Peter, Paul, or Jack because what happens to them are always so many attributes of the subject and of what can be encapsulated in a subject. He continues:

> Let's take an example. Since Julius Caesar will become perpetual dictator and master of the republic and will overthrow the freedom of the Romans, this action is contained in his notion, for we assume that it is the nature of such a perfect notion of a subject to contain everything, so that the predicate is included in the subject.

Then, a little farther on:

> For if someone were able to carry out the whole demonstration by virtue of which he could prove this connection between the subject, Caesar, and the predicate, his successful undertaking, he would in fact be showing that Caesar's future dictatorship is grounded in his notion or nature, that there is a reason why he
> [283] crossed the Rubicon rather than stopped at it and why he won rather than lost at Pharsalus and that it was reasonable, and consequently certain, that this should happen.[7]

We could produce many more quotations from this entire correspondence between Leibniz and Arnauld, but this one suffices to allow us to understand all that's essential in Leibniz's thought on this matter.

As I pointed out, if we want to understand Leibniz's thought completely, we have to go back to its Aristotelian origins.[8] The conception of science of someone like Aristotle or Plato is absolutely different from the one we have today. I already said the other day that for us, science is representative of things: the things are given first, sensible things, in space and time; science represents them more or less symbolically—not necessarily in a conventional way but always in a symbolical way. Science comes after the things. For Plato and for Aristotle, on the contrary, the things come after science. Science is given first, it hardly matters whether it's immanent or transcendent to the things, it's always internal to them. What is given first are the Ideas of the things, that is, it's scientific knowledge [*connaissances*], it's the science of things, and the things themselves are like a degradation of science: they're science descended, as it were, pulled down by *hylē*, descended into space and into time. I said that someone who could move, in one leap, as it were, into the world of science, into the Aristotelian and Platonic world of the *eidē*, this person would know all the absolute predicates, as it were, the real predicates, the genuine predicates that we can encapsulate in the subjects. But he wouldn't know everything that happens in things, he wouldn't be able to predict all their effects, he wouldn't be able to say that Caesar will cross the Rubicon, no, because thanks to the intervention of *hylē*, science is coupled with accidents in space and time, such that someone who entered into all the *eidē* wouldn't be able to determine a priori everything that happens in space and time. We know that the innovation of the moderns in general and of Leibniz in particular is the elimination of *hylē*.

If, then, we adopt the ancient conception of science minus the idea of *hylē* intervening, [284] what'll happen? We'll say that someone able to move into the Ideas of things, into their *eidē*, into their notions as Leibniz says, this person would see in the notions everything contained in them, all the events unfolding in space and time, which [events] are only the development of the notion itself. We are in space and time; we are in the blurry. There is a veil placed between us and the truth, and this is why we don't know the true subject and the true predicates. We are forced, temporarily at least and as long as the universal science Leibniz dreams of is not yet constituted, we are forced to make use of artificial predicates, artificial subjects to which we attach artificial predicates. But if we were able to lift the veil, we'd see the true subjects, the notions into which reality is truly divided, and within these subjects we'd see all the predicates that can be asserted of each of them. Which amounts to saying that in the idea of a being we'd read its past, its present, and its future.

We thus move quite naturally from Aristotle's view of science to Leibniz's view, simply by suppressing *hylē*, and we reach the conclusion that the knowledge of notions, of Ideas as the ancients said, that the knowledge of notions will provide us with the complete knowledge of everything that happens to beings. And the notions exist from all eternity.

Leibniz's idea, in short, is that the totality of a subject's predicates is equal to this subject because when we take a being, it's nothing more than the series of all its past, present, and future states—hence it results that, since the being is determined and the notion of the being is determined, everything that happens to it is determined as well, and determined necessarily.

Suppose that right now, I uttered words different from the ones I'm uttering, I articulated them differently, I made gestures different from the ones I'm making: the result would be that I wouldn't be the same being, it wouldn't be the same subject. It would undoubtedly [285] be a resembling being, as Leibniz says. Instead of Sextus, we'd have a "resembling Sextus," another Sextus, and there's an infinity of possible Sextuses, all more or less resembling the real Sextus, but for each of these possible Sextuses, everything he does and everything he will do in the possible [*dans le possible*] is contained in each of them just as all of the real Sextus's past, all of his present, and all of his future are contained in the real Sextus.[9]

Since I used a comparison borrowed from photography to analyze extension, I can use another one to analyze duration. This time, we'll have to think no longer simply of stereoscopic views and of one view for each substance, we'll have to think of a cinematographic film with thousands and thousands of successive views of one and the same thing.[10] For Leibniz, the subjects or the beings are the film of the cinematograph all rolled up on itself, if you will. Then, all the predicates we can assert of these subjects or, if you will, everything that happens to these beings, are different views juxtaposed on the film. Just as, given a roll of film, the smallest change to any of the views would suffice for it to no longer be the same roll, so, in the universe, in each of us, the slightest modification would suffice for it no longer to be the same person—but the moment it's the same person, everything they've done, everything they'll do, and everything that will ever happen to them, all that is contained in their notion. Their history is only the unrolling of their notion, which is really in the absolute, and the person is identical with their history.

This, gentlemen, is where the analysis of duration takes us. We can say that whereas the analysis of extension puts Leibniz on the path of a conception of reality analogous to that of Plotinus's Intelligibles, his analysis of duration puts him on the way to a conception of science that is quite close to that of a Plato, of an Aristotle, and of a Plotinus. We must always, I think, keep these two analyses in mind. I'm distinguishing them a lot more than Leibniz ever distinguished them himself. In his writings the two viewpoints constantly interpenetrate one another, but I think we have to dissociate them and we must always keep these analyses in mind if we want to understand the difference [286] between Leibniz and Spinoza, for at their core, the two doctrines resemble each other a lot. The two philosophers started from the same point: they started from Descartes; they set themselves the same goal: to unify Cartesianism completely, and to do so by taking it back to antiquity, by taking it back toward Plato, Aristotle, and Plotinus. So the analogies are very profound, the more we push the two systems, the more we see them ready to merge into one another.

Where is the difference? The difference consists in this: to obtain the unification, Spinoza placed himself immediately in unity. He immediately places himself in God, such that the big problem in Spinozism is to explain how there can be, I'm not saying something outside of God, but something that appears in itself outside of God, how the modes of thought can appear in themselves outside of God.[11]

Leibniz on the contrary went in the opposite direction. He didn't place himself immediately in unity, he looked for the unity by analyzing extension and duration.

And having started from multiplicity, he always necessarily preserved something of this starting point, he always had the multiplicity of substances. To be sure, the further we delve into these substances, the more we delve into their nature, the more we find them to be complementary to one another. They aren't independent, they can't be, each of them expressing what's in all the others. Not being independent, they aren't true substances, they aren't true beings: fundamentally, they are only aspects. If we pushed the doctrine, we'd find that they are aspects of God.

Consequently, the two systems are very close to being the same. The big difference is that Spinoza places himself immediately above and descends, while Leibniz places himself below and ascends, but both of them take the same route. The two systems, I repeat, are extremely close to one another.

This brings me to the conclusion of this study. What results from this study is that Leibniz's doctrine, where human freedom is concerned, must end up in a determination of our actions, in a determinism as rigorous, we can say, as radical as Spinoza's. This results from the very premises of the doctrine. Whether we consider the first or the [287] second of the two analyses we just saw, we come to the same conclusion. When we consider a state of a being at a given moment, the perception of a monad, the predicate of a subject, this state is complementary to all the rest of the universe, to all the states of all the other beings. It's absolutely determined by everything that is happening in all the rest of the universe. Although it's not influenced, it's determined by the rest. If we now place ourselves in the viewpoint of duration and no longer in that of extension, the determinism appears even more clearly. Once the notion of a being is posited, everything that will happen to it and everything it does is also posited, and in this way, we have been what we are from all eternity; from all eternity, we posit ourselves such as we must be.

So the determinism is radical. That can be proved a priori by starting from the premises of the doctrine, but Leibniz draws a posteriori arguments from it, on which I don't need to dwell since they're well known. You'll recall that Leibniz showed in many passages that the freedom of indifference or, as he says, the indifference of equilibrium, does not exist;[12] that there can be no real indetermination; that where we believe in indetermination, that where we believe that there are as many motives on one side as on the other, it's because we don't pay attention to the little perceptions, the imperceptible perceptions that determine us; that in reality there's a rigorous and perfect determination of everything we do; that when, for example, we leave the house, there's a determinant reason why we start walking with our right foot rather than our left foot or the other way around; that in this way, there are reasons, perfectly determinant causes for all of our actions; that if Descartes believed in indetermination, he was mistaken. In a passage in the *Theodicy*, Leibniz attributes this error to the education Descartes received at La Flèche.[13] Descartes was never able to free himself from this prejudice in favor of indetermination. The truth is that what we do is determined by what we've done, by what has already happened to us, and, basically, by what we are, by the very notion of our [288] being that we only develop in space and time.

Thus, whatever the testimony of consciousness might be, Leibniz criticized the proof from the intense inner feeling we have of our freedom. He declares that this "intense inner feeling" was only the ignorance of determinant perceptions—whatever this testimony might be, we are, in everything we do, what Leibniz calls "spiritual automatons."[14]

This is his doctrine. It is, as I said, a doctrine of necessity, of rigorous necessity. But the most remarkable and most interesting point is that in Leibniz's thought this is a doctrine of freedom—not only of freedom but of contingency. We're face to face here with an attempt of the highest interest, the renewal of the attempt that was very probably sketched in antiquity—I am saying "probably" because not many texts survived—probably sketched by Chrysippus. Moreover, in two or three passages in the *Theodicy*, Leibniz alludes to Chrysippus's doctrine according to which everything is determined but not necessary.[15] So he knows this doctrine, he interprets it in a certain way, which is probably the right way. I've adopted this interpretation here.[16] In a very precise way, he criticizes Cicero's interpretation, which he finds wanting.[17] What he tries to do, in short, is, with the most precise notion of necessity we have in modernity—especially since Descartes and since the scientific discoveries of the Renaissance—is, with this new notion of necessity, to do what Chrysippus did with the ancient notion of necessity, that is, in short, to define freedom and even contingency in terms of necessity. It's the same goal, it's the same method; that is, Leibniz, like Chrysippus, takes the idea of freedom and analyzes it into its elements. This is the method that the philosopher who wants to define freedom by necessity will necessarily follow. He'll take the idea of freedom and he will, through analysis, distinguish a certain number of elements. He'll show how, even in this nature where everything is perfectly determined, where everything is certain,
[289] as Leibniz says—for Leibniz likes the expression "certain" better than "determined" —even in a nature where everything is certain, there is nonetheless room for contingency and freedom, "contingency" and "freedom" being defined in a certain way. I'm saying that this is the trick [*artifice*] we necessarily end up with. At its core, this is only a trick since—I've constantly repeated this since the beginning of this course—if freedom is a real thing, it cannot be entirely analyzed. We must seek to analyze it, we'll manage to do so more and more but never completely. If freedom exists, we must attempt to express it in ideas, in concepts. This is possible to a certain extent and up to a certain point, but not completely. In fact, if we managed to analyze it completely, there'd be no freedom.[18] If we could express action entirely in terms of speculation, there'd no longer be any action, no *proprium quid*,[19] there'd be no freedom. Consequently, in short, freedom would only be a word, a name given to a certain kind of necessity. What is translating a thing into a concept? What is making something perfectly intelligible? What is analyzing a thing into ideas? It's bringing it back to a certain number of elements it has in common with other things. The ideas are genera, the ideas in no way have anything in common with a lot of terms.[20] If freedom could be entirely defined by ideas, there would be nothing in freedom that isn't held in common with terms other than freedom: there would be nothing proper to, nothing irreducible in freedom. So a priori we can say that an attempt that claims to define freedom in terms of necessity begins by analyzing freedom into ideas. A priori, too, we can say that a doctrine that will analyze freedom into ideas will, in short, bring freedom back to a certain aspect of necessity.

How does Leibniz go about this analysis? It's very simple: he declares that freedom is a thing that comprises a certain number of elements, three main elements: spontaneity, intelligence, and contingency. An act is free when it is spontaneous, when it is intelligent, and when it is contingent.

What is spontaneity? Leibniz defines it as the absence of constraint. What is constrained? It is that which has an external principle, that which is determined by [290] something else. Consequently, spontaneity is quite simply the property of being self-determining. A spontaneous act carried out is an act that emanates from the being carrying it out and from it alone, [one] that isn't the product of an external constraint.[21] Do we possess this kind of spontaneity? It's incontestable, since not only we but all beings, in Leibniz's theory, have this spontaneity. Substance develops by itself since there is no influence of things on one another; there's simply preestablished harmony. Substance develops by itself: all of a subject's predicates are included in this subject and emanate consequently exclusively from it. So we have spontaneity. Our actions are spontaneous, like those of animals. Animals, to be sure, aren't free: they lack the second condition, intelligence.

Are we intelligent? Yes, certainly, since humans are more than humans, they're minds. So humans possess intelligence. It's not hard, in fact, to show that intelligence is a condition of freedom and that it's realized in humans.

We still have to consider contingency, and it's here that the doctrine presents itself with a completely original character all its own, since, as for the other elements, other necessitarian philosophers already discovered them in freedom such as it is defined. But what's new and original, what's entirely Leibnizian, is that he says that our actions are absolutely certain in the sense of "determined," and nevertheless that they are not necessary, that they are contingent; they are certain, they are not necessary. This is the formula that comes back often in Leibniz. Everything I've done, everything I will do is certain, but it isn't necessary. Why? Because Leibniz defines contingency and necessity in his own way: what is necessary for him is that whose contrary implies a contradiction.[22] Thus, when I say that the sum of three angles of a triangle equals two right angles, this is necessary because the contrary proposition is a contradictory proposition, an absurd proposition; consequently, the contrary is impossible in the sense that the contrary is contradictory. But when I say that Caesar crossed the Rubicon, the contrary proposition —"Caesar did not cross the Rubicon"—is possible, it's not absurd, not contradictory. [291] Consequently, this action—crossing the Rubicon—is a contingent action, an action that's not necessary, even though it's determined and certain. It's certain but it's not necessary; it's not necessary because its contrary is possible since everything that's not contradictory is possible.

Gentlemen, here we have a definition that might be astonishing at first glance, a definition of contingency that can astonish. And the explanations that Leibniz provides for it do nothing, it seems at first glance, to dissipate the astonishment. For let's consider an action that a subject carries out. A different action, the opposite action, was possible because it was not absurd, nor contradictory; it was possible, but it couldn't be realized [*se réaliser*]. What prevented it from being realized? It's that it would have had to be compossible, as Leibniz says, with all the rest of what exists, and consequently, Caesar crossing the Rubicon, the action he carries out [would have needed] to be in harmony with all the rest of what is outlined in his notion and in the notions complementary to this notion, composing all the other beings. When I take the opposite action—Caesar not crossing the Rubicon—this is an action possible in itself, but it's not compossible with the rest of reality; consequently, it's an action seen in another nature, in another universe than ours, in a universe comprising a whole system of possibles complementary to that particular possible.

Leibniz tells us that the divine understanding conceives all the possibles and that it incorporates them in so many systems, and each system forms a possible world. The action I don't accomplish is a possible action, in the sense that it's part of one of the possible worlds represented in the divine understanding. Everything that doesn't imply a contradiction is possible; all the possibles are unified into systems; each of these systems forms a world; and God chooses the best of the possible worlds: that's the one he willed to be realized.

So when we come to clarify Leibniz's thought via the context, we find, in short, that
[292] the divine understanding conceives the possibles, all the possibles, that the divine will realizes the best system of possibles—from which it follows that the deeper we go into this conception of contingency and freedom, the more it seems we're dealing with absolute determination and necessity. However, this is only an appearance, and we must look behind the words for the completely unique vision of this point that Leibniz must have had, since he repeats so often, and in such definite terms, that everything is certain and yet nothing, at least in the realm of human actions, is necessary, that obviously he internally, I'd almost say subconsciously pictured matters to himself in a way a bit different from the way they appear when we stop at the letter of the texts.

First, there's one thing we mustn't lose sight of, which is that according to Leibniz, what isn't contradictory is possible, and that, therefore, the possibles posit themselves by themselves independently of God. Leibniz tells us that God's understanding is the seat of the possibles, but since it's the law of noncontradiction that makes it such that a possible is possible, and since this law is eternal like God himself, the possibles posit themselves by themselves from all eternity.

Second, what makes it such that a system of possibles realizes itself? What makes it such that our world has been realized, while all the other possible worlds are unrealized? It's that, Leibniz tells us, our world is the best of the possible worlds. But to evaluate [which is] the best of the possible worlds, does God need to weigh the possible worlds, as it were? Of course not, since for Leibniz the best is something that can be calculated and that has no need for someone to come inspect and judge it. The most perfect world is the world that contains the maximum of being; the best is the definition of existence; the best is what exists. What we call "existence" is just that, it's the highest perfection. So the possibles posit themselves by themselves and the best possible world realizes itself by itself, or rather, it is realized because it's the best possible that exists.

Then what becomes of Leibniz's God? Leibniz tells us that his understanding is the seat of the possibles, that his will is what realizes the best. The more we delve into

Leibniz's God, the more he appears to be—although Leibniz never said this, although [293]
he didn't want to believe this—Leibniz's God appears to us as being only the sum of the possibles and of existence.[23]

We have, to use the metaphor he himself takes at the end of *Theodicy*, speaking of something else, we have an immense pyramid whose base is lost in infinity.[24] This pyramid represents all possible worlds; the summit then is the real world. It's hard to picture Leibniz's God in any other form than in this form of the pyramid. We have to push Leibniz's doctrine to the limit, as mathematicians say. If we go that far, the doctrine of freedom is not as paradoxical, and also strange, as it appears at first: for the possibles exist, although Leibniz doesn't want to say it. The possibles have an existence as possibles. Reality is a certain highlighted possible, whose contours have been highlighted, whose contours have been emphasized. What happens for each of us? From all eternity, each posits itself as possible such as it is. Sextus posits himself from all eternity such as he is, and at the same time as the real Sextus posits himself, there are all the possible Sextuses, a little different or very different, the "resembling Sextuses," that posit themselves as more or less possible, but there is only one of the Sextuses, the one who is part of the best of the possible worlds, who is realized. The others as it were accompany the real one, if I may put it like that, they follow him as in a procession but in the form of simple possibles. He is bathed in an atmosphere of possibles that follow him. Beside the Sextus in flesh and blood, who acts as he acts, there are all the other Sextuses following behind him like so many phantoms. But these phantoms act completely differently from the way the true Sextus acts. In this sense, he is indeed free. Not only does he do what he does but he also does something else, he does all the other possibles. He does them in the possible, he doesn't do them in the real.

Here we have an extremely original theory of freedom, freedom being defined by spontaneity, by intelligence, and by contingency, contingency which here consists in that [while] what we do, we do in a way determined from all eternity, we can [do] something
else, in the sense that in the possible, we do do something else —not just something [294]
else but a thousand other things, an infinity of other things. All in all, this is a doctrine that spreads freedom out in the form of actions. Freedom is a power. An intellectualist like Leibniz cannot accept that, the idea of power, and so he spreads out all the possible actions, he turns them into so many accompaniments, as it were, of the action really performed.

I'm saying that this is an "interpretation" of Leibniz; but when we read the allegory of Sextus with which the *Theodicy* ends, we have the very clear impression that this is indeed what Leibniz thinks. You remember how this allegory ends:

> You accuse God of having made Sextus wicked, he was that way from all eternity. He has made himself wicked from all eternity; it's just that there are all the other Sextuses acting very differently from how Sextus has acted, having a different destiny. There are some who, instead of going to Rome, committing a crime, and being exiled, buy a house, a little garden, cultivate it, and live happily.[25]

There are thus all the possible Sextuses as it were surrounding the real Sextus. This I believe is the true meaning of Leibniz's thought.

Gentlemen, we've completed this presentation of the necessitarian metaphysical doctrines coming out of Descartes. For the second semester, which will be extremely short, which will comprise only a small number of lectures, we still have to say a word about Kant's doctrine of freedom, to show the path toward this doctrine, to show how Kant's theory of freedom develops from a necessary reaction—provoked by the atmosphere of reactions against these doctrines of necessity and under the influence of the moral ideas of the eighteenth century. And then, for that's where this very abbreviated presentation of the evolution of the problem of freedom will stop, it'll remain for us to find out—that'll be our dogmatic conclusion, that is what remains for us to see after Kant—how, it seems, the problem of freedom must be put today. That will be the object of the course in the second semester, which begins on Friday, May 5.

Notes

1. In the preceding lecture (193) and earlier, in discussing Plotinus (140).
2. The typescript says *traduit en quantités les grandeurs* here, "translates magnitudes into quantities," which does not seem right.
3. *Deixeketai* in the typescript. Rather than *diexerkhesthai*, this could also have been *diexienai*; both mean "to go through," literally and, importantly, figuratively, in the sense of "recounting in detail." Bergson is probably thinking of *Enneads* 3.8.9 here.
4. See the preceding lecture, 196 and 199n34—as indicated there, the passage is in "On Contingency."
5. See above, 189–90, and CE, 303/352.
6. All three of these quotations are from a draft of one of the letters that Leibniz would send to Antoine Arnauld on July 14, 1686 (PE, 69–77, here 73). Arnauld, now a demanding interlocutor of Leibniz's in their extensive correspondence, had formulated a series of objections to Descartes's *Meditations* some forty years earlier.
7. "Discourse on Metaphysics," in PE, §13: 44–5.
8. See the preceding lecture, 191–2.
9. Bergson is paraphrasing Leibniz's *Theodicy* 3.§§413–17: 369–73. The Sextus referred to is Sextus Tarquinius (son of Tarquinius Superbus, the last king of Rome), whom the oracle at Delphi foretold a criminal future (the rape of Lucretia).
10. For this famous comparison, see the January 20, 1905, lecture above, 62–63, and, especially, CE, 263–72/303–13.
11. CE, 301–3/350–2, and TFW, 213–14/160–1.
12. See, for instance, *Theodicy* 1.§49: 150 (on Buridan's ass) and 3.307: 312, and *New Essays on Human Understanding* 2.21.§36: 188.
13. Bergson is referring to *Theodicy* 3.§365:343–4. The Jesuits, who ran the Collège de La Flèche, were vocal defenders of the freedom of indifference, which suited their own theory of grace in the controversy with the Jansenists. On Descartes at the Collège, see the March 17, 1905, lecture, 150 and 158n4.

14. "Intense inner feeling" (*sentiment vif interne*, "intense inward sensation" in Huggard's translation) is a formula from the *Theodicy*, 1.§50: 150. The Cartesian doctrine Leibniz is criticizing can be found in the *Principles* 1.39 (PW I, 205–6/AT VIIIA, 19–20); see also the March 24, 1905, lecture above, 163. "Spiritual automaton" is an expression taken from Spinoza (*Treatise on the Emendation of the Intellect*, CWS 1, 37) but in a new sense. For Leibniz's use of it, see *Theodicy*, 1.§52: 151 and III.§403: 364–5.
15. On Chrysippus, see *Theodicy*, 2.§§168–70: 228–33, 2.§209:258–9, and 3.§§331–6: 324–7.
16. See the February 17, 1905, lecture above, 109–10.
17. Leibniz, *Theodicy*, 3.§331–3: 324–6. On Leibniz's reading, Cicero in *On Fate* saw in Chrysippus's position a "middle course" between the doctrine of the "ancient Stoics" who asserted determination, without, however, going as far as asserting necessity (the correct position, according to Leibniz, and one taken up by the Thomists), and a strict necessitarian position Cicero attributes to Democritus, Heraclitus, Empedocles, and even Aristotle (though Leibniz thinks this attribution to Aristotle is a mistake). Leibniz insists that Chrysippus be categorized with the "ancient Stoics" (he mentions Cleanthes in the text) and with the Thomists. For Cicero's discussion of Chrysippus, see *On Fate*, sections 4–8: 201–11; 13: 217–19 and 225–7; and 17–19: 235–43.
18. See the December 6, 1904, lecture above, 16–9, and especially TFW, 219–21/165–6.
19. "Something proper" to freedom; *proprium quid* is a Scholastic expression that refers to the distinction (which originates in Aristotle, *Topics* 1.5, 101b30–102b26: 169–70) between "property" and "accident."
20. While the phrase, *les idées n'ont point quelque chose de commun à beaucoup de termes*, is hard to understand, the thesis—confirmed by what follows—is hardly in doubt: an idea always has something in common with another idea. Analyzing freedom into ideas thus fails to see its singularity, its "irreducibility."
21. TFW, 172–3/130.
22. For this line of argument and for the example that follows, see Leibniz, "Discourse on Metaphysics," §13: 44–6.
23. In this analysis of the possibles' inherent tendency to be realized and in the reference to calculating the maximum and the minimum, Bergson has Leibniz's treatise "On the Ultimate Origination of Things" (PE, 149–55) in mind, a text he lectured on in 1898; see "Cours de Bergson sur le *De rerum originatione radicali* de Leibniz," ed. Matthias Vollet and Arnaud François, in *Annales Bergsoniennes* III: "Bergson et la science," ed. Frédéric Worms, 25–52 (Paris: Presses universitaires de France, 2007).
24. Leibniz, *Theodicy*, 3.§416: 372–73, where Leibniz is speaking of "something else" because, in his conception, the pyramid is not God himself.
25. Bergson is paraphrasing, rather than quoting, the words of the goddess Pallas, who is tasked with justifying to Theodorus the world her father, Jupiter, made; see Leibniz, *Theodicy*, 3.§§413–17: 369–73.

LECTURE 18
MAY 5, 1905

Ladies and gentlemen,[1] I can summarize the lectures of the first semester by saying that [295] what dominates in modern philosophy up to Kant as also in ancient philosophy is the belief in necessity much more than [the belief] in freedom in the sense of free will. In a way, philosophy is naturally necessitarian, and consequently reflective thought is naturally necessitarian.

At certain times, philosophy can open up a little, thrust forward by a moral idea, philosophy can open up a little to allow the belief in free will to slip in. But it closes back up very quickly, and this belief, I said, is pulverized into concepts, into distinct, definite ideas, so much so that in the end we find ourselves again face to face with necessity: a more comprehensive doctrine of necessity, no doubt, which widened to make room for a new belief, which in certain cases can even award itself the title of a theory of freedom, but it's no less a determinist theory, a theory of necessity. This is true of modern philosophy; this was true of ancient philosophy. From the beginning of ancient philosophy, we witness the hatching of the doctrine of necessity, and this natural belief of the mind even translates rather naively into Greek philosophy, for this philosophy tells us, in short, that things ought, "ought" to be necessitated, ought to be subject to an invariable and rational order.

The ancients, to be sure, thought that they wouldn't find this order in things such as they are, in sensible things. Not having studied them from the side where this order might be discovered, they concluded that this order belonged to the true ideas, to the [296] ideas that science must be about: the Ideas or the Forms; then the sensible world was as if in disarray, it was the world of the Ideas diminished, degraded, it was something lesser than the purely rational order, and this lack is what Aristotle calls *hylē*, matter. So there ought to be, in the things, a rational order perfectly realized, from which an absolute necessity would follow. In fact, this determinism is not realized, and it's not realized because of a principle: *hylē*, which in a way measures out the gap between what the things are and what they ought to be.

The old things changed with modern philosophy, at least in appearance. Modern philosophy is born to a large extent from modern science, and this science has focused entirely on the idea of physical law, the idea of law as it was in fact defined by people like Kepler, Galileo, because what yields definitions, in short, are discoveries. The idea of physical laws was defined the day there were physical laws.

What, in fact, is the great innovation, the great invention of the moderns on this point? I've already said it, but I can't repeat it too much. It's not, as has often been said, the invention of the experimental method.[2] The experimental method existed in antiquity, the ancients observed, they experimented as much as we do. To see this, all you have to do is read Aristotle's treatises. No, what characterizes this science is rather a limitation, is rather a focusing of the experimental method on one single point, which is measurement, the study of the quantitative variations of phenomena.

Now, this was above all a mathematical advance: what gave birth to this modern science was mathematics. The ancients didn't manage explicitly to extract the idea of the dependence of one magnitude in relation to other magnitudes, what we call the idea of functions, from their mathematics. The day the idea of functions was spelled out, the principle of physical laws was discovered, for that is what a physical law is: it's the
[297] statement of a constant function between variables. Now, the day some of these relations were formulated, that day, the hope arose to see the entire universe open up to a great mathematics, the hope to see all phenomena become functions of each other. And the mechanistic conception of nature[3] is a translation of this kind of algebraic dream: the universe would resemble a machine in which everything meshes perfectly and in where there is no play between the cogs, no room for indeterminism or contingency.

Thus, the idea of *hylē*—assuming it was an idea: for the ancients it's not an idea—matter, *hylē* disappeared forever. There could no longer be any question of the intervention, in nature, of a principle preventing things from being subjected to a purely rational order. The rational order was nature itself: it was in the relations among the phenomena, in the stability of the relations among variable things. This principle, *hylē*, disappeared and the rational order that the ancients had conceived—a rigorous order, in short, an order that, if it existed, had to impose necessary relations on coordinated things—this order as it were came down from heaven to earth, existed no longer only in the world of the Ideas but in the universe properly speaking. And the universe, nature, became the seat of a rigorous, mathematical necessity, of a kind the ancients were unfamiliar with. For while the Stoics believed in universal determinism, while they even provided the precise formula for a universal determinism, they thought this was a universal but not a mathematical determinism, that is, not one that is rigorously inflexible.

I said that Descartes's philosophy first of all reflected this mechanistic tendency of modern science. Descartes's philosophy is entirely permeated, it's as if imbued with the modern idea of physical laws, and while Descartes was not as great a physicist as he was a mathematician, we can say that his mathematics itself is imbued with the idea of physical laws since his great invention was that of analytical geometry, the geometry which considers figures, curves to, in short, express laws.[4] Since Descartes, a curve is the expression of a function, that is, of a relation of dependence between two or
[298] three variables. So the idea of laws, in the very sense in which physicists understand it, permeates all the way to Descartes's geometry, and Descartes's philosophy can be considered to have given a body to the dream I mentioned a moment ago, the dream of a universal mathematics encompassing the totality of things.[5]

Yes, but at the same time as science oriented minds in this direction—I'm saying "at the same time," but in fact this is well before it—another current was developing, taking shape: the belief in freedom, the belief in contingency and in indetermination, a belief having arisen here again, as [it had] earlier, in Pericles's century,[6] from ideas alien, all in all, to pure speculation, ideas that weren't exclusively theoretical or speculative. This belief, as I demonstrated, was introduced with the new current of ideas and feelings that coincided with the spread of Christianity. Its origins are religious and at the same time moral and even, we might say, social.

Freedom in the sense of free will reappeared, and it reappeared, moreover, much more complete and in a form much more profound, more self-conscious, than in the ancient Greeks and in Platonic-Aristotelian philosophy. Human freedom was in fact no longer, as in this philosophy, a stopgap. For in Greek philosophy, freedom is always a means for the human to find itself again, to conform again to its idea, and if there was no principle of degradation in the universe, if *hylē* didn't result in the degradation of the Idea, freedom would be useless. It's there only to put things back in place as much as possible, and we'd hardly say that it is a good: it's only a lesser evil. Freedom in the sense of the moderns, instead, is something more positive, and I showed that this has to do with freedom, in humans, being considered a power—we should circumscribe the meaning of this word—a creative power. Insofar as they are free, humans are the partners—I daren't say partners—the delegates of God, who, according to the Jewish tradition, is creative.[7] The idea of creation doesn't exist in Greek philosophy at all. So this freedom, freedom thus understood, is something more positive and more [299]
profound.

I said that Descartes takes up this idea of freedom and this inner feeling of freedom; and this is the other aspect of his philosophy. This philosophy, which from one side is essentially intellectualist, which from one side is mechanistic, from another side is voluntarist, [is] a positive conception of the role of the will in the world, and we find these two aspects unified and juxtaposed in Descartes. On this point, Descartes was not worried about an absolute logic, or at least not a simple logic. He undoubtedly didn't think that a complete unification was necessary, not in the sense that Spencer takes this word, that is, the oversimplification of things.[8] The mind no doubt has a tendency to demand it, but nothing proves that this tendency isn't an effect of laziness, the need, the desire it has to see [things] simply. What's certain is that the two tendencies, the two philosophies are intimately tied in with one another in Descartes. And he always stopped the first [tendency] at the point, at the precise moment when it would have contradicted the second. This is why his mechanism, although it is universal, is nonetheless relaxed enough, on certain points, to allow human freedom to slip in.

However, as I intimated, there was something in this that didn't conform to the ordinary habits of the mind, to the ordinary habits of philosophy. This coexistence of the two tendencies—intellectualist and voluntarist—had something, I wouldn't say abnormal, but exceptional about it, and it's quite natural that, after Descartes, the first tendency absorbed the second, and that is what we saw. I took the example of Spinoza and Leibniz—I could have selected others. We saw that in these two philosophies, to cite just these two among the many post-Cartesian philosophies, the idea of necessity expands, the doctrine of necessity takes up more and more space, it takes up all the space, it absorbs the belief in freedom—so much so that while these two doctrines preserve the word, even preserve, they say and they believe, the thing, the freedom at

[300] issue is defined in terms of necessity, and we are indeed, in short, dealing with strictly fatalistic or determinist doctrines.

This is where we stopped.

To be thorough on this point, we'd have to show how in the eighteenth century, throughout the eighteenth century, Descartes's philosophy is simplified, especially when it's in the hands of scientists, physicians, philosopher-physicians, and even some mathematicians.[9] We'd hardly dare say of philosophies like Spinoza's or Leibniz's that these are simplifications of Cartesianism: they undoubtedly eliminated an essential element, but [both] preserved, juxtaposed side by side, extension and thought. Undoubtedly, everything in the domain of extension happens mechanically, and undoubtedly, everything that happens in the domain of thought merely translates the mechanical necessity we encounter in the material world into another [kind of] necessity. Nevertheless, there is extension and there is thought, and reducing thought to extension is never an option. This reduction, this attempt at a reduction, is what takes place in the eighteenth century.

It's there that we see the idea take shape that thought, that consciousness is like an accident of extension, of matter. Matter is represented as being constituted by particles in motion. These particles, in certain conditions, constitute organisms; these organisms, in certain cases, have a nervous system, nerve centers; in these nerve centers, in certain cases, at certain moments, consciousness joins movement like a phenomenon, as the contemporaries say, like a kind of phosphorescence, in short, as an accident.[10] We can track this theory across the eighteenth century, and I'm not going back to this point because I pointed out the intermediaries last year in a course on the theory of memory.[11]

It's very intriguing to see how in France, in England, in Germany, all at the same time, a movement takes place by which one obtained, through simplification—it took a lot of simplifying to get there—this form of, in short, materialism from Cartesianism. And if,
[301] I wouldn't say our whole psychophysiology but certain works in our psychophysiology are as if imbued with this hypothesis, then this has to do—as I've shown as well—with this psychophysiology being inspired by the work of the philosopher-physicians of the eighteenth century. It emerged from there, and although it has made a lot of progress—since only in our time have psychology and pathology taken a precise form—while, therefore, as a science in the strict sense, our psychophysiology is far advanced over what was done in the eighteenth century, nonetheless, as a system of explanation, and insofar as it tries in certain cases, when it becomes a philosophy, to account for the very essence of phenomena, it hardly does anything more than reproduce—sometimes without criticism—these eighteenth-century philosophies, whose heritage it, as a philosophy, has accepted.

Here we have to distinguish very clearly between science and philosophy. In these matters, science is observation and experimentation, and no one can dispute the great discoveries of psychophysiology and especially of the current psychological pathology. But the philosophy that sometimes joins the science is something completely different. When it joins the science, it most often does so surreptitiously, without explicating itself as philosophy, and then, since it's not an explicit philosophy, an explicit metaphysics,

it's hardly anything other than the reproduction and elaboration of certain formulas from the philosophies of the eighteenth century, which are themselves simplifications of Cartesian philosophy and an as it were narrow-minded form of Cartesian philosophy. Last year, I tried to demonstrate this, there's no need to return to it. I'll thus limit myself to recalling that by "science" we understand that which is truly scientific, that is, the observations, the experiments. Well, what science constantly, incontestably shows us is that there is a relationship of interdependence between thought and consciousness on the one side and cerebral phenomena on the other. There is a relation of interdependence between the two: we don't know of any fact of consciousness that is not accompanied by a cerebral phenomenon. There's no profound lesion of consciousness that is not accompanied by a lesion—not always observed but no doubt observable— by a cerebral [302]
lesion. There is thus an interdependence between the two. That is indisputable.

But from there, it's a long way to concluding an equivalence between the two. "Interdependence" does not mean "equivalence." A garment hangs on a nail; the nail comes off; the garment falls: the garment depended on the nail, but that doesn't mean that it *is* the nail.[12] Similarly, the phenomena of consciousness are certainly linked to cerebral states, and the cerebral states cannot be taken away without the facts of consciousness falling off, as it were. But that doesn't mean at all—there aren't even the beginnings of a proof [here]—that the fact of consciousness is equivalent to the cerebral phenomenon, "equivalent" meaning that it follows the cerebral phenomenon in all of its modalities. That a determinate fact of consciousness corresponds to a determinate state is very probable, but that one determinate fact of consciousness corresponds to one determinate cerebral state is not certain, and it could be the case that several possible psychological phenomena correspond to the same cerebral state, in which case the mechanism could be rigorous in material nature, in the brain, without the mechanism therefore being rigorous in the world of consciousness.

Be that as it may, when we go as far as this, and when we transport a rigorous mechanism which we began by composing in the world of matter into the world of consciousness, we're doing metaphysics, and it's a metaphysics that at its core is nothing other than—we can lay out its history and follow its evolution—the simplification of Cartesian metaphysics.

This is what we'd have to show in detail in order to be thorough on this point. I'm limiting myself to recalling the conclusions we reached last year.

We'd have to add that in the eighteenth century, besides the philosopher–physicians, there were the scientists. We'd thus have to join at least a brief presentation of certain eighteenth-century scientists' ideas on universal mechanism to these elaborations on psychophysiological mechanism. We don't have time to give such a presentation or even just such a sketch. I'm limiting myself to citing a passage—the passage has been published more than once—from Laplace that is interesting because there we find the very formula [303]
of the universal mechanism of some current scientists and because, above all, we can see pointed out there the origin, the very source of this mechanism.

It's taken from the *Philosophical Essay on Probabilities*, from the first or second page of the introduction. I'm quoting the main passages: "All events, even those that on account of their rarity [or insignificance] seem not to obey the great laws of nature, are as necessary a consequence of these laws as the revolutions of the sun." You see the astronomical idea come in here. Then, a little further on:

> We ought then to consider the present state of the universe as the effect of its previous state and as the cause of that which is to follow. An intelligence that, at a given instant, could comprehend all the forces by which nature is animated and the respective situation of the beings that make it up, if moreover it were vast enough to submit these data to analysis, would encompass in the same formula the movements of the greatest bodies of the universe and those of the lightest atoms. For such an intelligence nothing would be uncertain, and the future, like the past, would be open to its eyes.[13]

Here, you see radical determinism coming about, and coming about as a consequence, and as an enormous extension of what I might call astronomical determinism: general determinism as it were emerged from astronomy, from planetary determinism. And—I've already referred to this point[14]—we have a tendency to picture the infinitely small like the infinitely large, and molecules, atoms as being subject, like the planets of our solar system, to forces that depend solely on speeds. Our science, in short, is built on this point, and it's natural that our science has a completely determinist tendency. The question is whether freedom can find a place in this mechanism when life appears and, all the more so, consciousness, reason. This is the whole question.

Nevertheless, a passage like that does show us the origin of the radical determinism
[304] certain scientists believe in when they become metaphysicians, for this is no longer science, it's metaphysics.

So this was the tendency of both science and of philosophy at the end of the eighteenth century.

But at the same time another current is taking shape, a current steered in the direction of the belief in freedom, a current whose origin, whose source was, like the source of all currents of this kind, in ideas or morals, either social or religious—social above all, perhaps.[15] We have to remember that Rousseau's *Social Contract* is founded entirely on the idea that the essence of society, the basis of society, is that each respects the freedom of the other. It goes without saying that the issue here is political freedom, and political freedom does not imply free will. We can demand that citizens be free without believing in freedom in the sense that philosophers have given to the word "freedom."

Nevertheless, a thinker who attributes to freedom, to political freedom, the importance Rousseau attributes to it, who makes it an irreducible and fundamental attribute of humanity, a psychological function, something that humans have at birth,[16] something we don't have the right to strip them of—this thinker, undoubtedly, can logically deny freedom, deny free will. The two things are not logically incompatible; but morally they are incompatible, and there's too much emphasis, the emphasis is placed too much on human freedom as what makes the human a special being in nature, the emphasis is placed too heavily for this same thinker to then be able to show us, in the human, a simple thing, a cog from the viewpoint of universal mechanism. We mustn't be surprised, then, to find in Rousseau's other writings very precise allusions, and more than allusions, the precise affirmation of human freedom and of freedom in the sense of free will. I could quote lots of passages, all of which, incidentally, would come from book 4 of *Émile*, the famous "Profession of Faith of a Savoyard Vicar":

> You will ask me . . . how I know that there are spontaneous motions. I will tell you that I know it because I sense it. I want to move my arm, and I move it without this movement's having another immediate cause than my will. It would be vain to try to use reason to destroy this feeling in me. It is stronger than any evidence. One [305]
> might just as well try to prove to me that I do not exist.[17]

Then comes a discussion of mechanism, which there would be lots of things to say about, but I don't have the time, I'll just quote the conclusion: "No material being is active by itself, and I am. One may very well argue with me about this; but I sense it, and this sentiment that speaks to me is stronger than the reason combating it."[18] So according to Rousseau, no argument can prevail over so profound a feeling.

Now, can this freedom we feel coincide with the mechanism of nature? On this point, Rousseau points us—and it's just than an indication, just an allusion a couple of pages later—he points us to the beginning of a solution:

> The principle of every action is in the will of a free being. One cannot go back beyond that. It is not the word *freedom* which means nothing; it is the word *necessity*. To suppose . . . some effect, which does not derive from an active principle is truly to suppose effects without cause; it is to fall into a vicious circle. Either there is no first impulse, or every first impulse has no prior cause; and there is no will without freedom. Humanity is therefore free in its actions.[19]

These are Rousseau's conclusions and this is his solution.

It's very remarkable to see the analogy between these ideas, and, I wouldn't say the ideas but the tendencies, the inspiration of Kant's *Critique of Pure Reason*. Undoubtedly, the differences are profound, very profound: Rousseau invokes the inner feeling, the testimony of consciousness; for Kant, this testimony of empirical consciousness holds no value, for him, consciousness points only to phenomena, not to absolute reality, not to freedom.[20] No doubt. But Kant does invoke, if not consciousness in the psychological sense, then at least moral consciousness, and in the passage from Rousseau moral consciousness has the last word.

For Kant, I can because I must: I must, therefore I can.[21] Freedom, in short, is proven [306]
by morality. On the other hand, Kant doesn't tell us, as Rousseau does, that necessity hangs on [*est suspendue à*] freedom—for that's what the last passage I quoted from Rousseau says: it means that things, in the material world, in nature, even in psychology in a certain sense, are connected to one another and compose the links of a chain, but the chain hangs on freedom. The first origin is freedom—Kant does not assert that this

is the case, but he does tell us in the *Critique of Pure Reason* that things might be like this, it's possible, and that will be, you'll remember, the solution to the third antinomy.[22]

Now, there's one thing in Kant that doesn't exist in Rousseau, it's the distinction between the phenomena and the world of things in themselves. You'll remember that Kant's conception of freedom rests on this distinction. So while the influence could, while it had to come, even, from Rousseau (and Rousseau's influence on Kant is indisputable), we do have to remember that in Kant's philosophy, there's an essential element completely irreducible to Rousseau's ideas—but that doesn't mean that the origin of this element is purely Kantian. Beside the current going in the direction of freedom, of the belief in freedom, in free will, which comes about in France in the eighteenth century, there's another current in England, which even precedes it, we see it at the beginning of the eighteenth century, and Kant certainly felt the effects of this one.

In the first half of the eighteenth century, Berkeley's philosophy comes about in England, and we mustn't be mistaken about the origin and significance of this philosophy.[23] We mustn't think of Berkeley, as people sometimes do, as a kind of dilettante who, for the fun of it, floats the apparently paradoxical thesis that material things don't exist in themselves and are only ideas of our mind. That's not it at all.

Berkeley had a constant objective, which is already indicated in the notes he wrote
[307] when he was still in college.[24] We must remember that Berkeley is a bishop who wants to justify religion and defend it. He's a moralist. Berkeley wants to refute materialism and mechanism in particular. His negation of the existence of material things outside of the mind means simply this: let's accept for a moment—and Berkeley contests this—let's accept that in the material world everything is perfectly determined, subject to necessary and mathematical laws, let's accept the mechanism taken from Descartes and Newton. I'm going to show you how this whole material universe, with the necessity to which it is subjected, exists only as a kind of intellectual phenomenon, a kind of dream, a beam of sunlight God has put in us. But this world has no existence outside of our mind, and consequently, if consciousness tells us, if this mind, when we ask it, tells us that we are free, if it feels itself to be free, it will be proved that at the base of this necessity, which is appearance, there is freedom, which is reality.

This is what Berkeley's immaterialism means, and his nominalism as well, for that is Berkeley's second thesis, which is less well known than the first: the assertion of the nonreality of abstract and general ideas.

When we look closely, in the texts, at this nominalist theory, when we gather all the passages that discuss it, we see that the general and abstract ideas whose objectivity Berkeley denies come down to a small number. He always cites the same examples: number, extension, movement, sometimes form. These are the three or four ideas at issue, these are the ideas of nominalism.

And what is he trying to establish concerning these ideas? That they are signs. The Cartesian or rather pseudo-Cartesian philosopher, the one he calls "minute philosopher"—the philosopher who looks at things in detail, the minute philosopher[25]—this philosopher takes signs to be things. He'll take extension, for example, he'll reason about extension, and because there, everything happens geometrically, he'll conclude

that everything in the universe happens geometrically. This amounts to reasoning about the symbol and to believing that the reasoning made about the symbol applies to the thing. For in reality, what exists is not extension, it's the concrete things, each possessing [308]
different qualities, and extension is not the common notation of these things, it's the common sign. And it's a big error to start from the sign, to reason about the sign, and to extend to the things reasonings that hold only for the signs.[26] This is absolutely the same as—the comparison isn't Berkeley's, but I've found no other—the same as if we represented all the sounds of a language by means of the signs of writing, all French words, for example, by the same written words. In writing, we would have a sign that would be to the spoken word what extension is to bodies in general. And we could say, considering that the signs are curved lines—the signs of writing are curved lines combined with each other in various ways, so the common attribute of signs of writing is the curved line—we could conclude that the spoken words are curved lines and that the French language is curved, which wouldn't make any sense. According to Berkeley, someone who, reasoning about extension, draws certain conclusions from it that he applies to the things, of which extension is the symbol, is making a reasoning like this.

And then, when we start from these premises and when we understand Berkeley's immaterialism and his nominalism in this way—two doctrines that converge on one point, the refutation of mechanism and of materialism—we can understand very well why Berkeley offers, in support of the belief in freedom, arguments based on feeling, on immediate intuition, like those he offers us in *Alciphron.*

This is one of the least read dialogues by Berkeley, dialogues that were very popular during their author's lifetime. We'd have to read nearly all of the seventh dialogue in *Alciphron*; I'm limiting myself to pointing out one or two pages. Alciphron, who is the minute philosopher, claims that the human is like an organ that external things play on or a puppet whose strings are pulled by external things, that in humans, consequently, everything happens mechanically, and his opponent, Euphranor, who represents Berkeley himself, responds:

> It is self-evident that there is such a thing as motion: and yet there have been [309]
> found philosophers who, by refined reasoning, would undertake to prove there is no such thing. Walking before them was thought the proper way to confute those ingenious men. It is no less evident that man is a free agent: and though, by abstracted reasonings, you should puzzle me, and seem to prove the contrary, yet, so long as I am conscious of my own actions, this inward evidence of plain fact

—notice this very curious expression—

> will bear me up against all your reasonings, however subtle and refined.[27]

And then Berkeley explains to us that the reasoning of determinism consists in taking concrete things and dividing them into abstract notions, breaking them down into abstract notions, breaking them up into many parts, of which many parts are abstractions, and one reasons indefinitely about these abstractions. They are signs, and one claims to apply the conclusions from reasonings obtained by multiplying these signs, [one claims to apply these conclusions] to the concrete whole one has broken into pieces: hence the illusion.

So here we have a theory of freedom that rests on speculative considerations: on nominalism first of all, and on immaterialism.

(1) We have no right to assert mechanism in nature, or at least we can state it only as symbolical.

(2) Nature exists only as a phenomenon of thought.

Out of these two theses, there is one that influenced the mind of Kant directly, and indirectly via Hume: the immaterialism. For at the extreme limit of Kantianism—Kant [himself] did not go this far—there would be a creation of nature by the mind, which is freedom and which, by creating nature, seeks to give itself, to give its freedom a stage on which it manifests.[28]

So we have two things, it seems. In Kantianism there is, above all, Kant himself. But Kantianism, after all, has certain sources, certain origins, and it's certain that the two main sources are these: Rousseau on one side, Berkeley and Hume on the other. In both
[310] cases, it's moral ideas, moral convictions, and, in Berkeley, religious ones, that distracted the belief in free will, that pulled it back toward philosophy.[29]

What remains for the last two lectures of this course is, for the next lecture, to sketch out very briefly Kant's theory of freedom; and, for the following one, which will be the last of these lectures, to present very summarily our conclusions.

Notes

1. This is the only time in the entire course that Bergson also addresses *Mesdames*.
2. See the December 16, 1904, lecture above, 31, and CE, 287/332.
3. The typescript reads "conception of mechanistic being." It seems unlikely that Bergson said this or something like "the conception of the mechanistic being of nature."
4. On this notion of physical laws, see above, 31 and 177; on Descartes's geometry, see 181.
5. "Universal mathematics," *mathesis universalis*, is a Cartesian expression; see the end of the fourth of his *Rules for the Direction of the Mind* (PW I, 19/AT X, 378).
6. That is to say, with Socrates; see the December 6, 1904, lecture above, 19–20.
7. This is humanity as *adjutor Dei*, as God's helper; see 1 Cor 3:9 (where it is rendered as "servants"), as well as the March 10, 1905, lecture, 144–5, and TS, 232/246.
8. This, coming out of Auguste Comte in particular, is Spencer's definition of the goal of philosophy: a "complete unification" of all the kinds of knowledge collected by the sciences. See Herbert Spencer, *First Principles*, 2nd ed. (London: Williams and Norgate, 1867), 2.2.§40: 141.
9. See CE, 305/355, ME, 47–51/38–41 and 232–4/192–4, and the final lecture in HTM.
10. Contemporary, that is, with these theories. In the eighteenth century, "phenomenon" often means a simple appearance, a rainbow, for example.

11. See the lecture of May 13, 1904, in HTM.
12. For this analogy see the 1910 Introduction (the preface to the seventh French edition) to *Matter and Memory* (MM, xi/4–5), and ME, 45–6/36.
13. Both quotations come from Pierre-Simon Laplace, *Philosophical Essay on Probabilities*, trans. Andrew I. Dale (New York: Springer, 1995), 2, Dale's interpolation. Bergson quotes from the same passage ("Laplace's demon") in CE, 40/38, to make a far-reaching point: he sees in it the paradigmatic formulation of our mind's tendency to believe that "everything is given" and that nothing has been created.
14. See the February 24, 1905, lecture above, 120–1.
15. See TS, 281–3/299–302.
16. Compare the opening sentence of Rousseau, *The Social Contract*, in *The Social Contract, and Other Later Political Writings*, ed. and trans. Victor Gourevitch (Cambridge: Cambridge University Press, 1997), 39–152, here 41.
17. Jean-Jacques Rousseau, *Emile or On Education*, trans. Alan Bloom (New York: Basic Books, 1979), 272.
18. Rousseau, *Emile*, 280.
19. Rousseau, *Emile*, 280–1 (modified).
20. Kant, CPR, §18: 250–1/B139–40/AA 3, 113.
21. Kant, CPR, 678/A 807/B835/AA 3, 524.
22. Kant, CPR, 535–7/A538–40/B566–8/AA 3, 366–7.
23. For an elaboration on Berkeley's philosophy which is quite close to this one, see CM, 134–42/125–33. This elaboration in turn inspired the course Bergson devoted to the *Principles of Human Knowledge* at the Collège de France in 1907–8 (see M, 748).
24. Bergson is referring to the *Philosophical Commentaries*, also known as the *Commonplace Book*, in *The Works of George Berkeley, Bishop of Cloyne*, ed. A. A. Luce, vol. 1, 1–139 (London: Nelson, 1948). Berkeley wrote these between 1705 and 1708 while he was still a student at Trinity College in Dublin. They were first published in 1871.
25. An allusion to the subtitle of Berkeley's text *Alciphron, or the Minute Philosopher*, published in 1732 and directed (primarily) against Mandeville and Shaftesbury. Bergson quotes from it in what follows.
26. Compare CM, 137–8/128.
27. Berkeley, *Alciphron*, in *Works* 3, VII.18: 314. The example of movement which one can prove by walking is clearly one of Bergson's favorites: see, for example, CM, 170–1/160–1.
28. Here, Bergson is probably thinking of Fichte's philosophy. See also the next lecture, 242 and esp. 249n8–9.
29. "Distract" (*distraire*) here in the sense of "to attract" or "to take in."

LECTURE 19
MAY 12, 1905

Gentlemen, in the last lecture, I explained to you that, in the mind of scientists especially, [311] Cartesian mechanism left behind one of the most simplified and thereby the most radical forms [of mechanism]. I also pointed out that, as a reaction against this mechanism pushed to the extreme and also thanks to a return to the inner feeling, the assertion of free will reappeared in a new form. It reappeared, moreover, more energetic and also more radical than it had ever been before; for in earlier[1] philosophies, all free will asked was to live side by side with mechanism and obtain a place in nature. The events of nature form a chain, but certain links can be missing, or certain links may slacken. And these points of discontinuity, these points of interruption in the chain or of the loosening of the linkage of phenomena, are those where freedom finds room to reside. But after the simplification of mechanism that makes it take on a radical and as it were extreme form, freedom and mechanism can no longer find space on the same plane in the same domain. In the linkage of natural phenomena, in the mechanism of nature, there are no more points where freedom might insert itself. Then, quite naturally, freedom seeks a place outside of this mechanism, outside of nature.

It's a quite remarkable fact found throughout the history of philosophy that the more emphatic the doctrine of necessity becomes, the more the doctrine of freedom or free will, which is posited over against necessity, also becomes radical and extreme. We saw the very modest form that the assertion of freedom took in ancient philosophy. In Greek [312] philosophy, freedom for the human is simply the means of returning to its Idea, that is, to itself, to become itself again. It's more a negative than a positive power, I said, a means of putting things back in place and of repairing, at least in regard to human nature, the disorder that an irrational principle introduced into it.

We saw that in the moderns freedom became something more than that, a positive power [*pouvoir*], the power [*puissance*] to create something, an emanation of God's creative power. But up to Descartes and including him, this is only the power of creating human actions—and still not all actions. God's share in what humans do must be taken into account: there's a share that's due to humanity, the most faithful Cartesians will say, and a share that's due to God. In any case, human freedom creates only human actions. But the solution we see established in the first half of the eighteenth century is a much more radical solution to the problem: freedom is more than the power to create human actions, it's the power to create everything. Mechanism does not have to make room, here and there, a little bit of room where it will reside. No, it's freedom that creates mechanism, which is its work, that serves as its support, and, in short, freedom is the ground of being itself, mechanism being only its representation.

Prior to Descartes, we catch, I'm saying, only a glimpse of this solution. It's not presented in a clear, precise, fixed form. In the last lecture, I showed how the moralists on the one hand, in France—or certain among them—and the metaphysicians on the other, in England, more or less blurrily catch a glimpse of this solution. There are several passages in *Émile* where [Rousseau] says that necessity as if depends on freedom. The facts of nature are linked to one another, but this chain cannot be understood on its own, it must be attached, attached to freedom. Freedom is thus the origin. Rousseau,
[313] to be sure, is not a metaphysician, he's a moralist, and while he seems to make necessity depend on freedom, he said nothing about the modalities of this dependence and the way in which this dependence is possible.

All in all, Rousseau's idea is a lot more vague. It could be expressed more or less in these terms, which are, incidentally, those, or almost, Rousseau uses. On the one hand, there's the belief in the necessity of the linkage of the phenomena of nature. This is what today we call the scientific postulate, the faith in reality, in the universality of science. Then, on the other hand, there's the belief in freedom, which is the natural feeling, which is given in immediate and inner experience. Rousseau's idea, now, on this point, clearly expressed, is that if one of these two beliefs must yield, must move it, as we'd say today, it's the one that serves as support for generalization, for science, it's not the one that is given in immediate and inner feeling. That is Rousseau's idea.

Berkeley's idea is a lot clearer in this sense because it's more metaphysical. We find Berkeley's idea implied, I said the other day, in the two theses that bear Berkeley's name, nominalism [and] idealism (or immaterialism). Berkeley's nominalism is the assertion that general ideas are words, are only symbols, an assertion that in fact he only ever supports with examples drawn from mechanism: numbers, figures, etc. For him, abstractions, generalities are only words. This thesis means that mechanism is a symbolic expression of reality, an inadequate symbolic expression, about which, undoubtedly, we can reason, but which is of such a nature that the reasonings we make about it will not necessarily link up with the things.

So mechanism is a symbolism, and a symbolism often empty as to the objects, as to the things that this mechanism links together. In a word, this nature, to which one claimed to make the mind subservient, this nature exists only in the mind itself, as a representation: the things are ideas of the mind, and thus at the basis of everything, there's the mind in which nature, in short, is contained. Mechanism is only the symbolic
[314] mode of expression, which does not correspond to the very core of things, such that it's not impossible that there's freedom in the very place of reality, of being. That's what Berkeley says expressly in his seventh dialogue in *Alciphron*, from which I read one or two passages the other day. He says there that all the abstractions of mechanism wouldn't be able to stand up to the inner feeling we have of our own free spontaneity.

There's no doubt, gentlemen, that Kant was very much under the influence of Rousseau and that of Berkeley—or that of David Hume who, for that matter, owes a lot to Berkeley. Kant was under the influence of Rousseau as a moralist and that of Berkeley as a theorist of knowledge. Berkeley's influence is visible throughout the *Critique of Pure Reason*. We just have to be careful not to believe that Berkeley gave Kant what's essential, for at its core, Berkeley's thesis is a negative rather than a positive thesis; it's positive in the terms, it's negative as to the core, as to the meaning.[2] I mean that Berkeley, for example when he turns mechanism into a simple symbolism that, in short, is empty—since the general ideas, the abstractions of extension, of number, etc., are only words—Berkeley doesn't explain why mechanistic science succeeds, why it can go so far into the knowledge of things, foresee the future to a large degree by using these symbols. Similarly, when he reduces things, material objects, to being only ideas of the mind, he doesn't explain—or at least he explains it only by a *deus ex machina*, by making God intervene here—he doesn't explain, in short, how and why these ideas, these representations that are there in different human intellects, these human dreams, if you like, which are so many perceptions of nature, he doesn't explain why these dreams concord with one another, concord so admirably that they join together in what we call the shared experience of all of humanity.[3]

So this theory is more negative than positive. He does point out what material objects aren't, what they mustn't be, what scientific mechanism isn't, mustn't be, but Berkeley doesn't say in a positive way what they are. That was Kant's great innovation, his great [315]
philosophical invention. Kant saw—and this truly was a stroke of genius—that when we put freedom in the very place of reality, we don't for all that compromise scientific mechanism, or at least that there's a way to do it without compromising the mechanism of science; that, on the contrary, we're able thereby to found this mechanism, give it an unshakeable basis; that this is the sole means, even, of unshakably founding mechanism, or, if you like, scientific dynamism,[4] in a word, knowledge of nature considered as something unified and systematic.

Well before Kant, [philosophers] sought to give mechanism a foundation, to say what the possibility of a unified and systematic science of the universe rests on. We can even say that all the great modern philosophers asked this question. Descartes made the mechanism rest on the divine will, on a free decree from God; the mechanism is preserved by means of a free decree of God continually renewed, repeated at every moment. Leibniz and Spinoza establish a much closer relationship between mechanism and a very different principle that they, too, will call God. The mechanism of nature is an expression of the divine nature. It's just that these were hypotheses, these were metaphysical constructions. [Philosophers] were grounding mechanism and science on a thing, on a being external to it.

Kant's solution consists in looking for the principle of scientific mechanism, the principle of the order of nature, in nature itself, on the condition of transposing nature.[5] Kant solved the problem by the transposition of the idea of nature, and here's how he did it: Kant started from the idea which is at the very origin of modern science and which I've already defined many times, the idea that general knowledge of nature is an extension of mathematics. We mustn't forget that Kant was steeped in Newton's physics, that for the greater part of his life, he was a pure Newtonian, he engaged in great speculations on the nature of the universe, on the origins of our universe, and that five years after the publication of the *Critique of Pure Reason*, he published the *First Principles of the Metaphysics of Nature*, which book, to his mind, was only the [316] introduction to a work of general physics, as we would say today, that would have been much more extensive.[6]

So Kant started out from the guiding and generative idea of Newtonian science, which is, in short, modern science. This idea, I said, is that physics extends mathematics, or, more exactly, that physics is a province carved out of mathematics. Mathematics is the study of functions in general. The role of physics, the role of knowledge of nature is to tell us, for such and such given phenomenon that varies in magnitude, what particular function it is of such and such other phenomenon with which the given phenomenon is interdependent. Consequently, knowledge of nature is this: to choose, from among the functions that mathematics studies, the one that fits with the study of such and such phenomenon. Mathematics, in short, is the basis, the wider basis on which this narrower science is built, [a science that] consequently [is] mathematical at its base, which is the knowledge of nature.

This is the starting point, explicit or implicit, the starting point of the *Critique of Pure Reason*. And then, this is what's properly Kantian: Kant's idea is that, since the issue is to provide a foundation for the science of nature, that is, in short, general physics, the knowledge of nature in general, since the issue is to provide physics with a foundation, the solution that fits this problem is the same as the one that fits the problem of discovering the foundation of mathematics. The two questions are interdependent, and must be resolved, if not in the same manner, then at least in an analogous way. This is what Kant considered to be his invention, and what he expressed by saying that, according to him, mathematical judgments are synthetic a priori judgments. In fact, before him, [philosophers] thought that judgments in mathematics and judgments in physics were of a different nature. In general, they considered mathematical truths to be analytic truths, that is, purely logical truths, while a physical truth is a truth that implies something more, the intervention of an author.[7] In a word, they considered
[317] mathematical judgments to be analytic and physical judgments to be synthetic. And the very ones who believed in the radical identity of these two kinds of judgments—Leibniz may have believed in it—those [philosophers] brought physics back to mathematics and not mathematics to physics: they thought that physical judgments were, basically, analytic, the difference being that the analysis that would have discovered the attribute of the subject was an analysis that must be pushed to infinity.[8]

Kant's great invention was to establish the link between physics and mathematics, or at least the identity in kind between mathematical judgments and physical judgments by basing himself on [the idea] that mathematical judgments are synthetic judgments. This is what he asserts from the very beginning of the *Critique of Pure Reason*,[9] which, in short, amounts to saying, to simplify Kant's thesis, that the solution the problem of the foundation of science is given, this solution is the same, or of the same nature, for physics and for mathematics. This is of the utmost importance, since it's clear that finding the foundation of mathematics is much easier than determining the foundation of physics and of the general mechanism of nature.[10]

Let's look at mathematics. What makes mathematics succeed? What makes it such that by reasoning, in accordance with certain a priori principles, about numbers, magnitudes, figures, etc. we end up at conclusions that are applicable to objects? For Kant, the objects of mathematics are determinations in space and time: numbers, figures, etc., all these things are determinations in space and time. Kant places space and time together on the same level.

This can be contested since one can argue that the time at issue, in mechanics especially, is never anything but space and that mechanics could be constituted without the idea of duration, without the idea of succession. This is what I've tried to show at length and in different ways.[11] So it's quite contestable, and one can argue that an analysis that holds for space doesn't hold at all for time if we take the word "time" in the sense of duration. In any case, I'll close this parenthesis.

For Kant, the objects of mathematics are thus determinations, are certain [318]
determinations, in space and time. Let's suppose that space and time, as Kant says, are only pure a priori forms of our sensibility, that is, let's suppose that space and time exist only within us and for us, as certain necessary conceptions of our faculty of perception. Let's suppose that we are made, we humans, such that we cannot perceive without making the perceived enter into certain frameworks that we bring with us, that are constitutive of our faculty of perception, and that are, precisely, space and time. So what would happen? To be known by us, everything that can be known would have to enter into these frames, through this prism that is constituted by space and time, and thereby the things would, in passing through, adopt all the determinations, all the modalities of space and time. We humans, we reason about these forms of space and of time, the forms we carry within us, with us. We reason at least about the forms—for example the figures—we cut out of [space and time]. We constitute a geometry. How does this geometry apply to real things? It applies to them necessarily, for what we call the "real things" are elements, materials that, to reach us, have passed as through a filter or, better, as through a colored glass, space and time, and they reach us colored by space and time. They reach us, consequently, with all the modalities, all the determinations of space and of time; hence the geometry we thus establish a priori applies necessarily to things. So what makes geometry, and mathematics more generally, possible is that mathematics is the study of certain determinations of space and of time and that the materials presented to our knowledge cannot reach this knowledge without passing through the frames that we call "space" and "time" and thereby adopting all their properties.

This, gentlemen, presented in more modern terms, is the doctrine developed in the
"transcendental aesthetics," the first part of of *the Critique of Pure Reason*, the part Kant [319]
thought—and not without reason—to be the most important. The rest follows from it, for if we conceive mathematics in this way, this is how a "pure physics," as Kant says, that is, a systematization, a systematic unity of nature, is explained.

When the materials supplied to our knowledge, having passed through the forms of space and of time, become objects laid out in space and time, then our understanding seizes them. And like our faculty of perception, the faculty of the understanding has its own nature, its own form. Our understanding, to speak like Kant, has its "categories": there are pure a priori concepts of the understanding as there are pure a priori forms of sensibility. Or, to speak more simply: our understanding is an understanding whose essential function is to unify things, to systematize. And it obtains this effect by making the objects it receives from space and time enter into certain frames aimed, precisely, at obtaining this unification. And these frames are the pure a priori concepts of our understanding, at the forefront of which we find the most important of them all, causality. By means of the causal relation, the understanding links up phenomena with other phenomena, objects with objects, and with this relation, and many others, the understanding ends up at an absolutely coherent and systematic unity of nature.

Thus, to summarize, there's a human nature, there's the human being, who is understanding and sensibility—and by sensibility we mean "faculty of perception." And then, what do we find face to face with the human? There's something unknowable, a reality about which we do not have and never will have any idea if we claim to grasp this reality in itself, there's what Kant calls the "things in themselves," the things grasped in themselves from the inside and not from the outside.[12] This knowledge is impossible because in order to reach this knowledge we'd have to enter into the things, we'd have to have, to speak Kant's language, an intellectual intuition of them. But there is no
[320] intellectual intuition. So we are face to face with a reality that in itself will elude us, the things in themselves.

There are two terms, then: the human, who is understanding and sensibility, then the things in themselves. These things in themselves, through a mechanism about which Kant never said anything precise—about which he couldn't say anything precise because it's something mysterious—the things in themselves irradiate, send us something, make a certain impression on our sensibility, an impression that in no way resembles them. This is what Kant calls "the manifold of appearances," the manifold of sensible intuition, something absolutely chaotic about which we have no idea, for we perceive this manifold of appearances only by means of the bodies that are in our space and in our time.[13] This manifold of appearances impresses on us, and by impressing on us, it scatters in our space and in our time, time and space that exist only within us and for us, that are part of our nature. This is how objects in space and time constitute. The understanding seizes these objects. It carries within it a power of organization. And just as our physical organism assimilates certain materials by means of certain juices that dissolve them, our understanding, by means of certain pure concepts, by means of certain categories, assimilates the materials that sensibility presents it with. This is how a perfectly unified science, a perfectly coherent science of the universe, is constituted.

The result of this, gentlemen, is that science can have an unshakeable confidence in itself. We can be sure that the deeper we go into the nature of things, the more we penetrate the interior of nature, the more we'll find order there, and a perfectly mathematical order, for the very simple reason that what goes deeper into nature is the mind, the understanding, and that the understanding cannot go deeper into nature without enlightening it with its natural light—and this light is of a mechanistic and mathematical nature. Our mind thus finds itself in nature.[14] What we call "nature" is only the mirror of the mind: the mind thus cannot not find in nature everything it needs
[321] to be satisfied. In this sense, science is absolutely certain to find, as it expands, the ever more complete confirmation of the a priori principles constitutive of it. It's just that this

science is wholly relative to our intellect, relative to our faculty of perception, relative to our faculty of thinking. Take away humans, take away humanity, take away all human consciousness, everything Kant calls "consciousness in general": what remains are the things in themselves, that is, something which has nothing to do with nature such as our science knows it.[15] Truth be told, nature and science are the same thing: nature cannot [not] be scientific because they're the same thing. If by "nature" we understand the canvas, the fabric of laws, that lies beneath the phenomena considered from the qualitative viewpoint, if this is what we understand by nature, then science and nature are the same thing. Posit this consciousness in general: you thereby posit nature, that is, a systematic unity of phenomena that perfectly fit with one another, and you posit science at the same time, because insofar as each of us makes an "objective judgment" about things, as Kant says, that is, a scientific judgment, each of us possesses this consciousness in general, each of us participates in this consciousness in general.

This is Kant's solution to the problem, an undoubtedly very novel and very profound solution, but an absolutely natural one in the sense that, in short, it's implied in a conception that all the great scientists of modernity had of science. None of them attained the explicit form that Kant gave to the idea, but all of them, or the majority of them, gravitate around this idea. It must be said that our science, modern science, as I've noted many times, is a science that bears on relations, on connections. Modern science was constituted around the idea that to know is to discover relations, to establish stable relations between variable terms—but, in short, a relation exists only in a mind.[16] Do you conceive that a relation between terms exists in itself? At most, we conceive that a thing, that a term exists by itself, that another term exists by itself; but a relation, a relationship [322]
between the terms, how could it exist in otherwise than in a mind? I conceive that A exists by itself, that B exists by itself, but the relation between A and B must have a mind to establish it. So a relation presupposes a mind to found it on, and, if nature is brought back to a system of relations—which is what modern science aims to do—it seems that nature must in a way rest on a mind that thus establishes connections between terms. And this is why Newton, reflecting on the conception of science as he understood it, the conception of this universal mechanism or, rather, of this universal dynamism, Newton, after having reduced things to being objects in space that act and react on one another, Newton turned this space into what he calls God's *sensorium*:[17] in short, it's God who supports the mechanic relations between things.

In the last lecture, I read a passage from a book by a scientist who was quite far away from Newton's ideas on God, Laplace. You remember the conception of mechanism according to Laplace. To formulate the universal mechanism of things, Laplace presupposed an intellect that in one sole formula would encompass the past and the future. This formula would be the key to everything. So to articulate mechanism, Laplace still presupposed an intellect. What Kant calls "understanding," "human sensibility," what he calls "human consciousness in general," is, in short, something intermediary between Newton's divine *sensorium* and Laplace's intellect. It's something intermediary, less than the one, more than the other. It's less than the divine *sensorium*, since for Kant, if we take away all human intellect, nothing of the mechanism of nature remains,[18] while

the divine *sensorium* is something that exists in itself and absolutely. So it's less than the divine *sensorium*. And it's more than Laplace's intellect, since this intellect, in the passage from Laplace I quoted the other day, this intellect is a spectator introduced into the mechanism of the world. Laplace didn't go as far as to say, he didn't make the concession, which, however, is inevitable, that an intellect of this kind is the support of mechanism, that we can understand mechanism only by making this intellect
[323] intervene, that mechanism exists only through an intellect that thinks it. Well, this is what Kant said, and his consciousness in general, which creates science and thereby the scientific order of nature, is a hypothesis around which, as you can see, scientists have turned without ever managing—it required something more than science, it required a metaphysical intuition—without ever managing exactly to get hold of it. Kant formulated the hypothesis of the necessity implied in his universal mechanism with the greatest rigor, with the highest level of precision.

So there we have Kant's conception of science. It results in human freedom not being impossible. Kant doesn't assert it in the *Critique of Pure Reason*, he doesn't assert human freedom, but he gives it as a possibility.[19] How is it possible? According to what I just said, nature is undoubtedly subject to determinism—although this isn't said exactly, at least not in the *Critique of Pure Reason*—but in the end nature is always considered to form a coherent and scientific whole, consequently nature is the seat of determinism. But what is nature? It's constituted by phenomena, that is, by what appears to us. Nature as nature exists only for our consciousness, and thus, what we today call "determinism," determinism exists, in short, only for the intellect, for our knowledge, as a function of our knowledge. It could be that there is freedom of action behind this determinism of knowledge. We could be free insofar as we act. It's just that we can know nothing of this freedom and of this action because to know is to perceive in space and time—it's something perceived [*un perçu*], which is always apperceived [*aperçu*] in space and time, bound, connected by the relation of cause to effect, causality taken in the sense of causality according to nature, that is, determinant causality. Consequently, everything we perceive of ourselves, of our actions, enters into the frame of necessity and appears to us as necessary.

When I take one of my actions, it's in space, it's in time above all, and insofar as it's in time, it's explained by the event that preceded it, which in turn was determined by
[324] the preceding event, and so on. Thus each action is integrated into the mechanism of nature and each is explained mechanically, or at least is explained necessarily by what today we call the "antecedents" and the "consequents." But when I consider all of my actions, from beginning to end, it could be that the totality of these actions was as it were sent out all at once, all together, into the world of phenomena, into the world that appears to my consciousness, and that this was the effect of a free decree of my will: my freedom would be endowed with another causality than causality according to nature. Causality according to nature is the determination of the consequent by the antecedent. This causality, it goes without saying, exists only in time, it implies time. But my freedom can be endowed with causality, with a causality sui generis that consists in purely and simply creating, in positing ourselves such as we are, and the nature of our understanding

condemns us to seeing only the development in time of this freedom, which is outside of the world of phenomena. This is why we appear to ourselves as necessary; nonetheless, we act or we appear to act as free beings.

In other words, there are two selves: there's the empirical self, the self that appears to us in consciousness, developing itself in time; then, there's the intelligible self, the core of ourselves,[20] the self outside of time, the one that our consciousness cannot reach because our consciousness, our knowledge, can reach only what has gone through the form of time.[21] This is the free self, creating its entire set of conducts by virtue of its free spontaneity. We have to be clear: there aren't in reality two selves, there isn't one self that exists in the sensible world—the self that develops its conduct in time—then another self that is somewhere else and that has chosen the character and the destiny of this temporal self. No, that's not it at all. Plato said something like that. You'll remember that, for Plato, the soul has chosen once and for all, in the intelligible world, both its character and its destiny.[22] But to say this is to put the soul into time, to suppose a before [325]
and an after: a moment when the soul chooses what it wants to be, then, the series of moments in which it develops the consequences of its choice. Kant never said or thought anything like that. No, the empirical self, the intelligible self are the same thing, but the same thing considered from the viewpoint of knowledge and the viewpoint of action: it's the intelligible self as it acts, it's the empirical self as it grasps itself through the series of actions, of thoughts, if you like. The actions I carry out in time unfold like a chain: they have something in common, and once my life is over, I'm very much able to say, considering my actions in their relations or even each by itself, I'm very much able to say what the moral value of my personality is. I occupy a certain moral level, I have a certain degree of morality represented by the series of my actions, by my conduct. What Kant calls "freedom," true freedom, is the choice of this moral level: it's a single act that doesn't imply a moment because it isn't in time, a single act but one of which we only see the dispersion, the refraction in time. This single act is the one that determines our moral value, that sets our moral level, that determines our place in the series of moral beings. Depending on whether we put ourselves in the viewpoint of morality or in the viewpoint of nature, we have two selves, the intelligible self and the empirical self. As for the intelligible self, we cannot know the mechanism of its action at all, since this action is timeless, but we see its effects, which are contemporaneous or, if you like, co-eternal with it, we see its effects in time.

There you have Kant's conception of freedom, and I believe that in this form, Kant's idea is quite intelligible, you can even say quite clear. The major objection you can raise against it can't be drawn from its alleged obscurity. No, the objection, rather, is this: it's that it's impossible to conceive how freedom thus understood is integrated into the mechanism of nature without breaking nature's unity.

I think about one of my actions. That action in time is explained by a prior action, which is itself integrated into the whole of nature and, in short, depends on the rest of [326]
nature. The intelligible self, what Kant calls the intelligible self, the one created by an act of will, this intelligible self as it were launches the series of its acts into time, which is what Kant calls its empirical character. But this series of actions, which constitutes the conduct

in time, this series of actions can only occupy the place left empty by the rest of all the phenomena of nature. Nature, according to Kant, is a great continuity of phenomena: in this continuity of phenomena, my conduct from beginning to end carves out, if you will, a certain surface. But the form of this surface is determined by all the rest of nature: I can occupy only the space left empty by all the rest of nature. From the moment that my conduct in time is interdependent with all the other phenomena, I don't understand how an act of my free will could have arbitrarily created, in an absolutely spontaneous manner, independently of any kind of consideration, created the character that it wills.

There we have, in short, the big difficulty. The truth is that if we place ourselves in Kant's viewpoint, if we accept his conception of science, freedom is possible. Ah! yes, but not the freedom of the individual, not individual freedom. For, according to Kant, what's constitutive of science? It's not me, it's not you, it's not individuals, it's human consciousness in general, science, and, in short, the order of nature is constituted in this impersonal human milieu. This human consciousness in general that creates the mechanism of nature—ah! that one can be considered to be tied to a creative principle: *this* consciousness in general can be free. We could easily—this is the solution immediately suggested by Kant's theory of knowledge—we could easily suppose that this consciousness in general emanates from a principle that, creating the mechanism of nature, thereby creates actions, actions it creates within the mechanism of nature as a whole. So that's freedom, it's no longer Peter's freedom or Paul's freedom, then, it's
[327] freedom in general. There are no freedoms, there is one freedom. This, it seems, is the conclusion that would have to come out of the *Critique of Pure Reason* if Kant hadn't insisted, for moral reasons, on safeguarding freedom in the sense we give the word, the freedom of individuals.

The truth is that if we posit the systematic unity of nature, the complete unification of all knowledge, freedom is possible, but not, it seems to me, the freedom of individuals. Must we sacrifice the freedom of individuals, or wouldn't it be better to sacrifice the belief in the absolute unity of nature, in the possible unification of all the sciences?[23] This is the question that poses itself, and I believe this is how the question poses itself today. This is the point I intend to develop in the next lecture—this will be the last lecture of this course, which will serve as our conclusion.

Notes

1. "Earlier" meaning earlier than the eighteenth century.
2. For this important distinction between positive and negative, see the February 24, 1905, lecture above, 121–2.
3. For this whole argument, see MM, 15–16/22–3.
4. Rather than "dynamism," Bergson might mean "determinism."
5. CE, 306/356.
6. More exactly, the title is *Metaphysische Anfangsgründe der Naturwissenschaft* (1786); see *Metaphysical Foundations of Natural Science*, trans. Michael Friedman, in *Theoretical*

Philosophy after 1781, ed. Henry Allison and Peter Heath, 171–270 (New York: Cambridge University Press, 2002). Once the lessons of the CPR had been learned, this work inquired into the basis of a metaphysics of nature. It did so in the same way as the "metaphysics of morals" (doctrine of right, doctrine of virtue) Kant later, in the eponymous work, constructed on the ground cleared by the *Critique of Practical Reason* (1788), mediated by the *Groundwork of Metaphysics of Morals*, published in 1785. All three texts, *Critique of Practical Reason*, *The Metaphysics of Morals*, and *Groundwork of the Metaphysics of Morals*, can be found in Immanuel Kant, *Practical Philosophy*, ed. and trans. Mary J. Gregor (New York: Cambridge University Press, 1999).

7. On the distinction between analytic judgments and synthetic judgments, see CPR, Introduction, 129–32/A6–10/B10–13/AA 3, 33–6.
8. On infinite analysis, see Leibniz, *Discourse on Metaphysics*, §8 and especially 13 (PE, 40–1 and 44–6). Kant attributes to "the Leibnizian-Wolffian philosophy" the thesis that, in principle, all judgments can be reduced to analytic judgments; see Kant, CPR, 186/A44/B61–2/AA 3, 66–7.
9. Kant, CPR, 109–11/Bxiv–xvii/AA 3, 36–8.
10. This is not to say that it is easily done. As Bergson is well aware, the foundations of mathematics are much in debate at the time he is teaching this course. See the April 7, 1905, lecture, and 197n6.
11. For instance, in TFW, 143–55/107–17, and in "Introduction to Metaphysics," in CM. For the objection to Kant in particular, see CM, 164–7/154–7.
12. CM, 188/178.
13. Kant, CPR, 155–6/A19–20/B33–4/AA 3, 49–50.
14. On the question of the agreement between the mind and nature, and for a non-Kantian response—the "nonrelativist" response, as Bergson would say—see CE, 167–72/187–93.
15. Kant, CPR, §20, 252/B143/AA 3, 155; 295/A176/B217/AA 3, 157; and 575/A614/B642/AA 3, 410. By "conscience in general," Bergson seems to be referring to what Kant describes as "the subject in its intelligible character" (CPR, 535–7/A538–41/B566–9/AA 3, 366–8), which is the subject of a longer discussion in the next and final lecture.
16. Compare CE, 306/356, where, in discussing Kant, Bergson notes: "A relation is nothing outside of the intellect that does the relating."
17. Space as "sensorium Dei": this expression—more precisely, "in Spatio infinito, tanquam Sensorio suo"—is found in the Clarke's 1706 Latin translation of Newton's *Opticks*. See Isaac Newton, *Optice: Sive De Reflexionibus, Refractionibus, Inflexionibus & Coloribus Lucis, Libri Tres*, trans. Samuel Clarke (London: Smith & Walford, 1706), 313. It appears at the end of query 20 in the third book, which does not feature in the first English edition of 1704, and the relevant passage in the second edition of 1718 (*Opticks: or, a Treatise of the Reflections, Refractions, Inflections and Colours of Light: The Second Edition, with Additions* [London: Innys, 1718], 379) elides the expression (though variants are found in queries 28 and 31). It would be at the heart of the controversy between Leibniz and Clarke; see the editor's summary in *Leibniz-Clarke Correspondence*, xv–xvi. For Bergson's reading of these debates, see MM, 254–7/216–18.
18. CE, 306/356.
19. Kant, CPR, 535–7/A538–41/B566–9/AA 3, 366–8.
20. The typescript reads *le moi de nous-mêmes*, "the self of ourselves," instead of *le noyau de nous-mêmes*, "the core of ourselves."

21. In the following lecture (243–4), Bergson returns to the Kantian notion of "the intelligible character."
22. See the January 13, 1905, lecture, 62.
23. CE, 171/192.

LECTURE 20
MAY 19, 1905

Gentlemen, in the last lecture I sketched, in very broad strokes, Kant's solution to the problem of freedom. That's where I will end the historical presentation of the evolution of the problem of freedom—for lack of time, first, and then because the discussions that arose in the nineteenth century around the problem of freedom are always more or less discussions of and commentaries on the Kantian solution. I'll add that the nineteenth-century discussions could not have been otherwise, for the very simple reason that the problem of freedom, as I've defined throughout this course, is the problem of the relationships between thought and action. We can say that Kant extracted the very quintessence of the conception of knowledge the moderns had prior to him, and that he extracted the quintessence of what we could call the modern conception of action. This is why we can argue about the Kantian solution, why we can contest it, refute it, we can even reject it—but it's not possible not to start from it and not to take it as our base of operations as it were. [329]

I'm saying that Kant extracted the quintessence, both of the conception his contemporaries had of science, and of the modern conception of action. First, of science. I said, in effect—and this was like the leitmotif of one half of this course, the one that comprised the theory of necessity—that what characterizes modern science since the great discoveries of Kepler, Galileo, Newton, Descartes, is the substitution of the knowledge of connections and relations for the knowledge of things, ideal things, moreover. Modern science bears on relations or, more precisely, on laws already known.[1] For the moderns, [330]
gravity is not, as it was for the ancients, about defining the thing "gravity," defining the concept "gravity," it's simply about finding a relation between certain variables—between, for example, the space traversed by a body that is falling in a vacuum, or almost,[2] and the duration of its fall: the relation between this duration and speed. So, in short, this science bears on laws or relations, more particularly and by preference on mathematical relations. This is why, from the dawn of this science and throughout all its developments up to and including Kant, we witness the evolution of the idea that science is or ought to be a perfectly unified system, a perfectly coherent system of mathematical relations connecting all the phenomena of nature to one another.

Now, to posit that nature, in regard to what is ordered about it, to posit that the order of nature is an order of relations, is—for better or worse, whether we want to or not—to give it as a base, give it as support a mind, for the very simple reason, as I said last time, that a relation exists only in a mind, through a mind. We may possibly conceive a thing, a being to exist outside of the mind. But a relation between beings, a relation between variations, that is something intellectual. To say that the order of nature is a system of relations is to say that nature is based on intellect [*à base d'intelligence*]. A physicist, a mathematician, reflecting on his work will necessarily, naturally, reach this conclusion. Newton, who had a very clear-cut conception of universal mathematicism, said that all things are in space, and that space is in God.[3] So, for him, God was the support of this mathematical mechanism. Leibniz says something in the same vein: *Deo calculante fit mundus*. The world is God calculating.[4] In fact, if the basis of the order of nature is mathematical relations, then it is calculation. We cannot conceive a calculation without someone who calculates, or relations without a mind that establishes these relations.

That's what everyone could see and could say, but what's Kant's own, what characterizes his philosophy, is that he reduced the postulate that this theory of science implied to the
[331] minimum.[5] To say that mathematical mechanism has God for its support is to go very far, it's to construct a metaphysics. Kant said with precision what supposition is necessary for this mechanism, this unity of nature, to be possible. He said what supposition is necessary but also what supposition is sufficient to presuppose: what's necessary is a mind, what's necessary is an intellect that supports nature, but according to him, it suffices that this be the human intellect.

Kant supposes that each of us is as if enveloped in an atmosphere of humanity. I reason, I judge, but all of that via participation in humanity, in the human intellect in general, which is like an atmosphere that surrounds [*environner*] me, that immerses me, and it's this atmosphere that Kant set out to explore.

Quite naturally, he distinguished two layers. There had to be two layers because the issue was to explain how nature is a system of scientific laws, which implies two things: mathematics and laws. A law is a relation in general, it's not necessarily a mathematical relation. The issue was to explain why nature is a system of relations in general and why, more precisely, these relations of one thing leading to another manage to take a mathematical form. For these relations to take a mathematical form, the terms being united must be measurable, that is, from a certain angle they must participate in magnitude, that is, they must be laid out, as it were, against a homogeneous background.

The first layer things must go through, refracting themselves, to reach my intellect, the layer where they take on homogeneity, virtual mathematism, everything necessary so they can be subjected to number and to measurement, is what Kant calls space and time, the a priori forms of sensibility, the forms of our faculty of perceiving. Then, once they have passed through this layer, the things, the materials that have thus settled on a homogeneous foundation, the materials enter into what Kant calls the pure a priori concepts of the understanding. That is, they pass through a second layer of humanity, what I'd call the layer of relations in general, relations that by themselves are not
[332] mathematical relations but that can be applied only to materials that have passed through the first layer, that thereby have become magnitudes and will necessarily be determined, specified, and as if reduced to mathematical relations. This is how, through this double passage, through this double refraction across our atmosphere, the materials presented to our future knowledge manage to constitute a well-connected nature. Take away the intellect, not my intellect, nor yours, not such and such intellect, take away human intellect in general, the human faculty of perceiving in general, in a word, what

I call the atmosphere of humanity we're steeped in, the atmosphere we breathe in, take away this human intellect in general in which each of us is placed necessarily when we make a genuine, scientific, [and] universal objective judgment:[6] nothing remains of human science, that goes without saying, but nothing remains of the order of nature either, nothing remains of nature considered in its framework, in its foundation, since what we call the order of nature and our science, for Kant, are the same thing.

So here we have extracted the quintessence of what Kant's contemporaries thought about the nature of knowledge in general. I'll add that Kant extracted the quintessence of the modern conception of action. In the first part of this course, I tried to show that what's primary, what's essential for the ancients is thought, is knowledge, and that action can be defined only in relation to knowledge. That is an idea implied in all of ancient philosophy that Plotinus gave its most forceful expression: any action, any production is only a weakening, a weakening of contemplation. In other words, morality coincides with science. The best action is the intellect elevating itself as high as possible, applying itself to its object with the most energy possible, and in any case, action can only be considered a diminishment of thought, of speculation. The ideal would be to think, and to think always; insofar as thought is distracted from itself, as it relaxes, so to speak, it acts. So action is the diminishment of thought and gravitates, as it were, around thought.

The idea implied in at least a part of modern philosophy, in a word what is modern, [333] truly modern in the modern conception of action, is the absolute opposite. First of all, morality is not science. These are two independent, in any case separate domains. Morality is not science. Then, if one of these two terms should have to take precedence over the other, it would be morality, it wouldn't be science, since what is real, what really exists in itself, is action. Action is reality itself, and what we call science is something that turns, that gravitates around action, whether it's our action or the divine thing-creating action, but in the end, it's action which is the foundation of science and science exists only relative to action.

I'm not saying that this is the idea of all modern philosophers, nor of even the majority of them. We saw that even in Descartes, who is clearly oriented in this direction, action and knowledge are juxtaposed in such a way that we are unable to say, in any formal way, that his is a theory of the primacy of action. However, the direction is quite clearly indicated. It's certain that after Descartes, we witness the development of doctrines like those of Spinoza and Leibniz, which in this regard are returns to the viewpoint of ancient philosophy. Nevertheless, what's really new and what contrasts with antiquity in the modern conception of science is just that, it's the theory of the primacy of action, action being the foundation of being, of knowledge, and it's not action which is tarnished with relativity.

There you have, in short, the two conceptions that Kant brought out and to which he gave their most precise and most rigorous form. And that's why I said that, the problem of freedom being the problem of the relationships between action and knowledge, it's very difficult to talk about it if we don't start from Kantianism and if we don't make Kantianism our base of operations.

Kant offered, of both action, of perfect action if it were possible, and of knowledge, if this knowledge were perfect, that is, if nature formed an absolutely unified system, both coherent and mathematical, he offered the most complete idea and the most rigorous [334] formula for both this action and this knowledge. Does it follow that we must accept Kant's theory of the relations of these two terms with one another, in short, Kant's conception of freedom? I don't think so, first of all because this conception, as I said at the end of the last lecture, this conception presents an internal difficulty that, it seems to me, is insurmountable unless we interpret the theory of knowledge we find in the *Critique of Pure Reason* in a completely different way. The difficulty is the following: if freedom is exactly, entirely what Kant said it is, it cannot be the freedom of a person, it cannot be Peter's freedom or Paul's, it cannot be the freedom, in short, we care about and with regard to which, be it to demonstrate its existence, be it to ascertain its impossibility once and for all, we start the discussion of the problem of freedom. This Kantian freedom cannot be the freedom of a person for the very simple reason that, for Kant, given his very conception of knowledge, his conception of action, freedom is the act by which the self posits itself, creates itself outside of time, and launches into time, while it creates itself—these aren't two successive acts—launches into time, into the sphere of knowledge, a series of facts that succeed one another, but these successive facts launched into the sphere of knowledge still have to find a way to reside there. How will they do this if all the other facts of nature don't make room for them? I'll try to explain this more clearly: each of the facts thus launched into the sphere of knowledge, if it's true that nature forms an absolutely unified, and coherent, system, each of these facts is explicable by all the other facts of nature; which amounts to saying that each of them is considered in the sphere of knowledge as determined by all the rest of nature; which amounts to saying that the act by which this fact is launched into knowable experience is an act compelled simply to fill in the place in nature left empty by all the rest; which amounts to saying that this freedom is illusory and that, in short, it's the rest of being that determines my being.

[335] Ah! Granted—and I did say this at the end of the last lecture—granted that freedom is possible in this conception, and even that it's the basis of things, but it's no longer the freedom of such and such an individual. There are no freedoms anymore, there is one freedom, the freedom of being in general. In this conception, I see very well that the principle of human consciousness in general, as Kant says, if there is one, is at the same time a free principle. Insofar as it is free, it will launch phenomena into space and into time that perfectly connect with one another, and insofar as it knows itself, it will present a nature in which everything is necessary. But this, then, is an impersonal freedom, just as it's an impersonal knowledge.[7] And freedom, in the sense our psychological consciousness gives to the term, is hard to reconcile, it even seems irreconcilable with Kant's conception of a perfectly coherent, in short, a scientific, mathematical unity of all the kinds of knowledge.

That is so true that what immediately emerged from Kant's philosophy is a philosophy that put freedom not in such and such a self, in such and such a person, but in the self in general, a self that's neither mine, nor yours, but the self in general.[8] It spoke of the self of freedom in general the way Kant speaks of knowledge in general. I'm well aware that Kant never accepted this interpretation,[9] but perhaps it imposes itself on us, given his premises. In any case, it's where it went immediately, naturally, almost necessarily after him.

This amounts to saying, more simply, that the freedom Kant speaks of is not and cannot be the freedom our psychological consciousness demands or that, in any case, it thinks it perceives, for what we think we perceive by means of consciousness is a freedom localized at certain moments of duration. To be free is to choose, to be free is, at least at certain moments, to solve the problem action is confronted with, it's to choose between several different paths. I'm not saying that this choice is continually, constantly offered to our action, and perhaps freedom is localized above all at certain moments of duration and in certain crises of our existence.[10] Nevertheless, it's true that the freedom we think we're aware of is a freedom in time and, even more specifically, localized at [336] certain moments of time.

There can be no question of this [kind of] freedom in Kant; freedom as he understands it is the creation by itself of a certain formula—I can find no other expression—of a certain formula that Kant calls the intelligible character,[11] a certain formula that at the same time as it creates itself, or rather—I can't say "at the same time" because this formula is not in time—a certain formula that then develops in time in the form of a series of actions that condition one another. It's the creation of this formula that the other day I called the choice of a certain moral level.[12] This is what our freedom is: a single, timeless act. And we get a glimpse of this one act only through its refraction in time. Consciousness tells us that there is something true in this conception of freedom, it would almost be true, if our freedom were something perfect, it would be that, but consciousness also tells us that Kant thereby grants us too much and too little.

He grants us too much because we do not completely and absolutely create ourselves. The very people who most believe in their freedom on the evidence of consciousness sense that there are snags, that the nature of our character doesn't come from us, that we must reckon with a host of things that are not us, and be it just psychological flaws or hereditary moral flaws (for, incidentally, vices are hereditary, not always, but they are much more transmissible through heredity than virtues are).[13] But what's certain is that we are not the complete authors of our character in the sense that Kant says, and, if it's true that our character is a kind of simple formula our existence comes down to, then this formula, to continue the mathematical comparison, contains coefficients that aren't created by us.

So Kant grants us too much by defining freedom in this way. I'll add that from another angle he grants us too little because we're well aware that if our freedom is real, then there must be, at least at certain moments of our existence, absolute possibilities to choose, points of bifurcation where we have the choice to switch tracks, the choice between [337] two or more different tracks, and that that's the case independently of anything that is given. Undoubtedly, we are subjected to [*nous subissons*] a fair bit of our character, but at certain moments we can absolutely break free of it.

In Kant, there can hardly be any question of these various switch points possible at a given moment in time, or, at least, if there is a question of them, they're already as it were contained in the one and undivided formula of our character, which he calls the intelligible character. I think that consciousness, if it's consciousness we consult, says something else and that at certain moments it's able to perceive one absolute real thing, and in this sense, within these limits, it is a genuine creation. In a word, if there is a formula, if our character consists in a formula as Kant said, this formula—I'm extending the mathematical comparison again—is a formula that evolves within the variables of indetermination, which amounts to saying that the formula doesn't say everything and that the main, the essential thing about our freedom, the freedom that, at one moment, translates into a given act, and, in short, into given acts at every moment, the essential thing about freedom[14] is not thereby explained. Finally, and to summarize everything: Kant doesn't take what I call the testimony of consciousness into account. For him, consciousness doesn't have jurisdiction, the [faculty][15] of knowledge doesn't have jurisdiction. What it tells us or doesn't tell us about our freedom must not be taken into account in the philosophical solution of the problem.

Why does consciousness, I mean psychological consciousness, lack jurisdiction in Kant's eyes? This is because Kant exactly aligns what we today call consciousness, inner perception, with external perception. For him, the faculty by which we know ourselves is aligned or nearly so—there's a nuance—but, in the end, it's nearly aligned with the faculty by which we know external objects. When we know an external object, we know it from the outside. We don't place ourselves in it, so we see only its exterior, the impression made on us; we only perceive of it a certain refraction through space and
[338] time. It's the same thing when we think about ourselves: we know ourselves, Kant said,[16] from the outside, because to know oneself is to take oneself as one's object; our self then becomes an object for us. In knowledge, we are external to ourselves as we are external to the rest of things. That's why in such matters Kant doesn't accept the testimony of inner consciousness.

But why doesn't he accept that external perception and inner perception are wholly different faculties? Why does he put them on the same plane, or almost? Why does consciousness not go farther, according to him, more deeply into the consciousness of our self, than the senses, or sensibility, as he says, in the perception of external objects? The reason is obvious: it's that for Kant, there's no difference in kind between duration such as I defined it earlier in this course, between duration and space.[17] Kant makes no difference between internal duration and the purely symbolic time that science talks about and that, in short, is only the space in which we line up successive phenomena. Kant makes no difference, in a word, between duration and space. Since he aligns time and space, since he puts them on the same plane, he thinks that we can speak of one as we do of the other, extend to duration everything that has been said about space.

Yet what is space? Space is a milieu in which the elements of knowledge, the materials that reach our consciousness are scattered, juxtaposed to one another, and form a multiplicity whose terms are external to one another. It's in this way that we see external objects in space and that we see a mass of elements that are external to one another, disjointed. To know an external object, to know an object physically, is to unite the disjointed, which can only be done by an operation of our mind, which brings in certain forms, certain categories rather, from the outside. It is to connect terms that, precisely because they have been connected from the outside, have only an, I'm not saying artificial coherence and unity but [one that's] relative to our mind, which unites them. For when it comes to our knowledge and facts laid out in space, purely physical facts, our knowledge of them is relative, since to know is to unite what is given as disjointed, and this unity [339] can be made only through the interposition of certain forms that belong to us and that are purely relative to our faculty of knowing.

But is that how things present themselves in duration? When we delve into ourselves by means of consciousness, what we find are not disjointed elements, juxtaposed to one another and in need of being connected by links we contribute ourselves. No, the unity is done, it's the unity of continuity, it's a unity where we undoubtedly find a multiplicity, a lot of different moments, but we encompass these moments only by means of abstraction. Here, we're not going from multiplicity to unity by an external and artificial unification, as when it comes to physical things. The unity is given, a multiple unity, the unity of continuity, and consequently, when we know this inner life in a unified form or relatively unified form, that is not the effect of a synthesis, of an operation properly speaking. No, all we do is note what is. All we do is place ourselves back in the current of our inner life.

This amounts to saying in different terms that while we have only relative knowledge of physical facts, since to know them is to unite them, and to unite them is to impose certain relations on them that come from us, that are concepts of our mind, when it comes to our inner life, our self, we have of it what I here have called an intuition, that is, direct and immediate knowledge from the inside and not from the outside, a knowledge that is the coincidence of that which knows with that which is known and with that which acts.

So if we separate duration and space this way, there are two very different modes of knowing: there's knowledge by relation, which is physical knowledge; then there's knowledge by intuition, which is psychological knowledge. Then there are lots of intermediaries between the two, for what we could call the biological knowledge we have of organic life, the idea we have of the organization of a living being, is something intermediary. It's very much the conception of a relation but not of an artificial relation [340] imposed from the outside, external to the terms united, no, it's a relation we conceive as internal: it's the unity of life being lived we sympathize with when we speak of the organization of a living being.[18] So between intuitive knowledge and discursive knowledge by relation, we could indeed imagine many intermediaries, but I won't pursue this point here.[19] Nevertheless, for Kant, duration and space are on the same plane and must be treated in the same way. Why are they on the same plane and why does Kant think that we have to treat them in the same way? Because Kant, precisely, accepts only one way of cognizing, one single means of knowing. For him, knowing always consists in synthesizing,[20] in establishing, from the outside, a unity between disjointed terms that is necessarily relative to our mind. For Kant, there's only one way of knowing. All things, all the materials of our knowledge, are laid out as it were on the same plane, which is the plane of space and of time. If we accept the viewpoint I just indicated of a series of degrees in knowledge, from discursive physical knowledge up to intuitive psychological knowledge, we accept different planes of experience: there are superimposed, ever-deeper planes of experience, there's a whole series of degrees between knowledge from the outside and knowledge from the inside.

The very relations Kant talks about, the causal relation for example, these relations can take many different forms or at least they can present many different degrees of tension.[21] In the physical world, causality means necessary determination, but to the extent that we go from the physical to the psychical, we see the connections between cause and effect becoming less and less tight. And when we reach the pure psychical, there's almost no more connection at all, causality being not a relation but a being, a production, ultimately what Kant called a creation.[22] So we go by degrees, by an imperceptible transition, from what Kant called causality according to nature, physical causality, to what he calls causality by freedom, which is creation. And this without any upheaval,
[341] without leaving the world of experience: it suffices to accept that experience is not laid out in its entirety on [one and] the same plane; that in the depths there are different planes of experience; and that we can thus, without any upheaval, by imperceptible transitions, pass from physical necessity to moral freedom, all of this being in nature, nature forming a whole—granted—but a whole in which the elements are not all equally packed tight against one another. There are points where the connection is relaxed, and consequently freedom can, without any contradiction, find its place in nature—on the condition, it goes without saying, that we don't consider knowledge as being laid out in its entirety on one and the same plane.

But that is what Kant does, and why does he do it? Going from one "why" to another "why," gentlemen, we come to the final "why." The reason for which Kant could not, must not conceive things otherwise than how he did conceive them, the ultimate reason, in short, is that Kant believes in a perfectly unified science, a perfectly coherent and systematic, and, in short, mathematical science of nature as a whole. This appears to be what was in the back of Kant's mind in the *Critique of Pure Reason*. Kant tells us what nature would be, if a perfectly unified, coherent and systematic, and, in short, mathematical knowledge of nature were possible. He believed in this perfect unity of nature. Why did he believe in it? He tells us himself:[23] because there is, inherent to our mind, a need to unify. Our mind is unification, and for our mind to be satisfied, there must be a possible unification and synthesis of all forms of knowledge. Undoubtedly—but as I just said, this unity might possibly exist without presupposing that all the terms are so tightly packed together and so systematically connected to one another. A nature with a whole series of degrees from necessity up to freedom is still a nature sufficiently unified to satisfy the demands of our understanding. So this reason is not the only one. The true reason is that Kant presented a theory of science such as, all in all, the majority of his contemporaries picture it, [where] science ought to be a kind of universal mathematics, as Leibniz said,[24] a system of relations that, in the final analysis, can take a mathematical form and that connect all the phenomena of the universe to one another.

[342] So the real question is what this conception is worth and whether this conception, which was in fact shared by the majority of scientists in Kant's time, which has remained shared by many scientists today, is, all in all, the definitive conception. There lies the whole problem of freedom.

If we go back to the origins of this conception—which is what you have to do to judge the value of an idea—if we go back to the origins of this conception, I don't think that we'd be able to find any other than the, I wouldn't say need, but an instinct of our intellect.[25] Our intellect is naturally led to believe first of all that it knows everything. That's its natural tendency. When we have accumulated knowledge, there comes a moment when we say: "this is it, I have nothing left to learn now." That's the natural tendency, it's what we would say if we gave in to the natural instinct. We don't say this because experience has shown, throughout the whole course of the history of the sciences, that what we knew was always very little compared to what remains to be learned. We thus resist this instinct and we end up saying: "I don't know everything." But the instinct reappears in another form. We say to ourselves: "I don't know everything, I don't possess all the subject matter of knowledge, but I do possess its form, I don't know everything but everything that's left for me to learn will be of the same nature, the same form as what I know already. All that's left for me to learn will resemble what I know and even what I know best." What do I know best? Mathematics, since this is the knowledge our mind has naturally. I said that mathematics is natural to us. So all that we have to learn will be of the same nature, the same form as what we know best, and consequently, it will be of a mathematical form.[26]

In the ancients, this instinct revealed itself in a form I pointed to several times in this course. What the ancients knew of mathematics was geometry, and overall, the ancient theory of science was constituted around the idea that everything we can know must resemble geometry.

Antiquity lived on the Platonic theory of ideas, for Aristotle said more or less the same thing as Plato, and Plotinus is very close to Aristotle. The ancient conception of [343] science is just that, namely that everything that we will ever be able to know will be of the same nature as geometry.

This conception of science, gentlemen, vanishes at the time of the great scientific discoveries of the Renaissance. People saw that what there was to be known weren't models like those of geometry. Yet that's what Plato's *eidē* were, they were models that were to the sensible world what geometrical figures are to the real forms of nature. People saw that science was not only that. What did these discoveries consist in? They were discoveries of physical laws, that is, mathematical relations, algebraic relations between certain variables. Then, quite naturally, by virtue of the same instinct that had led the ancients to say: "everything resembles geometry," the moderns say: "everything resembles algebra," and the modern theory of science up to Kant, in short, gravitates around this idea of a universal algebra.[27] Leibniz told us about this universal characteristic,[28] and Kant, in the *Critique of Pure Reason*, said in a definitive way what nature would have to be if this universal science with a mathematical foundation, a mathematical substrate were possible. But is this definition of science definitive? I don't think so, for the very simple reason that since Kant, science seems not to have taken this direction. What characterizes nineteenth-century science is the opposite tendency, the tendency to divide science up, and not only because it is convenient but by taking the natural articulations of reality into account.[29] During the nineteenth century, new sciences constituted themselves precisely by renouncing the algebraic form, the mathematical form: history constituted itself this way, social science, psychology, and even biology, which, all in all, did not found itself definitively as a science until the day it renounced Descartes's rule of reducing everything that happens in living beings to a simple problem of mechanics. All these sciences, in short, are based, however closely, on the hypothesis of freedom.

The historian, when he does history, reasons as if human actions depended on humans;
[344] so does the sociologist. The psychologist, when he does psychology, proceeds as if the will were a reality, as if there were free acts. The biologist, when he does biology, proceeds as if the living beings were capable of an effort. I'm well aware that a lot of scientists will say: "this is a provisional viewpoint and we'll eventually reach the mechanical; we'll reach the reduction of the biological, perhaps one day of the social, to simple mechanics." Yes, but let's ask whether, when we say this, we're doing anything other than returning to the belief, the illusion perhaps, but in the end, the belief of Kant's predecessors and contemporaries in this kind of universal algebra. Which seems to show that then, perhaps, they're no longer really scientists, they're no longer doing science, they're doing philosophy, and a philosophy, perhaps, that's outdated, because every time they proceed as scientists in their science, they proceed as if this reduction wasn't being made nor even possible. So we have to dwell not so much on what they say, but on what they do.[30] The procedures they employ, the methods they use, in short, are always founded on the idea of an independence of biology, of psychology, of social science, of history from physical-chemical science and from this alleged universal algebra.

So this, overall, seems to be the current orientation of science. And I really believe that if we considered the question from a theoretical, dogmatic viewpoint, if we considered living beings, conscious beings and matter in general, matter insofar as it's animated by physical and chemical forces, we'd reach theoretical conclusions of the same kind. We'd undoubtedly find a continuity in nature, but not a continuity due to formal and mathematical unity: no, we'd find organic life introducing itself among the purely physical-chemical forces, introducing itself by stealth, undoubtedly, in such a way that no law would be completely violated, but there are laws being avoided.[31] As soon as organic life appears, consciousness undoubtedly appears as well, and with consciousness a certain contingency, which grows as organic life complicates and finally becomes in the human the substrate of freedom in the strict sense of the word.

[345] But that, gentlemen, is a point I'm only gesturing at—moreover, I don't have to treat of it: the objective of this course was simply to show, first of all, that the problem of freedom is the problem of the relation of knowledge to action, that the difficulties with the problem have to do with the conflict that has always existed, that has existed until now, between reflective, systematic thought and intuition; that in this conflict, intuition necessarily comes off worse, that discursive thought always prevails until the day that, by a kind of inevitable eruption, intuition claims and reclaims its rights; then, finally—I was only able to sketch this point in the last lecture—that perhaps this conflict isn't destined to last forever, that discursive thought and intuition, which so far have been like two warring sisters, will perhaps be able to be reconciled in a science less simple than the one that runs through philosophy up to Kant, a much more complex, more comprehensive

science that would take all of experience into account,[32] that would no longer say a priori: "so far, we know facts reducible to such and such a form, and so this form is the definitive form that will suit all possible knowledge." No, science could become completely, radically empirical and take into account all experience, both internal as well as external, both the one that is an intuition and then gives [us], I believe, a thing in itself, as well as the one that is a knowledge from the outside, by relation.

In so comprehensive a conception of science, intuition and discursive thought could thus be reconciled. Such is the conclusion to which I steered this course.

It remains for me, because it has come to an end, gentlemen, to thank you, first for your diligence in attending the course, and then, and above all, for the constant and kind attention you never stopped giving it from beginning to end.

Notes

1. CE, 306/356.
2. This reading, "or almost," is uncertain; the typescript reads *ou autrement*, "or otherwise," which does not seem to make sense.
3. This is the idea of space as *sensorium Dei* Bergson talks about in the preceding lecture, 233; see also 237n27.
4. Or "a calculating God makes the world." The formula, which is at the heart of Couturat's interpretation of Leibniz (see the April 7, 1905, lecture above, 188 and 197n6), means that as God calculates (and by means of this calculation) the world comes into being. Bergson takes up and modifies the already abbreviated quotation on the title page of Couturat's *Logique de Leibniz*. Leibniz, in a manuscript note in his own copy of one of his early dialogues, "Dialogus de connexione inter res et verba" ("Dialogue on the Connection between Things and Words," written in 1677), writes: "Cum Deus calculat et cogitationem exercet, fit mundus." An English translation of this short work can be found as text 17 in *Philosophical Papers and Letters* under the title "Dialogue," 182–5, the remark at 185n4: "When God calculates and exercises his thought, the world is made."
5. CE, 306/356.
6. CE, 306/356.
7. Perhaps the word the typescript renders as *connaissance*, "knowledge," was *conscience*, "consciousness."
8. This mainly aims at Fichte's philosophy. Bergson explicitly refers to this aspect of Fichte's thought in CE, 306/356, and implicitly in "Introduction to Metaphysics," in CM, 204–5/194–6.
9. Bergson might be alluding to a text Kant had published in the *Allgemeine Literaturzeitung*, August 28, 1799, entitled "Declaration concerning Fichte's *Wissenschaftslehre*"; see Kant, *Correspondence*, ed. Arnulf Zweig (New York: Cambridge University Press, 1999), 559–61.
10. This is Renouvier's thesis, which Bergson opposes in TFW, 237–38n1/178n1, but partially accepts in his own way in "Life and Consciousness," in ME, 14–15/11, where he speaks of "moments of inward crisis."
11. Kant introduces the notion of "intelligible character" in his solution to the third antinomy in the CPR, 535–7/A538–41/B566–9/AA 3, 366–8.

12. See the May 12, 1905, lecture, 235.
13. It is unclear where Bergson takes this from.
14. The typescript says "necessity" instead of "freedom." In light of what immediately precedes it (the phrase is a repetition), this "necessity" can only be an unintended error by either Bergson or the stenographers.
15. Unreadable word in the typescript.
16. In terms borrowed from the opening pages of his own "Introduction to Metaphysics" (in CM, 188/178), Bergson seems to be alluding to the so-called B deduction, §18 ("What the Objective Unity of Self-Consciousness is"), of CPR, 250–1/B139–40/AA 3, 113.
17. See above, 15; for the argument concerning Kant, see "The Perception of Change," in CM, 164–7/154–7.
18. As noted earlier (78 and 80n22), both "organization" and "organic life" translate *organisation.*
19. Bergson does pursue it elsewhere: see especially "Philosophical Intuition" (CM, /119), "Introduction to Metaphysics" (CM, /211–16), and of course CE (308/359).
20. See Kant, CPR, 210–12/A76-80/B102–5/AA 3, 90–2.
21. Bergson devoted his 1900–1 course at the Collège de France to the causal relation (summarized in M, 439–41), as well as a "Note sur les origines psychologiques de notre croyance à la loi de causalité" (M, 419–28, and also EP, 213–22). See also CE, 71–3/73–5. On the question of tension, compare "Introduction to Metaphysics," in CM, 221/210–11 (where Bergson uses the verb *se tendre* rather than the noun *tension*).
22. Kant does in fact speak of creation (*Schöpfung*), but he does so to deny its possibility: if creation were possible, it would ruin the unity of experience; see Kant, CPR, 314/A206/B251/AA 3, 177.
23. Kant, CPR, 388–9/A301–2/B358–9/AA 3, 239.
24. Leibniz—for instance, in a short unfinished text of 1695 entitled, precisely, "Mathematica universalis"—takes up the Cartesian project of a universal mathematics, albeit by bending it in the direction of a "universal characteristic" (see 247 and 250n27).
25. In *Creative Evolution*, Bergson refers to this instinct as "the natural inclination of the intellect" (CE, table of contents) or as "the cinematographical mechanism of thought" (CE, 263–72/303–13).
26. According to *Creative Evolution*, the great modern notions, from Spinoza to Leibniz and up to the eighteenth-century French materialists, develop under the sign of this demand, which at the time is related more to "method" than to concepts: as philosophers and as scientists, "we should act as if its applicability"—the applicability of mathematics to reality—"were limitless—there will always be time to lower our expectations later" (CE, 299/347).
27. With regard to this distinction between geometry and algebra, Bergson will say in an allusion to the Cartesian project of a *mathesis universalis* in *Creative Evolution* that "in vain do they hold up before our eyes the brilliance of the perspective of a universal mathematics" (CE, 42/39).
28. As he does in the April 7, 1905, lecture above, 188, Bergson is alluding to the *Opuscules et fragments inédits* published by Couturat in 1903. These texts clearly made a great impression on him. A "universal characteristic" is a system of characteristics capable of universal validity, that is, a system that transcribes the universal forms of thought that lie this side of particular languages.

29. CM, 58/51.
30. Commenting on *The Two Sources*, Vladimir Jankélévitch considers this phrase to be a veritable watchword of Bergson's philosophy; see "Do Not Listen to What They Say, Look at What They Do," trans. Anne Hobart, *Critical Inquiry* 22, no. 3 (Spring 1996): 549–51. Compare also Jankélévitch, "With the Whole Soul," in *Henri Bergson*, ed. Alexandre Lefebvre and Nils F. Schott, 237–46 (Durham, NC: Duke University Press, 2015), 242.
31. *Mais il y a des lois tournées*. Compare CE, 94/99–100.
32. "The whole of experience," *experience intégrale*, like the philosophy that Bergson calls for at the very end of "Introduction to Metaphysics" (CM, 237/227).

BIBLIOGRAPHY

Works by Bergson

References to Bergson's works in the notes are given to the English first (see the bibliography for publication details), then to the French annotated edition published by Presses universitaires de France under the general editorship of Frédéric Worms since 2007, whose pagination follows that of earlier PUF editions.

CE *Creative Evolution* (*L'Evolution créatrice*)
CM *The Creative Mind* (*La Pensée et le mouvant*)
DS *Duration and Simultaneity* (*Durée et simultanéité*)
EP *Ecrits philosophiques*
F *Freedom (L'Evolution du problème de la liberté)*
HIT *Histoire de l'idée de temps*
HTM *Histoire des théories de la mémoire*
IT *L'idée de temps*
KW *Henri Bergson: Key Writings*
L *Laughter: Essay on the Meaning of the Comic* (*Le Rire: essai sur la signification du comique*)
M *Mélanges*
ME *Mind-Energy* (*L'Energie spirituelle*)
MM *Matter and Memory* (*Matière et mémoire*)
TFW *Time and Free Will* (*Essai sur les données immédiates de la conscience*)
TS *The Two Sources of Morality and Religion* (*Les Deux sources de la morale et de la religion*)

Works by other authors

Descartes

AT *Œuvres*
PW *The Philosophical Writings of Descartes*

Kant

AA *Kant's gesammelte Schriften*
CPR *Critique of Pure Reason*

References to CPR give the page number in the translation, followed by the pages in the first and second editions (A/B) and the Academy edition (AA).

Bibliography

Leibniz

PE *Philosophical Essays*
PPL *Philosophical Papers and Letters*

Spinoza

CWS *The Collected Works of Spinoza*

References to the *Ethics* use Curley's method of abbreviation (see CWS 1: xix–xx).

Biblical quotations are from the *New Revised Standard Version.* Works by Plato are cited using Stephanus numbering followed by page numbers in the edition by John M. Cooper. Works by Aristotle are cited using book and chapter numbers, where applicable, followed by Bekker numbering and page numbers in the edition by Jonathan Barnes.

Aeschylus. *Persians, Seven against Thebes, Suppliants, Prometheus Bound.* Translated by Alan H. Sommerstein. Cambridge, MA: Harvard University Press, 2008.

Alexander of Aphrodisias. *Alexander of Aphrodisias on Fate.* Translated by R. W. Sharples. London: Duckworth, 1983.

Alexander of Aphrodisias. *Alexander of Aphrodisias on Stoic Physics: A Study of the De Mixtione with Preliminary Essays, Text, Translation and Commentary.* Edited by Robert B. Todd. Leiden: Brill, 1976.

Aristotle. *The Complete Works of Aristotle: The Revised Oxford Translation.* Edited by Jonathan Barnes. 2 vols. Princeton: Princeton University Press, 1995.

Augustine. *City of God.* Translated by Philip Levine. Vol. 4. Cambridge, MA: Harvard University Press, 1966.

Azouvi, François. *La Gloire de Bergson: Essai sur le magistère philosophique.* Paris: Gallimard, 2007.

Baillet, Adrien. *La Vie de M. Descartes.* 2 vols. Paris: Horthemels, 1691.

Bentham, Jeremy. *An Introduction to the Principles of Morals and Legislation.* In *The Collected Works of Jeremy Bentham,* edited by J. H. Burns and H. L. A. Hart. Oxford: Oxford University Press, 1996.

Bergson, Henri. "Cours de Bergson sur le *De rerum originatione radicali* de Leibniz." Edited by Matthias Vollet and Arnaud François. In *Annales Bergsoniennes III:* "Bergson et la science", edited by Frédéric Worms, 25–52. Paris: Presses universitaires de France, 2007.

Bergson, Henri. *Creative Evolution.* Translated by Donald Landes. London: Routledge, 2023.

Bergson, Henri. *The Creative Mind.* Translated by Mabelle L. Andison. New York: Philosophical Library, 1946.

Bergson, Henri. *Duration and Simultaneity.* Translated by Leon Jacobson. Edited by Robin Durie. Manchester: Manchester University Press, 1999.

Bergson, Henri. *Écrits philosophiques.* Paris: Presses universitaires de France, 2011.

Bergson, Henri. *Henri Bergson: Key Writings.* Edited by Keith Ansell Pearson and John Ó Maoilearca. New York: Continuum, 2002.

Bergson, Henri. *Histoire de l'idée de temps: Cours au Collège de France 1902–1903.* Edited by Camille Riquier. Paris: Press universitaires de France, 2016.

Bergson, Henri. *Histoire des théories de la mémoire: Cours au Collège de France 1903–1904.* Edited by Arnaud François. Paris: Presses universitaires de France, 2018.

Bergson, Henri. *L'Évolution du problème de la liberté: Cours au Collège de France, 1904–1905.* Edited by Arnaud François. Paris: Presses universitaires de France, 2017.

Bergson, Henri. *L'idée de temps: Cours au Collège de France 1901–02.* Edited by Gabriel Meyer-Bisch. Paris: Presses universitaires de France, 2019.

Bergson, Henri. *Laughter: Essay on the Meaning of the Comic.* Translated by Cloudesley Brereton and Fred Rothwell. London: Macmillan, 1911.

Bergson, Henri. *Matter and Memory.* Translated by Nancy Margaret Paul and W. Scott Palmer. New York: Macmillan, 1911.

Bergson, Henri. *Mélanges.* Edited by André Robinet. Paris: Presses universitaires de France, 1972.

Bergson, Henri. *Mind-Energy.* Translated by H. Wildon Carr. New York: Henry Holt, 1920.

Bergson, Henri. *Time and Free Will.* Translated by F. L. Pogson. New York: Macmillan, 1910.

Bergson, Henri. *The Two Sources of Morality and Religion.* Translated by R. Ashley Audra and Cloudesley Brereton. Notre Dame: University of Notre Dame Press, 1977.

Berkeley, George. *The Works of George Berkeley, Bishop of Cloyne.* Edited by A. A. Luce and T. E. Jessop. 9 vols. London: Nelson, 1948–57.

Boutroux, Émile. *The Contingency of the Laws of Nature.* Translated by Fred Rothwell. Chicago: Open Court, 1920.

Bréhier, Émile. *Le Théorie des incorporels dans l'ancien stoïcisme.* Paris: Picard, 1908.

Carnot, Sadi. *Reflections on the Motive Power of Fire.* Edited by E. Mendoza. Mineola: Dover Publications, 1988.

Carroy, Jacqueline, and Henning Schmidgen. "Reaktionsversuche in Leipzig, Paris und Würzburg: Die deutsch-französische Geschichte eines psychologischen Experiments, 1890–1910." *Medizinhistorisches Journal* 39, no. 1 (2004): 27–55.

Chasle, Michel. *Aperçu historique sur l'origine et le développement des méthodes en géométrie.* Brussels: Hayez, 1837.

Cicero. *On the Orator, Book III, On Fate, Stoics Paradoxes, Divisions of Oratory.* Translated by H. Rackham. Cambridge, MA: Harvard University Press, 2004.

Couturat, Louis. *La Logique de Leibniz d'après des documents inédits.* Paris: Alcan, 1901.

Couturat, Louis. *Logique, mathématiques, langue universelle: Anthologie 1893–1917.* Edited by Michel Fichant. Lyon: ENS Éditions, 2018. https://books.openedition.org/enseditions/8171.

Couturat, Louis, ed. *Opuscules et fragments inédits de Leibniz.* Paris: Alcan, 1903.

Deleuze, Gilles, and Félix Guattari. *What is Philosophy?* Translated by Hugh Tomlinson and Graham Burchell. New York: Columbia University Press, 1994.

Descartes, René. *Œuvres de Descartes.* Edited by Charles Adam and Paul Tannery. 12 vols., 1897–1910. Paris: Vrin, 1964.

Descartes, René. *The Philosophical Writings of Descartes.* Translated by John Cottingham, Robert Stoothoff, and Dugald Murdoch. 3 vols. New York: Cambridge University Press, 1985–91.

Diogenes Laertius. *The Lives of the Eminent Philosophers*, Books VI–X. Translated by R. D. Hicks. Cambridge, MA: Harvard University Press, 2005.

Duhem, Pierre. *The Evolution of Mechanics.* Translated by Michael Cole. Alphen aan den Rijn: Sijthoff and Noordhoff, 1980.

Duns Scotus, *Ordinatio*, book 4. In *Opera omnia.* Edited by Commissio Scotistica. Vol. 14. Vatican City: Vatican Press, 2013.

Epictetus. *Encheiridion.* In *Discourses, Books 3-4. Fragments. The Encheiridion.* Translated by W. A. Oldfather. Cambridge, MA: Harvard University Press, 1928.

Fouillée, Alfred. *La philosophie de Platon: Exposition, histoire et critique de la théorie des Idées.* 2 vols. Paris: Ladrange, 1869.

Fouillée, Alfred. *La philosophie de Socrate.* Paris: Ladrange, 1874.

Fouillée, Alfred. *Psychologie des idées-forces*. Paris: Alcan, 1893.

François, Arnaud. "Vie et liberté." In *L'Évolution du problème de la liberté,: Cours au Collège de France, 1904-1905*, by Henri Bergson, 9–14. Paris: Presses universitaires de France, 2017.

Guerlac, Suzanne. *Thinking in Time: An Introduction to Henri Berson*. Ithaca: Cornell University Press, 2006.

Guyau, Jean-Marie. *La Morale d'Épicure et ses rapports avec les doctrines contemporaines*. Paris: Ballière, 1878.

Heraclitus. *The Fragments of the Work of Heraclitus of Ephesus on Nature*. Translated by G. T. W. Patrick. Baltimore: Murray, 1889.

Heraclitus. "Heraclitus." In *Early Greek Philosophy*, edited and translated by André Laks and Glenn W. Most. Vol. 3, *Early Ionian Thinkers, Part 2*, 114–337. Cambridge, MA: Harvard University Press, 2016.

Herodotus. *Herodotus in Four Volumes*. Translated by A. D. Goodley. Cambridge, MA: Harvard University Press, 1926.

Herring, Emily. "Henri Bergson, Celebrity." *Aeon*, May 6, 2019. https://aeon.co/essays/henri-bergson-the-philosopher-damned-for-his-female-fans

Homer. *The Iliad of Homer*. Translated by Richmond Lattimore. Chicago: University of Chicago Press, 2011.

Hörl, Erich. *Sacred Channels: The Archaic Illusion of Communication*. With a preface by Jean-Luc Nancy. Translated by Nils F. Schott. Amsterdam: Amsterdam University Press, 2018.

James, William. *The Will to Believe and Other Essays in Popular Philosophy*. In *The Works of William James*, edited by Frederick Burkhardt, Ignas K. Skrupskelis, and Fredson Bowers. Cambridge, MA: Harvard University Press, 1979.

Jankélévitch, Vladimir. *Henri Bergson*. Translated by Nils F. Schott. Edited by Alexandre Lefebvre and Nils F. Schott. Durham: Duke University Press, 2015.

Jankélévitch, Vladimir. "N'écoutez ce qu'il dissent, regardez ce qu'ils font" ("Don't listen to what they say, look at what they do"). Translated by Ann Hobart. *Critical Inquiry* 22, no. 3 (1996): 549–51.

Kahl, Wilhelm. *Die Lehre vom Primat des Willens bei Augustine, Duns Scotus und Descartes*. Strasbourg: Trübner, 1886.

Kant, Immanuel. *Correspondence*. Edited and translated by Arnulf Zweig. New York: Cambridge University Press, 1999.

Kant, Immanuel. *Critique of Pure Reason*. Edited by Paul Guyer and Alan Wood. New York: Cambridge University Press, 2009.

Kant, Immanuel. *Kant's gesammelte Schriften*. Edited by Wilhelm Dilthey et al. Berlin: Reimer [et al.], 1900–.

Kant, Immanuel. *Metaphysical Foundations of Natural Science*. Translated by Michael Friedman. In *Theoretical Philosophy after 1781*, edited by Henry Allison and Peter Heath, 171–270. New York: Cambridge University Press, 2002.

Kant, Immanuel. *Practical Philosophy*. Edited and translated by Mary J. Gregor. New York: Cambridge University Press, 1999.

Labaune, Christophe. "Bergson au Collège de France (exposition virtuelle)." *Colligere*, March 12, 2020. https://archibibscdf.hypotheses.org/?p=8177.

La Mettrie, Julien Offray de. *Machine Man and Other Writings*. Edited and translated by Ann Thomson. New York: Cambridge University Press, 2008.

Laplace, Pierre-Simon. *Philosophical Essay on Probabilities*. Translated by Andrew I. Dale. New York: Springer, 1995.

Lefebvre, Alexandre. *Human Rights as a Way of Life: On Bergson's Political Philosophy*. Stanford: Stanford University Press, 2013.

Lefebvre, Alexandre, and Nils F. Schott. "Closed and Open Societies." In *The Bergsonian Mind*, edited by Mark Sinclair and Yaron Wolf, 251–63. London: Routledge, 2022.

Lefebvre, Alexandre, and Nils F. Schott, eds. *Interpreting Bergson: Critical Essays*. Cambridge: Cambridge University Press, 2020.

Leibniz, Gottfried Wilhelm. *New Essays on Human Understanding*. Edited by Peter Remnant and Jonathan Bennett. New York: Cambridge University Press, 1996.

Leibniz, Gottfried Wilhelm. *Philosophical Essays*. Translated by Roger Ariew and Daniel Garber. Indianapolis: Hackett Publishing, 1989.

Leibniz, Gottfried Wilhelm. *Philosophical Papers and Letters*. Edited and translated by Leroy E. Loemker. 2nd ed. Dordrecht: Reidel, 1969.

Leibniz, Gottfried Wilhelm. *Sämtliche Schriften und Briefe*. Berlin: Akademie-Verlag, 1923–.

Leibniz, Gottfried Wilhelm. *Tentamina theodicææ de bonitate Dei, libertate hominis et origine mali Latine versa & notationibus*. Translated by Bartholomew Des Bosses. Frankfurt: Bencard, 1719.

Leibniz, Gottfried Wilhelm. *Theodicy*. Translated by E. M. Huggard. LaSalle: Open Court Publishing Company, 1985.

Leibniz, Gottfried Wilhelm, and Samuel Clarke. *The Leibniz–Clarke Correspondence*. Edited by H. G. Alexander. Manchester: Manchester University Press, 1956.

Lucretius. *De Rerum Natura*. Translated by W. H. D. Rouse. Cambridge, MA: Harvard University Press, 2006.

Lutosławski, Wincenty. *The Origin and Growth of Plato's Logic, with an Account of Plato's Style and the Chronology of His Writings*. London: Longman, Green, and Co., 1897.

Martin, Thomas-Henri. *Études sur le Timée de Platon*. 1841. Paris: Vrin, 1981.

McGrath, Larry. *Making Spirit Matter: Neurology, Psychology, and Selfhood in Modern France*. Chicago: Chicago University Press, 2020.

de la Mettrie, Julien Offray. *Machine Man and Other Writings*. Edited by Ann Thomson. New York: Cambridge University Press, 1996.

Mill, John Stuart. *Collected Works of John Stuart Mill*. Edited by J. M. Robson et al. 32 vols. Toronto: University of Toronto Press, 1963–91.

Nemisius. *On the Nature of Man*. Translated by R. W. Sharples and P. J. van der Eijk. Liverpool: Liverpool University Press, 2008.

Ovid. *Metamorphoses*. Translated by Frank Justus Miller. Revised by G. P. Goold. Cambridge, MA: Harvard University Press, 1916.

Pascal, Blaise. *Pensées*. Edited and translated by Roger Ariew. Indianapolis: Hackett, 2005.

Plato. *Plato: Complete Works*. Edited by John M. Cooper. Indianapolis: Hackett, 1997.

Plotinus. *Plotinus*. Edited and translated by Arthur H. Armstrong, rev. ed. Cambridge, MA: Harvard University Press, 1989.

Plutarch. *On the Generation of the Soul in the Timaeus*. Translated by Harold Cherniss. In *Moralia*. Vol. 13, pt. 1, *Platonic Essays*. Cambridge, MA: Harvard University Press, 1976.

Porphyry. *Porphyrii Philosophi Fragmenta*. Edited by Andrew Smith. Stuttgart: Teubner, 1993.

Riquier, Camille. "Presentation." In Henri Bergson, *Histoire de l'idée de temps: Cours au Collège de France 1902–1903*, 7–16. Paris: Press universitaires de France, 2016.

Rodier, Georges. "Sur une des origines de la philosophie de Leibniz." *Revue de métaphysique et de morale* 10, no. 5 (September–October 1902): 552–64.

Rousseau, Jean-Jacques. *Emile or On Education*. Translated by Alan Bloom. New York: Basic Books, 1979.

Rousseau, Jean-Jacques. *The Social Contract, and Other Later Political Writings*. Edited and translated by Victor Gourevitch. Cambridge: Cambridge University Press, 1997.

Russell, Bertrand. *A Critical Exposition of the Philosophy of Leibniz*. Cambridge: Cambridge University Press, 1900.

Schopenhauer, Arthur. *The World as Will and Representation*. Edited and translated by Judith Norman, Alistair Welchman, and Christopher Janaway. 2 vols. Cambridge: Cambridge University Press, 2010 and 2018.

Sinclair, Mark. *Bergson*. London: Routledge, 2019.

Sinclair, Mark, and Yaron Wolf, eds. *The Bergsonian Mind*. London: Routledge, 2022.

Soulez, Philippe, and Frédéric Worms. *Bergson*. Paris: Presses universitaires de France, 2002.

Surprenant, Céline. "Bergson at the Collège de France." In *The Bergsonian Mind*, edited by Mark Sinclair and Yaron Wolf, 28–41. London: Routledge, 2022.

Spencer, Herbert. *First Principles*. 2nd ed. London: Williams and Norgate, 1867.

Spinoza, Baruch. *The Collected Works of Spinoza*. Edited and translated by Edwin Curley. Princeton: Princeton University Press, 1985.

Stobaeus, Joannes. *Ioannis Stobaei Anthologium*. Edited by Kurt Wachsmuth and Otto Hense. 5 vols. Berlin: Weidmann, 1884–1912.

Tarde, Gabriel. *The Laws of Imitation*. Translated by Elsie Clews Parsons. New York: Holt, 1903.

Teichmüller, Gustav. *Neue Studien zur Geschichte der Begriffe*. Gotha: Perthes, 1876.

Teichmüller, Gustav. *Studien zur Geschichte der Begriffe*. Berlin: Weidmann, 1874.

Worms, Fréderic. "Présentation." In *Essai sur les données immédiates de la conscience*, by Henri Bergson, 7–13. Paris: Presses universitaires de France, 2007.

Xenophon. *Memorabilia, Oeconomicus, Symposium, Apology*. Translated by E. C. Marchant and O. J. Todd. Revised by Jeffrey Henderson. Cambridge, MA: Harvard University Press, 2013.

Yushkevich, Adolph-Andrei P., and Yu. Kh. Kopelevich. "La correspondance de Leibniz avec Goldbach." *Studia Leibnitiana* 20, no. 2 (1988): 175–89.

Zeller, Eduard. *Outlines of the History of Greek Philosophy*. Translated by Sarah Frances Alleyne and Evelyn Abbott. London: Longman, Green, and Co., 1886.

INDEX